Mary Wollstonecraft

A Critical Biography

Mary Wollstonecraft

A Critical Biography

by

Ralph M. Wardle

UNIVERSITY OF NEBRASKA PRESS · LINCOLN

Copyright © 1951 by the University of Kansas Press
All rights reserved
Library of Congress Catalog Card Number 51–12250
Manufactured in the United States of America

First Bison Book printing October, 1966

Bison Book edition published by arrangement with the University of Kansas Press.

TO
ANOTHER
MARY W.

Preface

The greatest debt which I have incurred in my preparation for this book is to Lord Abinger, of Clees Hall, Bures, Suffolk, who generously permitted me to examine his collection of the letters of Mary Wollstonecraft, her husband William Godwin, and her sister Elizabeth W. Bishop. These letters came into the hands of the Abinger family from Lady Shelley, aunt and foster-mother of the present Lord Abinger's grandmother. Since they had previously been consulted only by Charles Kegan Paul (who published all or parts of approximately one-third of them in his *William Godwin: His Friends and Contemporaries* in 1876), I was able to derive from them a good deal of information, both factual and interpretive, never before available to biographers of Mary Wollstonecraft. I have followed my own transcripts of the letters, since Paul's were often inaccurate, but have silently corrected errors in spelling or altered punctuation when I felt that doing so would prevent confusion or ambiguity.

I am, of course, indebted also to previous biographers of Mary Wollstonecraft and her associates and to the authors of dozens of standard works on eighteenth century history, political thought, and social backgrounds or on the history of education or feminism. I have picked many a good brain in my attempt to understand Mary Wollstonecraft, her period, and her position in intellectual history. Of them all, the late W. Clark Durant, editor of the modern edition of Godwin's *Memoirs* of his wife, proved most helpful; and, as my notes reveal, I have drawn repeatedly on the material about Mary Wollstonecraft which he assembled in the Supplement to his edition of the *Memoirs*.

I am grateful also to Miss Ethel I. Carr, of Canterbury, for her kindness in allowing me to examine the letters of Mary Wollstonecraft to Amelia Alderson Opie now in her possession, and to Miss Anne F. Wedd, of London, who not only allowed me access to the correspondence of Mary Hays which she inherited, but also gave me two of Mary Wollstonecraft's letters to Mary Hays, which I shall always treasure. Moreover, I am deeply indebted to Mrs.

Dorothy Bacon Woolsey, of Kent, Connecticut, for her suggestions and encouragement; to Mrs. Margery Beckingham, of London, for saving me many hours of labor by her efficient investigations; to Professor Benjamin Boyce, of Duke University, for reading and criticizing the book in manuscript; and to Professor Clyde K. Hyder, of the University of Kansas, for his invaluable criticism and aid in seeing the book through the press.

I wish to thank also, for their assistance, the officers and staffs of the following libraries, who have assisted me either directly or by correspondence: the Bodleian Library, the Boston Public Library, the British Museum, the Cornell University Library, the Harvard College Library, the Henry E. Huntington Library, the Library of Congress, the Mitchell Library of Sydney, N.S.W., the New York Public Library, the University of Omaha Library, and the Yale University Library. And I am obliged to the following publishers for permission to quote copyrighted materials: Messrs. Methuen & Co., Ltd., for quotations from Miss Wedd's edition of *The Love Letters of Mary Hays;* Messrs. G. Bell & Sons, Ltd., for a quotation from Roger Ingpen's edition of *The Letters of Percy Bysshe Shelley;* and Messrs. J. M. Dent & Sons, Ltd., for quotations from P. P. Howe's edition of *The Complete Works of William Hazlitt* and from F. K. Brown's *William Godwin.*

So much for acknowledgments. But I cannot close without congratulating myself on having had throughout my work the tireless assistance and encouragement of one who asks no acknowledgment. To her the book is affectionately dedicated.

R.M.W.

THE UNIVERSITY OF OMAHA
April 27, 1951

Contents

Contents

Mary Wollstonecraft

A Critical Biography

She had errors; but her errors, which were not those of a sordid mind, were connected and interwoven with the qualities most characteristic of her genius.—Godwin's Memoirs (Second Edition).

CHAPTER I

Education of a Rebel
(1759-1780)

*It is perhaps difficult to give you an idea of the
petty cares which obscured the morning of my life.*
—*The Wrongs of Woman.*

THE year 1759, the last but one of George II's reign, was a
year of extraordinary rejoicing for loyal Englishmen. It
was the fourth year of the Seven Years' War, and British
forces were gaining victory after victory in all quarters—at Lagos,
Quiberon Bay, Guadaloupe, Minden, Quebec, Ticonderoga, and
Fort Niagara. Horace Walpole jokingly complained that one must
inquire each morning what new triumph had been reported during the night for fear of missing one altogether. The war had
amply justified itself, for England's prestige abroad had never
been higher, and her citizens were well satisfied with the elder
Pitt's administration. Of course the war had crippled trade and
sent prices soaring. Poor people were hard put to it to buy even the
bare essentials of food and fuel. But that sort of trouble was an old
story: if they would only learn the rudiments of industry and
thrift, if they would stop swilling gin and enlist God's help, they
would soon find a way out of their difficulties.—So argued their
betters, who were too busy celebrating the long series of victories
to waste time in sympathy. Humanitarianism was not yet in vogue.

Edward John Wollstonecraft, the son of a Spitalfields "manufacturer" (doubtless a weaver) of Irish extraction, had reasons of
his own for rejoicing in the year 1759.[1] He had no occasion to
worry about rising prices; in fact he could look forward to a life
of ease. His father had died shortly before, leaving him a comfortable fortune—probably as much as £10,000—and his future
looked serene. He would never have to "work like a Spitalfields
weaver," as the phrase was; indeed he had decided to spend his

life as a gentleman farmer, and he was preparing to move to a pleasant farm not far from London. His young wife, Elizabeth Dickson,[2] had hailed from Ballyshannon, County Donegal, in Ireland, and she probably welcomed the chance to bring up her children away from the dust and grime of Spitalfields. Already she had a son, to whom she and her husband were devoted, and at the beginning of 1759 they were looking forward to the birth of a second child within a few weeks.

Presently their expectations were fulfilled. On April 27 Mrs. Wollstonecraft gave birth to a baby girl, whom they named Mary, and at about the same time they left London and settled on a farm in the Epping Forest.[3] Their troubles were soon to begin.

Wollstonecraft quickly learned that the life of a farmer, even a gentleman farmer with a substantial income, was much more exacting than he had supposed. It was especially difficult in the years 1760-80, for the Enclosure Acts were rapidly pre-empting vast areas formerly open to independent farmers and setting a price competition which they could not meet. Right beneath Wollstonecraft's nose the Epping Forest was being gradually enclosed, and whole families were abandoning their farms to work in the dismal stone mills which had begun to deface the countryside. But Wollstonecraft refused to be discouraged. And so he tried one farm after another, always positive that he would succeed in each new one as he took it over. In 1764 he left his first farm to move to another nearby, just off the Chelmsford Road and near the Whalebone. Then, after a year there, he moved again, this time to an acreage outside of Barking, in Essex, eight miles beyond the London city limits.

In the meantime his family was growing steadily. There were four children when he settled near Barking: Edward, Mary, Elizabeth (usually called Eliza or Bess), and Everina. And in 1768 a second son, James, was born.[4]

At Barking there was much to entertain the children: they could romp in the barnyard and fields or visit the marketplace and docks in the village. There were ruins of an ancient abbey there too, founded in the year 670 by St. Erkenwald, first Bishop of London. The Abbess of Barking had been the only woman of her rank in England to hold a seat in the Anglo-Saxon Witenagemot. In later years Mary Wollstonecraft would have delighted to learn of such a woman, but as yet she had no thought of these matters. She was only a lively little girl with auburn hair and brown eyes whose interests were confined to the passing show of village life. And she never forgot it. When she revisited the town with her husband in 1796, she went eagerly from the marketplace to the docks, intent on recalling her impressions of the place. "No person," Godwin later wrote, "reviewed with greater sensibility, the scenes of her childhood."[5]

But though the village pleased her, life at home must have worried her more and more, for all was far from well between her mother and father. Edward Wollstonecraft had found the farm near Barking no more profitable than the two in the Epping Forest. As his family grew larger, his expenses increased, and his inheritance dwindled. Gradually his temper grew morose, and he solaced himself by drinking heavily and tyrannizing over his docile wife. Mary could hardly have failed to observe the change in her father and its effect upon her mother's disposition. Doubtless their quarrels grew constantly more frequent, and the children learned to look for happiness outside of their home.

When Mary was nine years old—at Michaelmas, 1768—her father despaired of making the Barking farm succeed and sold it to buy a piece of property 150 miles north, near Beverley, in Yorkshire. There they remained for six years, from the time that Mary was nine until she was fifteen—a long stretch for the Wollstonecrafts. Indeed Mary lived there longer than she was ever to live anywhere else her whole life through. She had time to establish ties which would always bind her to the place, and in later years she considered herself a Yorkshirewoman and fell instinctively into the local idiom. "I must use my Yorkshire phrase," she wrote in 1794; "for, when my heart is warm, pop come the expressions of childhood into my head."[6] She learned to love Bev-

erley, a picturesque old town which was to charm Dorothy Wordsworth a few years later. There was a fine minster there, and many
churches, monasteries, and hospitals surviving from the historic
past. The countryside roundabout was beautiful too, and Mary
spent much of her time ranging the hills and fields, for she was a
high-spirited little girl who liked to romp with her brothers rather
than to play dolls with her small sisters.

Inevitably, however, she grew more sober and sensitive. Life
at the Wollstonecrafts' was becoming almost intolerable. There
were six children to provide for now, a third son, Charles, having
been born to the couple. And affairs were going from bad to worse,
for the new farm had proved just as unprofitable as the others. But
Wollstonecraft now vented his disappointment in brutal attacks
on his hunting dogs or his family. Years later Mary described to
her husband the overpowering revulsion she felt when she saw
her father abuse a dog. She must have suffered even more when
she saw him abuse her mother. And she soon grew used to the
sight. When drunk, Wollstonecraft could shift abruptly from extravagant fondness to brutality, and his wife and children learned
to be prepared for either extreme. Sometimes Mary was obliged
to rush between her parents to protect her mother from injury.
And nights when she feared an outburst from her father, she used
to sleep on the landing outside her mother's bedroom so that she
could protect her from harm if Wollstonecraft flew into a rage.

As for Mrs. Wollstonecraft, a timid woman by nature, she
gradually lost all dignity of character in the face of such treatment.
She had no control over her husband and could suggest no cure
for their difficulties except to talk vaguely of emigrating to a cottage in America, where life might prove easier and simpler.[7] The
more hopeless her prospects became, the less she seemed able to
cope with them—or with the everyday problems of raising a
family. She pampered her eldest son, Edward, even catering to his
whims at the cost of the other children. And she was unreasonably
severe with Mary, apparently considering it her maternal duty to
curb the girl's spirit. She demanded absolute obedience from her,

and often compelled her to sit indoors for three or four hours at
a time without speaking, as punishment for some slight display
of independence. The result was that Mary was frequently per-
plexed at the treatment which she received, and she developed a
morbid conviction of her own sinfulness. She resented her father's
unjustified brutality; but she perceived that her mother never
punished her without a specific reason, and she welcomed such
punishment as the only means of correcting her faults. Already
she was showing signs of the unhealthy introspection which was
to blight much of her later life.

Fortunately, however, her spirit was of too tough a fiber to be
crushed. Because she resented her father's tyranny, she gathered
strength to withstand his blows and eventually discerned that she
could counter most effectively if she met his outbursts with cold
contempt. Before long she was daring to challenge his authority,
to speak in defense of her rights and her mother's. And however
much anguish it may have cost her, her experience with her
father did much to shape the strongest qualities of her character
in later life. By suffering his tyranny and combating it, she learned
an abiding hatred for tyranny of all sorts and a fearlessness in fighting it. By witnessing her mother's abject servitude, she learned
resentment of the conditions which kept women in a state of submission. "At fifteen," she wrote to Godwin many years later, "I
resolved never to marry for interested motives, or to endure a life
of dependence." A pathetic decision for a girl of fifteen — and an
ominous one! Long before Mary had heard of the rights of men
or formulated the rights of women, she had developed a passion
for freedom and a dauntless courage which did much to shape her
later career.

Yet such qualities, valuable as they proved to be, came at the
cost of many wretched years. Mary's moments of bravery must
have been preceded and followed by hours of worry and fear.
She had no guide but herself, no support from outside. She did
not want to grow up to be a tyrant like her father or a slave
like her mother, and she had to discover for herself the right

course to normal maturity. And as she pondered over all the problems that confronted her, searching her soul for the right answers, she became ever more introspective.

She seems to have allowed small matters as well as large ones to worry her almost to distraction. In her novel *Mary,* much of which is patterned on her own early life, she wrote of her heroine:

Her mother's luke-warm manner of performing her religious duties, filled her with anguish; and when she observed her father's vices, the unbidden tears would flow. She was miserable when beggars were driven from the gate without being relieved; if she could do it unperceived, she would give them her own breakfast, and feel gratified, when, in consequence of it, she was pinched by hunger.

She had once, or twice, told her little secrets to her mother; they were laughed at, and she determined never to do it again. In this manner was she left to reflect on her own feelings; and so strengthened were they by being meditated on, that her character early became singular and permanent. Her understanding was strong and clear, when not clouded by her feelings; but she was too much the creature of impulse, and the slave of compassion.[8]

When life at home seemed intolerable, the fictitious Mary took refuge in wandering the nearby countryside, and her love of nature became fused with vague religious yearnings:

Sublime ideas filled her young mind—always connected with devotional sentiments; extemporary effusions of gratitude, and rhapsodies of praise would burst often from her, when she listened to the birds, or pursued the deer. She would gaze on the moon, and ramble through the gloomy path, observing the various shapes the clouds assumed, and listen to the sea that was not far distant. The wandering spirits, which she imagined inhabited every part of nature, were her constant friends and confidants. She began to consider the Great First Cause, formed just notions of his attributes, and, in particular, dwelt on his wisdom and goodness. Could she have loved her father or mother, had they returned her affection, she would not so soon, perhaps, have sought out a new world.[9]

Mary may also, like her heroine, have undergone a spiritual awakening at this period of her life. Perhaps she too was confirmed when she was fifteen and "hailed the morn and sung with wild delight" after the sleepless night before the ceremony. And perhaps she was "so much affected when she joined in the prayer for her eternal preservation, that she could hardly conceal her violent emotions."[10] Although she had read a good many romantic tales and imbibed a good many sentimental notions between the time she left Beverley and the time she wrote her novel, her heroine's rhapsodies may well reflect the intense feelings which she experienced as a girl.

But whether or not she underwent a spiritual awakening at Beverley, she certainly experienced an intellectual awakening during her years there. She received practically all her schooling at the day schools of the town, and she was probably an eager pupil. Yet her real education came to her through her own efforts. Meeting and solving her personal problems helped to broaden her mind, and reading sharpened it. Like the heroine of *Mary,* she "learned to think by wide reading"; and she corresponded with a Miss Masscy, evidently one of her teachers, who later published eleven of Mary's letters, written between 1773 and 1782, to demonstrate to young people how much they could improve their literary style if they applied themselves to the task.[11] Mary was eager to learn, and she had ability as well as ambition. A shrewd observer might have detected extraordinary potentialities in her, potentialities not normally expected in a girl of those times. For though she had gone to Beverley in 1768 as a child, by the time she left the town six years later she was a young woman of exceptional maturity, dissatisfied with the life she was leading and wanting only guidance for her expanding powers.

In 1774 the family moved south again and settled in Queen's Row, Hoxton, on the outskirts of London. Edward Wollstonecraft had decided at long last that he had had his fill of farming, and he was seeking to recoup his fortunes by a flyer in business. So once again the family was wrenched from its moorings and set down in a new environment—and a dreary one by contrast with Beverley. Though removed from the congestion of the city, Hoxton was by no means a pleasant place, for it contained several insane asylums and workhouses, great ugly structures which cluttered the landscape. There was a dissenting

academy at Hoxton too, and one of its students was a very sanc-
timonious young man of eighteen, William Godwin, who a
few years before had been edifying his pious family in Norfolk
by delivering weekly sermons from his high chair. Fortunately
for Mary, she was spared making his acquaintance until several
years later, when he had undergone many salutary changes.

She did, however, form two important friendships during
her stay at Hoxton. The first was with a neighbor in Queen's
Row, a deformed clergyman named Clare, who lived practically
as a recluse—leaving home so rarely that he had worn the same
pair of shoes for fourteen years. Clare and his wife were mild,
friendly people who welcomed Mary's company and entertained her in their home for weeks at a time. It was a desirable
arrangement on both sides: the Clares doubtless enjoyed the
youth and vitality which Mary brought into their house, and
for her part she found there much of what was wanting from
her own home life. Clare was an avid reader and a discrim-
inating critic, and he encouraged and improved Mary's half-
formed tastes. But even more important: both he and his wife
gave her the sort of affection which she craved. From them she
could learn how happy two human beings could be when
neither demanded submission from the other. This was, perhaps, her first real taste of the joys of contented domestic life,
her first knowledge of the power of human love.

Yet Mary still needed companionship. Mr. and Mrs. Clare could
help to satisfy her longing for affectionate parents, but they could
not take the place of a friend of her own age. They managed, however, to find such a friend for her. One day Mrs. Clare took Mary
on a trip to Newington Butts, south of London, to visit a family
named Blood. When they arrived at the Bloods' house, they found
Fanny, oldest of the family, busily feeding her little brothers and
sisters. Mary was enchanted at the sight, and she never forgot it.
Fanny, who was two years her senior, charmed her from the outset. Soon the two girls were fast friends.

They had much in common, for Fanny was an intelligent and

sensitive girl like Mary, and she too had family worries. Her father was shiftless and improvident, and her mother had long been baffled by the problem of raising a large family on an uncertain income. On Mary's side the friendship was intensified by profound admiration: she had never known a girl so talented as Fanny. She could sing, play, read, write, and draw well; in fact she was helping to support the family by selling her drawings. She was a good manager too, and had proved more efficient than either her father or her mother in supervising the household. By contrast Mary felt herself but a wild thing.

Because the girls could see each other only rarely, they corresponded. Soon Mary was asking Fanny to correct her letters, was trying to imitate her friend's handwriting and echo her style. Fanny was her model in all things. Even at home Mary tried to follow her example and insisted on more of a voice in family affairs. And when her parents objected, she threatened to leave home and earn her own living. She agreed to stay with them only when they promised to allow her a room of her own, where she could study in peace. Edward and Elizabeth Wollstonecraft must have been nonplussed at such demands. And they were certainly worried at the growing independence which the girl showed. She seemed almost determined to usurp their authority in the household.

Meanwhile Wollstonecraft's business venture had fared badly, and he decided after a year and a half at Hoxton that he would return to farming. This time he had chosen Wales as his location, and the family was obliged to decamp in the spring of 1776 and journey to Laugharne, at the mouth of the Taf River, in Carmarthenshire. Once again they found themselves in strange new surroundings. Yet they might have chosen worse places. Although Laugharne was a seaport of only about 1,000 inhabitants when they moved there, it had in Elizabethan days been one of the most important towns of Wales. Old Laugharne Castle had housed Percys, Herberts, and Devereux and had been despoiled by Cromwell's forces. The country roundabout was wildly romantic, with steep cliffs and mysterious caves, quite unlike anything the young Wollstonecrafts had ever encountered outside of storybooks. And the inhabitants had endless tales to tell of the glamorous past of their region or of the doings of the spirits who haunted the place. Yet Mary must have found her new life very lonely. She met the daughters of John Allen of Cresselly, Pembrokeshire, two of whom later married sons of Josiah Wedgwood, Senior, and another of whom was to become the second wife of Sir James Mackintosh. But they did not live within easy visiting distance of Laugharne, and Mary must have sorely missed Fanny Blood. It was perhaps now that, having been denied the room of her own which she was promised, she decided that she would hesitate no longer. She even went so far as to accept a position and to start packing her belongings; and she was dissuaded from her plan only when her mother, in tears, begged her to remain.

Fortunately the exile in Wales did not last long. In the summer of 1777, after little more than a year there, the family returned to England. This time Wollstonecraft despaired not only of succeeding as a farmer but even of earning a living in any way. He had apparently concluded that he could manage most economically if he merely lived on his income and avoided investing capital only to lose it. Though he seems to have retained the title to the farm at Laugharne and to have settled there in later years, he probably never again tried to support himself or his family by his own efforts. For the moment, however, his lack of objective was to Mary's advantage. Since one place was as good as another to him, she persuaded him to settle just south of London, in Walworth, probably in the house at 9 Manor Place owned by Thomas Taylor the Platonist.[12] There she was within easy visiting distance of Fanny Blood.

Soon, however, she found life at home unbearable. With her father in the house most of the day, there was endless quarreling and little of the security and love which a girl of her age needed. Her nerves were strained, and eventually her health was undermined. And so after a year at Walworth she decided that she would put up with such an existence no longer. Somehow she had heard of a position as companion to a Mrs. Dawson, a wealthy widow living at Bath. And nothing would stop her from taking it. She must have known that her life there would often be disagreeable; yet she could not afford to be fastidious. For a girl of her station there were only two approved vocations: teaching and serving as a companion. And since she was ill prepared to teach, she must resign herself to being a companion, however odious the job might prove at times.

Mary must have had qualms when she set off alone on the twenty-hour coach trip to Bath. It took real courage for a girl of her age to leave home without her parents' consent in those days. And Mr. and Mrs. Wollstonecraft not only disapproved of her scheme but bitterly resented it. Yet Mary did not submit. She was nineteen years old now, and convinced that she was quite able to fend for herself. For years she had longed for independence, and at last her hour had come.

Of course Bath did not turn itself out for the arrival of an unknown girl like Mary. The Abbey bells did not hail her arrival, nor did the "town waits" serenade her; such honors were reserved for more distinguished visitors. Yet she must have been dazzled by this, her first glimpse of high life. In 1778 Bath in "the season" was an education in itself for anyone who wished to learn the ways of the world. All fashionable England, from royalty down, conscientiously bathed and drank the waters there (when they could spare the time from the gayer diversions of the town); and the less fashionable aspired to make the trip at least once before they died. But Mary had no desire to shine in society, and she doubtless affected a hearty disdain for the endless parade of dissolute dukes, shameless fortune-hunters, simpering swains, creole heiresses, hopeful widows, rakes, nabobs, and befuddled bumpkins. She had no longing to join the carefree young ladies who cavorted about the town with but one apparent aim: to trap a husband. She was not looking for a master; she did not choose to fit into the pattern of life which had degraded her mother. All she wanted was a room of her own, a few shillings to spend as she saw fit, a few free hours to read and improve her mind—in short, a measure of independence. And at Bath she came closer to realizing it than anywhere else she had lived.

At first, apparently, she was well pleased with her new situation. She liked the town itself, and Mrs. Dawson seemed to be an intelligent sort of woman from whom she might learn a good deal. There was a calm and dignity about her new life such as she had scarcely known before. And it is reflected in a letter which she wrote, on her return from a holiday at Southampton with Mrs. Dawson, to a Miss Arden, probably a friend from her Beverley days, now governess or nurse in the family of Sir Mordant Martin of Bronham, Norfolk:

It is so long since I received your letter—that I am half ashamed to acknowledge the receipt of it. The only thing that I can say by way of excuse, is, that I was just going to Southampton, and had no opportunity of writing. After my arrival at that place, I had sufficient leisure; but as I had nothing of consequence to say to you, I put off writing 'till I return'd to Bath, that I might not put you to the expence of postage. So much by way of apology.—

As you kindly interest yourself about me, I know it will give you pleasure to hear, that I have received great benefit from my summer excursion. I was advised by one of the Faculty to bathe in the sea, and, it has been of signal service to me.—Has [sic] to the vivacity you talk of—'tis gone forever—and all I wish for, is a chearful settled frame of mind, which I use all my endeavors to attain, and hope in time I shall. I never let imaginary troubles disturb me—indeed so many real ones have occurred to harrass my mind and body, that it will require time to bring them into tune again. Tho' I mention this, I would not have you imagine that I repine at what has befalen me—Reason, as well as religion convinces me all has happen'd for the best. This is an old worn-out maxim; but 'tis not the less true—for I am persuaded misfortunes are of the greatest service, as they set things in the light they ought to be view'd in; and gives those that are tried by them, a kind of early old age.—

I have spent a very agreeable summer, S - - n is a very pleasant place in every sense of the word—The situation is delightful; and, the inhabitants polite, and hospitable. I received so much civility that I left it with regret, I am apt to get attach'd to places—and tho' backward and reserved in forming friendships, yet, I get sometimes so interested in the happiness of mere acquaintances, that it is the source of much pain to me.

I am quite agree[d] with you in admiring Bath, it is a most delightful place—yet, I imagine the prospects did not strike me in the manner they did you. And I will tell you why I think so: you came out of Yorkshire, and out of a part not very beautiful: while on the contrary I had very lately visited Wales—where Nature appears in the most romantic dress—tho' with respect

to its natural beauties I think Bath much inferior, yet as to the embellish-
ments of art, they are not [to] be compared, for I think the buildings here
are the most regular and elegant I have ever seen. I cannot say that I should
chuse a large town for my constant residence, if I was my own mistress, as I
am fond of the country; but if I was obliged to fix in one—in point of site
alone Bath would be as agreeable to me as any.

The family I am with here is a very worthy one, Mrs. Dawson has a
very good understanding—and she has seen a great deal of the world. I hope
to improve myself by her conversation, and I endeavor to render a circumstance (that at first was disagreeable,) useful to me.

Write to me soon and tell me you are merry and well—and I then will
laugh and sing.—The keen blast of adversity has not frozen my heart—so
far from it that I cannot be quite miserable while one of my fellow-creatures
enjoys some portion of content. That your's may not be a scanty share is the
sincere wish of your affectionate Friend

Mary Wollstonecraft

Bath Octr 17th

Pray send me some account of your old friend Miss Reed, when you write
make my compliments to her.—I am so unwilling to bid you adieu that I
have wrote to the bottom of my paper, tho' the watch has long since inform'd me 'tis past twelve o'clock.[13]

Though far from faultless in spelling, the letter is painstakingly
written and punctuated and shows far more care in composition
than most of those which Mary was to write after she turned
author. She seems to have been striving her utmost for correctness
—perhaps in an attempt to impress Miss Arden—and to have expressed herself as seemed becoming to a woman of education and
taste. In fact she appears somewhat self-conscious in her complaints
about her suffering and her lost vivacity and in the satisfaction
which she takes in describing her fortitude in the face of hardship.
Her revelations about her shyness and her love for her fellow-men,
together with her preference for nature above artifice, suggest that
she was adopting the pose of a woman of sensibility. Yet it was
probably a temporary pose; after all, she had only recently declared
her independence of her family and set out alone to seek her
fortune—neither of which acts was in the tradition of the sentimental heroine. Thus what the letter reveals, no doubt, is not the
real Mary, but the woman she would have chosen to be, at this
point in her existence, if she could have shaped her life and her
nature to suit her fancy.

In time the novelty wore off her new situation, and it became almost as disagreeable as the life she had fled. Mrs. Dawson proved to be an irascible old woman who had had a rapid succession of companions and who bragged that she had used them all outrageously. Mary was better able to control her than the others had been; she was, of course, used to temper tantrums. But later in life she looked back with loathing on the indignities which she had undergone. In *Thoughts on the Education of Daughters* she wrote:

Few are the modes of earning a subsistence [for a girl "fashionably educated and left without a fortune"], and those very humiliating. Perhaps to be an humble companion to some rich old cousin, or what is still worse, to live with strangers, who are so intolerably tyrannical, that none of their own relations can bear to live with them, though they should even expect a fortune in reversion. It is impossible to enumerate the many hours of anguish such a person must spend. Above the servants, yet considered by them as a spy, and ever reminded of her inferiority when in conversation with the superiors. If she cannot condescend to mean flattery, she has not a chance of being a favorite; and should any of the visitors take notice of her, and she for a moment forget her subordinate state, she is sure to be reminded of it.[14]

This was not the independence which Mary had dreamed of when she left her parents. Yet, with all its disadvantages, it was far better than life at home with a despotic father and a spineless mother. There must have been times when she was strongly tempted to quit Mrs. Dawson forever; but, having accepted the position, she persevered. She was willing to pay dear for even a vestige of independence.

Most of her time was probably spent in beguiling the hours for Mrs. Dawson. Yet there must have been occasional moments when she could close herself into her own room to read and think about her future. Although she may have been unsure of how she would spend the years ahead, she was doubtless determined to continue her studies so as to fit herself for a more dignified position. And if she had looked about her, she could have found in Bath several women who had managed to achieve positions of considerable dignity by dint of talent and determination. Mrs. Montagu, Queen of the Bluestockings, was in and out of the town during Mary's stay there. Fanny Burney, basking in the recent success of *Evelina,* spent the season of 1780 there as the guest of Hester Thrale, a perennial visitor. Mrs. Siddons, later Mary's dear friend, was enjoying success after success in a wide variety of parts at the theaters at Bath and Bristol; and Catherine Macaulay, the celebrated ladyhistorian, left the town suddenly in 1780, perhaps as a result of the scandal which blew up when she married a surgeon's mate less than half her age. Eventually Mary Wollstonecraft would be obliged to bow to none of these women for solid accomplishments; but for the moment she was wholly obscured by them. And while they shone in their glory, she clung to her shadows—reading, reflecting, preparing herself for brighter days.

She still heard from her family from time to time. She had not broken with them completely, yet her relations with them were evidently strained. They had not yet forgiven her for leaving home, and they evidently felt that she deliberately neglected them— perhaps even looked down on them. So at least Mary intimated in the letter which she wrote to her sister Eliza from Windsor, where she was apparently spending a holiday with Mrs. Dawson:

I this morning received your letter which was truly welcome to me, as I found by it you still remember me; but I must say, I should like to be remembered in a kinder manner. There is an air of irony through your whole epistle that hurts me exceedingly: I would willingly put the most favourable construction on it—yet, still it displeases me.—I hate formality and compliments, one affectionate word would give me more pleasure than all the pretty things that come from the head; but have nothing to say to the heart.—Two or three expressions in your last particularly displeased me, you mention my *condescension,* and early *enquiries*—I know not what to make of those words.—I did not answer my Father's letter because my stay at Bath was so uncertain, and besides, I was not willing a letter from him should come to that place after I had left it; but as soon as I was settled at Windsor I writ to him, and flattered myself I should be favoured with a line or two in return.—As to Everina's illness my Father only mentioned it in a careless manner to me, and I did not imagine it had been so bad, even now I am ignorant of the nature of her complaint tho' I am very anxious about it.

You don't do me justice in supposing I seldom think of you—the happiness of my family is nearer my heart than you imagine—perhaps, too near for my own health or peace—For my anxiety preys on me, and is of no use to you. You don't say a word of my mother. I take it for granted she is well—tho' of late she has not even desired to be remembered to me. Some time or the other, in this world or a better, she may be convinced of my regard—and then may think I deserve not to be thought so harshly of. But enough on this subject. Love me but as I love you, and I'll be contented.

Obviously Mary had been put on the defensive. It was not a position calculated to endear her family to her, yet her protestations of affection are probably sincere. In the years ahead she was to prove again and again that, however much her family might try her with their irresponsibility and their ingratitude, she was unfailingly loyal to them.

Mary's letter from Windsor was addressed to Eliza at Enfield, where the family had recently settled. For reasons of his own Edward Wollstonecraft had chosen to move again—and Mary protested in her letter that she could not "divine the reason of your taking a house now, when you must pay rent for two 'till Lady-day." It was such remarks, no doubt, which her parents and sisters resented—and such illogical behavior as she complained of that made Mary content to remain with Mrs. Dawson rather than return home. Yet she was apparently planning a visit to them while she was in the vicinity of London, for she added in a pathetic postscript to her letter: "Pray make my love and duty acceptable to every part of the family—and beg them all to receive me with smiling faces—for I cannot bear frowns—or sneers."

But however much the Wollstonecrafts may have frowned or sneered at Mary upon occasion, they called on her immediately when they faced a crisis. In 1780 they sent word from Enfield that her mother was dying and would have no one but Mary to nurse her. Elizabeth Wollstonecraft evidently knew in her heart which of her children was most reliable.

Mary left Bath at once. Forgetting her mother's coldness toward her, she rushed to Enfield and nearly exhausted herself in caring for the dying woman. Her prediction that her mother would at length think better of her was now fulfilled; yet Mary was not the person to gloat. She was truly a woman of sensibility—not the self-conscious sort of sensibility which she had cultivated in her letter to Miss Arden—not the "sensibility of the head," as she herself would have said later—but the sensibility of the heart, a warm and affectionate heart which was quick to forgive injuries and eager to serve those whom she loved. Her mother's present plight—as well as her whole life in retrospect—was pitiful; and Mary's heart always melted at the sight of a human being in trouble. "I think I love most people best when they are in adversity," she wrote later to a friend, "for pity is one of my prevailing passions."

Her father, of course, excited no such pity. She found him in no better state than she had left him. In the present crisis he was probably only an additional burden, for he was still idle and constantly underfoot. In *Mary* she wrote of her heroine's father during his wife's last illness:

He treated her with indifference; but when her illness at all interfered with his pleasures, he expostulated in the most cruel manner, and visibly harassed the invalid. Mary would then assiduously try to turn his attention to something else; and when sent out of the room, would watch at the door, until the storm was over, for unless it was, she could not rest.[15]

It was a long, trying time for Mary. Her mother demanded constant attention, and Mary never denied her. At last the ailing woman murmured apologetically, "A little patience, and all will be over."[16] Then slowly, wearily, she died as abjectly as she had lived.

When the funeral was over, Mary doubtless made plans to be off at once. Naturally she had no desire to stay on at Enfield and keep house for her father. Sooner or later he was married again—to a woman whom his children considered beneath them. And one by one the family drifted away. Edward, the oldest, was already married and practicing law in London, and he eventually articled his youngest brother, Charles, to him and took his sister Everina into his home to aid with the housekeeping. Eliza married a man named Bishop and settled in London, and James went to sea, apparently promising to revive the family fortunes in the course of a voyage across the Pacific.[17] As for Mary, she was probably one of the first to leave. But she did not return to Bath. She had evidently had her fill of life as a lady's companion and welcomed the opportunity to escape from it. Her future plans were no doubt hazy; perhaps she had decided that she should settle down quietly somewhere to prepare for a better position than she could command for the present. At all events she went to live with Fanny Blood and her family, who had moved to Walham Green, south of London, near Fulham.

Mary was twenty-one years old now and still striving to fill the gaps in her formal education. Yet, without realizing it, she had acquired a considerable education in human affairs. She had lived in Essex, in Yorkshire, on the outskirts of London, in Wales, and at Bath. She had lived on farms and in the city, by the sea and near the mountains. She had seen many ruins of the remote past of her nation's history and had viewed the most colorful sight that England could then afford: the gathering of the well and the ailing, the wise and the foolish, who disported themselves at "the national hospital," as Matt Bramble had called Bath. These experiences not only furnished her with material for later observations but broadened her horizons and matured her judgment. Now and later she was to gain from travel and experience what otherwise she could never have achieved in her time: the enduring values of a liberal education. Few girls of her class could have gained an education to match hers.

Moreover, conditions at home and elsewhere had taught her much. She had faced hardship and cruelty and learned to rise above them. She had discovered how to manage such apparently unmanageable people as her father and Mrs. Dawson. She had developed an indomitable courage and a determination which were to carry her far. Yet her experience had come at the cost of serenity. All the anguish of life with her parents, of constant moving, of insecurity, had levied its toll. As long as she lived she was plagued by chronic nervousness and irritability which she well knew stemmed from the worries of her early years. In 1795 after a period of despondence she wrote to her lover:

Fatigued during my youth by the most arduous struggles, not only to obtain independence, but to render myself useful, not merely pleasure, for which I had the most lively taste,—I mean the simple pleasures that flow from passion and affection,—escaped me, but the most melancholy views of life were impressed by a disappointed heart on my mind.[18]

It was small wonder that Mary subscribed wholeheartedly, when she became a teacher, to Locke's theory that man is the product of environment alone. Her own character seems at first glance to have been shaped wholly by experience. Yet on closer observation one reflects that she must have inherited from her hard-working Spitalfields grandparents or her Irish ancestors, if not from her parents, a fundamental stubbornness and a brave spirit of independence. Without them she would have quailed at her father's tyranny instead of rebelling against it. She would have despaired at the hopelessness of her situation as a young girl and sought refuge in a degrading marriage. Thanks, however, to her stubbornness and her independent spirit, she challenged her father's tyranny and fought her way to personal freedom. And later the same qualities enabled her to extend her private war against tyranny—especially the tyranny of the male—and to vindicate the rights of her sex.

CHAPTER II
Brief Triumph
(1780-1786)

*My heart would fain hold all the human race, and
every new affection would add to its comfort but for
the bitter alloy which will mix itself with every thing
here.*   —*Letter to George Blood.*

MARY'S two years at Walham Green were uneventful,
but probably far from peaceful.[1] Thanks to Mr. Blood's
chronic shiftlessness and improvidence, life for his family
was seldom free from worry. To be sure, he never descended to
such brutality as Mary had experienced from her father; but he
must have exasperated her constantly. A few years later, in letters
to his son George, she referred to him as a man "lost in the most
selfish sensuality," whose death would "deliver your mother from
one torment—poor woman!" And when she was living at his
house, she must have resented seeing him relaxed and contented
while his wife slaved at needlework for ridiculously low pay.
Fanny later wrote to Mary's sisters: "My mother used to sit at
work, in summer, from *four* in the morning 'till she could not see
at night, which with the assistance of one of her daughters did not
bring her more than half a guinea a week, and often not quite
that." And she added: "You may recollect that [Mary] was almost
blinded and sick to death after a job we did for Mrs. Bensley when
you were here." Evidently Mary was not content to sit idly by
while Fanny and her mother slaved.

But for all their efforts, the family could rarely have been out
of debt. One Christmas Mary was obliged to borrow twenty
pounds from her sister Eliza's husband to tide them over a particularly
difficult period. And afterwards, in a letter to her sister
Everina, she remarked: "I don't repent—for if I had not, the
Bloods would have been inevitably ruined .... You may suppose

my mind must have been very much distressed before I could submit to this—it added indeed to the misery of that *wretched time*—but there was no recourse . . . yet it made me miserable. I saw I was *entangling* myself with an *obligation*." Like most people in modest circumstances the Bloods must have been hard put to it to secure even the necessities of life: prices had been rising steadily ever since the beginning of the Seven Years' War, and wages had lagged far behind. Meanwhile taxes had increased; for the struggle with the American colonies had proved costly from the outset, and now the war in Europe was increasing the burden.

Naturally there was a general restiveness in the air. Ever since 1768-69, when the voters of Middlesex had been obliged to elect John Wilkes four times before he was admitted to his seat in Parliament, Englishmen of the middle and lower classes had been asking themselves what had become of the freedom which their forefathers had supposedly gained in the Bloodless Revolution. The revolution wrought in their own times had been industrial rather than political, and it seemed to have robbed them of their liberties. George III had managed to strengthen his power immeasurably, thanks to the outmoded system of Parliamentary representation which denied any share in government to thousands of Englishmen living in industrial centers. The poor were overtaxed and underprivileged: taxes on the necessities of life were exorbitant (the tariff on salt was 300 per cent), and laborers were forced to accept what wages their employers chose to offer them, since the Settlement Laws forbade their seeking work outside their own parishes without special permission. By 1780 the inevitable reaction had set in. It was the year of the Yorkshire Petition, of Burke's bills for economic reform, of the Duke of Richmond's proposal for manhood suffrage, annual Parliaments, and equal electoral districts. It was the year, too, of Dunning's shocking motion in Parliament "that the power of the Crown has increased, is increasing, and ought to be diminished." The yeast of democracy was acting in England.

Later in life Mary would have followed keenly these developments, but at present she probably ignored them. She had been brought up to think that such matters were not a woman's business, and she had not yet ventured to question the conventional attitude. In 1776 she had been busy trying to keep peace in her own family and had scarcely spared a thought to the revolution in America. And now in 1781-82 she was busy helping to preserve order in the Blood household. She had not yet learned what she and her radical friends were later to call "universal benevolence," and she was perfectly content to confine her efforts to a narrow area.

Thus she was, no doubt, reasonably happy at Walham Green. Her father could no longer tyrannize over her; Mrs. Dawson could no longer nag. She was obliged to live on a simpler scale than ever before in her life—perhaps even to endure actual want. Yet she probably repined very little, for her nature made her welcome hardship provided it gave her an opportunity to aid those whom she loved. And in the Blood family she had found three people on whom she could pour out her affection as freely as though they were of her own family. Her later letters to George Blood show that she had developed, as she herself said, a "motherly tenderness" for him, and that she felt a strong filial affection for Mrs. Blood, whom she often called "our mother." But of course it was companionship with Fanny which most delighted Mary. The two girls could read together and discuss their reading, could perhaps take an occasional trip up to London, only five miles away. Certainly a spinsterhood like this would be far preferable to a marriage like her mother's or Mrs. Blood's. Mary had responsibilities, but she was her own mistress.

Yet gradually her friendship for Fanny was to be overclouded. Living with the Bloods made Mary realize that her friend was not such a paragon of virtue as she had supposed. In the novel *Mary* the heroine's friend Ann proved to be

timid and irresolute, and rather fond of dissipation; grief only had power to make her reflect. In every thing it was not the great, but the beautiful, or the pretty, that caught her attention. And in composition, the polish of style, and harmony of numbers, interested her much more than the flights of genius, or abstracted speculations. She often wondered at the books Mary chose, who, though she had a lively imagination, would frequently study authors whose works were addressed to the understanding.[2]

Ann's manner toward her friend was often distant and abstracted —so much so as to make the fictitious Mary resentful, until she realized that her friend's coolness sprang from a disappointment in love. Then she felt an overpowering pity for the girl, and gradually assumed the role of her protector.

Probably the real Mary's friendship for Fanny ran much the same course; at least Fanny seems to have suffered from a disappointment in love, and Mary's attitude toward her eventually changed. For some time Fanny had been wooed rather halfheartedly by a man named Hugh Skeys, whom she dearly loved. Yet Skeys hesitated to marry her, apparently because he feared that his family would disapprove of the Bloods. So Fanny languished in neglect, and of course Mary felt a profound pity for her. Yet that pity implied a new relationship between the two girls. Fanny was no longer Mary's model; in fact Mary eventually realized that her friend's character was not so strong as she had supposed. And the more she undertook to direct Fanny's life, the more aware she grew of the girl's limitations. Thus the tables were turned, and Mary became the dominant one of the pair. Perhaps the truth of the matter was not that Fanny's character had grown weaker, but that Mary's had strengthened, thanks to the independence which she had won for herself. Indeed before long she was managing not only Fanny's affairs but those of the entire Blood family. Her self-confidence was growing apace.

Presently it received a new test. In November, 1782, affairs in the Wollstonecraft family reached another crisis, and again Mary was summoned to take charge. This time it was her sister Eliza Bishop who needed assistance, for she was ill at her home in London. She had just borne a daughter (named Mary in honor of her sister) and had failed to rally properly after her confinement; in fact she seemed for a while to have lost her mind. Of course Mary responded at once to the appeal for help. And when she reached the Bishops' house she found Eliza improved but still far from rational. "Her ideas are all disjointed," Mary wrote to Everina, "and a number of wild whims float on her imagination, and unconnected fall from her—something like strange dreams when judgment sleeps and fancy sports at a fine rate." Soon she had penetrated to the root of Eliza's trouble and concluded that it stemmed from a profound aversion which she had taken to her husband. Mary had seen enough of the man to sympathize wholeheartedly with her sister. "His friend Wood very justly said that he was either a 'lion or a spaniel,'" she told Everina; and though she pitied him, she was convinced that "misery must be his portion at any rate till he alters himself—and that would be a miracle."

Meanwhile she decided that Eliza would never regain her health or her reason until she escaped from her husband; and she set herself to the task of finding a means of escape. "I am convinced," she reported to Everina, "this is the only expedient to save Bess—and she declares she had rather be a teacher than stay here." But Mary was hard-pressed to find shelter for the frantic woman. Their father's house would never do, and she could hardly ask the Bloods to take Eliza and her baby into their narrow quarters. The logical place for her was their brother Edward's house. But Mary and he had never seen eye to eye, and she was chary of asking favors from him. "Do you think Edward will receive her?" she asked Everina, who was still living with her brother and his family. "Do speak to him," she begged. Then, perhaps mindful of her own more authoritative position in the family, she added: "Or if you imagine that I should have more influence on his mind, I will contrive to see you."

Evidently Edward refused to be a party to his sister's scheme, for Mary mentioned him no more. When next she wrote to Everina, she could report only that they had suffered through another "dismal day—long and dreary," with Bishop ill at home and misery haunting the whole house. Apparently she had tried to arbitrate the family quarrel, for she complained: "My spirits are

harried with listening to pros and cons, and my head is so confused that I sometimes say no when I ought to say yes. My heart
is almost broken with listening to B. while he *reasons* the case. I
cannot insult him with advice which he would never have wanted
if he was capable of attending to it." Affairs were growing worse,
and Mary's patience was nearly exhausted. Eliza, she remarked,
was "better and of course more sad."

Soon Fanny came to visit Mary at the Bishops', and the two
girls made plans for action. They would take the only possible
course: steal Eliza away, leaving her baby with Bishop, and then
find shelter where they could. It was an intrepid scheme, and to
carry it out Mary must flout all the sacred conventions clustering
about the bonds of matrimony and maternal love. She was deliberately interfering between a man and the woman God had given
him, separating a mother from the child she had borne. Rigidly
righteous folk would be scandalized at her conduct. To make
matters worse, Mary was still in debt to Bishop, for Fanny had
been able to repay only five guineas of the twenty pounds which
he had lent them. Yet she did not hesitate. She believed firmly
that unless Eliza escaped from her present environment she would
never regain her sanity; and she was convinced that the life and
happiness of a human being were holier than any abstract principle. Only shortly before, she had written to Everina: "May my
habitation never be fixed among the tribe that . . . draw fixed
conclusions from general rules—that attend to the literal meaning
only, and because a thing ought to be, expect that it will come to
pass." Now, as later in her life, her passion for freedom made her
spurn the restraints which society sought to impose upon her.

One day in January, 1783, while Bishop was away from home,
Fanny carried Mary's and Eliza's belongings to a brushmaker's
shop in the Strand, and the two sisters, with three guineas between
them, made their escape. They were terrified lest they be discovered, and according to Mary, Eliza "lost all presence of mind"
and "bit her *wedding ring* to pieces" in her terror. They took
separate coaches to avoid being traced, and drove to Hackney,

where Mary, posing as "Miss Johnson," took rooms with a Mrs. Dodds on Church Street. Their success was, as Mary herself admitted, "as much good luck as good management."

Now Mary had a chance to reflect on the possible consequences of her boldness. "My heart beats time with every carriage that rolls by," she wrote to Everina shortly after their arrival, "and a knocking at the door almost throws me into a *fit* .... I hope B. will not discover us, for I could sooner face a Lion—yet the door never opens but I expect to see him panting for breath." What, she asked, should she do if they were discovered? How would Edward advise her to manage matters? "Can [Bishop] force her?—but I'll not suppose it—yet I can think of nothing else." She was too nervous to go to bed, and she confessed that she feared Bishop quite as much as Eliza did. And to show Everina how completely distraught she was, she added in a postscript: "I almost wish for a husband—for I want somebody to support me."

In the days that followed Mary gradually mastered her fears. Though exhausted from the nervous strain and plagued by "a little periodical fever that keeps me warm these cold nights," she never swerved from her purpose of gaining Eliza's freedom. When Everina wrote that Bishop had called at their brother's house and demanded that Eliza return home for the baby's sake, Mary replied: "I know ... the generality will pity him and blame me—but however if we can snatch Bess from extreme wretchedness, what reason shall we have to rejoice." When Eliza pined for her child, Mary could "both pity and love her," but she forced a callous tone, admitting that "the poor brat ... had got a little hold on my affections," and hoping that "some time or other ... we shall get it." She had acted boldly and impulsively, as she well knew; but she had no notion of surrendering an inch of her gains. "What will be the issue of this affair," she wrote, "'tis impossible to say—but I am cheered with the hope that our poor girl will never again be in this man's power. Spite of the many vexations that have and still occur—my spirits do not sink. Supported by conscious rectitude, I smile at B.'s malice and almost thank him for it as it gives me fresh strength to pursue what I have begun with vigor."

In due time, of course, she tasted the ostracism which she had anticipated. Her brother Edward apparently disapproved strongly of her conduct, and a friend named Mrs. Brook "with grief of heart gave up my friendship." Old Mrs. Clare of Hoxton, who had ridden out to Hackney in the rain to offer the girls some money, approved "with *cautious words*"; but Mary feared that she might "advise a reconciliation" if she were to talk with Bishop. Fanny's friend Hugh Skeys, in whom Bishop had confided, at first thought that "there was not the most distant prospect of comfort" in the Bishop family; but later he sent word that *"poor B.* was puzzling himself to bring about a reconciliation," and that it might be advisable, since undoubtedly "he would now endeavour to make Mrs. B. happy." Still Mary was adamant. She had fully expected that others would conclude that "the strong affection of a sister *might* apologize for my conduct, but that the scheme was by no means a good one." And she was firm in her conviction that she had acted wisely. "All these disorders will give way to time . . . ," she wrote to Everina; "and the thought of having assisted to bring about so desirable an event will ever give me pleasure to think of."

Mary's self-confidence was, indeed, growing so rapidly that she must often have seemed rather obnoxious to those who were obliged to deal with her. If, as she said presently, she loved most people best when they were in adversity, it was perhaps because then she could manage their affairs for them. And though she acted always on impulse, she insisted that she was following the dictates of reason and the will of God. In one of her letters to Everina she wrote:

I am sorry but not surprised at your spirits being sunk. Nor do I wonder that the varnish that a sanguine temper gives to every object begins to wear off. The pictures that the imagination draws are so very delightful that we willingly let it predominate over reason till experience forces us to see the truth. The mind of man is formed to admire perfection, and perhaps our longing after it and the pleasure we take in observing a shadow of it is a *faint line* of that Image that was first stamped on the soul. Lost in sensual gratification, many think of this world only—and tho' we declare in general terms that there is no such thing as happiness on Earth, yet it requires severe disappointments to make us forbear to seek it and be contented with endeavoring to prepare for a better state. Don't suppose I am preaching when I say uniformity of conduct cannot in any degree be expected from those whose first motive of action is not pleasing the Supreme Being—and those who humbly rely on Providence will not only be supported in affliction but have a Peace imparted to them that is past all describing. This state is indeed a warfare, and we learn little that we don't smart in the attaining. The cant of weak enthusiasts have made the consolations of Religion and the assistance of the Holy Spirit appear to the inconsiderate ridiculous—but it is the only solid foundation of comfort that the weak efforts of reason will be assisted and our hearts and minds corrected and improved till the time arrives when we shall not only see *perfection* but see every creature about us happy.

When Mary finished writing these lines, she doubtless congratulated herself on her noble sentiments and the firm, sure tone of her expression. But Everina could be pardoned if she harbored the thought that her sister, at the age of twenty-four, seemed as stern and self-righteous as any Puritan preacher of sixty.

When at last Bishop gave up his attempts to regain his wife, and the scandal of the whole affair had died down, Mary was faced with a new problem: how to support Eliza. Realizing that Bishop would be unlikely to give his wife an allowance, she carefully considered several possibilities. "We have been racking our brains and cannot yet fix on any feasible plan," she wrote to Everina. "We once thought of going to Ireland & trying to keep a school or a little shop." But she had discarded the notion of opening a school because, as she said, "the MONIES did not answer"; and as for keeping shop, that was doubtless only a last resort. The two sisters could have gone to the Bloods' house; in fact Mr. Blood had urged them to do so. But Mary had apparently had enough of that arrangement, and presently she recalled a scheme which Fanny had suggested before Eliza's illness: hiring a small house together and supporting themselves by sewing and drawing. "With economy we can live on a guinea a week," Mary wrote optimistically to Everina, "and that sum we can with ease earn." It seemed like an ideal arrangement, for it would not only solve her problem and Eliza's but also rescue Fanny from her family.

But as soon as Fanny heard of Mary's decision, she had misgivings. Doubtless hesitant to acknowledge her timidity to Mary, she wrote to Everina that she had thought better of the suggestion since she first broached it. She recalled the difficulties which her mother had faced when she tried to earn a living by sewing. She feared that Edward Wollstonecraft, who had never approved of her, would oppose her living with his sisters. And as a substitute for this plan she repeated a suggestion made by Mrs. Clare: that Mary and Eliza open "a little shop of haberdashery and perfumery, in the neighbourhood of Hoxton, where they may be certain of meeting encouragement." Such a shop could be stocked for approximately fifty pounds, which sum Edward could doubtless raise for them. "However," Fanny added, "lest he should be averse from assisting them, from a notion that I should live with them, I solemnly declare that nothing is further from my intention;—and I wish you would take the earliest opportunity of assuring him, from me, *that on no account whatever will I ever live with them, unless fortune should make me quite independent,* which I never expect.—My health is so much impaired that I should only be a burthen on them—and for my own part, I don't spend a thought on what may become of me." Fanny's fears were well founded; she was in failing health, doubtless aggravated by Hugh Skeys's failure to marry her. But to Mary her friend's objections, when she heard of them, seemed timorous and cowardly. She was bitterly disappointed—and confirmed in her suspicion that Fanny was fundamentally weak in character. And though Mary could pity and love the weak, she could admire wholeheartedly only the strong.

At last, however, she decided to give up her plan and to risk opening a school instead. And having reached the decision, she persuaded Fanny to share in the venture, and they rented a house north of London, in Islington, then a country village. When few pupils appeared, they moved over to Newington Green. And there the school was an immediate success. Though they had taken a large house and were paying an "enormous" rent (as Mary later had reason to complain), they apparently were successful from the outset; and soon they had not only twenty day pupils but six boarders as well: a distant relative named Mrs. Campbell and her son, and a Mrs. Disney with her three children.[3] As if by magic all Mary's problems were suddenly solved. And before long she was able to summon Everina from her unpleasant surroundings at Edward's house and set her to work in the school too. Never had the future looked so promising.

Mary probably threw all her best efforts into her job as teacher. Since she had as yet no heterodox theories of education, the curriculum undoubtedly consisted of the three R's, plus perhaps music, drawing, and French. Yet because she was a conscientious woman, she must have been eager to learn as she was teaching, so that her work might become increasingly effective. All her reading in the past now stood her in good stead. Yet it had been directed toward no particular end. Now she doubtless needed to fill in gaps, to read up especially on matters directly related to her new vocation. Yet she would not have repined; she was never afraid of hard work, and she must have welcomed work which bore immediate results.

She was uncommonly fortunate in the location she had chosen for her school. She would have had to search far to find a more congenial spot than Newington Green. Although it was near enough to London to afford the attractions of the city, it was a restful place, consisting of "a piece of open grass with a few ancient elms and quaint Elizabethan houses round it."[4] Yet for all its seclusion, it was a remarkably stimulating neighborhood. On the north side of the Green stood a little brick chapel attended by a congregation of English Presbyterians of liberal sympathies who had as their afternoon preacher or "lecturer" the Reverend Richard Price, a Welshman by birth who since 1758 had lived in a house on the south side of the Green.[5] He and his friend Joseph Priestley, a frequent visitor at his house, were generally recognized as the leading liberal philosophers of England.

When Mary moved to Newington Green, Price, then sixty years old, had reached the pinnacle of his career. His *Observations on the Nature of Civil Liberty, the Principles of Government, and the Justice and Policy of the War with America,* published in 1776, had sold over 60,000 copies in its first year and prompted replies from some thirty writers, including Edmund Burke, the Archbishop of York, and John Wesley. Earlier he had distinguished himself as a critic of England's financial structure, and he was commonly hailed as the Father of Life Insurance, the Sinking Fund, and Old Age Pensions. In recognition of his achievements he had been elected a Fellow of the Royal Society, voted the freedom of the City of London, and awarded a Doctorate of Divinity by the University of Aberdeen and a Doctorate of Laws by Yale University, the latter in a special ceremony at which he and George Washington were the only ones so honored. In 1788 he had been invited to emigrate to America and direct the finances of the new nation. He was, indeed, a spectacular figure, quite the most famous man whom Mary had ever met. Yet he allowed distinction to sit lightly on his shoulders. He always insisted that he had been led into political or financial controversies against his will, and that he preferred to live quietly at the Green, dabbling in his laboratory, preaching God's word, and writing an occasional moral treatise. Though he knew or corresponded with many of the leading thinkers of the day—such men as Hume, Franklin, Jefferson, Condorcet, Necker, and Turgot—he was happiest with his neighbors on the Green, where he could challenge a friend to a hopping race to Stoke Newington parish church, display his ability to leap over a honeysuckle bush, enjoy a daily dip in nearby Peerless Pool, or drop in on his friends after supper in his dressing gown.

Mary soon became acquainted with Price and his neighbors. She was especially friendly with Mrs. James Burgh, widow of a Scotsman who for many years had conducted a school at the southeast corner of the Green,[6] and who was remembered as the author of the posthumous *Political Disquisitions,* a notable contribution to the liberal cause. Mary must also have known Thomas Rogers, the wealthy London banker, who lived with his eight children two houses south of Price.[7] Though born an Anglican and a Tory, Rogers had married into a Non-conformist family and had gradually been converted to liberal opinions in both religion and politics. He too had favored the American colonists in their revolution; in fact when he first heard of the Battle of Lexington, he put on mourning. One of his sons was the celebrated Samuel Rogers, who was to distinguish himself as a poet and a patron of less affluent (though often more gifted) writers.

In time Mary was occasionally attending the services at Price's little chapel, where she occupied the pew next to the Rogers family. She may have been friendly with two of their relatives, Miss Mary Mitchell and Mrs. Mildred Worthington, who since the death of Mrs. Rogers had served as housekeeper and governess to the family. Yet she would not have been confined to the company of women; a true democracy prevailed at the Green. Women were accepted there as reasonable human beings! Indeed there was an amazing congeniality about the whole neighborhood. Samuel Rogers later said that Dr. Price could induce in all his fellows "a frame of mind as heavenly as his own";[8] and Price's nephew, returning to Wales after a long stay at the Green, dreaded leaving his "heavenly-minded friends at Newington Green, among whom such unbounded love reigns."[9] Mary was not obliged to agree with the principles advocated by her new friends: their "heavenly-mindedness" included tolerance. Indeed Price was, for those days, a marvel of tolerance. He remained a friend of Hume and Priestley even while he was engaged in public controversy with them; and (test of tests!) he was devoted to his invalid wife, who remained a staunch Anglican to her death. No, Mary was not obliged to accept her friends' opinions. Her alert mind, her healthy curiosity, and her eagerness to aid her fellows were sufficient recommendations. Yet she could hardly have lived in their midst without being somehow affected by their way of looking at life. Their lively minds and their affable spirits must have delighted her. Never before had she met people whom she could admire so thoroughly.

Price, above all, must have charmed and influenced her, much as Mr. Clare had charmed and influenced her when she lived at Hoxton. Here was another man who was the direct antithesis of most of the men whom Mary had known best: her father, Mr. Blood, and her brother-in-law Bishop. He was, according to Samuel Rogers, "slim in person, and rather below the common size, but possessed of great muscular strength and remarkable activity. With strong features, and a very intelligent eye, his countenance was the mirror of his mind; and when lighted up by conversation his features were peculiarly pleasing."[10] He was strong but did not use his strength to tyrannize; he was brilliant but showed no disdain for those less gifted. And he and Mary had much in common: both had lived in Wales, both were generous almost to a fault, and both had an omnivorous curiosity. Price could talk to Mary about literature, composition, ethics, mathematics, politics, and a score of other subjects which she must have thirsted to understand more thoroughly. He could fascinate her with demonstrations of the telescope, the microscope, and the electrical machine in his laboratory. She must have listened entranced as the old man talked on in his absent-minded way, shifting his wig about on his head, folding and unfolding his cocked hat, and twisting his legs one around the other. He knew so much, and she so little! But from him she could glean innumerable bits of information to supplement her limited education and render her teaching more effective. She could learn new wisdom too; and she was perhaps a better teacher and a finer woman for her chance to observe that true humility is an ornament to even the ablest and most successful of human beings. Her own little successes had left her with an overweening self-confidence, and she could profit by this opportunity to compare her achievements—and her estimate of herself —with those of a man who had far outdistanced her.

Just how much Price helped to mold Mary's opinions is dubious. Though Godwin insists that she had no "superstitious adherence to his doctrines,"[11] she may well have learned from him to regard her orthodox religion more critically. In the long run she was to go beyond Price's "low Arianism" in religious liberalism, but she may well have been first tempted to question her old principles by his provocative conversations and sermons. In politics too she eventually subscribed to more radical theories than Price held, but she may have learned from him to criticize the established order. She was ripe for such criticism, surely, after years of finding fault with the established order in her own home and others'. She may have read Price's *Observations on the Nature of Civil Liberty* or his *Observations on the Importance of the American Revolution* (published in 1784, soon after Mary moved to the Green) or she may have read James Burgh's *Political Disquisitions,* which must have circulated freely in the neighborhood. Had she read any one of these books, she would have been struck by their close analysis of political problems or their occasional impassioned pleas for more equitable government. Yet probably at this point in her career she would have been more puzzled than enlightened by the books; they assumed a knowledge of and interest in politics such as Mary could hardly have acquired as yet. And since her letters and her early works show no trace of liberal theories—since she was not to express any interest in politics or sympathy with democratic doctrines until after she had settled in London in 1787—it is reasonable to assume that Mary was not converted to the new faith during her stay at Newington Green. But it is more than likely that Price and his friends prepared the way for her later conversion.

On the whole, life at the Green moved along smoothly. Mary was probably worried from time to time about her father's affairs. He had gradually fallen into debt and of course was not above appealing to his successful daughter for aid. But she probably did not mind sending him money now and again provided she was not obliged to live with him. She had much to be thankful for. She was busy with work which she enjoyed, and she was aiding Eliza, Everina, and Fanny. She had found at Newington Green not only independence, but also a means of aiding others; and that more than anything else must have gratified her. She could look with pride at the little haven which she had created for her

sisters and her friend, and could reflect joyfully that her scheme of
opening the school, however rash in appearance, had proved wise.
All had indeed turned out well. Who could have suspected a year
or two before, when Mary had been living quietly with the Bloods,
that she would so soon be mistress of a school of her own and
friend of such a man as Dr. Price? She had emerged from all the
petty cares which had shadowed her earlier years; she had made
of life what life should be. And now she could relax from the
intense efforts which had carried her so far; she could enjoy work
and companionship—and even love.

Price and the devout residents of the Green were not her only
friends. Her letters of the period refer to a Mrs. Cockburn, a Mr.
Sowerby, a Mr. and Mrs. Poole, a Mr. Church, and an Anglican
clergyman named John Hewlett. Hewlett was something of a
literary man; at least he was to become so in 1786, when he published his first book, a volume of *Sermons on Different Subjects*.
It was perhaps through him that Mary was taken one day to call
on the great Dr. Johnson shortly before his death. The old man
evidently took a fancy to her, for he invited her to call again. And
Mary must have been thrilled at the chance to converse with him.
At this point in her life he must have represented all that was wise
and good in the mind of man; it was only later that she concluded
that, for all his wisdom and goodness, he was fundamentally an
intellectual coward incapable of appreciating the power of poetry
or music.[12]

Hewlett may also have introduced her to another Church of
England clergyman, who was to make a deeper mark on her life.
This was the Reverend Joshua Waterhouse, then resident at Cambridge, where he was about to receive his Baccalaureate of Theology
at St. Catherine's College.[13] Because Mary's letters to Waterhouse
have been lost, there is no way of knowing how they met or how
far their friendship progressed. On the surface Waterhouse seems
like the last man in the world who would have attracted Mary
Wollstonecraft. Yet apparently he did. She who had "almost
wished for a husband" only when she sorely needed protection

had evidently undergone a change of heart. But for Joshua Water-house, of all people! He was, to be sure, a clergyman; but he was a dashing creature, considered one of the handsomest and best-dressed men of his college and used to mingling in the most fash-ionable society of Bath and Bristol with his friend Sir John Danvers of Swithlands. Yet Mary certainly loved him, though perhaps against her better judgment. For all her supposed self-sufficiency, she was not above being dazzled by a debonair man of the world who had little to recommend him apart from his physical appear-ance and his urbanity.

Thus Mary had much to take up her mind during her first years at Newington Green. And from time to time new cares were thrust upon her. Fanny's health was a constant worry. She seemed to be growing steadily weaker, and was showing symptoms of tuberculosis. Was the Green a bad place for her? Should they move elsewhere? Then, providentially, came the long-delayed proposal from Hugh Skeys, who had accepted a position in Lisbon. Since marriage would doubtless revive Fanny's spirits and since Lisbon was considered a healthful place for consumptives, Mary urged her to accept at once. (Indeed the proposal seems so well timed that one wonders if Mary could have prompted Skeys.) Soon pre-parations for Fanny's passage were made, and she left England early in 1785 and was married in Lisbon on February 24, shortly after her arrival.

Mary must have missed her friend grievously; Fanny had al-ways meant more to her than either of her own sisters. Yet she rejoiced at the thought that Fanny would soon regain her health. And soon she was able to congratulate herself once again that her impulse had been justified. On March 30 Fanny was writing from Lisbon to Eliza and Everina that her spitting of blood had stopped and her cough had improved noticeably. And though she com-plained of "an extreme depression of spirits," which prevented her from writing oftener, she admitted that her distresses were largely imaginary, and she gave a cheerful picture of her new life. "I shall remain in town . . . a month or two," she wrote, "as I find it agrees with me, even tho' I play the rake here, and have a crowd of visitors almost every evening." As for her new husband, he was, she said, "a good sort of a creature," who had "sense enough to let his cat of a wife follow her own inclinations in *almost* every thing"; and she signed her letter gaily: "Frances—(Heigh ho!) *Skeys.*" Her husband was probably just as well pleased with his bargain, for Mary reported triumphantly in a letter to Fanny's brother George: "Skeys has received congratulatory letters from most of his friends and relations in Ireland, and he now regrets that he did not marry sooner. All his mighty fears had no foundation— so that if he had had courage to have braved the world's dread laugh, and ventured to have acted for himself, he might have spared Fanny many griefs, the *scars* of which will *never* be obliterated."

With Fanny in Portugal Mary felt more than ever obliged to take the Blood family under her wing. Before long Mr. Blood was out of work, and she was doing her utmost to find a job for him. Then George fell into difficulties. He had been articled to an attorney named Palmer, who lived near Newington Green. And when Palmer was arrested for forgery and George feared that he might be implicated, Mary took him in at the school. Nor was that the end of the affair. One day while George was staying at the school, bailiffs called and asked for information about him. But Mary was undaunted. She helped him to escape from the school and saw him off on a coach going west. And presently she was writing to him in Dublin, informing him that the bailiffs had called not about the forgery case but to arrest him on a charge of bastardy brought by Palmer's maidservant. "I suppose the child is P.'s, or many fathers may dispute the honor," she observed realistically. Then: "Let that be as it will, the recent affair of Mary Ann would have given this some colour of truth." Apparently George had been in such difficulties before, and yet Mary was not too squeamish to befriend him.

In doing so she was brought once again face to face with the criticism of conventional folk. Evidently most of her acquaintances

disapproved of her aiding George, for she wrote in one of her
letters to him:

Mrs. Campbell (who has all the constancy that attends on folly—and in
whose mind when any principle is fixt it remains for ever) has long disliked you. This confined ill-humour has at last broken out, and she has sufficiently railed at your *vices,* and the *encouragement* I have given them—and
this to the Morphys, who she is very intimate with. They have repeated her
stories to their neighbours—so they have ran all over the Green—and I am
assured in a very gross manner. I called on Mrs. Poole. She was very rude.
As you know the woman you can easily conceive how she would behave. I
believe she would have scolded me in the true vulgar female style—if I had
not assumed the Princess. Mr. Carter was full of enquiries and impertinently
curious. The Poet [perhaps Samuel Rogers] was the only one that seemed
at all concerned about you.

But Mary cared not; she was positive that she had acted wisely.
And she continued to correspond with George, often inundating
him with advice against prodigality, homilies on the ardors of the
true Christian life, and assurances that she had "a motherly tenderness" for him. By September she was able to announce to him
that Fanny had found him a position in Lisbon, adding: "I hope
to see you before the year is out, as I am determined to be with her
on a certain occasion, if I can possibly contrive it." Fanny had written that she was pregnant, and Mary resolved, whatever the cost,
to be with her when she was confined. In her weakened state
childbirth might prove to be a greater tax than her constitution
could bear. She would need the tenderest care possible, and Mary
dared not trust her to strange hands.

Here was a new worry. Indeed Mary's worries were rapidly increasing during the year 1785. For the first time life seems suddenly to have overwhelmed her. Early in July she complained of
illness. "I have been very ill," she wrote to George Blood, "—and
gone through the usual physical operations, have been bled and
blistered, yet still I am not well. My harassed mind will in time
wear out my body. I have been so hunted down by cares, and see
so many that I must encounter, that my spirits are quite depressed.
I have lost all relish for life—and my almost broken heart is only
cheared by the prospect of death. I may be years a-dying tho', and

so I ought to be patient—for at this time to wish myself away would be selfish." And in the conclusion of her letter: "Adieu to the village delights. I almost hate the Green, for it seems the grave of all my comforts."

What had happened? Surely her father's difficulties could not suddenly have plunged her into such a despondent state; nor could loneliness for Fanny or George. She may well have been having financial trouble with the school, or may have been irked (as she no doubt was) by the constant company of her sisters. Yet such annoyances would hardly have occasioned such profound depression in one who had weathered as many hardships as Mary had. And it was not a momentary depression. Within three weeks of her first complaint she was writing to George: "I am resigned to my fate, but 'tis that gloomy kind of resignation that is akin to despair. My heart—my affection cannot fix here, and without some one to love, this world is a desart to me. Perhaps tenderness weakens the mind, and is not fit for a state of trial." And less than a month later: "My 'social comforts drop away'—for I now seldom see Church or any other rational creature who I can love. Labour and sorrow fill up my time, and so I toil through this vale of tears —and all this leads to an end which will be happy if I faint not."

Surely something drastic had happened to provoke such despair; and the talk about love and the heart offers a hint of the probable cause of Mary's wretchedness. Sooner or later her friendship with Joshua Waterhouse broke off, and it may well have ended only shortly before the lugubrious note crept into her letters. Why it was terminated, no one knows; indeed mystery shrouds the whole affair. Mary may have been jilted, or she may have concluded that her beloved was too selfish or worldly. "Before true passion, I am convinced, every thing but a sense of duty moves," she wrote to George Blood in July, 1785, after commenting on Skeys's delay in marrying Fanny. Had a sense of duty made Mary stifle her passion for a man of whom she could not approve?

Her letters to her sisters and George Blood offer no tangible evidence to solve the mystery. Yet there is some evidence that her remarks about Waterhouse have been carefully expunged by a later censor, eager to spare her any further notoriety than she was to suffer when Godwin told the world about her affairs with Imlay and himself. The surviving letters of 1785 seem not to have been tampered with, but those of 1786 and 1787 show clearly that someone had censored them. For example, in her letter of May 1, 1786, to George Blood, she wrote, after lamenting his sister's death: "My poor heart still throbs with *selfish* anguish. It is formed for friendship and confidence—yet how often is it wounded." The next sixteen lines of the letter have been crossed out by a later hand and so carefully written over with *g*'s and *l*'s that the original words are utterly illegible. Immediately following the canceled lines are the words: "I am however melancholy rather than unhappy now my hopes of happiness are extinct." Surely the censor did not go to such pains to conceal Mary's lamentations on the death of her friend; it is quite likely, however, that she here discussed whatever other matters were plaguing her. And elsewhere one can find hints, overlooked perhaps by the censor, that Mary was suffering from a disappointment in love. On July 6, 1786, she wrote to George: "Give my love to your father and mother—and you may give the same to Neptune. I have done with all resentments—and perhaps I was as much to blame in expecting too much as he in doing too little. I looked for what was not to be found." This sounds like a reference to a bygone love affair—and "Neptune" would be a likely pseudonym for *Water*house. In the following year, when Mary was about to go to Dublin, she wrote to George: "Is Neptune still in Dublin?" And after her arrival she wrote in a letter to her sister Everina: "I must not forget to tell you that Neptune enquired after me—yet could not find time to visit me. At the Rotunda, where Lady K. took me one evening, he was coming up to speak to me. I was in the *party* of a . . . ." But the next third of a page has been torn away—doubtless by the conscientious censor. The evidence, therefore, is tenuous; and though Mary's letters to Waterhouse were found among his possessions after he was murdered in a brewing tub in 1827, they have since disappeared, and specific information about the affair is almost certainly unobtainable. One may, however, safely assume that, whatever the circumstances, it came to an abrupt end in 1785. And probably Mary's disappointment in love did much to plunge her into the Slough of Despond, in which she wallowed for the next two years.

When the time for Fanny's confinement drew near, Mary must have welcomed the chance to leave the Green and submerge her woes in service to her friend. But once again she encountered opposition. Her neighbor Mrs. Cockburn apparently believed that the trip would be a foolish waste of money, and even went so far as to say that she would prevent Mary from having three new lodgers on whom she was counting. But Mrs. Burgh warmly defended Mary's desire to nurse her friend, and presently she provided her with the money needed for her trip—though Mary always thought that Dr. Price had actually furnished it.

Late in 1785 Mary sailed for Lisbon. Her ship was only thirteen days en route, but it suffered such rough weather that the captain feared that the mast would be lost. "The wind was so high and the sea so boisterous," Mary wrote back to her sisters, "the water came in at the cabin windows, and the ship rolled about in such a manner it was dangerous to stir." But Mary was always a good sailor, and she weathered the voyage without mishap. Most of the time, no doubt, she was below deck—not cowering in her cabin, but serving others. "The woman was sea-sick the whole time," she reported to her sisters, "and the poor invalid so oppressed by his complaints I never expected he would live to see Lisbon. I have supported him hours together gasping for breath, and at night if I had been inclined to sleep, his dreadful cough would have kept me awake."

When she reached Lisbon, Fanny was already in labor. Four hours later she bore a son. "The child is alive and well," Mary wrote, "and considering the *very very* low state Fanny was reduced to, she is better than could be expected . . . . [She] is so worn out her recovery would be almost a resurrection, and my reason will scarce allow me to think 'tis possible." Later she added: "Fanny has been so exceedingly ill since I wrote the above I intirely gave her up . . . . Yesterday afternoon some of the most alarming symptoms a little abated, and she had a comfortable night—yet I rejoice with trembling lips—and am afraid to indulge hope. She is very low." Mary tended her assiduously and "laboured to be resigned." Then on November 29, just as Fanny seemed to be rallying, she collapsed and died in her friend's arms.

This was doubtless the harshest blow that Mary had ever borne. Fanny had meant more to her than her parents ever had; she had been her closest friend, closer by far than either Eliza or Everina. Mary owed to her much that was strongest and noblest in her own character; above all, her burning desire to better herself and to minister to others. She would miss her sorely, more than she would ever miss Joshua Waterhouse. As long as she lived, she honored the memory of her friend. She named her first child after Fanny; she treasured a ring of her hair always,[14] and in her *Letters Written during a Short Residence in Sweden, Norway, and Denmark*, published in the year before her own death, she wrote feelingly: "The grave has closed over a dear friend, the friend of my youth; still she is present with me, and I hear her soft voice warbling as I stray over the heath."[15]

The combination of the two misfortunes, Fanny's death and Waterhouse's defection, must have seemed unbearable. All Mary's self-assurance vanished; she complained in her letters that she had little to hope for in life, that she was a wounded spirit destined to a solitary existence, that she had lost all relish for pleasure and longed only for death, "Friendship—*even* friendship, the medicine, the *cordial* of life," she mourned, "was imperfect." And so she directed her gaze toward a better world and found consolation for the ardors of her life only by repeating that she was toiling her way to heaven by the thorniest path available.

But all her lamentation failed to relieve her from her depression of spirits; on the contrary she sank deeper and deeper into despondency. And as she did so, she found her misfortunes ever more fascinating and gloried in her martyrdom. Her introspection grew increasingly morbid and the fiber of her spirit more flaccid. The courage which had carried her so far and which had promised so much in the future seemed suddenly to be dissipated; and for months after Fanny's death Mary's letters were black with despair.

Mary stayed on in Lisbon for about three weeks after Fanny's death. Godwin claims that "she was admitted into the best company the English factory afforded";[16] but she would hardly have gone often into society. Yet she had ample opportunity to observe conditions among the Portuguese and to see for herself how debased eighteenth century European civilization could be. Like most English travelers of the period she must have been struck by the shocking contrast offered by the city of Lisbon: the beauty of the tier upon tier of white buildings as seen from a ship at anchor on the Tagus—and the ruin and filth disclosed when one disembarked and strolled through the streets. She must have been horrified to find building after building still in the ruins to which it had been reduced by the great earthquake thirty years before. She must have been revolted by the streets littered with offal, on which dozens of stray dogs fed; by the ill-heated houses infested with flies. And she was certainly appalled at the ignorance of the people. In *Mary* she was to write:

The Portuguese are certainly the most uncivilized nation in Europe. Dr. Johnson would have said, "They have the least mind." And can such serve their Creator in spirit and truth? No, the gross ritual of Romish ceremonies is all they can comprehend: they can do penance, but not conquer their revenge, or lust. Religion, or love, has never humanized their hearts; they want the vital part; the mere body worships. Taste is unknown; Gothic finery, and unnatural decorations, which they term ornaments, are conspicuous in their churches and dress. Reverence for mental excellence is only to be found in a polished nation.[17]

What Mary saw in Portugal made a profound impression upon her; it confirmed her belief that the world was in a sorry mess and encouraged her to subscribe eventually to the doctrines of eighteenth century progress and enlightenment. She never forgot her brief stay in Portugal. In her *Rights of Woman* she cited that nation as the worst possible example of ignorance and immodesty:

there, she claimed, "men attend the levees of equivocal beings, to
sigh for more than female languor"; there well-bred women
"would think their charms insulted, if, when left alone with a
man, he did not, at least, attempt to be grossly familiar with their
persons."[18] Mary's experience in Portugal was, indeed, one more
contribution to her education. It was, one might almost say, like
a "field trip" to the Middle Ages (the Inquisition had enjoyed
absolute power there until 1751), and it left her acutely aware of
the results of ignorance and tyranny. And though she was at the
moment in no frame of mind to declare war on ignorance and
tyranny, the lesson which she learned in Portugal was eventually
to implement her attack when she had found a fighting faith.

After Fanny had been buried and her baby had died, Mary had
no call to remain in Lisbon. She must have been anxious to return
to her school, and quite willing to leave Hugh Skeys, whom she
inwardly blamed for Fanny's death. Accordingly, shortly before
Christmas she embarked on her trip homeward.

The crossing this time was even worse than the first. The ship
was a month in passage, and Mary said later that she never expected
to see land again. She added characteristically: "If it had pleased
Heaven to have called me home—what a world of cares I should
have missed." Yet for all her complaints she seems to have retained in her sorrow some of the fearless courage which had long
sustained her. One day her ship encountered a French vessel in
danger of foundering, and Mary's captain refused to take its
passengers aboard his ship, maintaining that he had barely enough
food for his own charges. Immediately Mary intervened and
threatened to report him as soon as they reached land if he failed
to rescue the Frenchmen. And once again she carried the day.

At last the ship reached port. England must have looked good
to Mary after four weeks in benighted Portugal and four more
on a stormy sea. But she was disheartened when she reached
Newington Green. The school was in bad straits. The enrollment
had fallen off, and Mrs. Disney was preparing to depart with her
three children after a quarrel with Eliza and Everina. Presently

she went off in a huff, leaving her final bill unpaid; and Mary, who had been running close to the margin, found herself unable to meet her current bills. Meanwhile the "enormous" rent for the house was about to fall due, and she had no idea how she could pay it. And to make matters worse, Mr. Blood was still out of work, and he and his family were as usual looking to her for help. No wonder she felt herself utterly overwhelmed. Her eyes were troubling her, and she claimed that her memory had gone. Where could she turn for help? What would become of Eliza if she were forced to give up the school? On February 5, 1786, she wrote to George Blood, who had returned to Dublin from Lisbon: "My constitution is impaired, I hope I shan't live long—yet I may be a tedious time dying." And when he wrote back that he was settled in a new position in Dublin and suggested that she flee her creditors and join him in Ireland, she replied later in the month:

I am indeed very much distressed at present, and my future prospects are still more gloomy—yet nothing should induce me to fly from England. My creditors have a right to do what they please with me, should I not be able to satisfy their demands. I am almost afraid to look forward, tho' I am convinced that the same Providence that brought me through past difficulties, will still continue to protect me. Should our present plan fail, I cannot even guess what the girls will do. My brother, I am sure, will not receive them, and they are not calculated to struggle with the world. Eliza, in particular, is very helpless. Their situation has made me very uneasy,—and as to your father and mother, they have been a continual weight on my spirits. You have removed part of the load, for I now hope you would be able to keep them from perishing, should my affairs grow desperate,—and this hope has made me very grateful—for often when I have thought of death as the only end of my sorrows and cares, I earnestly wished to see them settled before I went to *rest*. Indeed I am very far from being well. I have a pain in my side, and a whole train of nervous complaints, which render me very uncomfortable. My spirits are very very low, and [I] am so opprest by continual anxiety 'tis a labour to me to [do] any thing. My former employments are quite irksome to me. If something decisive was to happen I should be better; but 'tis this suspense, this dread of I cannot tell what, which harasses me.

But for all her complaints, Mary could not afford, for very long at a time, to repine. She needed money, and if the school failed to yield it, she must find a new source of income. She was tormented by the demands of her creditors and distressed by the thought that she had been unable to pay the Bloods' rent for the last quarter. And the result was that she suddenly decided to turn author. She would write a book on the subject which she best understood: the education of young women. In short order she dashed off her *Thoughts on the Education of Daughters* and sold it to the bookseller Joseph Johnson, to whom she was introduced by her friend John Hewlett. With the proceeds she paid Mr. and Mrs. Blood's passage to Dublin, where George could provide a home for them, and where Mr. Blood would perhaps be better able to find and keep a job. Now one at least of her cares was removed, thanks to her ingenuity. It was a much-needed stroke of good fortune—or, as Mary wrote to George Blood, "a most Providential thing, and an answer to my fervent prayers."

Thoughts on the Education of Daughters: with Reflections on Female Conduct, in the More Important Duties of Life was a curious mélange of short essays which might or might not concern either education or daughters. They were set down in helter-skelter order, the chapter headings running thus: The Nursery; Moral Discipline; Exterior Accomplishments; Artificial Manners; Dress; The Fine Arts; Reading; Boarding-Schools; The Temper; Unfortunate Situation of Females, Fashionably Educated, and Left without a Fortune; Love; Matrimony; Desultory Thoughts; The Benefits which Arise from Disappointments; On the Treatment of Servants; The Observance of Sunday; On the Misfortune of Fluctuating Principles; Benevolence; Card-Playing; The Theatre; and Public Places. The essays themselves have little more unity than the book. Mary skipped from topic to topic with little attention to even the elementary rules of structure or transition. She had only a faint notion of the craft which she had so casually adopted. In fact even her grammar was weak.

The ideas which she expressed in the book had doubtless been forming in her mind for some time. They were by no means confined to education in the limited sense—the training given girls in school. Rather, Mary wanted to write about what teachers had no time to do and what parents were failing to do for young women. As she said:

Parents have mostly some weighty business in hand, which they make a pretext to themselves for neglecting the arduous task of educating their children; they are therefore sent to school, and the allowance for them is so low, that the person who undertakes the charge must have more than she can possibly attend to; of course, the mechanical parts of education can only be observed.[19]

The book was in effect a harassed teacher's reprimand to erring parents. Mary accepted as axiomatic Locke's theory that environment alone shapes the man, and she hoped to correct the faults of contemporary men—or women—by improving their home environment.

In some respects *Thoughts on the Education of Daughters* foreshadowed Mary's later work in *The Rights of Woman*. She begged that girls be trained to be mothers, not fashionable ornaments to society. She urged women to suckle their children, to show them affection, and to cultivate in them a taste for the beauties of nature and a fondness for animals. And she lamented the frailty of her sex, especially their preoccupation with polite manners, their trivial conversation, and their love of fine clothes. Moreover she declared emphatically that "the marriage state is too often a state of discord"—primarily because women have never been prepared for life properly. As she put it:

Women are said to be the weaker vessel, and many are the miseries which this weakness brings on them. Men have in some respects very much the advantage. If they have a tolerable understanding, it has a chance to be cultivated . . . . Nothing, I am sure, calls forth the faculties so much as the being obliged to struggle with the world; and this is not a woman's province in a married state.[20]

All these ideas Mary was later to emphasize and develop in *The Rights of Woman*. Here they appear at random as she skims over the surface of the problem of female education. Her book shows that she was dissatisfied with the status of her sex, but that as yet she had not formulated her objections or traced them to the basic human rights to which women as well as men were entitled. Mary already had a wealth of material for the work which was to make her famous, but she still wanted a thesis.

Today the book is interesting primarily as a reflection of a side of Mary's character seldom revealed by her letters. The impression it gives is that the author is a sensible old maid. She has no use for pretension or ornament; she damns elaborate dress and cosmetics; she deplores such affectations as a pretended love of music; and she condones "exterior accomplishments" only insofar as they may make a girl "in some measure independent of the senses." Nor is sincerity her only plea; she begs for common sense as well. "I am very far from thinking love irresistible, and not to be conquered," she remarks flatly.[21] Or: "Universal benevolence is the first duty, and we should be careful not to let any passion so engross our thoughts, as to prevent our practising it."[22]

Yet there are poignant hints that Mary's attitude of solid common sense conceals a powerful internal conflict. She may well have had her experience with Joshua Waterhouse in mind when she wrote:

The heart is very treacherous, and if we do not guard its first emotions, we shall not afterwards be able to prevent its sighing for impossibilities. If there are any insuperable bars to an union in the common way, try to dismiss the dangerous tenderness, or it will undermine your comfort, and betray you into many errors. To attempt to raise ourselves above human beings is ridiculous; we cannot extirpate our passions, nor is it necessary that we should, though it may be wise sometimes not to stray too near a precipice, lest we fall over before we are aware.[23]

Elsewhere she admits the power of the passions and the difficulty which faces anyone determined to control them by means of reason. "I think there is not a subject that admits so little of reasoning on as love," she declares almost wistfully.[24] And in one sentence she seems to lay bare her very heart: "Perhaps a delicate mind is not susceptible of a greater degree of misery, putting guilt out of the question, than what must arise from the consciousness of loving a person whom their reason does not approve."[25] Every now and again the reader is brought up short with the realization that Mary

is speaking from her own bitter experience, that her attitude of
solid common sense has been hard won.

In religion her thinking seems as yet conventional. She is bla-
tantly pious and often repeats the familiar laments about the ardors
of earthly life. Yet she never questions the wisdom of Divine Will.
No matter how severe the suffering in this life, religion can always
assuage it. Indeed she accepts suffering as man's lot on earth and
regards this world as only a proving-ground for the next. "[God]
never wounds but to heal," she declares; or: "The main business
of our lives is to learn to be virtuous."[26] And doubtless recalling
her own recent disappointments, she writes:

How earnestly does a mind full of sensibility look for disinterested friendship, and long to meet with good unalloyed. When fortune smiles they hug
the dear delusion; but dream not that it is one. The painted cloud disappears
suddenly, the scene is changed, and what an aching void is left in the heart!
a void which only religion can fill up—and how few seek this internal
comfort.[27]

Or again:

A young mind looks round for love and friendship; but love and friendship
fly from poverty: expect them not if you are poor! The mind must then sink
into meanness, and accommodate itself to its new state, or dare to be unhappy.
Yet I think no reflecting person would give up the experience and improvement they have gained, to have avoided the misfortunes; on the contrary,
they are thankfully ranked among the choicest blessings of life, when we
are not under their immediate pressure.[28]

Mary's philosophy is admirable, perhaps, for its courageous accep-
tance of suffering; the trouble is that she leaves no room for joy.
To her, life is devoid of happiness; the only satisfaction it affords
is that of battling bravely against overwhelming odds. Her religion
is always austere; it is certainly not deism, nor is it either pure
Church of England or pure Calvinism. It can perhaps best be
described as her own compound of philosophical scraps which she
had gleaned from her early years of churchgoing, from attendance
at the Chapel on Newington Green, and perhaps from her reading.
But at bottom it is truly the desperate resignation of a baffled
idealist.

Beneath her surface resignation, however, Mary could not help resenting conditions in the world as she found it; she was annoyed particularly by the plight of her sex. On the one hand she could say: "A woman cannot reasonably be unhappy, if she is attached to a man of sense and goodness, though he may not be all she could wish";[29] but on the other hand she obviously resented the subjection of her sex, especially their dependence on marriage. As yet, however, she did not presume to offer any scheme to rectify the faults of the social system. To be sure, she urged that women be given intellectual improvement; but by "intellectual improvement" she apparently meant religious training. And her only specific suggestion for the improvement of female education is that the mistress of a household be provided with "a little knowledge of physic."

Yet though Mary's rebellion was still inchoate, her book suggests that she was a woman of firm convictions, considerable energy, and strong passions. Obviously she did not spend all her time in idle lamentation. Whether she is stating dictatorially that "most women, and men too, have no character at all,"[30] or bemoaning the false emotionalism of contemporary tragedies, or ridiculing the clichés of literary criticism, she is always positive. "I am sick of hearing of the sublimity of Milton, the elegance and harmony of Pope, and the original, untaught genius of Shakespear," she declares.[31] And the reader feels that if ever this woman seizes on a conviction which she values wholeheartedly, she will fight for it to the death.

As yet, however, she had not found such a conviction. *Thoughts on the Education of Daughters* was obviously a potboiler scribbled off for the sake of the ten guineas which it would yield. She sent it forth with the lame apology: "If [my book] should prove useful to one fellow-creature, and beguile any hours, which sorrow has made heavy, I shall think I have not been employed in vain."[32] And of course it attracted little attention when it appeared early in 1787. The *Monthly Review* alone seems to have noticed it, in a few brief, though favorable, lines. Yet presently it appeared in another edition in Dublin, bound up with Fénelon's *Instructions to Governesses* and an anonymous *Address to Mothers*. Mary had begun to find a public, however narrow.

On May 22, 1786, shortly after she had finished her book, Mary wrote to George Blood to ask if his parents had reached Dublin safely. Of herself she had no cheerful news to report. "My affairs are hastening to a crisis," she told him. "The money that is due to me on account of the Disneys would very nearly have discharged all my debts; but I have little hopes of getting it—and this disappointment distresses me beyond measure, as some of my creditors cannot well afford to wait for their money." She had given up all hope of making her school a success and was planning to disband it. "Everina and Eliza are both endeavoring to go out into the world," she wrote, "the one as a companion, and the other as a teacher—and I believe I shall continue some time on the Green. I intend taking a little cheap lodging, and living without a servant, and the few scholars I have will maintain me." Then she lapsed into her old complaints: her "constitution is much impaired," she has "not much to hope for in life," she has done "with all worldly pursuits, or wishes." And she closed with the melancholy observation: "The prison walls are decaying—and the prisoner will ere long get free."

When next she wrote to George,[33] she was about to leave the school and move to a room in Mrs. Cockburn's house with Eliza. She was planning to discharge her servant and was sending Everina back to their brother's house in London. And though the Bloods had urged her to join them in Dublin and remain at their house as long as she chose, she explained confidentially to George that she could not bear the thought of being under obligation to anyone—least of all a selfish person like his father. She was determined, moreover, not to leave England until she had discharged her debts. She still hoped to find a situation for Eliza, and she planned to support herself in "the most rigid oeconomy" from the tuition of the pupils who remained with her. Of course such prospects depressed her, and she complained of loneliness, "nervous complaints," and a general apathy toward life. "I am sick of every thing under the sun," she mourned, "for verily every thing is grievous to me. All our pursuits are vain—only the end which they bring us to is of consequence."

Yet before long her head was again full of schemes. In her next letter she wrote that she had been offered two positions as governess—one in Wales and the other with the family of Lord Kingsborough, of Mitchelstown, County Cork, Ireland. She well knew the disadvantages of life in such a situation. In *Thoughts on the Education of Daughters,* after dwelling on the hardships of teaching, she had written:

A governess to young ladies is equally disagreeable. It is ten to one if they meet with a reasonable mother; and if she is not so, she will be continually finding fault to prove she is not ignorant, and be displeased if her pupils do not improve, but angry if the proper methods are taken to make them do so. The children treat them with disrespect, and often with insolence. In the mean time life glides away, and the spirits with it; "and when youth and genial years are flown," they have nothing to subsist on; or, perhaps, on some extraordinary occasion, some small allowance may be made for them, which is thought a great charity.[34]

Yet the position in Ireland was strongly recommended by a friend, the wife of the Reverend John Prior, a teacher at Eton, and it seemed too good to be rejected. It would pay forty pounds a year, half of which, Mary estimated, she could save to pay her debts and aid Eliza. If she could be sure of a fixed income, she could promise her creditors a given sum at regular intervals; but in her present situation she could do nothing but fend them off. Of course they were becoming always more insistent, and she was subjected now to "insults which my unprotected situation naturally produces." Only the day before she wrote to George, a man who had come to demand the money that was due him had "behaved . . . with great rudeness." The position with the Kingsborough family seemed her only salvation. "*Duty* impels me to consider about it and not too hastily to reject it," she told George, "and yet only duty would influence me if [I] accepted of it."

As usual duty triumphed, and by August 25 she had written that she would take the position. Meanwhile her friend Mrs. Burgh had found Eliza a situation at a boarding school operated by a Mrs. Sampel, at Market Harborough, in Leicestershire; and so Mary was free to go to Ireland as soon as she was needed. She was still at Newington Green, waiting for a call from Mrs. Prior, at whose house she was to meet the Misses King, Lord Kingsborough's daughters, in order to travel with them to Mitchelstown. Meanwhile she was continuing to teach eleven pupils and was feverishly taking French lessons to prepare herself for her new duties. Yet with all this activity she found time to make herself a new gown for the trip (since she had no money to spend on clothes) and to brood at length over the unpaid debts which she must leave behind her. "How shall I be able to satisfy my creditors, I cannot even guess," she wrote to George Blood, "and it harasses me beyond measure. I owe near eighty or ninety pounds and some of the debts I would give the world to pay."

On September 23 she was still waiting for word to go to Eton and was busy with final preparations for her journey. Thanks apparently to a loan from faithful Mrs. Burgh, she had been able to settle her "trifling debts" and to buy what was absolutely necessary for her trip. A Miss Mason, formerly an employee of the school, was staying with her and helping her to make a great coat; and Mrs. Cockburn had presented her with a gay blue hat. Indeed she had much to be thankful for. And though she could not forget that her brother Edward had "behaved very rude" to her and offered her no assistance whatsoever in her need, she was consoled by the thought that "though many have disappointed me, others have gone beyond my hope or expectation." "I wish to remember it," she wrote to Eliza, now settled at Mrs. Sampel's school, "for I like to encourage an affection for all mankind—and the unkindness of some individuals now and then, made me turn, sick, from all social affections."

At last she was summoned to the Priors' house at Eton. But once there, she was obliged to resume her waiting, for the King girls failed to appear when they were expected. By October 9, when she wrote to her sister Everina, she was in a dismal frame of mind. "How grateful to me was your tender unaffected letter," she wrote. "I wept over it—for I was in a melting mood . . . . A whole train of nervous disorders have taken possession of me—and they appear to arise so much from the mind, I have little hopes of being better." On the preceding Friday, she reported, when she received news that Everina would be unable to visit her as expected, she had almost fainted under the disappointment; and she had been very ill in consequence. And as she went on to describe her prospects for the immediate future, she grew increasingly despondent. She would be obliged to travel west by postchaise, she complained, with the King girls in her charge. She would probably be left alone with them at Mitchelstown for weeks at a time while their parents stayed at their town house in Dublin, 170 miles away. The only ray of hope she could perceive rose from the favorable impression of Lady Kingsborough which she had formed after reading one of her letters to Mrs. Prior. "She says," Mary wrote to Everina, ". . . that those who have hitherto had the care of [the children] have neglected their minds and only attended to the ornamental part of their education, which she thinks ought ever to be a secondary consideration. These sentiments prejudice me in her favor more than any thing I have heard of her—for I cannot venture to depend on the opinion of people who are dazzled by her superior station in life."

Yet despite her depression Mary was still trying to locate a position for Everina in order to rescue her from their brother Edward's house. "How earnestly I wish you out of his house!" she wrote. "If you possibly can, try to exert yourself—or you will fall a prey to melancholy. You require kindness and look round for domestic comfort and congenial souls—but those you are with are the merest earth worms." And somehow the emphatic turn of phrase and the wholesome advice—"exert yourself—or you will fall a prey to melancholy"—reveal that beneath all Mary's gloom her energetic spirit was not only alive but active. It was a hardy spirit, as it needs must be, and it had carried Mary through many a difficult year. And though when she sat down to take stock of her misfortunes, she may truly have longed for death as an end to all her woes, she could have had little time for sitting still and pitying herself. She was still full of schemes to release herself from difficulties and to insure herself a brighter future.

During her stay at Eton she had her first opportunity to observe one of the great English public schools. As a teacher she would naturally be interested to learn about the place; and she happened along at a colorful period in the history of the college. Dr. Jonathan Davies, the headmaster, was an affable person in society but a martinet in office; not long before Mary's visit his assistant masters had actually gone "on strike" to protest conditions in the school, and the pupils had taken the opportunity to stage a revolt which caused considerable damage to the buildings and sent the headmaster scuttling for safety through the back gate. Yet, as always, Eton attracted many of the most promising young men of England. Outstanding among them when Mary visited the school was young George Canning, a solitary boy highly respected by the students, whose fame had brought the great Charles James Fox down from London in an attempt to convert him to the Whig party. Canning and his friends John Hookham Frere, "Bobus" Smith, and Charles Ellis were undoubtedly busy during Mary's visit bringing out the first issue of their famous magazine, the *Microcosm,* which appeared only a week or two after her departure.

Yet Mary's impression of Eton was anything but favorable. Had she made a study of the curriculum, she would certainly have found ground for complaint. For one thing she would have deplored the overemphasis on the classics and the neglect of natural history. The system hardly prepared young men for life; in fact it turned out some strange anomalies—Canning, for instance, who could write Sapphics without a flaw in quantity, but who was dumbfounded to learn, years after his graduation, that a frog developed from a tadpole. But Mary was less concerned with educational theory now than she was to be later in her life—and she was distressed primarily by the inane worldliness which she encountered among the teachers at the school. "I could not live the life they live at Eton," she wrote to Everina, "—nothing but dress and ridicule going forward—and I really believe their fondness for ridicule tends to make them affected—the women in their manners, and the men in their conversation—for witlings abound— and *puns* fly about like crackers, tho' you would scarcely guess they had any meaning in them, if you did not hear the noise they create." She felt herself "quite alone in a crowd," but she comforted herself with the thought that her "thoughts and wishes tend to that land where the God of love will wipe away all tears from our eyes."

At last, late in October, 1786, word came that the King girls would not meet her at Eton after all, and she set out alone on the weary journey to her new home. "*Home,* delightful word," she exclaimed in her last letter to Everina, "—but what a different one that will be—how unlike the one I have in my 'mind's eye.'" She was twenty-seven years old now, and apparently resigned to a lonely spinsterhood, convinced that she had but a few more years to live, and hopeful only of relief in the grave. At least so she claimed in her letters—and reiterated the claims until her correspondents must have become heartily weary of them. But certainly her letters were misleading. Mary's dauntless spirit was far from quenched. It had already carried her from an obscure post as lady's companion at Bath to a position as mistress of her own school, respected by her distinguished neighbors at Newington Green. And it was still carrying her along in the face of great odds.

After all, she had accomplished a good deal during the months in which she had allegedly been overwhelmed by sorrow: she had been to Lisbon to tend Fanny Blood in her last hours, had dissolved her unsuccessful school and hunted for positions for her sisters, had staved off her creditors, sent Mr. and Mrs. Blood to Ireland, taught her classes, studied French, made clothes, and performed a score of other duties. And with it all she had found time to write a book—not a long book or a great one, but a book that showed reflective thought and common sense, and, above all, energy—in both content and style. Indeed Mary had proved again and again that she was still a woman of tireless energy, even while she was protesting in her letters that her energies were exhausted. Undoubtedly there were moments when her hardships seemed insuperable. She had endured in Fanny's death and Waterhouse's defection and the failure of the school and the loss of her valued independence quite enough to overpower anyone plagued, as she was, by a weak constitution and unsteady nerves. Yet she was confronted always by manifold duties, and she fulfilled them regularly, whatever the cost to her energies. For whether she realized it or not, those energies were alive and active; and if properly channeled, they could rescue her now as they had done before.

Nor was energy her only asset. She was endowed with powers of reflection, too, and a basic fund of good common sense. Too often, however, they were swayed completely by her passions—the passions which had nearly driven her frantic when she encountered disappointment, and which prompted the tiresome lamentation of her letters. Yet, uncontrollable as they often were, they too deserved to be reckoned among her assets. Had she not been of so passionate a nature, she could never have achieved what she was destined to achieve. To do so, she needed energy and reflective power and common sense and passion. And of course she needed also a goal to strive for.

During the weeks before her departure for Ireland she seems at first glance to have had no goal save to pay her debts and resign herself to heaven. Yet, according to Godwin, she had a fixed purpose in mind: to save as much as she could and, as soon as possible, launch herself on a literary career. *Thoughts on the Education of Daughters* had proved to her that she could write—and sell her writing; it had given her a new goal. And if she could reach that goal, she would enjoy not only the independence which she so craved, but perhaps something even rarer for one of her sex—distinction.

CHAPTER III
Return to Bondage
(1786-1787)

"An accumulation of disappointments and misfortunes seems to suit the habit of my mind."
—*Letter to Imlay.*

MARY'S trip to Ireland proved to be surprisingly pleasant. The weather was clear, "the prospects delightful"; and she confessed that she would truly have enjoyed her journey "if I had not dwelt on the *end* of it."[1] She had as a companion an agreeable young clergyman who was going to Ireland as a tutor, and she was pleased to report that he was "intelligent and had that kind of politeness which arises from sensibility." She stopped off for a few days at Dublin to visit the Blood family and their friend Betty Delane, and then was conducted to Mitchelstown by the Kingsborough family butler.

When at last she reached the castle, she suffered dire misgivings. "I entered the great gates with the same kind of feeling as I should have if I was going into the Bastille," she wrote to Everina on October 30, 1786, shortly after her arrival. And she complained that there was "such a solemn kind of stupidity about this place as froze my very blood." Of course she was lonely. "I hear a fiddle below," she wrote; "the servants are dancing—and the rest of the family diverting themselves. I only am melancholy and alone." She was spending her time "in sorrow—and unavailing tears"; life still seemed "a frightful vision and equally disjointed"; and she found her only consolation in her old attitude of desperate resignation. "I must labor for content," she told her sister, "and try to reconcile myself to a state which is contrary to every feeling of my soul."

Had she been in a more receptive frame of mind, she might have exulted in her new surroundings. The Kingsboroughs'

castle stood on the edge of an abrupt cliff overlooking a wide river
and a broad valley encircled by mountains. From her window she
could look out on the Galties, a rugged range of mountains famous
for caves and crater lakes. She granted, indeed, that the scenery
"would please me when any thing of the kind could rouse my
attention." But for the present she was too wretched to respond to
the beauties of nature.

She was, on the whole, fortunate also in her employers. Robert
King, Viscount Kingsborough and later second Earl of Kingston,
was well above the average of his class in intelligence and liberality.
Though absolute master of a territory some hundred miles square,
he was a benevolent despot, eager to improve his land and better
the living conditions of his tenants. Nine years before Mary's
arrival in Ireland he had hired as manager of his estates the Eng-
lishman Arthur Young, who was later to become the foremost
authority on agriculture in Great Britain. Gradually they ousted
the middlemen, whose claims kept the tenants constantly in debt,
and erected offices and hothouses to put the farms on a scientific
basis. Moreover, Kingsborough gave saplings to tenants who
promised to plant them and awarded prizes to those who made
most improvements on their land. For such benevolences Mary
must have admired him, but in her letters she remarked only that
"his countenance does not promise much more than good humour,
and a little *fun* not refined." And her estimate was probably just,
for Arthur Young observed that "his manner and carriage were
remarkably easy, agreeable, and polite, having the finish of a perfect gentleman; he wanted, however, steadiness and perseverance
even in his best designs, and was easily wrought upon by persons
of inferior abilities."[2]

Lady Kingsborough, born Caroline Fitzgerald, her husband's
cousin, was to Mary "a *clever* woman, and a well-meaning one;
but not of the order of being that I could love." She was apparently
affable and democratic; she even played chess with Arthur Young
evenings after dinner while he was staying at the castle. But
though Mary acknowledged that she was "very civil, nay, kind,"

she added: "Yet I cannot help fearing her." Her Ladyship had little love for her husband[3] and apparently not much more for her children; and for the latter fault especially Mary could not forgive her. In her first letter from Ireland she wrote: "I have not seen much of her as she is confined to her room by a sort throat—but I have seen half [a] dozen of her companions—I mean not her children, but her dogs. To see a woman without any softness in her manners caressing animals, and using infantine expressions—is, you may conceive, very absurd and ludicrous—but a fine Lady is [a] new species to me of animals." And later: "All her children have been ill—very disagreeable fevers. Her Ladyship visited them in a *formal* way—though their situation called forth my tenderness—and I endeavored to amuse them while she lavished awkward fondness on her dogs . . . . I am almost tormented to death by dogs." Mary could not forgive such conduct; and her considered appraisal of Lady Kingsborough was: "In short [she] is a fine Lady without fancy or sensibility."

Life at the castle was seldom dull; in fact the place teemed with activity—but of course not the sort that Mary could approve. She complained that Her Ladyship was surrounded by "a *host* of females"—"her step mother, and three sisters, and *Mrses.* and *Misses* without number," who chattered incessantly about nothing at all. To Mary's eyes they seemed like abandoned worldlings. "I see Ladies put on rouge without any mauvais honte—and make up their faces for the day," she wrote to Everina. "Five hours—and who could do it in less?—do many, I assure you, spend in dressing —without including preparations for bed, washing with Milk of roses, &c &c." And later she thanked heaven that she was not "so unfortunate as to be born a Lady of quality," and solemnly assured her sister: "You cannot conceive, my dear Girl, the dissipated lives the women of quality lead." Yet however much they might scandalize her, she had to admit that they had always been gracious toward her. "[They] labor to be civil to me," she wrote; "but we move in so different a sphere, I feel grateful for their attention; but not amused . . . . I am treated like a gentlewoman—but I cannot easily forget my inferior station—and this something betwixt and between is rather awkward." And though she remarked that the last governess had been treated like a servant and that she herself was "a GREAT favorite" of the family, she could not resign herself to her new life. She had, she felt, lost her freedom; and without it she could never achieve anything like contentment.

She found her only comfort in her work with the three girls in her charge. At first they had resented the thought of having an English governess, and she in turn had looked upon them as "wild Irish, unformed and not very pleasing." But when the girls discovered how affectionate a creature Mary could be, they grew fond of her, and she of them. The eldest, Margaret, became her favorite. "My sweet little girl is now playing and singing to me," she wrote one day to Eliza. "She has a good ear and some taste and feeling." But she was forced to add that the child had great faults which Mary feared she would never conquer. And the more she grew attached to Margaret, the more she suffered from the conviction that the girl was being badly brought up. "She has a wonderful capacity," Mary wrote, "but she has such a multiplicity of employments it has not room to expand itself—and in all probability will be lost in a heap of rubbish mis-called accomplishments. I am grieved at being obliged to continue so wrong a system." Sometimes she almost wished the girls were "novel readers and romantic"; she was oppressed by their knowledge of isolated facts, by the number of languages and the "*cart*loads of history" which they had mastered. But most of all she was distressed by their attitude toward their mother. Margaret, she claimed, was afraid of Lady Kingsborough. And she lamented that "such a creature should be ruled with a rod of iron, when tenderness would lead her anywhere." In time, according to Godwin, Mary "insisted upon the unbounded exercise of her own discretion" in teaching the girls, and discarded many of the rules which their mother had made, preferring "to govern them by their affections only."[4] Yet the task must have been truly disheartening: she could not in a few months undo the harm done over a period of years. And in the long run her affection for the three girls only intensified her unhappiness.

And so she continued to suffer. Wherever she looked, she found cause for tears. Outside the castle she was confronted with the misery of the peasants, who were still poverty-stricken despite Lord Kingsborough's attempts to aid them. Their rude cabins overflowed with the two unfailing products of the country: pigs and children. "I believe there are more pigs in Mitchelstown than human beings," Arthur Young declared, "and yet propagation is the only trade that flourished here for ages."[5] Inside the castle Mary saw, by contrast, the easy gaiety of the idle rich; for Lord and Lady Kingsborough kept a constant open house for their relatives and friends. "Confined to the society of a set of silly females," she wrote wearily, "I have no social converse—and their boisterous spirits and unmeaning laughter exhausts me, not forgetting hourly domestic bickerings. The topics of matrimony and dress take their turn, not in a very *sentimental* style—alas, poor sentiment! it has no residence here." Before long she developed a thoroughgoing scorn for the class which she was seeing at such disadvantage. "You have a *sneaking* kindness, you say, for people of quality . . . ," she wrote to her sister Eliza. "Shall I try to remember the titles of all the Lords and Viscounts I am in company with, not forgetting the clever things they say? I would sooner tell you a tale of some humbler creatures. I intend visiting the poor cabbins as Miss K. is allowed to assist the poor. I shall make a point of finding them out."

Mary had ample time to reflect on the scenes she was witnessing, and they were bound to strengthen her belief that the world was in a sorry mess. What had the Kingsboroughs and their fine friends done to merit wealth and ease? And what had the peasants done to deserve misery? Surely all was not right in a world where such injustice prevailed. Undoubtedly God would in His own time make all men equal sharers in His bounty. But meanwhile was there no way to rectify the evils of this life? At Newington Green Mary had doubtless heard a good deal about democracy and the rights of men. At Lisbon she had seen the deplorable results of absolute monarchy. And now in Ireland, under the rule of His Majesty King George III, a constitutional monarch, she found conditions little better. Surely something was radically wrong with the social structure.—But what could a poor governess do to remedy it?

The winter of 1786-87 passed slowly, and Mary continued to be tormented by cares. She feared lest she prove unequal to her task. She suspected that Mr. Prior had misrepresented her, that the Kingsboroughs thought her better grounded in French than she actually was. And though she tried to study the language whenever she could, she complained that she "went but slowly on," and that "this unwearied application to business" undermined her health. In November she was "very ill—and so low-spirited my tears flow in torrents almost insensibly." She had tried drinking ass's milk to increase her strength, but it seemed to do her no good. She was, as usual, worrying about her debts—and hoping that she would not die before she had paid them. And she was lonely—"a sojourner in a strange land," "an exile—and in a new world." "I am sometimes so low spirited, I think anything *like* pleasure will never revisit me," she wrote in January, 1787. "I go to the nursery. *Something like* maternal fondness fills my bosom. The children cluster about me. One catches a kiss, another lisps my long name— while a sweet little boy, who is conscious that he is a favorite, calls himself my Tom. At the sight of their mother they tremble and run to me for protection. This renders them dear to me—and I discover the kind of happiness I was formed to enjoy." Sometimes Mary strove to "make allowance and *adapt* myself—talk of getting husbands for the *Ladies*—and the *dogs*—and [to be] wonderfully entertaining." But then she would flee to her own room to "form figures in the fire, listen to the wind, or view the Galties," and thus *"waste* away [the hours] in apathy or misery."

Actually she was in a more comfortable situation than she had enjoyed for some months. Her sisters and the Blood family were no longer depending on her, and she was well treated at the Kingsboroughs'. Of course she could not quickly forget the sorrows of the past two years; and she was probably depressed at the thought of a future alone—and perhaps childless, as her description of herself in the nursery seems to imply. Her only cause for immediate concern was a lawsuit against a man named Roebuck, which her brother Edward was apparently handling for her.[6] In a candid moment she wrote to Everina: "According to the general notion of things—I have no reason to complain. Mine, at present, might be termed comparative rather than positive misery." And undoubtedly her "comparative misery" was due primarily to her lack of independence; after her brief taste of freedom at Newington Green, she was in bondage again—and her whole being rebelled at the thought. Perhaps, too, complaining had become second nature to her; perhaps she rather enjoyed rehearsing her sorrows. Certainly it is worth noting that her letters to her sister Eliza were much less gloomy than those she wrote to Everina. In fact she once told the latter: "I would not write thus to Eliza—she cannot discriminate; but to you I *cannot* be reserved—and I hope the dreadful contagion will not infect you." And she seems to imply that Everina is a woman of sensibility who will sympathize with—perhaps even enjoy—the outpourings of a distressed spirit.

Surely she was not always so glum as her letters would suggest. Occasionally, in the middle of one of her complaining letters, she tells of her little social successes, describing how eagerly the ladies of the castle listen to her, or remarking ironically that they think she has "an angelic temper." She was, as she had admitted, "a GREAT favorite" with these fine people, and the little King girls were devoted to her. In truth she was now, as later, a woman of great personal charm who endeared herself to those she met. Like many women of great charm, she doubtless was something of an actress; and in her letters to Everina she was almost certainly playing a part. Yet it was not her only part: she could play also the part demanded of her by the fine folk at the castle—and with the children she could perhaps be herself.

Evidently Lord and Lady Kingsborough felt that Mary deserved extraordinary treatment. Though they were accustomed, as

Mary had said, to regarding their governess as a servant, they treated Mary almost as one of the family. When the time came for their departure for Dublin for the social season, they decided to take her and the children along with them. And although she had been in their employ only three months, they gave her a few days' leave to visit the Baillie family, relatives of the Bloods, in Tipperary.

The removal to Dublin took place in February, 1787. Mary and the children went first, and the rest of the family followed a few days later. Of course she was pleased at the change. Not only was she near the Bloods again, but she could meet and associate with young women of her own station; and she saw much of the Bloods' friend Betty Delane from the outset. She had pleasanter quarters too: "A fine school room—the use of one of the drawing rooms where the Harpsichord is—and a parlour to receive my MALE visitors in." Moreover she enjoyed more freedom, now that Lady Kingsborough was abroad much of the day visiting friends. And the result was that she could tell Everina that she was more "tranquil." "I commune with my own spirit," she wrote, "—and am detached from the world. I have plenty of books. I am now reading some philosophical lectures, and metaphysical sermons—for my own *private* improvement." And on another occasion: "Books are my only relaxation. Yet I do not read much—I think, and think, and these reveries do not tend to fit me for enjoying the *common* pleasures of this world.—What does it signify? I am going home! . . . I am only alive to *attendrisement*. Certainly I must be in love—for I am grown 'thin and lean, pale and wan.' "

Actually she did not spend all her leisure time in solitude. She went to the theater now and again, and Lady Kingsborough took her to a two-day Handel festival. She was even invited to some of the parties which the King family gave and attended, and there were many of them. The court at Dublin was uncommonly gay in the late 'eighties, and fashionable people entertained lavishly. Several years afterwards, in her *Letters Written during a Short Residence in Sweden, Norway, and Denmark,* she wrote that Dublin was the most hospitable city she had ever visited—though she remarked, rather uncharitably, that hospitality revealed not "goodness of heart" but "indolence or vacancy of a head."[7] There were large parties or balls almost every night of the week, and the Kingsboroughs, who were outranked by few, were seldom excluded. At one party Mary fell into conversation with a woman of fashion who was interested enough to inquire her name—and appalled to learn that she had been wasting her charms on a mere governess. And on another occasion Mary went with Lady Kingsborough, Betty Delane, and a friend of the Kingsboroughs named Miss Moore to a masquerade—Mary and Her Ladyship in dominoes, Miss Delane as a forsaken shepherdess, and Miss Moore "in the habit of one of the females of the new discovered Islands." "As it was taken for granted the stranger who was just arrived, could not speak the language," Mary reported in one of her letters, "I was to be her interpreter, which afforded me an ample field for satire . . . . The lights, the novelty of the scene, and every thing together contributed to make me *more* than half mad. I gave full scope to a satirical vein."

But sooner or later Mary relapsed into her mood of complaint. In describing her success at the masquerade, she explained that she was still melancholy every morning, but that by evening she developed a fever which "gives me *false* spirits." On other occasions during her stay in Dublin she complained of "a violent pain in my side, which affected my breath"; of a "fit of trembling" which lasted all day; of "a rising in my throat, which I know to be a nervous affection"; of faintness and even spasms. Somewhat against her will Lady Kingsborough induced her to consult the family physician, who diagnosed her ailment as "a constant nervous fever." "I am sure he is right," Mary wrote with apparent satisfaction. And in a later letter:

Indeed it is impossible to enumerate the various complaints I am troubled with; and how much my mind is harassed by them. I know they all arise from disordered nerves, that are injured beyond a *possibility* of receiving *any* aid from medicine. There is no cure for a broken heart! It is true, it may languidly perform its *animal* functions—but it can no longer be *inflated* with hope. The nervous fever I am subject to has increased my natural sensibility to such a degree I may with reason complain of the irritability of my nerves. I want a tender nurse—I want—but it matters not. The Will of Heaven be done—I am resigned. I do not imagine that any of my complaints promise a hasty dissolution—though they render me very uncomfortable . . . .

Obviously by now Mary was completely enamored of sorrow. She was fascinated with her "disordered nerves" and her "broken heart," and she delighted in writing about the grating of the harsh world against her tender sensibilities. On May 11, 1787, she wrote to Everina:

"That vivacity which increases with age is not far from madness," says Rochefoucault. I then am mad—deprived of the only comforts I can relish, I give way to whim. And yet when the most sprightly sallies burst from me, the tear frequently trembles in my eye, and the long drawn sigh eases my full heart—so my eyes roll in the wild way you have *seen* them. A deadly paleness overspreads my countenance—and yet so weak am I a sudden thought or any *recollected* emotion of tenderness will occasion the most painful suffusion. You know not, my dear Girl, of what materials this strange inconsistent heart of mine is formed, and how alive it is to tenderness and misery. Since I have been here I have turned over several pages in the vast volume of human nature, and what is the amount? Vanity and vexation of spirit—and yet I am *tied* to my fellow-creatures by partaking of their weaknesses. I rail at a fault—sicken at the sight—and find it stirring within me. New sympathies and feelings *start* up. I know not myself.—"'Tis these whims," Mr. Ogle tells me, "render me interesting"—and Mrs. Ogle with a placid smile quotes some of my own sentiments—while I cry the physician *cannot* heal himself.

It is a pretty scene, fit for a novel of sensibility, and Mary doubtless fancied herself as the heroine of such a novel. The Mr. Ogle mentioned was a friend of the Kingsboroughs who enjoyed a local reputation as a writer of sentimental verse. Mary had earlier described him to Everina as "a *genius,* and *unhappy*," adding: "Such a man, you may suppose, would catch your sister's eye." Such a man might also inspire Mary to sentimental flights, just as Everina herself did. For Mary had less to say these days about life as a "thorny path" leading to everlasting bliss: her lamentations spring not from evangelical piety but from sensibility, the quality which she used so often as a criterion of her new friends' merits. And there can be no doubt that Mary was enjoying her new role of sentimental heroine. She probably agreed with Mr. Ogle that distress made her "interesting." She was reading *Emile*, she had reported soon after her arrival in Dublin, and had found that Rousseau "rambles into that *chimerical* world in which I have too often wandered—and draws the usual conclusion that all is vanity and vexation of spirit." Mary seems, for a time at least, to have lost her grip on common sense—and it is difficult to keep from losing all patience with her.

Certainly she was not yet free of cares; but they were petty cares compared with those of the past. Her debts continued to worry her, and she was increasingly concerned about the money which her brother had now collected from her suit against Roebuck, but which he had failed to turn over, as agreed, to Mrs. Burgh. She was angry with him, too, because he seemed to be trying to rid himself of Everina, who was still staying at his house. Yet Mary's most immediate worry seems to have proved, on the whole, to be a source of grim satisfaction to her. This was her silent struggle with Lady Kingsborough, who had grown increasingly "haughty and disagreeable" since their arrival in Dublin. Her Ladyship was doubtless jealous of the affection which her governess had won from the little girls in her charge. She may also have sensed that Mary disdained her and her frivolous friends and was hardly grateful for the condescension which they had shown her. As for Mary, she resented being obliged to neglect her pupils on days when a ball was to take place, and being expected to join the servants in last-minute alterations of Lady Kingsborough's gown. The antagonism between the two women grew constantly, and on one or two occasions Her Ladyship was so rude when guests were present that Mary resolved never again to join the company in the drawing room. Lady Kingsborough was apparently piqued at this display of independence; and one day when her father-in-law, the old Earl of Kingston, was visiting the house, she repeatedly urged Mary to go down to the drawing room to see him. Much against her will Mary finally complied rather than create a scene. But as soon as it was time for the younger men to come in from dinner, Her Ladyship "used several arts" to dismiss

her. And when Mr. Ogle, Lady Kingsborough's favorite, entered
and paid Mary marked attention, Her Ladyship was obviously
irked. To Mary, however, the incident yielded some satisfaction;
"for to tell you a secret," she wrote in a letter to Everina, "she is
afraid of me. Why she wishes to keep me I cannot guess—for she
cannot bear that any one should take notice of me." And two
months later: "Lady K. and I are on much better terms than ever
we were.—To tell the truth she is afraid of me . . . . [She] keeps in
her temper surprisingly before me and really labors to be civil.
The defect is in her nature. She is devoid of sensibility." Mary must
have known, however, that her position with the Kingsboroughs
was precarious.

As spring approached, she dreaded the return to Mitchelstown;
and taking advantage of her power over Lady Kingsborough, she
urged that the family spend the summer on the Continent. "I do
not like Ireland," she had written to her sister. "The family pride
which reigns here produces the worst effects. They are in general
proud and mean, the servile respect that is universally paid to
people of quality disgusts me, and the minute attention to propriety
stops the growth of virtue. As a nation I do not *admire* the Irish
. . . . In short I should not chuse this Kingdom for my residence, if
I could subsist any where else." And though she had at first tried
to find positions for her sisters in Dublin, she now advised them
not to consider leaving England. Indeed she may have been cast-
ing about for a means of escape for herself. In April she wrote to
Joseph Johnson, who had just published her *Thoughts on the
Education of Daughters,* that she was "still an invalid" and had
begun to believe that she "ought never to expect to enjoy health."
She complained of being "confined almost entirely to the society
of children" and "counteracted in my endeavours to improve
them." "How can I be reconciled to life," she asked, "when it is
always a painful warfare, and when I am deprived of all the pleasures I relish?—I allude to rational conversations, and domestic
affections. Here, alone, a poor solitary individual in a strange land,
tied to one spot, and subject to the caprice of another, can I be

contented?"[8] Again she was magnifying her troubles—but this time, perhaps, with a purpose. She may well have been hoping that she could make herself "interesting" to Johnson—so interesting that he would be prompted to rescue her from her plight by offering her steady work in London.

But presently, in late May or early June of 1787, the King ménage was off again—this time to Bath and Bristol Hot Wells, where they were to spend the early part of the summer. The move must have been welcome to Mary, for she was now thoroughly homesick for her own land. "I never before felt what it was to love my country," she had written; "but now I have a value for it based on rational grounds, and my feelings concur to fix it. I never see an English face without feeling tenderness." But the chance to return to England was as nothing compared to the unexpected good fortune which she reported in a letter to Eliza dated from Bristol on June 27:

I have *every* reason to think I shall be able to pay my debts before I again leave the Kingdom. *A friend* whose name I am not *permitted* to mention has insisted on lending me the money. I shall certainly borrow it—and as I shall then reckon myself rich, I hope to contrive for you and Everina to spend the winter-vacation together, as the only alleviation I can devise to render your confinement tolerable. With respect to this money matter you must not enquire, or expect any other explanation—yet let me tell you, dear Girl, the manner in which this favor has been conferred on me *greatly* enhanced the obligation. I could have no scruple—and I rejoiced to meet with a fellow-creature whom I could admire for doing a *disinterested* act of kindness. In short it is a present; but I would not have it mentioned to *any* creature. The lending it was first mentioned as the most delicate way of reconciling me to it. I intend paying Sowerby—and every body; and as Lady K. is in my debt I shall be able to afford to visit you and Everina.

Yet even these bright prospects failed to cheer her for more than a moment, and presently she was complaining:

My nerves daily grow worse and worse—yet I strive to occupy my mind even when duty does not force me to do it. In a trifling way I net purses, and intend having two smart ones to present to you and Everina—and when I have more strength I read Philosophy—and write (I *hope* you have not forgot that I am an Author) yet many are the hours that are loaden with cares. I shake my head but it remains heavy—and I *ruminate* without digesting.

No one who had read this and the many similar passages from Mary's letters during her stay in Ireland would be surprised that she was indeed writing—a sentimental novel, largely about herself. She had been reading *Emile* in Ireland and probably had access, in the King household, to any number of the sentimental novels then in vogue. Shortly before, she had acted out a sentimental scene for the edification of the Ogles with gratifying success. Now she would try her hand at a more sustained experiment in the same genre. Fortunately this experiment proved her salvation. She poured her distress into print for all the world to see and admire; and in doing so she purged her mind of the sentimental affectation which was threatening to atrophy her energies. With it out of her system she could resume life with the zest which had accomplished so much for her in the past. In short, writing a sentimental novel proved to be far more healthful than trying to live one.

The title of the novel, *Mary, a Fiction,* suggests that the book was at least partly autobiographical; and so it was. That part, the story of the heroine's friendship for a girl named Ann, was obviously patterned on Mary's friendship with Fanny Blood. And there are other similarities: the heroine's parents have the same first names and much the same characters as Mary's own mother and father; and the rather worldly hero, Henry, whom the fictitious Mary loved but could not marry, may have been an idealized portrait of Joshua Waterhouse. Most of the plot, however, is imaginary. It concerns the life of a sensitive, intelligent girl, the daughter of rich and fashionable parents, who is forced to marry a young man named Charles in order to settle a dispute over an estate. Immediately after the ceremony the bridegroom sets out on the grand tour of Europe, leaving his bride to fend for herself. She is bitterly unhappy, of course, but finds consolation in her friendship for Ann. And when Ann's health fails, the two girls go to Lisbon in an attempt to cure her. But the trip is taken in vain, and presently Ann dies, leaving Mary among strangers. Soon, however, she meets and falls in love with Henry, a man who has known the world only to renounce it. Like a good sentimental hero, he first appears playing a Scottish ballad on his violin:

He brought such a thrilling sound out of the instrument, that Mary started, and looking at him with more attention than she had done before . . . saw, in a face rather ugly, strong lines of genius. His manners were awkward, that kind of awkwardness which is often found in literary men: he seemed a thinker, and delivered his opinions in elegant expressions, and musical tones of voice.[9]

Of course Mary conceals her love for months; and, in an attempt to master her sorrow, she devotes all her energies to caring for a sick woman. As a result she presently comes down with a dangerous fever—at about the time Henry falls into "a consumption." And when at last the two meet again, they confess their undying love. ("Dear enthusiastic creature," Henry whispers in one of their rendezvous, "how you steal into my soul!")[10] But Mary's marriage stands between them, and they can only take the Sacrament together as a symbol of their spiritual union. Soon afterwards Henry dies, and Mary devotes herself to his mother, traveling here and there with her in search of health. But eventually, despite her feeling of revulsion for Charles, her nominal husband, duty impels her to return to him. When they meet again, the reader is told,

she gave him her hand—the struggle was almost more than she could endure. She tried to appear calm; time mellowed her grief, and mitigated her torments; but when her husband would take her hand, or mention anything like love, she would instantly feel a sickness, a faintness at her heart, and wish, involuntarily, that the earth would open and swallow her.[11]

And so she spends the rest of her life in good works, ever looking forward, as the author wrote in her final sentence, "to that world, *where there is neither marrying,* nor giving in marriage."

In many ways the novel offered Mary an ideal means of escape from the life which she found so unpleasant. Not only did it tell of human existence on a higher spiritual plane than that which she saw daily, but it glorified and sentimentalized many details of her own life and character. The setting is considerably more picturesque than that in which Mary had spent most of her life: the heroine's house looks out on cloud-capped mountains, "little bubbling cascades," and an ivy-covered castle formerly occupied by her ancestors. Moreover, the fictitious Mary shares her creator's intelligence and "sensibility," but is blessed with a much richer income. She is not obliged to teach or serve as a companion or governess; she is free to spend her time as she wishes and can devote herself wholly to charity. This was just the sort of life that Mary would have chosen for herself, had she been free to choose; and she no doubt enjoyed imagining it. She must have been consoled in her loneliness by visualizing such an existence and thinking how much she could have made of life had she been given the opportunities which Lady Kingsborough and her friends were so wantonly wasting.

To a modern reader Mary's novel seems like sentimental nonsense. It idealizes the woman of sensibility who is disdainful of this world, eager to serve her fellow-sufferers, and confident of a reward in heaven. Such conscious nobility is less admired in our day than in the late eighteenth century, and a modern psychologist would certainly trace the heroine's self-sacrifice to motives quite different from those which Mary provided. Her preoccupation with sorrow, too, is at times almost pathological; for Mary worked always on the assumption that nothing was more "interesting" than distress. Of Ann she wrote: "This disappointment [the neglect of a former suitor] spread a sadness over her countenance, and made it interesting."[12] She piled woe upon woe and then regaled her reader with the heroine's rhapsodic commentary on her misfortunes; and she seems to have admired the fictitious Mary not for her strength of character but for her ability to suffer and to put her suffering into words.

As a reflection of Mary Wollstonecraft's spiritual and emotional biography, however, the book is valuable; for the fictitious Mary, like the real one, had found little joy in her parents, had been suddenly exalted by her friendship for another woman, had fallen in love with a man whom she could not marry, and had concluded that her only satisfaction in life would rise from service to others. She seems, in fact, to be trying to say that she is laying bare her

soul (though she gets considerably entangled in figures of speech)
when she writes in the Advertisement to her novel:

> Those compositions only have power to delight, and carry us willing
> captives, where the soul of the author is exhibited, and animates the hidden
> springs. Lost in a pleasing enthusiasm, they live in the scenes they represent;
> and do not measure their steps in a beaten track, solicitous to gather expected
> flowers, and bind them in a wreath, according to the prescribed rules of art.
> These chosen few, wish to speak for themselves, and not to be an echo—
> even of the sweetest sounds—or the reflector of the most sublime beams.
> The paradise they ramble in, must be of their own creating—or the prospect
> soon grows insipid, and not varied by a vivifying principle, fades and dies.[13]

Mary reveals herself again to be a devotee of the school of sensibility, which she defines as "the most exquisite feeling of which
the human soul is susceptible." "When it pervades us," she adds,
"we feel happy; and could it last unmixed, we might form some
conjecture of the bliss of those paradisiacal days, when the obedient
passions were under the dominion of reason, and the impulses
of the heart did not need correction."[14] Yet once in a great while
Mary's old-maidish common sense reasserts itself. "If my readers
would excuse the sportiveness of fancy, and give me credit for
genius," she observes at one point in the book, "I would go on and
tell them such tales as would force the sweet tears of sensibility to
flow in copious showers down beautiful cheeks, to the discom-
posure of rouge, &c., &c. Nay, I would make it so interesting, that
the fair peruser should beg the hair-dresser to settle the curls himself, and not interrupt her."[15] Obviously there was still a conflict in
Mary's spirit; she had not sworn complete allegiance to the hazy
doctrines of sensibility.

Moreover, the book reveals not only Mary's spiritual and emotional biography but also the progress of her thinking; and it bears
out the impression imparted by *Thoughts on the Education of
Daughters* that as yet she had not abandoned the orthodox opinions
taught her in her childhood. Though she is dissatisfied with the
world as she finds it, she has no remedy to offer. She still looks for
improvement not to any sweeping change in the social structure
but to man's translation to a better life after death. Her religion

likewise shows little evidence of speculative thought: she is perhaps more tolerant than the average young woman of her time, but she has not yet begun to question her orthodox creed. Surely it was no believer in "rational religion" who wrote in the account of the heroine's visit to Lisbon:

The Roman Catholic ceremonies attracted her attention, and gave rise to conversations when they all met; and one of the gentlemen continually introduced deistical notions, when he ridiculed the pageantry they all were surprised at observing. Mary thought of both the subjects, the Romish tenets, and the deistical doubts; and though not a skeptic, thought it right to examine the evidence on which her faith was built. She read Butler's Analogy, and some other authors: and these researches made her a christian from conviction, and she learned charity, particularly with respect to sectaries; saw that apparently good and solid arguments might take their rise from different points of view; and she rejoiced to find that those she should not concur with had some reason on their side.[10]

In the matter of feminine rights, however, she had apparently begun to think for herself. She had formulated no theory, but she had at least learned to resent the common attitude which gentlemen showed toward the opposite sex. After meeting the fictitious Mary, one of the characters in the novel "doubted whether heaven was peopled with spirits masculine; and almost forgot that he had called the sex 'the pretty play things that render life tolerable.' "[17] And in the Advertisement to the book Mary inserted the acid statement:

In an artless tale, without episodes, the mind of a woman, who has thinking powers is displayed. The female organs have been thought too weak for this arduous employment; and experience seems to justify the assertion. Without arguing physically about *possibilities*—in a fiction, such a being may be allowed to exist . . . .[18]

Again it is clear that though Mary had in her mind and her heart the germs of her later theories, she had not yet found the culture which would bring them to maturity.

As a reflection of life, however, *Mary* is practically worthless. The author's mind was in no state to see life clearly and see it whole, and her conception of human existence was too warped to permit her to evolve anything but a negative philosophy. As a

result she presented only a segment of life distorted by the unhealthy values of a sentimentalist; and apart from its autobiographical interest the book is not worth the time demanded to read it.
When it was published in 1788, it received little attention. The
reviewers seem to have ignored it altogether, and the public seems
never to have demanded a second edition. In fact, after Mary's
reputation had been established, Joseph Johnson advertised it regularly in her new publications, apparently hoping that her admirers
would be beguiled into buying up his surplus stock. In 1797 Mary
herself told her sister that she considered the book "a crude production," adding that she did not "very willingly put it in the way
of people whose good opinion, as a writer, I wish for." Yet if she
thought seriously about the matter, she might have concluded that
though the book was indeed, as she said, "an imperfect sketch," and
though it had done nothing to spread her fame, it had proved to
be a valuable investment in time. Thanks to it she had been enabled
to rid her mind of the morbid introspection which encrusted it.
Now at last her real energies would be able to reassert themselves.

In midsummer of 1787 the Kingsboroughs and their entourage
went up to London to prepare for a trip to the Continent. Mary's
wishes had apparently prevailed! But before they set out, she asked
for a few days' vacation to visit her two sisters, whom she had not
seen for nearly a year. She was granted permission and was on the
point of leaving. But when Lady Kingsborough saw how distressed
little Margaret was at the thought of parting from Mary for only a
few days, she lost all patience. Why should she put up with this
woman who had captured her children's affections—who so often
made her feel uncomfortable, and even guilty? And, doubtless in
a futile effort to prove her own superiority, she discharged Mary
on the spot.

The This was a sudden change in the course of events. Yet Mary
was not completely taken aback. "I long since imagined that my
departure would be sudden," she wrote later to Everina. She must
have known that Lady Kingsborough would eventually find a

pretext to be rid of her. And she doubtless had few regrets, for her year with the Kingsboroughs must have seemed like time wasted. Actually, however, the experience had added one more bit to her education in the ways of the world. Hitherto she had seen British life at many social levels, but never the highest. Now she had seen that, and had unconsciously stored up material for later use. Whatever respect for the aristocracy she may have acquired in her childhood was now dissipated. She now knew the worst faults of the leisured class, and she was often to recur to them in her writings. And in *The Rights of Woman* she took everlasting revenge on Lady Kingsborough in her picture of the fine lady who ignores her children to lavish affection on her dogs.[19]

The only tie that bound Mary to the Kingsboroughs was her love for Margaret. In the year that they had been together the little girl had been intermittently ill, and in tending her Mary had grown increasingly fond of her. Now that they must part, she must have been upset not only because she would miss the child but also because she could but fear what would become of her when left to the care of her mother or ordinary hirelings. Shortly before the family had left Dublin Mary had written: "Margaret is really a fine girl and so much attached to me I govern her completely. Yet her violence of temper teases me, though I myself never feel the effects of it. She sees her mother's faults and sometimes ridicules them. I try to curb her, but fear she will launch out when out of my sight." Unfortunately, though, Mary had no alternative but to bid her "little favorite" farewell. Yet she did not forget the girl. After she was settled in London she wrote to Joseph Johnson: "I had, the other day, the satisfaction of again receiving a letter from my poor, dear Margaret.—With all a mother's fondness I could transcribe a part of it .... I miss her innocent caresses—and sometimes indulge a pleasing hope, that she may be allowed to cheer my childless age—if I am to live to be old."[20] And although they probably never met again, Margaret remembered her governess affectionately, and years later befriended Mary's daughter when they were both living in Italy.[21]

Once her connection with the Kingsboroughs was dissolved, Mary probably did not hesitate. In August she went with the manuscript of her novel to consult Joseph Johnson. She had published one book; why should she not write others for a living? To her delight Johnson accepted her novel, provided her with lodgings at his house for two or three weeks, and promised her steady work as soon as she could settle in London. Naturally she was elated. The break with Lady Kingsborough had been a blessing. Now she could begin life anew; now she could realize her true merits. The years of slavery were over; henceforth she could lose herself and submerge her sorrows in congenial work.

But first she must make her postponed visit to her sisters. And so she went down to Henley, in Oxfordshire, and stayed with Everina at Miss Rowden's school, where she had recently accepted a position. While she was there she wrote to Johnson that she was busy comparing a French translation of the Bible with the King James Version, telling stories to the schoolchildren, wandering the fields to observe "the falling leaves, . . . the singing of a robin, or the noise of a water-mill, . . . at the same time perhaps discussing some knotty point, or straying from this *tiny* world to new systems." Certainly Mary was now trying to make herself interesting to her future employer; she was writing as she thought a lady-novelist should write. But in the next paragraph she revealed that beneath the sentimental varnish her old spirit was reviving:

I often think of my new plan of life; and, lest my sister should try to prevail on me to alter it, I have avoided mentioning it to her. I am determined!— Your sex generally laugh at female determinations; but let me tell you, I never yet resolved to do any thing of consequence, that I did not adhere resolutely to it, till I had accomplished my purpose, improbable as it might have appeared to a more timid mind.[22]

A week later, from Market Harborough, where she was spending a few days with Eliza, she wrote again to Johnson. This time she described her coach trip from Henley with "three opulent tradesmen" whose "conversation was not calculated to beguile the way, when the sable curtain concealed the beauties of nature." Of course she had "shrunk away" from their mundane talk, and she remarked that she "was not surprised by any glimpse of the sublime, or beautiful" in their conversation. But for all her delicacy, one of the tradesmen told her that she would make "a useful partner in a good *firm*."[23] Mary passed the remark along to Johnson for what it was worth. And since he was a shrewd man, he may have found it more truly revealing of Mary's character than all her sentimental claptrap.

By Michaelmas, 1787, Mary was settled in the house which Johnson had rented for her at 49 George (now Dolben) Street, off Blackfriars Road on the Surrey side of the river. And before long she was busy seeing her novel through the press, planning her *Original Stories* for children, and doubtless trying to finish off another piece of fiction which she had named "The Cave of Fancy."

This was another attempt in the sentimental vein. It began with the sentence: "Ye who expect constancy where every thing is changing, and peace in the midst of tumult, attend to the voice of experience, and mark in time the footsteps of disappointment; or life will be lost in desultory wishes, and death arrive before the dawn of wisdom."[24] Then followed an account of a "hoary sage" named Sagestus, who spends his nights in the Cave of Fancy, where he can converse with "various spirits, which inhabit the different regions of nature." One morning he emerges from his cave to find the ground strewn with the bodies of the victims of a shipwreck, and he proceeds to analyze their characters from a quick study of their faces and bodies. Only one person has survived, a little girl whom the sage adopts and names Sagesta.

Evidently the rest of the tale was to be taken up with an account of the education of Sagesta. But Mary failed to complete it. The only portion which survives is a story told by the sage as a part of Sagesta's preparation for life. It is the lugubrious history of a girl who falls in love with a married man and tries to extinguish her love by marrying another man, to whom her family is indebted. But her attempt to conquer her first love fails; and only many years later does she learn that she can find contentment in life

solely by serving others. Once again Mary seems to be charting
the course which she has taken to conquer her love for Joshua
Waterhouse; once again she tells the story of a girl who cannot
marry the man she loves. And once again her treatment of the
subject is often mawkishly sentimental. Yet despite the world-
weariness and resignation expressed in the tale, there is an occasional trace of Mary's reviving spirit. At one point in the narrative
she quotes Gray's lines beginning "Full many a flower is born to
blush unseen," and then denies the claim sharply. No true poet
remains "mute" and "inglorious," she insists; rather, "those only
grovel who have not power to fly."[25] She might well have added
that she herself had just finished a whole year of groveling as a
governess to the Kingsboroughs—and that now, if ever, she must
try her wings. She might even have gone on to reflect that her old
sentimental flights would never carry her far—that if she genuinely wished to soar, she must aim higher than she had done in
Mary.

Surely it was no accident that "The Cave of Fancy" was never
finished; for it was a product of the dead past, and Mary's eyes
were fixed on the future.

CHAPTER IV
New Directions
(1787-1790)

Let me tell you, I never yet resolved to do any thing of consequence, that I did not adhere resolutely to it, till I had accomplished my purpose, improbable as it might have appeared to a more timid mind.

—Letter to Joseph Johnson.

WHEN Mary settled down in her house on George Street in 1787 England was enjoying a period of renewed prosperity. The American Revolution had ended with the Treaty of Versailles four years earlier, and the ominous rumblings across the Channel in France were still faint. The younger Pitt, who had been born in the same year as Mary, had served four years as Prime Minister and had proved himself friendly toward the people and willing to reform the government to their specifications. He had done much to repair the feeble financial structure, which had been shaken by the war and the hostility of European countries; and he had even succeeded in accumulating a surplus of half a million pounds in the treasury. To the majority of Englishmen the return to national solvency alone was enough to recommend Pitt and his administration. And since England's inventive genius was regularly supplying the world with mechanical contrivances of all sorts, she once more commanded the respect which she had lost during the war with the Colonies. All in all, most Englishmen were satisfied with the *status quo*.

Londoners were particularly pleased with the national prosperity. Because of it their city was growing steadily. They cared not that it was becoming a dirty, overgrown metropolis; what mattered was that it was increasing in size and importance, bidding fair to rival Paris itself. The sedan chair, as Horace Walpole remarked, was now almost extinct; distances had become so great that a vehicle borne by human power was impractical. And although the smoke from the nearby lime kilns was a constant nuisance, the city was undergoing vast improvements. Visitors from the Continent were dazzled by the new pavements and the street lights; indeed the Prince of Monaco, arriving in London for the first time, assumed that the city had been specially illuminated in his honor.

Social conditions had improved too, and travelers marveled at the paucity of beggars, streetwalkers, and drunkards in the city. Thanks partly to heavy taxes on alcoholic liquors, Londoners were drinking far less than they had earlier in the century. And thanks to the labors of John Howard and his associates, morality had improved among the lower classes and poverty had declined. Howard's reforms had, to be sure, made a few thoughtful Londoners suddenly aware of the faults of their social system; they realized, as never before, how much reform was needed. And in their zeal they sometimes complained bitterly of the deterioration of society, blind to the signal increase in morality in their own time. Mary herself had bewailed the depravity of London in her novel, when she described the heroine's return from Lisbon:

As she passed through the streets in an hackney-coach, disgust and horror alternately filled her mind. She met some women drunk; and the manners of those who attacked the sailors, made her shrink into herself and exclaim, are these my fellow creatures! . . . She saw vulgarity, dirt, and vice—her soul sickened; this was the first time such complicated misery had obtruded itself on her sight.—Forgetting her own griefs, she gave the world a much indebted tear; mourned for a world in ruins.[1]

But Mary had been content merely to shed a tear. Like most contemporary critics, she had not yet learned to diagnose the disease she deplored. When she went up to London in the fall of 1787 she was probably too much absorbed with her personal plans to be seriously concerned about society. London, grimy and sinful as it was, must have looked good to her after her exile in Ireland. She was never to share the Romantics' longing for rural solitude; she loved nature, but she demanded stimulating companionship. And so she must have thrilled at the prospect of being a real Londoner (not, as before, a dweller on the fringes of the city) and sharing in the activity of the great metropolis.

If she had paused to gauge the literary competition which she was about to encounter, she would have found little to challenge her. The great men of the Johnsonian Era were fast dying off; the Bluestockings were in their nonage; Wordsworth and Coleridge were still schoolboys. Of the poets of the period who are now remembered, Blake and Burns were scarcely known, Cowper had abandoned creative work to translate Homer, and Crabbe had begun his twenty-two-year silence. The reigning laureate was Thomas Warton, and the most popular poets were William Hayley, author of the cumbersome *Triumph of Temper;* the satirist "Peter Pindar"; and Robert Merry, leader of the absurd Della Cruscans. In prose fiction, drama, and the essay the situation was much the same; as Leslie Stephen expressed it, "The giants of those days were dwarfs compared to their predecessors or their successors."[2]

Yet even among the dwarfs Mary was to fill an inconspicuous place. As yet she had written nothing of great promise, and Joseph Johnson could scarcely have suspected what powers she would eventually display. Although he had accepted her novel and commissioned her to write a book of children's stories, he seems to have intended her primarily as a hack writer.[3] And soon he was encouraging her to try her hand at translation, assuring her that such work would prove the easiest and surest means of securing a steady income. It was a modest beginning, but Mary was content to proceed by slow degrees. For the present at least, she regarded her new trade as a means to an end rather than an end in itself. Though translating might be arduous work, she could console herself that it was far less trying than any means of livelihood she had yet attempted. Surely she would have no cause to complain if she could attain her objectives of gaining complete independence and losing herself in her work—in the job itself and in the chance to aid her sisters.

On November 7, 1787, soon after her arrival in her new house, she wrote to Everina at Henley to report her attempts to locate a better position for her. At the same time she announced that she had sent twenty pounds to Mrs. Burgh but that she would probably be unable to discharge her debt to Sowerby or pay Eliza's fare to town for the holidays. Apparently the gift which was to settle all Mary's debts had failed to materialize—or perhaps she had spent it on her initial expenses in London. At all events she was undaunted, now that her future looked so promising. And presently she was revealing to Everina the plans which she had thus far concealed from everyone. First she swore her sister to absolute secrecy. None of their friends must know about this new scheme, she said; she was in no mood to receive pity or advice. Then she proceeded:

Mr. Johnson, whose uncommon kindness, I believe, has saved me from despair and vexations I shrink back from—and *feared* to encounter, assures me that if I exert my talents in writing I may support myself in a comfortable way. I am then going to be the first of a new genus—I tremble at the attempt, yet if I fail I *only* suffer, and should I succeed, my dear Girls will ever in sickness have a home and a refuge where for a few months in the year, they may forget the cares that disturb the rest.

Of course Mary was stretching the truth a bit in her desire to dramatize her secret. She was not "the first of a new genus"; in fact there were several women of letters—Fanny Burney, Mrs. Trimmer, Hannah Cowley, Hannah More, and Mrs. Barbauld, to name a few—who were making a very decent living by their pens. But Mary, understandably, wanted to startle her sisters. And after telling Everina that she wished to be "a mother to you both," she concluded, still with an eye to dramatic effect: "You know I am not born to tread in the beaten track—the peculiar bent of my nature pushes me on."

A few days later she wrote: "I have *done* with the delusion of fancy. I only live to be useful. Benevolence must fill every void in my heart." And she reported that, though she had a room for her sisters, she had no bed. She assured them, however, that she would get one as soon as possible, and that they must plan to spend their vacations with her. She was full of schemes again, and obviously happier than she had been in months. It was good, surely, to be bustling again, to be making plans for which one could feel a hearty enthusiasm. And though she had not yet ceased to dramatize herself, her new attitude was far healthier than the one which she had adopted in her letters from Ireland. Instead of fancying herself a creature too sensitive to withstand the trials of daily life, she was exulting in her power to achieve.

Everina and Eliza were not slow in taking advantage of Mary's hospitality. On January 1, 1788, when she wrote to George Blood, her two sisters were visiting her and had brought their problems for her to solve. Everina had resigned from Miss Rowden's school and had no idea where she could find another job. Eliza had retained her position at Market Harborough but was dissatisfied with it, and Mary was hoping to find her "a more comfortable school." And she had an additional responsibility in Caroline, the wayward daughter of Mr. and Mrs. Blood, who had left their home some months before. "Last week," Mary told George,

Mrs. Burgh wrote to me, to inform me that the parish officers of Islington had been with her to enquire where your father resided that they might *pass* Caroline to him. She was taken up in a *dreadful* situation—and they now permit her to remain in the workhouse, on conditions *I* pay them half a crown a week, 'till I write to her father. What is to be done, my dear boy? I cannot allow them again to turn her out—nor will I see her. If she knew where I lived, she would come to me, and be a burden I could *not* bear.

On January 17 Mary wrote again to George, this time suggesting that Caroline be left where she was in order to "spare you and our mother the uneasiness [her] presence will of course produce." "I will try to board her at the work-house," she continued, "and buy her a few clothes to cover her, if your father will contrive to send me ten pounds." Thus one of her problems was solved—though with more inconvenience to herself than to the Bloods. And she told George in the same letter that she had hopes of finding a better position for Eliza before long and that she was planning to send Everina to Paris for a few months to "catch the French accent." Yet Mary did not complain of her cares; on the contrary she doubtless welcomed them. They were a healthy outlet for her energies and for her innate urge to direct—and mother

—her family and friends. And her new activity had apparently proved healthful, for she told George that she was "in better health than I have enjoyed for some years."

Soon she was too busy to dramatize herself. The next few years were the busiest of her whole life. Before the first six months of 1788 had elapsed,[4] she had published the novel *Mary* and the children's book *Original Stories*, and was doubtless at work on her first translation.

Original Stories from Real Life; with Conversations, Calculated to Regulate the Affections, and Form the Mind to Truth and Goodness was, like its models, Thomas Day's *Sandford and Merton* and Sarah Trimmer's *History of the Robins*, a loosely strung narrative designed to inculcate the virtues in children by means of precept and example. The stories concern two girls, Mary and Caroline, whose father has put them under the care of a widowed relative, Mrs. Mason, who proves to be a preceptress of terrifying zeal. Though described as "a woman of tenderness and discernment," she strikes a modern reader as a heartless virago. Convinced that Mary's "turn for ridicule" and Caroline's vanity must be corrected, and equally convinced that her own experience has fitted her to rectify others' faults, she approaches her task with utter confidence. By precept and example, one as relentless as the other, she instructs them in the principles of humility, temperance, charity, fortitude, piety, promptness, industry, and kindness to servants and animals. And never does she falter. When she finds a lark with broken wings, she ends its misery by firmly placing "her foot on the bird's head, turning her own another way."[5] When the girls wonder at her equanimity in allowing a caterpillar and a spider to crawl over her hand, she lectures them on the necessity of being kind to all God's creatures, and concludes: "You are often troublesome—I am stronger than you—yet I do not kill you."[6] When her charges are horrified at her tale of the injustice suffered by a man known as Crazy Robin, and one of the girls cries, "Did you ever hear of any thing so cruel?" she replies: "Yes . . . and as we walk home I will relate an instance of still greater barbarity."[7] Mrs. Mason "was never in a passion," her creator assures us; yet the children cannot go to sleep, one night when she is displeased with them, for thinking of her eyes. Small wonder, when she has just "dismissed" them with the grave remark: "I give you to-night a kiss of peace, an affectionate one you have not deserved."[8] When she approves of their behavior, she says, "Give me your hands, my little girls, . . . you have acted like rational creatures."[9] When she finally returns them to their father, she bids them good-bye with the chilling words: "You are now candidates for my friendship, and on your advancement in virtue my regard will in future depend." She confesses, however: "I tremble for you, my dear girls, for you must now practise by yourselves some of the virtues which I have been endeavouring to inculcate."[10] For all her faith in herself as teacher and example, she is still far from sure of her pupils' steadfastness.

A modern reader immediately wonders: Was Mrs. Mason Mary? Are these the principles by which she taught the youngsters at Newington Green and Mitchelstown? Hardly so; little Margaret King's lasting affection for her would seem to disprove it, as would Mary's motherly fondness for the girl. (Mrs. Mason was never motherly!) Surely Mary's letters suggest that she had little of Mrs. Mason's adamant self-satisfaction and a much larger share of common humanity. Yet there are points of similarity between the two: Mrs. Mason's stern religion, with its stoic insistence that life is a "vale of tears," is like Mary's; so is her belief that young children should be taught to bow to the superior wisdom of their parents—though Mary herself was probably subtler in impressing the doctrine on her pupils.

Why, then, did Mary create such a character? Perhaps because she worked from such models as Thomas Day's Mr. Barlow and Mrs. Trimmer's Papa and Mamma Redbreast and Mrs. Benson, and because she herself at the age of twenty-nine had little real understanding of human nature—or genuine sense of humor. Perhaps too because she had revolted too suddenly from the senti-

mentality of *Mary*. Indeed Mrs. Mason and the heroine of *Mary,*
who appeared before the public almost simultaneously, reveal the
two extremes between which Mary was always to vacillate. For the
moment she had discarded her pose of sensibility; and she was
perhaps trying to convince herself that reason, if followed unswerv-
ingly, could control her unruly emotions.

Most of the faults of *Original Stories* are directly traceable to
the intense seriousness with which Mary wrote. She sought not to
delight young readers but to instruct them and to undo the harm
done by negligent parents. She was approaching from a new angle
the problem which she had already attacked in *Thoughts on the
Education of Daughters.* "Good habits, imperceptibly fixed, are
far preferable to the precepts of reason," she remarked in her Preface; "but, as this task requires more judgment than generally
falls to the lot of parents, substitutes must be sought for, and medi-
cines given, when regimen would have answered the purpose
much better." And presently: "But to wish that parents would,
themselves, mould the ductile passions, is a chimerical wish, for
the present generation have their own passions to combat with,
and fastidious pleasures to pursue, neglecting those pointed out by
nature . . . ."[11] When Joseph Johnson objected that such remarks
might well antagonize prospective buyers, Mary wrote to him:
"I cannot *now* concur with you, I mean with respect to the preface,
and have not altered it . . . . A general rule *only* extends to the
majority—and, believe me, the few judicious parents who may
peruse my book, will not feel themselves hurt—and the weak are
too vain to mind what is said in a book intended for children."[12]

Whatever children may have thought of the book, parents
seem to have approved of it; at least they bought it in sufficient
quantities to justify a second edition, with engravings by William
Blake, in 1791; a Dublin edition in the same year; a German translation in 1795; a third London edition in 1796; and a second Dublin edition in 1799. The popularity of the book lasted even into
the nineteenth century, and it went through four editions in thirty-
five years.[13] Probably it seemed less formidable to its first readers

than it does now. In those days anyone who wanted to amuse a child gave him a toy; books, which came relatively high (*Original Stories* cost two shillings without the Blake engravings and two-and-six with them), were reserved for nobler purposes. And Mary's book was not, after all, much sterner stuff than *Sandford and Merton* or *The History of the Robins;* in some respects it showed a healthier tissue, since it lacked their relentless opposition of the model child and the scapegrace. Indeed, at a time when "Sermons for Children" were generally considered to be legitimate "entertainment" for young minds, *Original Stories* must have seemed to many parents rather frivolous. And if they had been brought up, as many were, on James Janeway's *Holy and Exemplary Lives and Joyful Deaths of Several Young Children,* it must have seemed downright insipid.

Of course Mary had few opportunities in *Original Stories* to reveal what change, if any, her opinions had undergone during the first few months of her stay in London. Yet the very absence of liberal ideas implies that she had not been swept off her feet by the "new philosophy." Mrs. Mason, like any enlightened lady of her time, is charitable to those beneath her in rank and wealth. "Perhaps the greatest pleasure I have ever received," she tells her protégées, "has arisen from the habitual exercise of charity, in its various branches."[14] But her notion of charity is confined to the "alms-giving" which Mary was later to decry.[15] Though she professes to believe in the brotherhood of all God's creatures, Mrs. Mason never for a moment suspects that brotherhood demands equality; in fact she prides herself on her generosity in allowing a family of hay-makers to sleep in her barn each summer; and when she visits the poor, she judiciously dresses in simple clothing so that they will not be tempted to covet the privileges of her class.

As for the matter which presently absorbed Mary's attention, the equality of the sexes, it would have been utterly out of place in *Original Stories.* Indeed, when reprimanding one of the girls for her slowness in dressing, Mrs. Mason says: "Fathers, and men in general, complain of this inattention; they have always to wait

for females. Learn to avoid this fault, however insignificant it
may appear in your eyes, for that habit cannot be of little consequence that sometimes weakens esteem."[16] The statement is in-
nocuous enough, but the overtones are obvious: females cannot
well afford to tax the patience of "fathers, and men in general."
Mary was not yet ready to demand equality for her sex. In fact the
only evidence of a change in her thinking is her veneration for
reason in the person of Mrs. Mason.

With all its faults *Original Stories* was the most successful book
Mary had written. With the money which she received for it and
her novel she apparently set to work at once to better her sisters'
fortunes. In mid-February of 1788 she packed Everina off to Paris,
only to receive presently "two long letters from her, full of accounts
of disasters and difficulties, which must necessarily occur in a
strange country." But Mary ignored her complaints and presently
was, in effect, employing her sister as her Paris representative. On
March 22 she wrote to her:

Pray enquire of the *literary* man about some particulars, relative to M.
Necker, the late Minister, which I shall mention. He has written a book
entitled De l'importance des opinions Religeuses. It pleases me, and I want
to know the character of the man in domestic life and public estimation &c
and the opinion the French have of his literary abilities.

And she enclosed a letter to be forwarded to Necker himself—
probably a request for permission to translate his new book into
English. Mary urged her sister to "gather together all the news you
can with respect to literature, and send it to me—for I am almost
as deeply immersed in study as the Baron himself." "Many motives
impel me besides sheer love of knowledge," she explained. And
undoubtedly she had in mind, as one of those motives, the forth-
coming *Analytical Review,* the new magazine which Joseph Johnson and Thomas Christie first issued in May, 1788, and which was
to be her mainstay in the years immediately ahead. With books to
read, reviews to write, and her first job of translation under way,
Mary was busier than ever in her life before. There was little time

now for brooding over the sorrows of the past. In fact when she wrote to George Blood on May 16 she told him triumphantly:

I have lately been very busy translating a work of importance, and have made a very advantageous contract for another. Besides, I have had a variety of other employments. In short, my dear Boy, I succeed beyond my most sanguine hopes, and really believe I shall clear above two hundred pounds this year, which will supply amply all *my* wants and enable me to defray the Expences of Everina's journey, and let her remain in Paris longer than I at first intended. I am thankful to Heaven for enabling me to be useful, and this consideration sweetens my toil, for I have been very diligent . . . . I have had some difficulties at the onset which imperceptibly melt away as I encounter them—and I daily earn more money with less trouble.

Yet busy as she was, she could not write all the time; and whenever she could escape from her duties, she made her way to Joseph Johnson's rooms at 72 St. Paul's Churchyard. There she was introduced to an unusually stimulating group of people. Most of them were Johnson's regular clients, men and women of liberal sympathies who met regularly for dinner in the "quaintly shaped upstair room, with walls not at right angles"[17] above his shop. None of them were "radicals" like Godwin or Tom Paine or William Blake, all of whom were eventually to write for Johnson; but they were friends of freedom and democracy who enjoyed good talk. And it was with them, rather than at Vauxhall or Ranelagh or such pleasure spots, that Mary spent her leisure time.

Johnson himself was an extraordinarily affable man. A comparative stranger remarked that "his good-humoured face, with a cordial shake of the hand, and 'How d'ye do, sir? I dine at three,' always disarms me."[18] And his dinners were merry affairs: one of his frequent guests, Mrs. Anna Laetitia Barbauld, told her brother that she was almost afraid to name the hour at which some of the parties broke up.[19] When Johnson first met Mary he seems to have treated her with reserve—perhaps because he was a bit alarmed by her effusive letters. But Mary assured Everina that "his sensible conversation would soon wear away the impression that a formality, or rather stiffness of manners, first makes to his disadvantage." And she added: "I am sure you would love him did you know with what *tenderness* and humanity he has behaved to me."

Before long Mary regarded him as her protector and dearest friend; and she spent "many of her afternoons and most of her evenings" at his rooms.[20] In one of her letters she assured him that he was "a *man* before [he was] a bookseller," and she frequently unburdened her troubles to him. Twice in her letters she told him that he had filled for her the part of both father and brother.[21] But she never offered even a hint of any romantic attachment for him, and it would be idle to assume that she felt any. Mary had put that sort of thing behind her—or so she thought.

Soon she was accepted as a colleague by all Johnson's cronies: John Bonnycastle, the mathematician; George Fordyce, the physician who was to attend Mary in her last illness; George Anderson, the classical scholar; and perhaps Alexander Geddes, the Biblical scholar, and Henry Fuseli, the Swiss "painter of nightmares."[22] She met Mrs. Trimmer too, spent a day at her house, and "found her a truly respectable woman." But she seems to have preferred the company of the men. They were an able group, and, thanks to their variety of interests, they must have made lively company.

None of them could have passed for heroes of romance; in fact most of them were decidedly eccentric. According to Leigh Hunt, Bonnycastle looked so much like a horse "that a bag of corn would have hung well on him."[23] Fordyce, a deliberate Scot who punctuated his speech with long pauses, was famed for his disregard for manners and dress and for his habit of eating, by conviction, only one meal a day—but that a huge one.[24] Geddes, the renegade priest who had analyzed the Bible so closely as to be frowned on by both Protestants and Catholics, was unkempt and irascible, and when in a temper (often caused by a trifling disagreement) would "bellow and rush at his antagonist like a wild bull."[25] And Fuseli, who was attracting much notice by his grotesque contributions to Boydell's Shakespeare Gallery, must already have shown some signs of the "gnarled, hard, and distorted" features, the "stalking and straddle-legged" gait, the "aspiring and gigantic" gestures, and the "uncouth and dwarfish" physique which Hazlitt later derided in his essay "On the Old Age of Artists." All these men were strange company for a young woman of Mary's age, but she probably admired even their eccentricities. Twice in the year 1788 she remarked, in her writings, on the vapidity of mere "bodily beauty."[26]

But though she was doubtless happier than ever before in her life, the blue devils sometimes plagued her. On March 3, 1788, in a letter to George Blood, she complained of "the return of some of my old nervous complaints." "Even now I am suffering," she wrote.

A nervous head-ache torments me, and I am ready to throw down my pen—almost unable to direct it. My thoughts are frozen—I cannot thaw them—or force them to flow glibly from my pen. I shall write nothing but tautology. Well—Well—Nature will sometimes prevail, 'spite of reason, and the thick blood lagging in the veins give melancholy power to harass the mind; or produce a listlessness which destroys every active purpose of the soul.—I am not however going to complain; for I have abundant reason to be thankful to Providence for the many comforts I at present enjoy, and the evils I have escaped.

In her notes to Johnson, too, she complained of being "very low spirited" or "sick with vexation," and again and again she thanked him for having sustained her even when she was most petulant and unreasonable. No longer, however, did she seem to find morbid satisfaction in her sorrow; no longer did she bewail the ardors of earthly life and hail death as a release. In fact Mary was probably undergoing a thorough spiritual shake-up. It was at about this time that she gave up regular church attendance—probably because she had begun to question the beliefs which she had hitherto accepted as incontrovertible. Perhaps Johnson and his circle had helped to bring about the change; perhaps it sprang from her growing devotion to reason and a natural desire to test her old beliefs by rational standards. Whatever the cause, it was a change for the better. She had already shifted her attention from herself to others, and in so doing had revived her paralyzed energies and set them to work to aid her family and friends. But before she could bring those energies to complete fruition, she must gain

faith in the possibilities of earthly life. Before she could extend her
benevolence to all mankind, she must be convinced of the basic
truth of humanistic philosophy.

Meanwhile she was deprived of the austere consolations of her
old religion, and her mind was naturally unsettled. What *was* the
purpose of life, she wondered, if it was not a preparation for the
next world? "I acknowledge that life is but a jest—and often a
frightful dream," she wrote to Johnson, "—yet catch myself every
day searching for something serious—and feel real misery from
the disappointment."[27] In March, in a letter to George Blood, she
told of hearing her old friend John Hewlett preach "a sermon,
which he wrote to oblige me, on the recognition of our friends in
a future state." Perhaps she had appealed to Hewlett, as one who
held fairly orthodox beliefs, to help bolster up her tottering faith.
Certainly she did not abandon her old convictions without a struggle; in fact she never wholly abandoned them. In July, 1788, for
example, she wrote Joseph Johnson that, while reading Dr. Johnson's sermon on the death of his wife, she "seemed (suddenly) to
find my *soul* again." And she added in a postscript: "I believe [Dr.
Johnson] is somewhere—*where* my soul has been gadding perhaps;—but *you* do not live on conjectures."[28] Such speculations
were, however, a good deal less comforting than the assurance
which she had lost; and her uncertainty must have cost her many
a pang.

Yet she was determined not to slip into disillusionment; she
was striving as never before to master herself. But when she turned
to reason as a means of self-control, she was often disappointed.
"I am trying to brace my nerves that I may be industrious," she
wrote to Johnson. But she added: "I am afraid reason is not a good
bracer—for I have been reasoning a long time with my untoward
spirits—and yet my hand trembles."[29] In the course of her soul-
searching, however, she learned to understand the complexities of
her nature better than she ever had before. And in one of her letters to Johnson she anatomized herself shrewdly in these few lines:

I am a mere animal, and instinctive emotions too often silence the suggestions of reason .... I am a strange compound of weakness and resolution! However, if I must suffer, I will endeavour to suffer in silence. There is certainly a great defect in my mind—my wayward heart creates its own misery.—Why I am made thus I cannot tell; and, till I can form some idea of the whole of my existence, I must be content to weep and dance like a child—long for a toy, and be tired of it as soon as I get it.

We must each of us wear a fool's cap; but mine, alas! has lost its bells, and is grown so heavy, I find it intolerably troublesome.[30]

Surely this passage records one of the most lucid flashes of self-understanding that Mary ever experienced. There is here, to be sure, a hint of her old self-dramatization and self-pity, and more than a hint of her lifelong neuroticism; but for all her self-consciousness she penetrates fearlessly to the very roots of her nature. She can discern no real purpose in life; she knows that she is too often swayed by her emotions, and yet she realizes that she cannot live by reason alone. Still, recognizing her shortcomings as she does, and learning to view herself objectively, she leaves some hope that she will eventually master her "wayward heart" and her "instinctive emotions" and direct them to a purposeful end.

All in all Mary was profiting by her busy life in London and by her new friendships. She was abandoning her narrow religious doctrines, she was seeking to discover some sort of satisfaction from a life well led, and she had concluded that she must seek to discipline herself. But more important: she had achieved some degree of sincerity; she had outgrown her former fascination with her every emotion, her studied display of her inmost self. Her native common sense had come to the surface again, and she was a better woman as a result. Indeed she was probably able to master her energies oftener than her letters to Johnson would suggest. She accomplished much during her first year in London, and she could have had little time for introspection. Most of the time she must have stifled her doubts to immerse herself in her work and her service for others. She had, after all, a healthier mind and a good deal more reason to relish life than ever before; and like many mortals she may have been able to ignore the apparent aimlessness of human existence so long as she could detect an immediate purpose in her own.

She had plenty of work now to fill her time. Indeed she was busier than ever, since she had become a regular contributor to Johnson's new *Analytical Review*. Though she doubtless wrote for the magazine from its inception in May, 1788, her contributions were not signed until the July issue.[31] Thereafter she was a regular contributor, assigned at first to the department of fiction, travel books, and literature for or about women or children. In these first months her articles were usually brief: between July and December, 1788, she wrote nineteen signed reviews which covered only forty-four pages in all, a good many of which were devoted to summaries and excerpts.

Mary's early reviews were hardly remarkable for their content. She usually relied on common-sense criticism, praising the tame *Letter from a Lady to her Daughter, on the Manner of Passing Sunday Rationally and Agreeably* (August, 1788), but damning the new novels, which she accused of affectation or nonsense likely to turn the heads of young lady readers. In her review of Charlotte Smith's *Emmeline* (July, 1788) she deprecates the author's fondness for overworking the passions of her characters, and laments that "our young females" should be encouraged to think that "useless sorrow" is more commendable than "rational resignation." In her review of the anonymous *School for Fathers* (October, 1788) she lauds the author (presumably a woman) for her modesty, but objects to her overstressing the hero's physical beauty. In short, Mary was usually content to judge a work on moral grounds alone; only twice in the first four and a half years of her reviewing for the *Analytical* did she attempt aesthetic criticism of novels.[32] Her view of literature was that of the austere school-ma'am who refuses to truckle with any book which is not somehow uplifting.

Mary's thinking about matters of politics and religion scarcely affects her early reviews, for they seldom touch on such topics. They were the province of older and sager members of the staff.

Now and again, however, one of her articles contains a hint which confirms the impression left by her early writings: that thus far her political and religious opinions were only mildly liberal. In her review of A. W. Costigan's *Sketches of Society and Manners in Portugal* (August, 1788), for example, she blames Portuguese depravity on the climate, "want of rational employments," "a childish cruel religion," "the system of dissimulation it has introduced," "Moorish customs," and—at the end of the list—"an arbitrary government." A year or two later she would almost certainly have placed the last item first; and she might well have been content to mention it and no other. Elsewhere, in her review of the Reverend Samuel S. Smith's *Essay on the Causes of the Variety of Complexion and Figure in the Human Species* (December, 1788), she suggests that she has not yet lost all her faith in revealed religion; at least she declines to discuss "vague conjectures, which shake our confidence in the validity of the Mosaical account, and consequently lead to a distrust of revelation." Mary's own faith may by this time have been severely shaken. Yet, perhaps because she had found no substitute for her old doctrines, she was not ready to discuss the matter publicly.

On only one score do her reviews show individuality: her style is distinctly her own. She may annoy a modern reader by her fondness for clichés and her conscious rhetoric. But compared with the other reviews in the *Analytical,* Mary's work is refreshing. Her sprawling sentences, though sometimes confusing, are a relief from her colleagues' studied periods; and the exhausted reader of the magazine welcomes them despite their prosy ideas and their artificialities. There is a liveliness about them which the formlessness, the rhetorical flights, even the triteness cannot conceal. Mary's style is indeed the woman herself; she too was wanting in control, often confused, a bit pretentious, a strange mixture of imitation and originality—but never tiresome. It is to Joseph Johnson's credit that, though he may have tried to direct Mary's thinking, he let her write as she chose.

As a matter of fact, though, Johnson may have been powerless in such matters. From the outset Mary made clear to him that she would not write at anyone else's dictation. She refused to alter her Preface to *Original Stories* to please prospective buyers, or to review Dr. Johnson's sermon on the death of his wife "in any other way" than that which she had first adopted.[33] And before many issues of the *Analytical* had appeared, she was writing to the editor to suggest what policy he should follow toward the rival *Critical Review* and *Monthly Review*.[34] Mary was not the woman to surrender herself to others' suggestions.

Toward the end of 1788 Johnson published her first translation anonymously. It was an ambitious job: Necker's *De l'Importance des Opinions Réligeuses,* a book which had been addressed to the French Academy and which was, accordingly, expressed in language of extraordinary complexity. Though a modern reader would scarcely be tempted beyond the first page, it was widely read in 1788—primarily, perhaps, because it was such a singular product to issue from the mind of a Minister of Finance. In content it was an odd mixture of reason and intuition: Necker was severely rational when he tried to prove that religion is necessary to the well-being of man, but appealed only to "feeling" when he went on to demonstrate that God exists.

In the brief Advertisement which preceded Mary's translation she announced that she had taken "some liberties . . . which seemed necessary to preserve the spirit of the original." She might better have apologized for not taking more. For though she usually translated accurately and idiomatically, she sometimes perpetrated such clumsy phrases as "that unquiet love of a long celebrity," "promissory notes, of which it is necessary to await the distant expiration," and "we associate ourselves with delight to all the beauties of nature." And, what was worse, she occasionally wrote sentences which are practically unintelligible. For example:

In short, very often, perhaps the dupes of their own heart, [philosophical writers] have been induced to believe, that, because they were at the same time irreligious by system, and just by character and habit, religion and virtue have not a necessary union; and if it be true, that in the grand interests of life, the slightest doubt has some influence on our actions, would it be possible, that at the time when they would seek to shake religious opinions even when they are ridiculed in conversation, they would still endeavour to preserve a secret connexion with them, by the propriety of their conduct?[35]

Yet in Mary's defense it must be said that she often improved on her original. Though her style was sometimes puzzling, Necker's was often so: his sentences were hopelessly complicated, and his paragraphs were interminable. Mary often omitted superfluous phrases or supplied others which would clarify the meaning. She simplified her reader's task by breaking up Necker's longest sentences and paragraphs, excising much of his empty rhetoric, and compressing repetitious passages. The liberties which she took were almost always justified. She had learned a good deal about the craft of writing since the days of *Thoughts on the Education of Daughters*.

Of the Importance of Religious Opinions was, however, Mary's first translation, and she was understandably timid. Doubtless she felt very audacious when she presumed to improve on the famous Necker.[36] In her own review of the translation in the *Analytical* for January, 1789, she wrote: "The book is certainly very unequally written; in one page easy flowing eloquence gives dignity and interest to the diction, in another the thoughts are laboured, and bombast swells the turgid periods. These remarks will account for some liberties occasionally taken, and we think very properly, by the translator."[37] But for all her changes, the essay as translated was often labored and sometimes utterly confusing. Johnson never reissued it, though it appeared in two American editions, one published at Philadelphia in 1791 and the other at Boston in 1796.

Mary could have profited little from her translation beyond whatever sum she was paid for her work. Her enforced study of Necker's opinions and his style would have taught her little that she did not already know. Yet she must have derived genuine satisfaction from the thought that Johnson had assigned her so important and difficult a piece of translation. She must have rejoiced at the thought that she had fulfilled conscientiously the task assigned to her. Surely her confidence in her own powers had not been misplaced!

During the year 1788 Johnson engaged Mary on two less important bits of hack work. She began a translation of Campe's *New Robinson Crusoe,* a series of selections from Defoe with supplementary "conversations" on the significance of the passages. But she abandoned work on it when another translation of the same book was published anonymously by Stockdale and Company.[38] At about the same time she compiled an anthology, *The Female Reader; or Miscellaneous Pieces, in Prose and Verse; Selected from the Best Writers, and Disposed under Proper Heads; for the Improvement of Young Women.* The book, which was an imitation of one of the popular textbooks of the time, "Enfield's Speaker," was published in 1789 as the work of "Mr. Creswick, Teacher of Elocution." Since Mary's task was largely to select passages from other published works, she had little chance to show her originality save in the "Preface, containing some Hints on Female Education" and perhaps the two prayers signed "O," which may have been her work.[39] Unfortunately no copy of the book seems to have survived.

During the following year, 1789, Mary devoted practically all her time to the *Analytical.* In the first five months of the year she contributed more than forty reviews, averaging roughly a page (of very small type) each. She added biography and moral philosophy to the list of topics under her jurisdiction, but the spirit of her reviews remained unchanged: she continued to praise books for young people if they seemed reasonably moral and sensible, and to assail the immorality and affectation of the new novels. At times she even apologized for the monotony of her articles, assuring the reader that her task of reading such trash was an unmitigated bore.

The June number of the *Analytical,* however, was a banner issue for Mary. She wrote the second, third, and fourth articles and thirty-three lesser ones. In one of them, a review of Dr. Hugh Downman's didactic poem "Infancy, or the Management of Children," she paused to deplore the ignorance of women in her time. Hitherto she had been content with genteel suggestions for improving the education of girls, but now she faced the grim truth about her sex. Mary was painfully aware of how hard it was for a woman to secure an education in her time—and she well knew how much the lack of education penalized women. She and her sisters had been thrown on the world with no intellectual resources, and they had been obliged to snatch at whatever means of support they could find. Eliza had married, Everina had lived as a dependent in her brother's household, and Mary herself had served as companion, teacher, and governess. They had explored all the paths normally open to women of their class, and they had met with little but misery. It was practically impossible for a woman to attain such a degree of independence as a proud spirit like Mary's demanded. Yet she had achieved it; she had even won the respect of a few thoughtful men. But she had not forgotten the fate which confronted the great majority of women who lacked her initiative. She was not yet ready to plead for the emancipation of her sex, but at least she was conscious of the need for some sort of reform.

Mary's increasing literary activity must have brought her a fairly respectable income; yet she never had a penny to spare. "I have had a number of draw-backs on my spirits and purse," she wrote to George Blood in February, 1789. And she asked him to remind his father that Caroline's board at the workhouse was long overdue. Mary had paid it, however, and she asked George to send the money to Mrs. Fitzgerald, Lady Kingsborough's stepmother. Mary had borrowed ten guineas from her for Betty Delane, who had apparently forgotten all about the loan. But Mary had not, and she felt obliged to repay it. "Do not tell your father," she warned George, "for his notions of justice are so lax, he would call honesty romance." Doubtless much of Mary's income was spent on her sisters. Everina was still in France—at Mary's expense, of course— and Eliza was settled at a school in Putney conducted by a Frenchwoman named Mrs. Bregantz. But she seems to have been living there as a "parlour boarder" rather than a teacher, and doubtless she too was at least partially dependent on Mary's support. Yet there was no word of complaint in Mary's letter to George. On the contrary, she wrote joyfully: "Blessed be that Power who gave me an active mind! If it does not smooth, it enables me to jump over the rough places in life . . . . Still I cry avaunt despair—and I push forward."

But on April 16, when next she wrote to George, she was "envolved in numberless difficulties" and considerably upset. This time it was her brother Charles who was troubling her. Mary had taken him in once before, when he had fallen out with his brother Edward and left his employ. She had managed then to article him to another attorney. But now he had been discharged from that post, and she was bitterly disappointed and hurt. He had evidently gone to Ireland, for she wrote:

Before you receive this, or very soon after, you will see Charles—he will tell you some of my vexations. Those *very* severe ones he has brought on me I suppose he will throw into the shade; but I will not prejudice you against him though he has wounded a heart that was full of anxiety on his account— and *disappointed* hope, which my benevolence makes me regret, more than reason can justify. Let me now request you to have an eye on his conduct, and if you can get him into any employment you will relieve me from a heavy weight of care. *Pray* write soon. I am so agitated now, and so unwell, I cannot write.

Yet for all her disappointment, her energies still sustained her, and she prayed heaven to grant her patience that she might overcome her difficulties.

And so she kept busy, as indeed she must in order to meet all her obligations. In the second half of the year 1789 her reviews for the *Analytical* resumed their normal rate and bulk, but in content they showed significant changes. For one thing she was steadily expanding the scope of her department; she was reviewing plays and operas regularly, and in December she undertook to criticize her old friend Dr. Price's *Discourse on the Love of Our Country,* the sermon which was to kindle flames of controversy all over England. Meanwhile her articles were reflecting a more daring and independent spirit than she had hitherto displayed. Her review of *La Vie Privée du Cardinal Dubois* in the August issue assailed the faults of the French aristocracy, attributing them to "the nature of that government." In October her review of the third volume of *Sandford and Merton* showed a knowledge of contemporary educational authorities and an eagerness to test them by her own experience. She seems to have been pondering the question of human independence and speculating on the extent to which it can be secured by means of education. And since this tendency becomes ever more marked in the following months, it is perhaps safe to assume that it stemmed from the world-shaking events across the Channel. For in July, 1789, with the storming of the Bastille, France was plunged into the revolution which many forward-looking Englishmen believed and hoped to be the first step toward the emancipation of mankind. As Godwin put it, the French Revolution had "a conspicuous effect in the progress of Mary's reflections."[40]

For Mary's purposes, indeed, the French Revolution was ideally timed. It burst upon her just as she was rounding out her apprenticeship to her new trade, just as she was seeking for a new creed and a broad outlet for her energies. Its spirit was ideally adapted to hers. As she had told Joseph Johnson, she was "not fond of groveling"; and at the moment she was glorying in her independence after years of bondage. Though the American Revolution had, in its time, seemed like the dawn of a new era, it had taken place in a remote country when Mary could hardly have comprehended its significance. But now freedom was coming to Europe, and Mary was old enough and wise enough to appreciate the meaning of the exciting events—and woman enough to be thrilled by them. Only a few months before, she had rejected her melancholy piety and tried to convince herself that reason could serve both as guide and as justification for human existence. But reason had proved cold comfort; it was, as she complained, "not a good bracer." The French Revolution, however, represented not *cold* reason, but reason in action, reason which recognized men's longings and tried to achieve them. The abstract rights of men, which she had heard so much about at Newington Green and at Johnson's dinner parties, were now about to be realized; and suddenly they made sense to her. Her whole life had been a struggle for just such rights. If all men could gain those rights, there would be an end to the tyranny and injustice which made life seem a thorny path. There would be no such discrepancies as she had seen between peasant and lord in Ireland. No nation would suffer in the grip of one man—perhaps a madman like George III, her own monarch. Instead, every man would be his own master; love would replace hatred; and heaven would reign on earth.

To Mary the Revolution must have seemed like a happy fusion of all that she had been taught to respect by her sage London friends, and all that she cherished by nature. It was Voltaire and Rousseau too, rationalism and enthusiasm; it appealed to her head and her heart, and for once she was not obliged to compromise between them. And so she, like many of her countrymen, looked hopefully to France as the great proving-ground. Once established there, freedom could easily be carried across to England and gradually spread throughout the world. It was indeed bliss to be alive —even for a sensible old maid.

Mary's whole view of life must suddenly have been enlarged. Instead of working to secure comfort and freedom for herself and her sisters, she could now exert herself for the emancipation of mankind. She had passed from private benevolence to public benevolence, a step which she later regarded as evidence of thorough maturity in man or woman. Now at last she had found the direction and the momentum which her life had wanted. Before long she would find also the occasion and the means to advance the great cause which she had espoused.

And yet, though she must have talked Revolution almost constantly, she wrote about it very little at first. She was, after all, only a woman, and nobody cared what she thought about the breathtaking events abroad. So she went on with her chores, translating what came her way, reviewing the silly new novels, and thinking and saying what she hardly dared write. It was exasperating, and at times she boiled over with irritation at her tiresome task. In November, 1789, she concluded a review of a particularly vapid novel by a young lady: "Pray Miss, write no more!"

Meanwhile Johnson must have been watching Mary's progress attentively. When he received a poorly composed translation of the Dutch Madame de Cambon's *Young Grandison,* a series of letters characterizing the model child, he turned it over to Mary for revision.[41] Presently he asked her to translate an abridgment of Lavater's popular *Physiognomie,* which had been dedicated to Fuseli. The book was, however, never published. Probably Mary abandoned work on it midway when Thomas Holcroft's translation of the book appeared late in 1789.[42]

During the first half of the year 1790 Mary continued to broaden the scope of her work as a reviewer. She tried her hand at criticism of music (witness her seventeen page review of Dr. Burney's *General History of Music,* the leading article in the February issue) and even esthetics (witness her review of William Gilpin's *Observations Chiefly Relative to Picturesque Beauty* in the January issue). And though she had nothing to say about the rights of men, she shows in her reviews of two books for young ladies that she is giving some thought to the status of women. She questions the conventional attitude toward her sex and shows familiarity with Dr. Gregory, Dr. Fordyce, and Mrs. Chapone, all of whom had written popular books on female education.[43]

Throughout these busy months Mary was seldom free from cares. By spring or early summer of 1790 Everina had returned from France, and she doubtless took refuge at Mary's house, as she and Eliza usually did when they were at loose ends. Soon, however, she was settled at Mrs. Bregantz's school, where Eliza was by now probably one of the regular staff. Yet the two apparently did not make enough to support themselves; at least Mary wrote in an undated letter of this period that she would try to borrow some money from Johnson for them. Then presently her father appealed to her for help. She tried to manage his property for him, but it was by now so much reduced that she was forced to supply him with money from her own earnings. No wonder she complained to Johnson that she was "over head and ears in debt."

With all her responsibilities, Mary was bound to neglect something. And as one might expect, she chose to neglect herself. Her house was still barrenly furnished, and she spent little on clothing. John Knowles, biographer of Fuseli, claims that she "scarcely touched animal food" for years and eventually became a "philosophical sloven," wearing a coarse cloth dress, black worsted stockings, and a beaver hat, "with her hair hanging lank about her shoulders."[44] Probably she even prided herself on her unkempt appearance; it was the fashion among literary ladies.

But though she might neglect her person, she was determined to improve her mind. Such effort was one of the most lasting satisfactions of life, she had found, and it was essential to her livelihood as well. "I really want a German grammar," she wrote to Johnson, "as I intend to attempt to learn that language—and I will tell you the reason why.—While I live, I am persuaded, I must exert my understanding to procure an independence, and render myself useful. To make the task easier, I ought to store my mind with knowledge—The seed-time is passing away."[45] And so she taught herself German, and presently was translating Salzmann's *Moralisches Elementarbuch*. She studied Italian too, probably in the hope of doing more translating; but she refused to make one translation from the Italian when Johnson offered her the job, because the book was in manuscript and she felt uncertain of her understanding of the language.[46]

She still suffered occasional periods of illness and depression. In a letter to Eliza she complained of "this dreadful complicated, lingering illness" and claimed that she had never before been ailing for so long at a time. Yet she added: "It is not of illness I complain. I could bear it, but I am very unhappy at being thus idle." But such complaints grew rarer. All in all she was probably better satisfied with life than she ever had been before. She had much to console her: she was happy to be serving others, proud of her own plain living and high thinking, and probably triumphant at her victory over a social system designed to make a woman like herself miserable. There was indeed only one thing that she lacked, and that she had long since driven from her mind. Surely Joshua Waterhouse was now a dead issue. On that score she was resigned. But though she could hardly hope ever to enjoy a husband and children and the domestic comforts, she had found fairly adequate substitutes in independence, service, and resolute devotion to a noble cause.

In August, 1790, Mary took a long-due vacation and went down to Warminster, in Wiltshire, to stay with a Reverend Mr. Gabell and his wife. From there she wrote three letters to Everina. In the first, dated August 23, she reported her arrival at the Gabells' house and remarked that they were a devoted and exemplary couple—and she must have mused to herself that they had found a kind of happiness which must ever be denied to her. But in her second letter she seemed rather bored with the Gabells' company, and she told Everina: "My die is cast!—I could not now resign intellectual pursuits for domestic comforts—and yet I think I could form an idea of more *elegant* felicity—where mind chastened sensation, and rational converse gave a little dignity to fondness." By the time she wrote again on September 10 she had had her fill of her host and hostess and their connubial bliss. "Whenever I read Milton's description of paradise," she wrote, "the happiness which he so poetically describes fills me with benevolent satisfaction—yet, I cannot help viewing them, I mean the first pair—as if they were my inferiors—inferiors because they could find happiness in a world like this. A feeling of the same kind frequently intrudes on me here." At thirty-one Mary was resigned to the prospect of spinsterhood. And she had convinced herself that she could never be contented with the passive existence of an ordinary married woman, that her nature demanded more of life than the common pleasures could supply. It was all a very pretty piece of rationalization.

Perhaps, indeed, she had just reached a momentous decision. During the last six months of the year 1790 her work for the *Analytical* continued much as before: though she wrote fewer reviews, they concerned more important books and were given more prominent positions in the magazine. But one of those reviews overshadows all the rest: that was her fourteen-page discussion of Catherine Macaulay Graham's *Letters on Education,* the leading article in the November issue. In it Mary summarized and quoted lavishly, and agreed with the author's defense of private education, her complaints against contemporary parents, her confidence in freedom of the will—in fact with practically everything in the book. Yet more important than her criticism of the principles expressed is her tribute to the author's genius—"so unusual in a woman." Here was one who had been strong enough to break the shackles which society had clamped on her sex. Why should not a younger woman aspire to her place? Surely there was room in the world of letters for another woman used to thinking for herself. Why waste one's time in reviewing and hack writing when there was so much that needed to be said, so much that an intelligent woman could tell the world?

Presently Mary spoke out. In the Appendix to Volume VIII of the *Analytical,* which accompanied the December issue of the magazine, she praised Robert Merry's liberal sentiments (though she deplored his affectations) in his new poem "The Laurel of Liberty"; and in a footnote she angrily contrasted the rights of men and the supposititious rights of nobles. It was her first declaration, in the *Analytical,* of her espousal of the cause of freedom. But already she had declared herself much more fully and explicitly in her audacious *Vindication of the Rights of Men,* written in reply to Edmund Burke's *Reflections on the Revolution in France.* Soon rival reviewers were scolding away, advising her not to meddle in men's affairs. But Mary had no notion of retiring, now that she had entered the lists. She had found suddenly a means of achieving real distinction—and, incidentally, of gaining such satisfaction from life as she had scarcely dared hope for.

CHAPTER V

Success
(1790-1791)

My die is cast!—I could not now resign intellectual pursuits for domestic comforts . . . .
—Letter to Everina Wollstonecraft.

MARY had begun her reply to Burke's *Reflections* with no sympathy whatsoever. In fact she remarked in her Advertisement to *A Vindication of the Rights of Men* that she had read his book for amusement rather than information. But her amusement must have been short-lived. She who had so recently been converted heart and soul to democratic doctrines was naturally infuriated at what was generally regarded as Burke's abandonment of the liberal cause. She must have been shocked to find that a man of intelligence, especially one who had befriended the American revolutionists, could deny that all men were entitled to govern themselves. And so she went to work almost immediately to answer his arguments. Joseph Johnson agreed to publish her book and began seeing it though the press before Mary had completed half the manuscript.[1]

Then she had misgivings. Perhaps she asked herself why a nobody like herself should presume to challenge the opinions of a man of Burke's stature. She was only a woman, and politics was the affair of men. At all events she lost interest in her task, and one evening she announced to Johnson that she could not complete it. Then she waited for his disapproval. To her surprise, however, he told her to stop work immediately if she found the job too arduous. He would, he assured her, gladly destroy the pages already in print. Mary, who had anticipated resentment and scoldings, returned home determined to finish her book. Thereafter she wrote rapidly; and four or five weeks after the publication of Burke's *Reflections,* the anonymous first edition of the *Vindication* was on sale at Johnson's shop.

Mary's book was only a minor contribution to a pamphlet war which had already waged for nearly a year. It began with Dr. Price's sermon "On the Love of Our Country," delivered at the meeting-house in the Old Jewry on November 4, 1789, before the Society for Commemorating the Glorious Revolution of 1688. Like many other liberal Englishmen who had supported the American Revolution, Price regarded the events across the Channel as proof that the world had entered on a new era. Yet his sermon was hardly incendiary. He merely pointed out that true love of one's country should include an earnest desire to improve its constitution, itemized a few flaws in the British Constitution which had not been remedied by the Bloodless Revolution, and concluded with the stirring benediction:

Lord, now lettest thou thy servant depart in peace, for mine eyes have seen thy salvation. I have lived to see a diffusion of knowledge which has undermined superstition and error—I have lived to see the rights of men better understood than ever; and nations panting for liberty, which seemed to have lost the idea of it.—I have lived to see THIRTY MILLIONS of people, indignant and resolute, spurning at slavery, and demanding liberty with an irresistible voice; their king led in triumph and an arbitrary monarch surrendering himself to his subjects.—After sharing in the benefits of one Revolution, I have been spared to be a witness to two other Revolutions, both glorious.—And now methinks I see the ardour for liberty catching and spreading; a general amendment beginning in human affairs; the dominion of kings changed for the dominion of laws, and the dominion of priests giving way to the dominion of reason and conscience.[2]

The effect of the sermon was considerably intensified by a congratulatory address to the French National Assembly, which Price initiated and the audience drafted on the spot. When it was published with the sermon, the lovers of law and order, the defenders of the *status quo,* were immediately on the alert. They saw in Price's sermon as well as the congratulatory address dark threats against the sovereignty of the English King and Church, and within a few weeks the presses were choked with replies to Price, many of them signed with such pseudonyms as "Anti-

Price," "A True Whig," or "A Clergyman of the Church of England." Soon there were replies to those replies—though Price himself never deigned to defend or modify his original statements —and the reviews seethed with the controversy. Then just as it seemed to have simmered out, Edmund Burke set it once more a-boiling with his *Reflections on the Revolution in France*, published on November 1, 1790.

The *Reflections* was far more than a reply to Price; it contained not only strictures on his sermon but also a searching critique of the new government in France and an impassioned plea to Englishmen not to discard the institutions which time had proved and consecrated. Burke censured Price for discussing politics in a church, accused him of loving dissent more than he loved truth, and assured the French people that the sentiments of the Society for Commemorating the Glorious Revolution by no means represented English opinion. He questioned Price's assumptions too: his claim that the English king owes his crown to the people, and that they may change their government at will. Indeed Burke discussed such points more fully and thoroughly than Price had, and he cited English constitutional history to support his arguments. His book was many times as long as Price's sermon and in every respect more fully developed.

The bulk of the book was devoted to a careful analysis of the new French government in theory and practice, with incidental observations on the differences between it and the English government. Burke charged the new powers in France with "frauds, impostures, violences, rapines, burnings, murders, confiscations, compulsory paper currencies, and every description of tyranny and cruelty"—and with blind chauvinism for insisting on annihilating all traces of the old regime. He was outraged at the revolutionists' blithe assumption that any man is fit to govern himself, let alone his neighbors, and at their failure to realize that the science of government cannot be mastered in a day or even in a generation. He was convinced, moreover, that the new system would never succeed in achieving true liberty. To him the whole spirit of the Revolution was destructive rather than creative; it was, he maintained, extirpating the spirit of religion and the spirit of chivalry on which European civilization had long been founded.

But always his primary concern was with his own country rather than France. England, he feared, was in danger of being misled into a similar political debauch. Contagion was in the air —and he believed that thoughtful Englishmen could not afford to ignore it. In a moment of relaxed good humor he remarked, "Whenever our neighbour's house is on fire, it cannot be amiss for the engines to play a little on our own." But usually he was not in a good-humored mood; rather, he was alarmed; for to him Price's sermon was only one indication of the growing school of radicalism in English politics.

Had he chosen to trace the principles of the new school to their source, he would have found himself confronted with the figure of John Locke, the philosopher of the Bloodless Revolution. But he did not. To him the new philosophy was un-English and un-clean; and perhaps worse: it was manifestly impractical. As a realistic politician he looked to history rather than abstract prin-ciples as the basis for his theories. He could not for a moment be-lieve that the rights of men could be fixed once and for all. Nor could he believe that a stable government could be scrambled together by amateurs (even clear-headed amateurs!) without benefit of the experience of professional statesmen.

Of course the *Reflections* eclipsed all other replies to Price not only in its thoroughness but also in its expression. Burke could be incisive or dazzling, could write the simplest and clearest exposi-tion or the most impassioned prose; and in the *Reflections* he fought with all the weapons that he had mastered in years of ex-perience. His famous lament for the humiliation of Marie Antoi-nette, though inspired by the mistaken notion that Price had gloat-ed over the Queen's misfortunes,[3] is one of the most splendid bits of rhetoric in English literature. Yet however brilliant it may appear when viewed across the gap of a century and a half, it seemed to many of Burke's contemporaries like sheer moonshine; they refused to be stirred by his admiration for the Queen, which had supposedly burned for seventeen years from the fuel of a fleeting glimpse. And to those who were rejoicing at the death of chivalry and all that it represented, his tribute was ludicrous. Gillray, the cartoonist, sketched Burke amorously languishing over the side of Marie Antoinette's sedan chair. Tom Paine charged that the great orator "pitied the plumage but forgot the dying bird." But Mary Wollstonecraft was neither amused nor disdainful; she was infuriated.

In the Advertisement to *A Vindication of the Rights of Men, in a Letter to the Right Honourable Edmund Burke* Mary declared that her "indignation was roused by the sophistical arguments" of Burke's essay. Actually, however, she had more than one score to settle with him. Not only had he libeled her old friend Richard Price, but he had demonstrated his reverence for tradition (or "Gothic survivals," as she was fond of saying), his belief in the doctrine of "inbred sentiments," and his faith in a civilization based on the preservation of property rights; and all these notions she deplored. She could not conceive how an intelligent man could subscribe to such principles, how a supposed friend of the American Revolution could condemn the French, how a master of English prose style could prostitute his talents to the service of tyranny and ignorance. To make matters worse, she recalled that in his *Philosophical Enquiry into the Origin of Our Ideas of the Sublime and Beautiful* Burke had claimed that the beauty of women depended in large measure on their physical littleness and weakness.—And suddenly Mary thought she understood: Burke was not the great man that people had supposed him; what talents and virtues he had once possessed had been dissipated, and now there remained only the fine words and the grand manner to be applied to evil causes. And on that assumption she wrote her *Vindication of the Rights of Men*.

As a reply to Burke's arguments her book was hardly successful. In her Advertisement she wrote apologetically: "Not having leisure or patience to follow this desultory writer through all the

devious tracks in which his fancy started fresh game, I have confined my strictures, in a great measure, to the grand principles at
which he has levelled many ingenious arguments in a very specious garb."[4] This was perhaps a euphemistic way of warning
her readers that they must not expect any very close analysis of
Burke's reasoning. Her answers to his criticisms of Price were, by
and large, negligible: she maintained that Blackstone "seemed"
to agree that the King of England did indeed owe his Crown to
the people, and she defended Price's love of dissent by saying that
he hoped to use it as an instrument in finding truth. As for her
replies to Burke's thoroughgoing critique of the new French government, they are usually flimsy. Probably she realized that her
ignorance of the science of government and of conditions in
France would betray her. In any case she usually contented herself with comparing statements in the *Reflections* with earlier
statements by Burke to prove his inconsistency. For example, she
contrasted his professed respect for George III with his desire to
dethrone the King during his "illness." At other times she tried to
disprove Burke's claims by elaborate hypothetical arguments. But
more often she sidestepped the real issues. When, for example,
she discussed Burke's denunciation of the seizure of church property in France, she declared that the seizure had hurt no one, that
the Church had earned its disgrace by ignoring men's rights, and
that leveling the rank of clergymen would in general prove bene-
ficial. Then, shifting her attack, she charged that Burke defended
the Church so warmly because he admired its weakness—just as
he admired weakness in women. And she asked : If seizing church
property is wrong because it is "unlawful," what of emancipation
of slaves or abolition of the caste system in India—could they not
be proved wrong on the same principle?

Mary succeeds best as a critic of Burke when she attacks his
assumption that England enjoyed a government so equitable that
it demanded little or no reform. Then she is on familiar ground.
She cites the records of Edward III and Richard II and asks if laws
enacted in such reigns are likely to be perfect beyond need of

reform. She examines the contemporary scene for evidences of injustice, and of course she finds many. Surely, she argues, all is not well in a nation where the property of poor farmers can be despoiled at will by wealthy huntsmen, where men can be impressed into the naval service, where parents can tyrannize over their children and in their eagerness to perpetuate their wealth condone the vices of primogeniture. She calls attention to the venality of men in high offices, the vices of fashionable women, the ineffectiveness of the clergy; and she does not hesitate to speak frankly. In criticism of this sort Mary was at her best. Yet always her arguments led eventually to abuse of Burke. Instead of proving that the faults of the English social system could be remedied only by drastic change—or that Burke was blind to the faults of that system—she usually flayed him as one whose fondness for the aristocracy makes him insensitive to the sufferings of common men. When, for example, she attacks the law which condemned to death any man who killed a deer, she rails:

But it was the poor man with only his native dignity who was thus oppressed . . . —and a *gentleman* of lively imagination must borrow some drapery from fancy before he can love or pity a *man*.—Misery, to reach your heart, I perceive, must have its cap and bells; your tears are reserved, very *naturally* considering your character, for the declamation of the theatre, or for the downfall of queens.[5]

The words are charged with dynamite, but grossly unfair. Mary was stirring up her readers' prejudices rather than constructing a reasonable case against her adversary.

Probably Mary resorted to such tactics when she was unsure of herself. She must have realized that she had, after all, nothing new or original to say about the theories on which governments were based. She defined the rights of man as "such a degree of liberty, civil and religious, as is compatible with the liberty of the other individuals whom he is united with in a social compact,"[6] and she claimed that no government had ever achieved such rights. But she went no further than that in her discussion of basic doctrines. Indeed the theory to which she was subscribing was fairly new to her. She had long since been subjected to scraps of it in the conversation or writings of Dr. Price and the habitués of Johnson's bookshop, or in Rousseau and Locke (whose educational works she had evidently read). But she had only recently been converted to implicit belief in democratic principles, and she had probably not studied the authorities on the subject. It was on that account, no doubt, that she relied on name-calling rather than logical reasoning throughout her essay—and based her arguments not on sober analysis of the political or social structure but on impassioned pleas for the underprivileged. After all, Mary's work in this book was a marked departure from anything she had done in the past, and she probably did not feel entirely at ease in it.

That may account, in part, for the weak structure of the *Vindication*. Part of its disorganization is doubtless due to Mary's haste in writing it; part is due to her usual lack of planning. She never hesitated to veer from her central purpose to discuss any one of a dozen subjects dear to her: the vices of wealthy women, the tyranny of the male sex, the faults of contemporary education, the absurdity of the theory of "inbred sentiments," or the importance of reason and imagination in human thinking. It was an easy, rambling method of procedure, but it did not make for a powerful thesis; and the more one reads of the *Vindication,* the more convinced he becomes that Mary's argument is hard to follow primarily because it was hazy in her own mind and she often chose to dodge the central issue.

Yet for all its faults of reasoning and structure, the essay is powerful. It is made so primarily by the searing vituperation which Mary poured upon Burke—so strong that Godwin later felt compelled to apologize for it.[7] For though she charged Burke with disrespect for Dr. Price, she seldom sought to temper her own personal remarks. She claimed that she did not "war with an individual," but actually her essay derived most of its power from sheer abuse. She acknowledged at the outset that Burke was a "good" man, however misled. But as her anger mastered her, she discarded all restraint. She branded her antagonist as a reactionary, a sentimentalist, and a sophist; she accused him of insincerity, hypocrisy, snobbishness, even venality; she questioned his judgment and his good sense, and belabored him alike for conscious sensationalism and heartless disdain. But let her speak for herself:

> When you call yourself a friend of liberty, ask your own heart whether it would not be more consistent to style yourself the champion of property, the adorer of the golden image which power has set up?—And, when you are examining your heart, if it would not be too much like mathematical drudgery, to which a fine imagination very reluctantly stoops, enquire further, how it is consistent with the vulgar notions of honesty, and the foundation of morality—truth; for a man to boast of his virtue and independence, when he cannot forget that he is at the moment enjoying the wages of falsehood [a footnote adds: "See Mr. Burke's Bills for œconomical reform"]; and that, in a skulking, unmanly way, he has secured himself a pension of fifteen hundred pounds per annum on the Irish establishment.[8]

The charges are unfair, and the tone is strident; but the paragraph accomplishes its purpose—at least it would sway the sympathies of any uninformed reader.

And there are many such passages. Mary's envoy to Burke (though considerably weakened in its effect by the five pages of afterthoughts which follow it) is a masterpiece of its kind:

> Man preys on man; and you mourn for the idle tapestry that decorated a gothic pile, and the dronish bell that summoned the fat priest to prayer. You mourn for the empty pageant of a name, when slavery flaps her wing, and the sick heart retires to die in lonely wilds, far from the abodes of man . . . . Hell stalks abroad;—the lash resounds on the slave's naked sides; and the sick wretch, who can no longer earn the sour bread of unremitting labour, steals to a ditch to bid the world a long good night—or, neglected in some ostentatious hospital, breathes its last amidst the laugh of mercenary attendants.
>
> Such misery demands more than tears—I pause to recollect myself; and smother the contempt I feel rising for your rhetorical flourishes and infantine sensibility.[9]

Again, though Mary's charges are unjust, the effect is telling. Small wonder that she made her mark at once as a controversial writer! Her indignation welled forth in loosely constructed sentences laden with words rich in ironic or resentful overtones. To a modern reader she seems to have relied too much on the mere piling up of words, to have been content too often with trite phrases. Yet despite the overloading and the triteness, despite the conscious rhetoric (which she deplored so cordially when she encountered it in Burke's essay), Mary's writing was powerful—powerful not for its logic or its truth or its structure, but powerful as oratory or lush poetry can be, by the overwhelming richness of its expression. In short, Mary had proved herself a formidable propagandist in this, her first attempt; she argued best not by logic but by emotional appeal or by metaphor. Even when she tried hardest to be reasonable, she often resorted to a telling phrase to accomplish her purpose. When, for example, she wished to disprove Burke's claim that the French erred in discarding all traces of their former government, she succeeded best in the simple question: "Why was it a duty to repair an ancient castle, built in barbarous ages, of Gothic materials?"[10]

In short, Mary's *Vindication of the Rights of Men* was dominated throughout by emotion rather than reason; it was a triumph not of critical analysis but of rather obvious propaganda. Try as she might, Mary could not write the careful logical analysis which Burke's *Reflections* demanded (and which it presently received in Tom Paine's *Rights of Man*). That is not to say that her work was not sincere; she certainly meant every word she wrote. But she was evidently too infuriated to dissect Burke's essay in cold blood. She had just been converted to the doctrine of the rights of men, and her blood boiled at the discovery that an enlightened statesman like Edmund Burke could fail to share her new faith. Doubtless the truth was that she herself had been attracted to democratic principles not by her intelligence alone but by her sympathies; she subscribed to the rights of man not because they were reasonable but because they were humane.

The book was an immediate success. The anonymous first edition evidently sold out at once, and on December 14 a second edition appeared with Mary's name on the title-page.[11] All the best reviews of the day discussed it in their pages—of course with varying reactions. The *Analytical* was naturally favorable; it agreed with practically everything that Mary had said and praised her "just sentiments," "lively and animated remarks," and "elegant and nervous language," maintaining that the literary merits of her essay would render it good reading even after the present controversy had subsided. The liberal *Monthly Review* approved Mary's ideas, her warmth, and her positiveness, but regretted that her points should have been obscured by faults of style and irrelevancy. The *Critical Review,* sworn foe of the *Analytical,* offered only carping criticism—with a chivalrous apology for so addressing a woman. And the sedate old *Gentleman's Magazine* poohpoohed everything about the book: its lack of reason, its absurd assumption that men will be happier if free, and the very notion of a woman's posing as an authority on the rights of men.[12] But what the reviewers said was unimportant; obviously all of them had approached Mary's essay with preconceived opinions and merely wrote what their editors and readers demanded that they write of such an essay. What mattered was that they all said something, that they were not expected to ignore the work of this upstart young woman who had hitherto hardly presumed to trespass on the field of legitimate literature, much less the field of politics. Mary had proved her right to the public ear, and now she would retain it despite her sex. Almost overnight she found herself ranged with such prominent liberals as Joseph Priestley, James Mackintosh, Mrs. Macaulay, and Tom Paine, all of whom had written or were preparing answers to Burke's *Reflections.*

Today, of course, the book has been practically forgotten. In fact it was soon drowned in the flood of other replies to Burke. Regardless of the opinion of the reviewer in the *Analytical,* its literary merits were insufficient to keep it alive after the subject matter had lost its interest. At best it can be regarded as an interesting compendium to the superior *Reflections;* a curious scholar might combine the two—as Hazlitt's friend Joseph Fawcett bound the *Reflections* and Paine's *Rights of Man* together, claiming that the two combined made one whole book.

Yet ephemeral as it was, the *Vindication of the Rights of Men* made a vast difference in Mary's life. Thanks to it, she had arrived;

her name became familiar to book-buyers, and soon Johnson was entrusting her with more important assignments than he had given her hitherto. Naturally Mary sensed her new importance, and naturally too, she relished it. For the first time in her life she could feel a measure of self-assurance which rose from contentment rather than dogged determination.

Meanwhile her family was troubling her less than usual. Everina and Eliza were both employed at Mrs. Bregantz's school, and Charles had gone to Wales, where his father had promised to find him a position in the Excise. To be sure, she had the care of her brother James, who stayed with her for a while after his return from the sea, and then went at her expense to Woolwich to study mathematics under John Bonnycastle so that he could qualify for a higher rating. Her greatest worry, however, was for her friend Johnson, who told her one evening that he was settling his affairs because he believed himself to be in danger of suffering a paralytic stroke. Mary was beside herself with grief at the thought, and she spent a restless, feverish night in consequence. On the following day Everina sent word that she must come at once to Putney, and Mary hastened to her sisters only to learn that she had been summoned about a very trivial matter—it seemed especially trivial in comparison with the news which she had received the night before. As a result she lost her temper, and in the argument that followed she probably expressed her feelings frankly. A few days later she wrote to Eliza to apologize for her conduct. But her letter showed clearly that she was exasperated with her sisters and their perpetual dependence on her. "Before I came to Putney," she wrote,

I had been very uneasy; but after Miss B. left town, I gave way to the hope, that respecting you I should have a little peace—and for *some* years I have not had this satisfactory feeling. Indeed this hope had had a good effect on my mind. . . . If I had not cared for my sisters, who certainly do not adore me, the two last years of my life might have passed tranquilly, not embittered by pecuniary cares.

This quarrel was eventually patched up, but thereafter relations between Mary and her sisters were often strained. She probably found their petty troubles irksome now that she had extended her benevolence to all mankind. And they doubtless resented her self-assurance and outspokenness. Indeed there was a very real danger now that Mary's self-assurance would become as objectionable as it had been during her early years at Newington Green. She could not seem to take success gracefully.

Thanks partially to her regained self-confidence, however, the next year was doubtless the happiest she had ever known. Her time was partly taken up with completing her last piece of hack work, a three-volume translation of the first volume of Christian Gotthilf Salzmann's *Moralisches Elementarbuch,* another book of stories for children.[13] The first volume of the translation had appeared in October, 1790, shortly before the publication of *The Rights of Men;* now followed the second and third volumes, on January 1 and March 14 respectively.[14] This was, indeed, no ordinary translation; it was embellished with fifty-one engravings by William Blake adapted from the originals by Daniel Chodowiecki in the German version, and it sold for ten shillings, six pence. The success of this fine edition was probably responsible for Johnson's issuing the second edition of *Original Stories* with a set of engravings by Blake. He was of course a poor choice for the task, and in his hands the stolid, implacable Mrs. Mason became a willowy and ethereal creature whose feet barely clung to the ground.

Elements of Morality, as Mary named her translation, was her best piece of hack work. Of course her task was considerably easier than translating *The Importance of Religious Opinions,* for Salzmann's book offered few linguistic difficulties. Moreover, since her last attempt at translation, Mary's powers of expression had improved and her self-assurance had increased; and both had their effect. The new translation was smooth and idiomatic at all times, and never slavish. Not only did she compress and expand when she saw fit to do so, but she introduced original material—sometimes an illustrative anecdote, sometimes a whole incident and its accompanying homily, or sometimes a theory of her own.

There were, to be sure, far fewer changes in the last volume of the book than in the first; and it is conceivable that Mary, who at first gave her best efforts to the translation, lost interest in it after she had made her mark as a polemical writer. It would indeed be disheartening to turn from a tilt with Edmund Burke to the task of diverting children with the product of another man's mind.

In the prefatory Advertisement to *Elements of Morality* Mary announced that she had taken some liberties with the text, and cited two examples: the shift of scene from Germany to England, and the introduction of a story about the American Indians. The first demanded many minor changes; for example, the characters are not Herr Hermann, his wife Sophie, and their children Luise and Ludwig, but Mr. and Mrs. Jones, Mary, and Charles. Customs and scenery must change too; even behavior is anglicized, for Mary evidently realized that she could not permit her Anglo-Saxon characters to weep, kiss each other, and fall on each other's necks in the indiscriminate manner of the romantic Germans in Salzmann's book. As for the story about the Indians, it is actually not so much an insertion as an alteration of the details of a story told by Salzmann. He tells about a soldier frightened by what he thought to be the Devil, and Mary tells about a soldier frightened by what he thought to be Indians. She doubtless made the change because she disapproved of telling children stories about the Devil.[15] But she added a new twist by allowing the soldier to be rescued by a real Indian—and then expatiating on the brotherhood of mankind.

Other changes are more significant. Generally Mary retains Salzmann's supplementary moral comments, for he draws his morals effectively, if less forcefully than Mary's Mrs. Mason. Now and again, however, she inserted a point or two of her own; for example, in stressing filial obedience she dwells on the weakness of a child's mind (to explain why he should obey) when Salzmann does not.[16] And elsewhere she implies that children should be given an increasing amount of liberty as they mature and become better able to govern themselves.[17]

There is little opportunity in the translation to discern how Mary's religion had been affected by her new theories. But at least once she suggests that she no longer subscribes wholly to the doctrines of revealed religion, for she translates Salzmann's sentence *"Auf mein Gebet schickte mir Gott einen Freund zu, der mir ein Mittel zeigte, meine Zahnschmerzen los zu werden"* as "My prayer so calmed my mind, that I patiently endured the most excrutiating anguish, till a friend pointed out a remedy."[18] In matters of political or social theory, however, there are numerous hints of Mary's change. Though she followed Salzmann in apologizing for the privileges of the rich (by saying that they have duties as well, and that they provide employment for the poor), she occasionally refused to go so far as to echo his admiration for the splendor of aristocratic life. When the children in Salzmann's book call their father to see a fine coach, Herr Hermann rises at once to see it the better; in Mary's translation, however, Mr. Jones disdains the fine equipage, and though he rises, he does so only because he "was willing to indulge them." When the occupant of the coach proves to be a noble friend of the father's, Salzmann pauses to describe the gold lace on his clothing; but Mary ignores the detail. When Salzmann describes the nobleman's mansion, he says, *"Kein Fürst hätte sich schämen dürfen in demselben zu wohnen";* but Mary omits the sentence.[19] But perhaps the most interesting change occurs in a later section of the book: there Salzmann explains a poor man's helplessness by saying that he lost three fingers in the last war; Mary, however, says that he lost the use of his hands while working in a white lead factory.[20] Obviously she did not confine her propaganda to her controversial writings.

Elements of Morality proved to be one of Mary's longest-lasting successes. It reappeared in two London editions in 1792 and 1793, and across the ocean it was published in a single volume by Carter and Wilkinson of Providence, Rhode Island, in 1795, and in two volumes by Hoff and Kammerer of Philadelphia in 1796.[21] Moreover, the popularity of the book persisted. It was reissued in Baltimore in 1811, in Edinburgh in 1821, and in Boston (without acknowledgment of the translator's name) in 1850; and it was included in Miss C. M. Yonge's *Storehouse of Stories,* published by Macmillan in 1872.

Thanks to her new translation and to *The Rights of Men* Mary now found herself one of Johnson's leading contributors and, consequently, a prominent figure in the group of writers who congregated in the rooms above his shop. The tone of the group had changed considerably since Mary's arrival in London. Johnson's liberalism had consistently attracted writers of radical opinions who would not have been welcomed in most publishers' offices. The genteel (and often pious) friends of the American Revolution—Priestley, Price, Mrs. Barbauld, and the like—had been succeeded by such stormy petrels as Tom Paine, William Godwin, and William Blake. Mary, as the leading feminine member of the group, knew them all well and doubtless entered eagerly into their exchange of ideas.

Of them all, Blake probably made least impression on her. Even in Johnson's coterie he must have been regarded as eccentric. And his association with the group was brief; for after he had finished the plates for *Elements of Morality* and *Original Stories* and submitted his *French Revolution, Book I* for publication, he was off on his own again. Johnson had doubtless hired him as an engraver because his rates were low rather than because his genius was appreciated. His *Songs of Innocence,* published two years earlier, was little known, and his *Songs of Experience* and most of his prophetic books had not yet been published. To all appearances he was just another hack, distinguished only by his outlandish behavior and his alleged powers of "double vision." Certainly it would have been difficult for Johnson's hard-headed contributors to take him seriously; his fat little body and his round, smiling face—topped with a liberty cap—were not calculated to impress rational folk. Of all the group Mary might best have appreciated his peculiar talents, and earlier or later in her life she might have recognized and respected his sensitive nature. At the moment, however, she was probably trying to appear as hardheaded as her colleagues.

Shortly before, she had written in a review of Swedenborg's *Marriages in Heaven*:

As it would be highly absurd to attempt to give an analytical account of a book, that with all due humility we profess appears to us unintelligible, we shall only inform our readers, that there are marriages in heaven, and that those heavenly pairs are not strangers to conjugal pleasures; and still more wonderful, never feel weariness or disgust: "spiritual fruits of love and wisdom proceedeth from these mystic yet quite terrestrial unions &c. &c." As we have never been in the celestial kingdom, we do not pretend to contradict the assertions so confidently presented, and plausibly strung together; yet we cannot help lamenting, that such ingenious reveries should ever be treated seriously.[22]

Mary may well have regarded Blake's brand of mysticism with the same tolerant irony. Yet she may have had a profound influence on him. Blake was less sure of himself than Mary and was gathering new ideas which he would later fuse into his poetry. Mr. Mark Schorer is doubtless right in naming Mary's *Rights of Woman* as a "focus" for the theories of love and marriage which Blake later professed.[23]

From Tom Paine Mary may have learned a great deal; yet for him too she apparently felt some disdain. She would, of course, have refused to be bothered by his physical appearance, which many people found revolting—his face, rough as a Seville orange (as the Reverend James Hurdis said), the "strange ideotish obliquity" of his eyes, and his "carelessly frized" hair "tied by a slip of ribbon loosely behind."[24] And she must have admired his shrewd mind and his uncompromising support of the principles which she cherished. Yet though she knew him well in London and later in Paris, she left only one hint of her attitude toward him. It appears in her review of Francis Oldys's *Life of Paine* in the *Analytical* for October, 1791. She defended Paine against Oldys's prejudice and pointed out his inaccuracy—though she insisted that "we know nothing of Thomas Paine's private life." Yet even as she was berating the biographer for dwelling on Paine's careless grammar, she remarked that "Mr. Paine continually offends against the subjunctive mood." It is a small matter, of course, and yet it probably reflects Mary's self-confidence—which by this time was not far from smugness. Mary was becoming increasingly sure of herself and increasingly intolerant of others. And to at least one of her new friends her self-satisfied air was to seem downright obnoxious.

That man was William Godwin, who was to have a profound influence on Mary's life and her posthumous reputation. In the *Memoirs* he tells about their first encounter, which took place at Johnson's rooms on November 13, 1791. He had changed a good deal since the days when he had been studying theology at Hoxton while Mary lived nearby with her family on Queen's Row. He had renounced not only the ministry but all religion as well. He had abandoned conventional political ideas too for a theory of his own. And though he had as yet confined his controversial writing to journals, he had made London aware of his ideas, was known to be preparing a startling exposition of them, and was welcomed in the best liberal circles.

Godwin had invited himself to Johnson's in order to make the acquaintance of Tom Paine, whose *Rights of Man* he had helped to revise after Johnson declined to publish it in its original form. The two men had never conversed, and Godwin was eager to explore Paine's mind. But in vain; for Paine was a taciturn person, and Mary was not. "I, of consequence, heard her very frequently," Godwin later observed, "when I wished to hear Paine." In fact the conversation was confined almost wholly to Mary and Godwin, and they disagreed on practically every subject introduced. Indeed she spoke so disparagingly of several men whom he respected that he left the gathering thoroughly disgruntled. "We met two or three times in the course of the following year," he remarked in the *Memoirs,* "but made a very small degree of progress towards a cordial acquaintance."[25]

Mary had, of course, other friends, most of whom she saw regularly at Johnson's. There were Thomas Christie, co-founder of the *Analytical Review,* and his wife; there were the handsome Americans, Joel and Ruth Barlow—he a poet of proved abilities, now about to publish his *Advice to the Privileged Orders;* there was Dr. Priestley, philosopher and discoverer of "dephlogisticated air" (oxygen), who settled temporarily in London after his house and chapel in Birmingham were burned to the ground during the Riots of July, 1791; and of course there were Johnson, Fuseli, and other veteran members of their circle.

Occasionally Mary was still plagued by her family. To be sure, Eliza left Mrs. Bregantz's school in May to accept a position as governess at Upton Castle, in Wales; and Everina went in October to Waterford, Ireland, as governess to the family of a Mr. Samuel Boyse. And at about the same time James finished his studies under Bonnycastle and returned to sea. But no sooner did she have these three settled than other responsibilities arose. In fact Eliza, who visited her father at Laugharne on her way to Upton Castle, wrote back that he and Charles were in a sorry plight:

The sight of my father's ghostly visage haunts me night and day; for he is really worn to a mere skeleton, [and] has a dreadful cough that makes my blood run cold whenever I *listen* to it; and that is the *greater part* of the night, or else he *groans* most dreadfully; yet he declares he has good nights. There cannot be a more melancholy sight than to see him not able to walk ten yards without *panting* for breath; and continually falling—still he is able to ride ten miles every day; and eat, and *drink* very hearty. . . . When I beg him to be more careful in money matters he declares he will go to London and force Ned, or when I tell him how Mary has been distressed, in order to make him *save in trifles,* he is in a passion; and exhausts himself . . . .

Charles is half naked and is treated by my father in the way he deserves (for he is at him perpetually) he never even tried to get him into the excise or any where else. He is actually altered rather for the better, drinks never any thing but water and is much thinner, and all submission.

Then a few weeks later, after Eliza was settled in her *"Haven"* (as Upton Castle had seemed to her in prospect), she was writing to complain of the monotony of her new life and the parsimony of her employers. So once again Mary bestirred herself. She tried to find a position in India for Charles and a situation in France for Eliza, so that she could qualify for a position as a French teacher back in England. And of course she continued to contribute to the support of her father. On January 2, 1792, she wrote to George Blood: "Respecting my father I live in continual fear of having him thrown upon me for his whole support; for though E[dward] is once more in business, and even in a flourishing way, I am told, yet he is going on in the old track, and it does not require great foresight to say what must be the consequence. However, I do not disturb myself by anticipating an evil, which no forethought can ward off." Yet with all these cares Mary still felt that she could afford to take into her home a little girl named Ann, niece of Hugh Skeys's second wife.[26] She referred to the child as "my daughter" and doubtless hoped to realize through her something of the joy of motherhood which fate had denied her. Yet the care of the child was one more drain on Mary's income, which still failed to meet her expenses. On October 6, 1791, she wrote to George Blood to ask for a loan of ten pounds to settle a debt which was to fall due on the 19th. She was short of money after outfitting Everina for her trip to Ireland, she explained, and she disliked to ask Johnson to lend her more than she already owed him. Yet she seemed cheerful. "Excepting Mr. J. I do not owe twenty pounds," she declared. "This winter I shall *try hard* to lessen *the pounds* that stand against me in his books."

And so she worked steadily. Actually she must have been earning a rather good income by this time. In the year 1791 she had, in addition to her payments for *The Rights of Men, Elements of Morality,* and the new edition of *Original Stories,* a regular stipend from her duties as reader for Johnson and editorial assistant on the staff of the *Analytical.*[27] Early in the year her usual signatures appeared less frequently in the sections of the magazine which she had previously almost monopolized, and new initials—M.D., C., H., D.M., and O.—took their place. Evidently, though, she still maintained control over these departments but was allowed to assign the reviews to other writers. This must have been a welcome change after her three years of furious reading and writing against a deadline. It must have been heartening, too, to know that Johnson was recognizing and rewarding her talents.

Mary's own contributions now contained frequent hints of her political interests. In January, 1791, when she reviewed *Lindor and Adelaide,* an anti-Jacobin propaganda novel, she deplored the author's hatred of innovation and the rights of man. In a review of *Memoirs of de Richelieu,* in July, she bitterly assailed Louis XIV and Orleans. And in a review of Brissot's *Travels in North America,* in the September issue of the magazine, she commended the author's quest for "men who had recovered their freedom." She even tackled two books in the realm of political affairs: David Ramsay's *History of the American Revolution* in June and Rabaut St. Etienne's *Address to the English Nation* in September. Obviously Mary had "arrived." No longer need she chafe at the affectation or immorality of silly novels. No longer need she pick major flaws in minor works. All other interests had faded to the vanishing point in comparison with her new duty of preaching the gospel of freedom.

Yet her reviews rarely expressed original ideas; she had adopted her new standards from pioneers in the field, and for her own part she was content to apply them to individual cases. But in one respect she showed her independence. For while Godwin and Tom Paine and the others basked in the sunshine of pure reason, she occasionally withdrew to the shaded groves of the emotions. She still knelt occasionally at the shrine of Rousseau—and worshiped devoutly that aspect of Rousseau's genius which the pure rationalists disdained. To be sure, she continued to decry false sentiment (the sentiment which came from the head, she claimed, rather than from the heart); but at the same time she honored sincere sentiment when she felt she had found it. She lauded Brissot's "sacred overflowings of an honest heart" and mourned that such enthusiasm was so little appreciated. And to a writer who sought to apologize for Rousseau she wrote:

A defence of Rousseau appears to us unnecessary—for surely he speaks to the heart, and whoever reading his works can doubt whether he wrote from it—had better take up some other book . . . . It is impossible to peruse his simple descriptions without loving the man in spite of the weaknesses of character that he himself depicts, which never appear to have risen from depravity of heart . . . .[28]

And elsewhere, when she found an author praising the rationalist Shaftesbury, she declined to quote him,

because we think, that however noble and true the sentiments may be, which represent virtue as desirable for its own sake, those sentiments appear in rather suspicious garb in his affected inflated periods; and this parade of words, has ever led the writer of this article to suspect, that his heart was unmoved whilst his head fabricated the lifeless rhapsody, which might be called a non-conductor, so little does it contain of that subtile fluid, which running along Rousseau's lines, finds the nearest way to the heart.[29]

This is odd talk for an apostle of pure reason. But of course Mary never was that. Try as she might, she could not subscribe wholeheartedly to a purely rationalistic view of life. She was too much the creature of her emotions, too much a human being. Latterly she had tried to rise above her emotions, even to ignore her humanity—or at least her femininity. But it was high time for a reversion to type.

Presently it came. For one thing, she decided that her dingy house on George Street was no fit setting for a woman of her fame and accomplishments; and at Michaelmas, 1791—despite her indebtedness to Johnson—she moved to a larger and finer house on Store Street, in the respectable neighborhood of Bedford Square. She began to dress better too; there was a satisfaction, she found, in squandering a bit of money on oneself. And it was a real delight to prove to skeptics that an intelligent woman need not be a fright. Mary had fine auburn hair, good features, and a trim figure which could be charmingly feminine. Now that she had proved that her wits were what was commonly called "masculine," she could afford to discard her old coarse gown, arrange her hair becomingly, and indulge in a bit of harmless vanity. She must have been amused to see how people stared when they were told that the winsome, animated young woman across the room was the sharp-tongued author of *A Vindication of the Rights of Men*.

Nor was that the last they were to hear of her. Shortly after she settled in Store Street, she began the task for which she had been unconsciously preparing for many years. In November the *Analytical* contained no articles signed with one of her signatures;

in December there was only a very brief one. Johnson, of course, knew what was brewing, but the subscribers to the magazine could hardly have guessed. A few weeks back the *St. James Chronicle* had contained a letter from one "Jenny Sarcasm" observing that "the answerers of Burke" were "all *bachelors* or *old maids*," and complaining that the rights of women were being generally neglected in the universal furore over the rights of men.[30] It was all very amusing indeed. Yet the truth was that one of those old maids was scribbling away busily on a vindication of the rights of her sex.

CHAPTER VI

"A Vindication of the Rights of Woman"

(1792)

*The neglected education of my fellow-creatures
is the grand source of the misery I deplore.*
—*Introduction to* The Rights of Woman.

WRITING *A Vindication of the Rights of Woman* was undoubtedly the easiest task of Mary's literary career. Now if ever she must have been full of her subject. Encouraged by the success of her *Rights of Men* and confident of her ability to handle this new subject, she must have rushed headlong through the task. According to Godwin, she spent only six weeks in actual composition, but she had evidently been deliberating on the subject for several months before she began writing.[1] And in a sense she had been preparing for this, her greatest work, ever since she first took up writing as a profession. *Thoughts on the Education of Daughters* was the first step; then *Mary, Original Stories,* and the reviews in the *Analytical* of books for or about women—all had shown interest in the education or social position of her sex. Even in *The Rights of Men* she had digressed occasionally to deplore the effects of wealth and rank in shaping the minds of fashionable ladies, or to chide Burke for his fondness for physical littleness and weakness in women.[2] Indeed Mary's thinking had for years been directed toward the subject which she now undertook, and the whole course of her life seems to have formed her powers for it.

She had learned long years before that she had been born into a man's world; no one knew better than she that men could be tyrants. She could not forget her father's shameless treatment of his wife, or the hardships suffered by Mrs. Blood and Eliza Bishop.

She knew, too, how hard it was for an unmarried woman without means to achieve any degree of independence. She and her sisters had been forced to take in sewing, to humor an irascible old woman, to teach other people's children, or to live as a hanger-on in an older brother's family. Nor had her experience been confined to her own family and friends; she had seen for herself that the lot of a Portuguese peasant woman was a good deal harsher than her own, and that the life of an Irish society lady (though considerably easier) was not much more enviable. Not until she settled in London did Mary find any lasting personal freedom. There she learned that independence is "the grand blessing of life" and the foundation of all other blessings. Having provided herself with something like a man's education, having equipped herself to earn her living in a man's world, Mary was jubilant. Now she wanted to show other women how to achieve independence and self-respect. Thus it was that she evolved her argument: that women *deserve* equality with men and should be given the education necessary to achieve it. Her whole life led to this conclusion; and no one could have expressed it with more conviction than a schoolteacher like Mary who knew from her own experience what hardships women faced and who had learned from the ablest thinkers of the time the doctrine of the rights of man—his innate rights to liberty and equality. Once she had reached this conclusion, all her experience in the past merely confirmed it. And she burned to realize for her sex the freedom—economic and intellectual— which she had achieved for herself.

The overwhelming majority of Englishwomen of the time had known no such freedom. Most of the advantages which their sex had gained during the late Middle Ages and the Renaissance, largely because of worship of the Virgin, had been swept away in England with the triumph of Puritanism. Devout Christian gentlemen could find good Biblical precedent for their disdainful attitude toward women: St. Paul had enjoined on the sex the virtues of silence and submission as a means of atoning for their share in man's fall from grace.³ Actually the gentlemen may have been a bit afraid of women and their subtle powers. So at least one would gather from the statute which Parliament passed in the year 1770, declaring that "all women of whatever age, rank, profession, or degree, whether virgin maid or widow, that shall from and after such Act impose upon, seduce, and betray into matrimony any of His Majesty's subjects by means of scent, paints, cosmetics, washes, artificial teeth, false hair, Spanish wool, iron stays, hoops, high-heeled shoes, or bolstered hips, shall incur the penalty of the law now in force against witchcraft and like misdemeanours, and that the marriage upon conviction shall stand null and void." More-over, the common law of England ruled that whatever property a woman owned before marriage or might receive thereafter became automatically her husband's. Sir William Blackstone, in the chap-ter "Of Husband and Wife" in his *Commentaries on the Laws of England,* explained the ruling by maintaining that when women became one with their husbands they lost their legal identity; and he claimed that the law was designed for women's protection and benefit. Dr. Johnson, however, had a different explanation: "Na-ture has given women so much power," he declared, "that the law has wisely given them little."⁴ But whatever the reason, the fact remained that English common law allowed women little real freedom—and, incidentally, left wealthy girls a prey to un-scrupulous fortune-hunters seeking to settle themselves in life by means of an advantageous marriage.

Mrs. Mary R. Beard has recently pointed out, in *Woman as Force in History,* that dozens of women in England managed, by premarital contracts, to outwit the law and retain control of their own property. Yet there were certainly dozens of others who were married off by eager parents with no contracts to safeguard their property rights, and there must have been still others who, like the heroine of Defoe's *Roxana,* refused to marry because they were afraid of losing control of their property. Unfortunately such cases are, of course, unrecorded. But there were also thousands of women of the period who had no private property to be safeguarded. Mary Wollstonecraft and her sisters—indeed all the women whom she knew best—belonged to that group; and it was for them, above all, that she wrote. She had little to say about property rights; as Mrs. Beard remarks, "The objects of her special aspersions were customs and opinions, not specific provisions of law affecting women, married and single."[5] She was attacking the attitude which most men of the time showed toward her sex, and she traced it to the inadequate education of women. The vast majority of women in her century had been given only a slender education and had been encouraged to display little positive virtue or intelligence. Naturally they failed to command respect from men; and Mary believed that they never would until their minds were properly trained and disciplined. It is not surprising, then, that she offered "no program of legislation guaranteed to bring about [women's] 'emancipation.' "[6] She asked, rather, for the sort of education which would enable women of her class to be good wives and mothers if they married, or to earn a respectable living if they remained single. Only by means of education, she believed, could they achieve the personal freedom and self-respect which she had won for herself and which she coveted for her whole sex.

Probably, in her zeal for her cause, she sketched an exaggerated picture of the plight of women in her time. Yet she was not far from wrong in her claim that they were rarely treated with genuine respect. Mary had read a good deal in eighteenth century literature, and she had found that most writers either showed outright disdain for women or echoed Burke in condescending praise of their weakness. Thackeray makes Henry Esmond complain: "There's not a writer of my time of any note, with the exception of poor Dick Steele, that does not speak of a woman as of a slave, and scorn and use her as such."[7] The generalization is doubtless too sweeping; yet a quick look at the writers of the early years of the century reveals statements which would horrify Mary. When she read Pope's epistle "On the Characters of Women," she found the "snarling poet" (as she called him) declaring that "every woman is at heart a rake," dominated by "the love of pleasure and the love of sway"—that, in fact, "most women have no characters at all." In Swift's "Letter to a Very Young Lady on Her Marriage" she could find her sex described as "a sort of Species hardly a degree above a Monkey." Mary would hardly appreciate the humor of such remarks. Nor would she have been amused when she found Addison, in his essay "On Patches" (No. 81 of the *Spectator*), quoting with approval that part of Pericles' Funeral Oration in which he advised the Athenian Women: "Aspire only to those virtues that are peculiar to your sex; follow your natural modesty, and think it your greatest commendation not to be talked of one way or other."

In more recent literature too the same attitudes had prevailed. Chesterfield wrote in his "Letters to his Son" that women were to be regarded as "only children of a larger growth" and declared that he had never known a woman to act "consequentially" for twenty-four hours together. "A man of sense only trifles with them, plays with them, humours and flatters them, as he does with a sprightly, forward child," his Lordship continued, "but he neither consults them about, nor trusts them with, serious matters; though he often makes them believe that he does both; which is the thing in the world that they are proud of; for they love mightily to be dabbling in business (which by the way they always spoil); and being justly distrustful, that men in general look upon them in a trifling light, they almost adore that man, who talks more seriously to them, and who seems to consult and trust them; I say, who seems, for weak men really do, but wise ones only seem to do it."[8] Such remarks were enough to make Mary's blood boil; and she encountered them again and again in her reading. For although the popular novels and plays of the second half of the century showed a growing interest in women, they idealized always the heroine who knew her place and kept it. In *Tom Jones,* for example, the benevolent Squire Allworthy praised Sophia Western's lack of "pretense to wit" and her "deference to the understandings of men." And Mary, who prided herself on her own wit and understanding, could but deplore such criteria of virtue. She wanted women to develop positive virtues, to be more than pretty ornaments to society. And she would not have agreed with Dr. Johnson that "women have all the liberty they should wish to have" or that "one [sex] or other must have the superiority";[9] she wanted men and women to live in a democratic partnership founded on mutual respect, and she knew that half-educated women could never command respect.

The majority of women of the eighteenth century accepted their inferior status without complaint. Even the Bluestockings, who had managed to gain a sort of equality with men, were careful not to press the point. Probably they were more eager to retain their own position than to extend it to other women—at the risk of stirring up a dissension which might rob them of their privileges. At least they made no attempt to proselytize for their sex. Mrs. Barbauld, in a dainty poem "To a Lady, with Some Painted Flowers," assured the recipient: "Your BEST, your SWEETEST empire is—to PLEASE." And when she was asked to head a projected girls' school where foreign languages were to be taught, she declined immediately and made it emphatically clear that she disapproved of any scheme of general education for women. Hannah More, to be sure, wrote a book entitled *Strictures on the Modern System of Female Education*; yet she confined herself largely to the suggestion that women be taught propriety, convinced that if they were truly moral, there would be no need for a reform in their status. Certainly she did not want anything like freedom for her sex. "I am sure I have as much liberty as I can make use of, now I am an old maid," she wrote to Horace Walpole in 1792; "and when I was a young one, I had, I dare say, more than was good for me."[10] Most intelligent women would probably have agreed with Lady Mary Wortley Montagu, who insisted that "learning is necessary to the happiness of women, and ignorance the common foundation of their errors," but who advised that a young girl conceal what learning she had "with as much solicitude as she would hide crookedness or lameness."[11] Women were so used to being treated with condescension or disdain that they had grown servile. They accepted subjection as their lot in life and stifled whatever rebellion they felt. To be feminine was to be docile.

The conventional attitude toward women was summed up in two very popular books of the day: Dr. James Fordyce's *Sermons to Young Women* (1765) and Dr. John Gregory's *Father's Legacy to His Daughters* (1774). They sold by the thousands; and no wonder, for in them girls could learn specifically what two Christian gentlemen of unquestionable moral standards believed to be the duties of women—that is to say, how they could render themselves pleasing to men.

Dr. Fordyce, the brother of Mary's friend Dr. George Fordyce, recommended "the retiring graces." He urged his readers to be meek, timid, yielding, complacent, sweet, benign, and tender, modeling themselves on Milton's Eve (before the Temptation, of course). "With the character of a Christian woman," he declared, "nothing, methinks, can better correspond than a propensity to melt into affectionate sorrow."[12] He warned girls against indulging in any sort of strenuous exercise because it might deprive them of their valued softness. And to enhance the values of piety he remarked:

Never perhaps does a fine woman strike more deeply, than when composed into a pious recollection, and possessed with the noblest considerations, she assumes, without knowing it, superior dignity and new graces; so that the beauties of holiness seem to radiate about her, and the by-standers are almost induced to fancy her already worshipping amongst her kindred angels.[13]

To be sure, Fordyce suggested that young ladies study history, travels, geography, astronomy, noble fiction (such as the *Spectator*), and "the most obvious branches both of Natural and Moral Philosophy." But he added:

You yourselves, I think, will allow that war, commerce, politics, exercises of strength and dexterity, abstract philosophy, and all the abstruser sciences, are most properly the province of men. I am sure those masculine women, that would plead for your sharing any part of this province equally with us, do not understand your true interests.[14]

Obviously Fordyce considered women who wanted to study abstract philosophy to be as "masculine" as those who wanted to serve in the army.

Sometimes Dr. Gregory seems more enlightened than Fordyce. He urges that women be men's companions and equals—though he adds: "to soften our hearts and polish our manners." By and large he seems to give women credit for good sense; yet he advises them to conceal it. In fact his *Legacy to His Daughters* cautions young women to conceal not only their good sense but whatever wit or learning they may possess; and it warns them that they must resist the temptation to fall in love until they are sure of being loved in return. Obviously dissimulation plays a strong part in the Gregory code of etiquette; in fact, he goes so far as to say that if women are truly wise, they will never reveal the full extent of their love. He virtually admits, in short, that, though women (at least his daughters) may not be so flighty as most men assume, they will do well to cultivate an appearance of flightiness. To be sure, he seems often to be trying to aid intelligent women to reconcile themselves to the position which society has accorded them. Yet though he perhaps deserves some credit for his realistic approach to the subject, his realism is fundamentally cynical: most men are deceivers, he says in effect, and women cannot afford to be too honest.

The women for whom such books were written were certainly not slaves. They had their little liberties and their little triumphs, but always they were obliged to confine themselves to such liberties and triumphs as were approved in the code by which they lived. They were bound, as Mary said, in "silken fetters." They were reminded constantly of what was expected of them as daughters and wives, and nobody thought to inquire what they expected of their fathers and husbands. It was a pleasant state of affairs for the woman who had no ambition or self-respect; but for a Mary Wollstonecraft it was downright humiliating.

Yet the women who suffered only the mild subjection imposed by convention were not in the worst plight. The real slaves were the poor wretches whose husbands did not try to behave like Christian gentlemen. Fielding describes Squire Western's dead wife as one who had worn out her life as a "faithful upper servant" to her husband, only to be rewarded with unrestrained contempt. The Squire could never forget that she had once presumed to ask him to take her on a trip up to London; and he made sure that she would never again forget her place. There were many other women of the time—most of them in the lower classes— who lived lives just as dismal. Dorothy Antrobus Gray, mother of the poet, lived dutifully with her brutal husband for nearly thirty years before her patience finally snapped and she appealed for protection of the law. She had, she declared, supported herself by her millinery shop all those years and had defrayed almost all the cost of rearing and educating her son, "notwithstanding which, almost ever since [her husband] hath been married, he hath used her in the most inhuman manner, by beating, kicking, punching, and with the most vile and abusive language, that she hath been in the utmost fear and danger of her life, and hath been obliged this last year to quit her bed, and lie with her sister."[15] But of course the law did not interfere in matters between husband and wife, and Mrs. Gray was promptly notified that the courts could do nothing to remedy her "unhappy circumstance." Her case was perhaps exceptional, but it was certainly not unique: there must have been many a cowardly husband who was willing to take advantage of his legal right to tyrannize over his wife. Such wives were treated, surely, not as overgrown children but as slaves, and the law seemed designed to enforce their subjection. When one reflects that Mary Wollstonecraft's own mother suffered such subjection, the daughter can be forgiven if she seems to use the word "slaves" too often or too freely. The warmth of her feelings understandably prevented her from adhering always to cold facts.

Mary was not alone in deploring the position of women or in blaming their faulty education for it. For over a hundred years alert Englishmen had been arguing that women should be given a better education to render them more rational beings. As early as 1673 Mrs. Makin had published *An Essay to Revive the Ancient Education of Gentlewomen,* and in 1694 Mary Astell had advocated, in her *Serious Proposal to Ladies,* a sort of convent where serious-minded women might retire for study and contemplation. Three years later Daniel Defoe had included in his *Essay on Projects* a suggestion for an academy for women, where they might study whatever subjects they chose. And he observed: "We reproach the sex every day with folly and impertinence, while I am confident, had they the advantages of education equal to us, they would be guilty of less than ourselves." Then Sir Richard Steele took up the cause; and in the *Tatler* and the *Spectator* he urged that women be treated more respectfully, and pleaded for a better education for them. "The general mistake among us in the educating our children," he wrote in *Spectator* No. 66, "is, that in our daughters we take care of their persons and neglect their minds; in our sons, we are so intent upon adorning their minds that we wholly neglect their bodies."[16] Even men like Addison and Swift, who were often disdainful of contemporary women, advocated that they be given a better education to render them more tolerable companions.[17]

By far the most vigorous champion of women's rights in the first half of the eighteenth century was a woman who signed herself "Sophia" and who is sometimes identified with Lady Mary Wortley Montagu. In her first book, *Woman Not Inferior to Man* (1739), Sophia argued not only for a better education for women but also for an independent position in society. She maintained that women had achieved less than men only because they had been given less education—and went so far as to refer to her sex as slaves. But she believed that women were inherently more "responsible" than men and that, if relieved of their bondage to household duties, they would make good teachers, physicians, lawyers (because they are good talkers!), even soldiers—and more sensible philosophers. And when "A Gentleman" replied with arch condescension in *Man Superior to Woman,* Sophia countered boldly with *Woman's Superior Excellence to Man* (1740), acknowledging the faults of women but blaming them directly on inadequate education and the tyranny of men.

Among Mary's contemporaries there were several in France who had written in behalf of women. Antoine Léonard Thomas's *Essay on the Character, Customs, and Minds of Women in Different Centuries* (1772) had shown sympathy with the sex without offering any really constructive criticism.[18] But Olympe de Gouges had spoken boldly in defense of her sex in her various publications (one of which was called *A Declaration of the Rights of Woman*). And Condorcet had advocated better education for women in the first of his *Memoirs on Public Instruction* (1790). But Mary was probably familiar with none of these works. She was certainly familiar, however, with another treatment of the subject, Catherine Macaulay's *Letters on Education;* in fact she had reviewed the book for the *Analytical* with enthusiastic approval. And there can be no doubt that she was considerably indebted to it for the formation of her own thesis.[19] For though *Letters on Education* was not primarily concerned with the education of women, Mrs. Macaulay had a good deal to say on the subject: she denied that there was any fundamental difference in character between the sexes and maintained that they should be given the same education. She also attributed women's weaknesses to their faulty education and social position, advocated that they be taught not only light accomplishments but solid virtues, and urged that they develop more strength so that they might be better mothers. Mrs. Macaulay deplored the common practice of training girls only to please their husbands; and she demonstrated that, because they had been denied their rights, they had contrived by ignoble means to achieve a kind of sovereignty by utilizing their powers of pleasing. Yet she did not despair of her sex; she believed that they would gladly sacrifice their privileges if they were granted their rights. And she warned men that, if they wished women to improve, they must improve themselves; specifically she demanded that men be modest as the first step toward improvement in women.—Obviously Mrs. Macaulay was far ahead of her generation in her thinking on this subject. Obviously, too, Mary had studied her book attentively, for in *The Rights of Woman* she was to repeat and develop almost every point which Mrs. Macaulay had made. Unfortunately for the author, *Letters on Education* appeared only after Mrs. Macaulay had sacrificed her extraordinary popularity by her second marriage. And it remained for Mary Wollstonecraft to circulate many of the ideas advanced in the *Letters.*

The immediate cause of *A Vindication of the Rights of Woman* was Talleyrand's *Report on Public Instruction,* an outline of the projected plan of national education under the new French constitution. Ignoring what Condorcet had said on the subject, Talleyrand declared that French girls should be educated with their brothers in the public schools only until they reached the age of eight; thereafter they should remain at home, where their interests and activities would normally center as long as they lived. Mary dedicated her book to Talleyrand and prefaced it with a letter, addressed to him, in which she urged him and his compatriots not to debar women from their just rights. "If," she wrote, "the abstract rights of man will bear discussion and explanation, those of woman, by a parity of reasoning, will not shrink from the same test."[20] Then she plunged into the task which was to establish her fame.

She began by reaffirming her faith in liberal doctrines. The ills of the world she traced to "arbitrary power," and to illustrate her point she examined the vocations in which men were subordinated to authority—the army, the navy, and the clergy—and found, she alleged, ample justification for her claim. She was convinced that subordination weakened morality and that men could never become truly virtuous so long as they were denied their natural rights of freedom and equality. Yet she could not believe that God had created man only to abandon him to his own blind courses: she was confident that men would one day see reason and work their way toward perfection. Eventually, she believed, monarchy, which had long been outgrown in the progress of civilization, would be exterminated; eventually all men would rebel against brute force and disregard the false idols of "expediency" and "prescription." They would realize what Mary had learned by harsh experience, that independence is "the grand blessing of life," and that "the more equality there is established among men, the more virtue and happiness will reign in society."[21]

When she turned to the plight of women in her time, she found ample confirmation, she claimed, for her theories about subordination. True, women were ignorant and foolish; but what was more natural, considering their position in society? They were regarded as mere "gentle domestic brutes," too weak to be capable of any active virtue. They were treated as children, kept in ignorance, denied any opportunity to learn self-discipline, and taught only superficial manners rather than fundamental moral principles. Inevitably they sensed that they would be powerless until they could attract a male "protector," and they instinctively employed every art to snare him. Everything conspired to keep them intellectually inferior to men; their only salvation was to develop a "spaniel-like affection" which would in time nauseate a man. And what then? They had been trained to be "pleasing at the expense of every solid virtue," to be mistresses rather than wives or mothers; and when their masters tired of them, such women often sought love elsewhere. At best they could compensate for their subordination by tyrannizing over their children and servants. It was a lamentable state of affairs, and it was intensified in Mary's eyes by her conviction that it degraded not only the women but their husbands too, since few men were strong enough to rise above the harmful effects of wielding power over others.

No doubt Mary's picture was overdrawn. She was still a woman of intense feelings despite her professed devotion to reason; and in her writing she was still a propagandist. But she was a sincere propagandist, burningly sincere; she wrote from a heart so filled with righteous indignation as sometimes to distort her perspective and make her treat exceptional cases—the worst exceptions—as if they were typical. Yet for all her overstatement, she was getting at the root of a matter which needed correction.

Mary must have felt a real vocation in this, the task which was to perpetuate her name. There were few women in her generation fearless enough to say what needed to be said. Indeed there were few who resented their position as she did. They were, she claimed, reconciled to their lot by the meaningless homage paid to their sex—a homage usually granted with condescension which served only to emphasize their subjection. The result was that their moral fiber grew ever more flaccid until most of them were too weak to assert their rights. It was not surprising, then, that they had failed to secure their own emancipation. They were so used to obedience, Mary claimed, that they had forgotten—or never learned—how to act independently. Occasionally she granted that they might really be incapable of thinking for themselves, that they might deserve their bondage. But until they had been given a fair chance to display their merits, she refused to admit that they deserved to be subjected.

When she sought for a rational justification for the state of her sex, Mary was nonplussed. Was it because of the Biblical tale that Eve had been created from Adam's rib for his pleasure and comfort? Surely, she retorted, no rational person could credit that myth. Was it because women were truly "overgrown children" incapable of intellectual attainments? She was very doubtful.— No, the reason for woman's subordination was simply that she had been forced to it by her environment and education. She had been regarded always as a woman, never as a human being; she had been treated as a species apart, unable to conduct herself like a reasonable creature. Women had been trained only for love; they had been taught that marriage was their ultimate goal in life and had been led to believe that they could attain it only by exerting their cunning—by devoting hours to needlework and artful dressing, and by exaggerating their weaknesses in order to flatter men's pride in their strength. Indeed women had hardly been educated at all, but often taught only pretty accomplishments which might catch the eye of a prospective husband. As Mary wrote in the first page of the Introduction to her book, "The neglected education of my fellow-creatures is the grand source of the misery I deplore."

When in the course of her argument she came to examining contemporary writers on the subject of female education, she found ample evidence to confirm her theory. All of them, it seemed to her, had worked from the premise that women were divinely appointed to be subordinate to men and that they must rely on physical and intellectual weakness at all times. Rousseau, her old favorite, she discussed most fully, declaring that she applauded his scheme of education for Emile but could only deplore his neglect of Sophie. She was naturally infuriated when she found in Rousseau such a passage as the following:

To please, to be useful to us, to make us love and esteem them, to educate us when young, and take care of us when grown up, to advise, to console us, to render our lives easy and agreeable: these are the duties of women at all times, and what they should be taught in their infancy. So long as we fail to recur to this principle, we run wide of the mark, and all the precepts which are given them contribute neither to their happiness nor our own.[22]

Mary resented his picture of Sophie as one whose mind is "pleasing but not brilliant, and thorough but not deep," who finds needlework to be the occupation best suited to her talents, and who passively accepts the religion chosen for her by those wiser than herself. And Mary had no patience with Rousseau when he insisted that the education of women should always be "relative" to that of men. Indeed she quarreled with him about practically every point which he made. She bristled when she found him placidly observing that "a young Englishwoman [should] cultivate her agreeable talents, in order to please her future husband, with as much care and assiduity as a young Circassian cultivates her's, to fit her for the Haram of an Eastern bashaw."[23] And after every long passage of *Emile* which she inserted in her book, she added an angry commentary. When Rousseau claimed that at maturity men attain "a degree of perfection of mind" denied to women, she cried: "But, alas! husbands, as well as their helpmates, are often only overgrown children."[24] When he claimed that girls naturally choose to play with dolls rather than to romp the fields, she contradicted him, arguing that most *rational* women had shown a decided fondness in childhood for romping the fields. And she added cogently: "I have, probably, had an opportunity of observing more girls in their infancy than J. J. Rousseau."[25] She was revolted by his worst intimations—and indeed many of them are shocking. For Rousseau was so faithful to his belief in women's inferiority that he did not scruple to say that their conversation should be agreeable but not necessarily sensible, their dress modest yet provocative, and their manner obedient even at the cost of fortitude and honesty. He accused them of enjoying their weakness because it gave them a pretext for yielding to their natural appetites. He advised them to learn how to suffer injustice from their husbands and how to appear more docile than they really were. And he candidly admitted that they needed only enough reason to enable them to preserve their chastity and to justify their husbands' choice in the eyes of the world. In short, as Mary charged, Rousseau wanted women to develop only their beauty and their "subtlety"; he never once suggested that they cultivate true virtue. And she showed that his reasoning was at fault when, after insisting that women be educated wholly for love, he acknowledged that love is transient and that children are the most lasting tie between husband and wife. Or again when she found him remarking that women should "reflect" so as not to bore their husbands:

"What," asked Mary, "has she to reflect about who must obey?"[26]

When she turned to the best-known writers on female education in her own country, she found their precepts little better. The
inflated style of Fordyce's *Sermons for Young Women* offended
her from the outset; so too did his praise of meekness and docility,
his warning against physical exercise, and his description of the
irresistible charms of a young woman at prayer. Gregory's *A
Father's Legacy to His Daughters* she sometimes admired, but she
objected to his stress on decorum (she would have substituted
reason, of course) and his advice that women conceal their wit,
their reason, and their true affections. Such dissimulation she abhorred; and she declared that, though the *Legacy* might be expressed in tender paternal terms, "it all comes home to the same
point, and whoever is at the trouble to analyze these sentiments,
will find the first principles not quite so delicate as the super-
structure."[27] And when she encountered Dr. Gregory's warning
that well-bred young ladies should not dance with spirit, she
burst out:

In the name of truth and common sense, why should not one woman
acknowledge that she can take more exercise than another? or, in other
words, that she has a sound constitution; and why, to dampen innocent
vivacity, is she darkly to be told that men will draw conclusions which she
little thinks of?[28]

Chapter V of *The Rights of Woman,* which contained most
of Mary's strictures on Rousseau, Fordyce, and Gregory, also included slighting notices of Mrs. Piozzi, Madame de Staël, and
Madame de Genlis, all of whom were guilty of echoing men's degrading opinions of their sex or otherwise offending against the
rational principles which Mary cherished. She offered high praise,
however, to the writings of Mrs. Chapone and to Mrs. Macaulay,
"the woman of the greatest abilities, undoubtedly, that this country has ever produced," who stood as living proof that female
reason was capable of full development. In a footnote Mary added:
"Coinciding in opinion with Mrs. Macaulay relative to many
branches of education, I refer to her valuable work, instead of

quoting her sentiments to support my own."[29] This was doubtless Mary's acknowledgment of her debt to the woman whose *Letters on Education* had aided her to formulate the arguments of *The Rights of Woman.*

Unfortunately there had been few Chapones or Macaulays; the great majority of writers on female education had kept it always "relative" to that of men. The result, Mary believed, was that women had grown physically and morally weaker and had developed none of the virtues which would render them useful to society. They had failed as wives because they could not interest the minds of their husbands. They had failed as mothers because they were physically and mentally unprepared to shoulder the duties demanded of them. To be sure, all women had not accepted this state of affairs passively: some vigorous souls had refused to confine themselves to the limited areas normally open to them. Then they had exercised their charms to control men—often men in high position—and had wrought much mischief because they did not know how to wield the power which they had usurped. Such women Mary admired no more than their subjected sisters; she sought not power for women, but freedom. She wanted them to be neither men's slaves nor their tyrants, but their equals, their friends and companions. But wherever she looked she found little equality between the sexes, and her passion for reform made her burn to correct the evils which confronted her.

But rational education, Mary believed, would correct these evils. Like most of her predecessors in the field she advocated an education based on a new attitude toward her sex and directed toward the development of positive virtues. She sought for women that perfection of nature which grew out of an ideal combination of knowledge, reason, and virtue; and she believed that education could accomplish that combination. She was willing to concede that the superior strength of men would probably enable them to attain a higher degree of virtue than women could achieve, but she was convinced that the virtues of the two sexes should be the same in kind if not in degree. "Women . . . may have different duties to fulfil," she allowed; "but they are *human* duties, and the principles that should regulate the discharge of them, I sturdily maintain, must be the same."[30] She pleaded for co-education so that boys and girls would learn to regard each other as equals and companions. She advocated national public education in day schools open to all classes of society, where children would be taught the fundamentals of knowledge together and later allowed either to learn a trade or, if their abilities justified it, to study "experimental philosophy," literature, psychology, history, ethics, and esthetics—in short, to receive a liberal education. She urged too that all schools offer a program of physical education, so that the students' bodies might be developed along with their minds. And she asked that, until these reforms were put into effect, men's judgment of the powers of women be suspended.

Mary anticipated remarkable changes, once her system was adopted. Not only would it prepare men and women for true democratic living, but also it would render them true companions. Their marriages would be based not merely on evanescent sexual passion but on lasting friendship. Wives educated to talk intelligently with their husbands would not waste their efforts in trying to rekindle dying passions. And there would be other and nobler consequences of the new education. For women should develop their minds not only so that they might hold their husbands' affections, but also so that they might be more virtuous. She was convinced that active virtue relied always on reason, that "it is vain to attempt to keep the heart pure, unless the head is furnished with ideas."[31] And if women were to fulfill their duties as mothers, they must be truly virtuous. Mary believed that children's characters are formed before they reach the age of seven, and she shuddered to think of the lasting damage being done by addle-headed or immoral mothers. In fact her plea for better education for women was in reality, as she made clear, a plea for humanity: she wanted to prevent half-educated women from halting the progress of mankind toward perfection by harming themselves and their children. Nor did she stop with mortal life. She argued that women deprived of a rational education were handicapped not only in this world but in the next as well. Salvation, she maintained, rose from virtue—and virtue from reason. Thus if women were poorly educated, they were in effect denied the opportunity to perfect their souls and render them fit for immortality. But women properly educated would be prepared to enter heaven and to fulfill their duties there.

Though Mary's claims for education may seem extravagant, no one today would deny that both her diagnosis of the faults of her sex and the remedy which she wished to apply were sound. To her first readers, however, her arguments seemed often absurd. Though observant critics of society had long advocated a better education for women, the average man was reluctant to acknowledge that women's minds were capable of the "enlargement" which Mary urged. She was obliged, therefore, to develop her thesis in great (and often tiresome) detail—to demonstrate the relationship between education and morality, and to prove whenever possible that women were not, as Swift had once suggested, incapable of arriving "in point of learning, to the perfection of a School-boy." And she could find little concrete evidence for her claims; for though she could single out the achievements of a few distinguished women, she was striving always to prove that the great majority of women would be improved by education. She had always to caution her readers that she had no desire to breed a generation of independent and unattached women like herself, but that she sought to develop wiser and more virtuous wives and mothers. Again and again she repeated that education would lead women to a more serious interest in "domestic pursuits" rather than to a longing for distinction in the world; indeed she contended that women would be less likely to crave distinction if they were granted solid intellectual resources. Hers was a difficult case to present, but her zest for it never flagged. She had everything to gain and nothing to lose. Though she was realistic enough to know that her reforms could not be achieved quickly in England—that it would take years to uproot the old prejudices about women or to persuade her sex to sacrifice their supposed privileges—still she hoped that individual men and women might try to apply her principles. And her highest hope was always that she could persuade the French to adopt her theories and include women in their plans for universal education and emancipation.

Mary did not limit herself entirely to an appeal for more education for women. She believed that, once they had achieved intellectual equality with men, they should be given political and economic equality as well. As she put it, she wanted to reform the law that made man and wife one and then treated the wife as a nonentity. She believed that the law should guarantee women protection so that they will not be obliged to depend wholly on their husbands' bounty; it should allow them also to "fulfill the duties of a citizen, or be despised." She even imagined (though she admitted that her notion might "excite laughter") that in the glorious future women might "have representatives, instead of being arbitrarily governed."[32] Yet she merely touched upon such matters in passing, and hinted that in later volumes of her book she would develop them more fully.[33] She was concerned here with woman's position in the family and in the course of human progress toward heavenly perfection. And though she urged that women be allowed to achieve economic independence by means of an honorable vocation—and went so far as to advocate that exceptionally talented women be permitted to study medicine or business—she had relatively little to say on the subject. She was seeking to develop not "heroines," she claimed, but "rational creatures"; she was not asking for careers for distinguished women but hoped only to improve the lot of the average woman of her class. And although she was interested in opening new fields of activity to women so that they could support themselves when necessary, she stated explicitly that most women should remain with their families and should direct all their wisdom and energy to their tasks as mothers. "Whatever tends to incapacitate the maternal character," she declared, "takes woman out of her sphere."[34]

But whatever the objective in view, the first step to be taken was always the same: education. Without it women could never hope to realize the other reforms which she urged. Without it reason and the will of God would never actuate their behavior— or the behavior of their husbands and children, indeed of all humanity. In order to achieve a truly rational civilization and to realize the millennium of earthly perfection, women must be made wise and free. Until they are, they can only retard human progress.—And quite apart from all these fine theories, Mary would have repeated: women have a *right* to knowledge and liberty. If they have been endowed with immortal souls, they *deserve* a better education, an independent position in society, a fair share of dignity and respect, all of which were virtually inaccessible to them. Mary was indeed vindicating the rights of her sex. She was outlining their duties too, but she believed that their first duty was to themselves. And at the same time she was assisting in the advance of civilization toward realization of the divine plan. "Rousseau exerts himself to prove that all *was* right originally," she wrote; "a crowd of authors that all *is* now right: and I, that all will *be* right."[35] Thus in *The Rights of Woman,* as never before, Mary could rejoice that she was working for the benefit of her sex, for humanity, and for God.

Throughout the pages of her book Mary burns with the sincerity of her subject. She who had become so absorbed in herself and her success after the publication of *The Rights of Men* certainly lost herself in this new task. She was now aghast at the deplorable state of women in her time, now agog at the dazzling prospect of perfect society and emancipated woman in the future. Writing the book must have been one of the most thrilling experiences she had ever known. She was tasting the joys of eager, spontaneous creation, creation which was effortless because she had a wealth of material to draw from, and because she was convinced that her message had inestimable value.—And yet the book is tedious reading. Did she write it in six weeks? Then would she had spent six years on it!

Its worst fault is lack of organization. Mary darts now forward, now backward, in her argument; she strays off into matters of incidental interest and often loses her way completely. And the reader is left breathless and bewildered. The thesis, which might have been effectively developed in 100 pages, is buried under the weight of 452 quarto pages in the first edition. Perhaps she was writing with the press, as in *The Rights of Men;* that would explain part of her confusion. But the greater part of it was doubtless due to her usual want of mental discipline. She often apologized for the "desultory" nature of her writing, as though she had deliberately jotted down her thoughts without imposing upon them any clear plan. The truth of the matter, however, is probably that her natural ebullience resisted control in writing as in life. Her letters to her friends acknowledged the difficulty repeatedly; and even in *The Rights of Woman* she mentioned "that sanguine ardour, which it has been the business of my life to depress."[36]

Mary's style, too, is annoying. Though she announced at the outset that she would not "polish her phrases," she could not resist the chance to turn a fine period; to exhort her readers in grand terms to the cause of love or religion or what-not; to apostrophize Love or Religion or What-not; or to display her rhetorical virtuosity in whatever fashion came most easily to hand. As always, her writing abounded in clichés or in far-fetched metaphors which served only to cloud her meaning. She could seldom round off a subject without a high-sounding peroration, seldom relax into simple, direct language when her subject required it. Occasionally, however, when she was exasperated, she burst out with a homely tartness of expression which is refreshing. For example:

Fragile in every sense of the word, [women] are obliged to look up to man for every comfort. In the most trifling dangers they cling to their support, with parasitical tenacity, piteously demanding succour; and their *natural* protector extends his arm, or lifts up his voice, to guard the lovely trembler—from what? Perhaps the frown of an old cow, or the jump of a mouse; a rat, would be a serious danger. In the name of reason, and even common sense, what can save such beings from contempt; even though they be soft and fair.[37]

Unfortunately such passages are rare. They suggest how lively Mary's writing might have been had she allowed her real nature to express itself—instead of straining to echo the idiom of a moribund literary convention. Even such a passage of outraged candor does not reveal Mary as a craftsman in style; it merely shows that her vigorous personality now and then broke through her artifice. Mary had written or translated seven books and reviewed a good two hundred before *The Rights of Woman* appeared, but she still had much to learn about the craft of writing.

Yet despite its discursiveness and its artificialities, *The Rights of Woman* is a great book. Though many of Mary's arguments were not original—though she may have been indebted to Locke or Helvétius, to the Encyclopedists or her radical English friends, to Thomas Day and Rousseau, and certainly to Talleyrand and Mrs. Macaulay—the development and application of her arguments was distinctly her own, drawn from her experience. So too was her central thesis: that women as well as men are entitled by birthright to liberty and equality, and that if their rights are withheld, they will deter the progress of civilization. Truly Mary enjoyed at least one flash of genius, and that came when she recognized the similarity between the plight of oppressed womankind and that of oppressed mankind, and concluded that the solutions were identical. *The Rights of Woman* was regarded in 1792 as radical and revolutionary, of course; but what was more important: it was new and original. It was so new, in fact, that nearly a century elapsed before its tenets were applied. And when later feminists formulated their bills of rights, they introduced no points which Mary had not anticipated.

Naturally the book attracted wide attention when it appeared, and it extended Mary's fame much further than *The Rights of Men* had. Before the year 1792 had ended, Joseph Johnson had published a second edition, American editions had appeared in Boston and Philadelphia, and a French translation had been published at Paris and Lyons. Meanwhile Mary had achieved a new kind of immortality when George Dyer, later historian of Cambridge University and a friend of Charles Lamb, wrote in an "Ode to Liberty":

> . . . dost thou, sweet enthusiast! choose to warm
> With more than manly fire the female breast?
> And urge thy Wollstonecraft to break the charm,
> Where beauty lies in durance vile opprest?[38]

The first reviews of the book, oddly enough, were generally favorable. The *Analytical* was of course enthusiastic; its critic "D." devoted the leading articles of two issues (March, 1792, and the Supplement to Volume XIII) to a summary of the book with extensive excerpts. In his fervor he even went so far as to describe Mary's style as "strong and impressive." The *General Magazine,* the *Literary Magazine,* the *New York Magazine,* and the *Monthly Review* all praised the book, with only occasional minor reservations.[39] And the staid *Gentleman's Magazine,* which had poohpoohed the notion of a woman's defending the rights of men, simply ignored the new book.

The attitude of the general reading public was probably less favorable. The book seems to have been widely read: Mrs. Anne MacVicar Grant, writing on January 2, 1794, from Glasgow, announced that it was "so run after here, that there is no keeping it long enough to read it leisurely."[40] But Aaron Burr, who admired the book intensely and seems to have tried to rear his daughter Theodosia according to its principles, complained in February, 1793, that he had "not yet met a single person who had discovered or would allow the merit of this book."[41]

Of the distinguished women of the time Anna Seward, the "Swan of Lichfield," seems to have been most enthusiastic. She wrote in a letter to a friend on February 26, 1792:

Have you read that wonderful book, The Rights of Woman. It has, by turns, pleased and displeased, startled and half-convinced me that its author is oftener right than wrong. Though the ideas of absolute equality in the sexes are carried too far, and though they certainly militate against St. Paul's maxims concerning that important compact, yet do they expose a train of mischievous mistakes in the education of females;—and on that momentous theme this work affords much better rules than can be found in the sophist Rousseau, or in the plausible Gregory. It applies the spear of Ithuriel to their systems.[42]

Hannah More informed Horace Walpole that she was "invincibly resolved" not to read the book, adding that to her way of thinking "there is something fantastic and absurd in the very title."[43] But Hannah Cowley was only amused at the thought. In the Advertisement to her play *A Day in Turkey* she wrote: "I protest I know nothing about politics;—will Miss Wolstonecraft forgive me—whose book contains such a body of mind as I hardly ever met with—if I say that politics are *unfeminine*? I never in my life could attend to their discussion."[44]

These reactions were no doubt typical. Conventional people were either enraged or amused at the book. Those who were most offended were bothered not only by Mary's liberal opinions but by her frankness as well: squeamish folk could hardly stomach Mary's insistence that women should not conceal their "natural appetites," her candid admission that she had discussed anatomy openly with men, or her passing allusions to homosexuality. Horace Walpole lauded Hannah More's determination not to read *The Rights of Woman,* declared that he himself would not even look at it, and classed Mary with Tom Paine and Horne Tooke as one of "the philosophizing serpents we have in our bosom." And later he described her as "a hyena in petticoats."[45] Eliza Bishop wrote to her sister Everina in June, 1793: "Did I tell you how much the gentry of Pembroke are shocked at M.'s book? Every one declares it the most indecent Rhapsody that ever was penned by man or woman." Yet probably the majority of those who were most emphatic in denunciation of the book had, like Walpole and Hannah More, never read it. To them women's rights were vaguely associated with free love, and they would not even give Mary a hearing.

Most gentlemen doubtless dismissed Mary's book with a complacent guffaw. Most ladies, mindful of all they had been taught, would scarcely have dared not to echo that guffaw in a genteel titter—or to treat it with a coy mixture of awe and ridicule such as Mrs. Cowley displayed. Two contemporary writers found the general interest in human rights so uproariously funny that they promptly burlesqued Mary's book and Paine's *Rights of Man* in *A Sketch of the Rights of Boys and Girls* and *A Vindication of the Rights of Brutes,* which were based on the ironic assumption that the general emancipation should extend not only to men and women but also to children—and even the brute creation.

A Sketch of the Rights of Boys and Girls, purportedly written by "Launcelot Light" of Westminster School and "Laetitia Look-about" of Queen's Square, Bloomsbury, was a travesty not only of Mary's book and Paine's but of Joel Barlow's *Advice to the Privileged Orders* as well. The sections concerned with the emancipation of girls, written by "Miss Lookabout," began with a mock approval of the doctrine of female emancipation and concluded that "if girls were permitted without restraint to do from their childhood what they liked, they could not possibly go astray."[46] Later the author advanced some theories of her own, which she considered to be quite in harmony with the theory of sexual equality: she argued that girls and boys should be brought up together so that they will "know more," she urged that girls wear breeches and burn their embroidery frames, she recommended that they read *Tom Jones* and *La Nouvelle Héloïse.* And she concluded in high irony:

And thou too, friend of our sex, respectable Woolstoncroft, (is not this very like Rousseau?) what do we not owe to your affectionate eagerness to assist and improve us. May the second part of your truly chaste and valuable performance, hasten to be united to its first. Thus will mankind, womankind I mean, be aided by a plain and simple code of instruction; in which all foolish prejudices are overturned; and in which women are taught to regard with becoming scorn the means by which they have till now captivated, namely, softness of beauty, grace and elegance of manner, and the pursuit of more delicate employments.[47]

A Vindication of the Rights of Brutes, probably the work of Thomas Taylor the Platonist, said to be the Wollstonecraft family's landlord at Walworth, was a good deal heavier-handed than *The Rights of Boys and Girls*. Occasionally the irony was mildly effective, as when the author wrote: "Mrs. Woolstoncraft, who though a virgin, is the mother of this theory, often I am told, eats beef for mutton; and I myself am frequently so lost, as when reading the best productions of the moderns, to imagine they are nonsensical, when at the same time they are the progeny of the most consummate wisdom and wit."[48] On the whole, though, the satire was labored; and it sometimes became scurrilous, notably when the author recalled that in the "Introductory Address" to Mary's *Elements of Morality* parents had been urged to teach their children the purpose of the sexual organs. But the man who wrote the burlesque was obviously a scholar rather than a humorist, and much of the time his normal interests intruded upon his purposes as a satirist. He devoted far too much time to an elaborate "proof" of his thesis that animals are reasonable creatures and deserve to share in the rights of men. He summarized and quoted at length the arguments of the Neo-Platonist Porphyry in favor of abstaining from animal food, and he cited Plutarch extensively to bear out his contention that animals have extraordinary powers which would be useful to men. His satire was directed at the historical method of proof rather than at liberal principles, and he seems at times to be trying to revive the old battle between the ancients and the moderns. And it was only after several chapters in which Mary and Paine had been almost completely ignored that he concluded:

And thus much may suffice, for an historical proof, that brutes are equal to men. It only now remains (and this must be the province of some abler hand) to demonstrate the same great truth in a similar manner, of vegetables, minerals, and even the most apparently contemptible clod of earth; that thus this sublime theory being copiously and accurately discussed, and its truth established by an indisputable series of facts, government may be entirely subverted, subordination abolished, and all things every where, and in every respect, be common to all.[49]

The very existence of these two burlesques proves that Mary's book was not ignored; and it would be wrong to assume that it was greeted only with wrath or amusement. Among the people whom Mary respected, *The Rights of Woman* was recognized as a valuable contribution to human thinking, and Mary herself was hailed as living proof of her claims about the mentality of her sex. Her position among the liberal thinkers of her time was now assured, and she was honored as the champion of womankind. Robert Southey dedicated his poem *The Triumph of Woman* to her in 1795, and six years later he declared that he had "never praised living being yet, except Mary Wollstonecraft."[50] Liberal novelists like Robert Bage and Charlotte Smith cited Mary's work and introduced into their novels enlightened women who tried to apply her theories in their lives. And in America Charles Brockden Brown, in his *Alcuin* (1798), echoed Mary's arguments and her appeal for a more rational attitude toward women—although Judith Sargeant Murray had claimed in *The Gleaner* that American women were already "improving on the opinions of a Wollstonecraft."[51]

Mary must have been thrilled at the thought of this, her latest achievement. Even the wrath or ridicule of her foes could hardly have distressed her, since she believed that their lack of sympathy merely proved their blind prejudice. After all, she had not expected immediate results from her book; she had admitted that women could not hope to enjoy freedom until men did. She would probably not have despaired even at the savage attacks launched at her after her death, when the horrors of the French Revolution had convinced most Englishmen that all revolutionary theories were conceived in iniquity. For Mary looked always to the future. And even though her book languished in comparative neglect while Fordyce's *Sermons* and Gregory's *Legacy* flourished,[52] even though Thomas Gisborne's timid *Enquiry into the Duties of the Female Sex,* published in the year of Mary's death, outsold *The Rights of Woman* for years, she would doubtless have been confident that the last laugh would be hers. And she was right.

Since *The Rights of Woman* is Mary's most original book and her most thoroughgoing discussion of any one problem, and since she often digressed to topics of slight relevance, it reveals a good deal about her thinking when she had reached the peak of her career. For one thing, she alluded to more works by other authors than in any of her other books. And those allusions suggest something about the sort of education which she had managed to gain through her own efforts.

Where had Mary garnered the ideas which led to her fearless defense of her sex? What was she reading besides the third-rate books which she was obliged to review for the *Analytical*? Of course she was familiar with Talleyrand's *Report on Public Instruction* and with such authorities on female education as Rousseau, Fordyce, and Gregory. She reveals, too, that she had at least dipped into the works of a number of others who had declared themselves on the position of women: Mrs. Piozzi, Madame de Staël, Madame de Genlis, Mrs. Chapone, Mrs. Macaulay, and the Reverend Vicesimus Knox. But what else? The answer is revealing.

Mary alludes to only two writers, Swedenborg and Thomas Day, whose works she had reviewed in the *Analytical*. Of other contemporaries she quotes Cowper's and Mrs. Barbauld's verse, Chesterfield's *Letters*, Hume's essays, a translation of one of Forster's travel books, Lord Monboddo's *Origin and Progress of Language*, and Adam Smith's *Theory of Moral Sentiments*; and she cites Boswell's *Life of Johnson*, Johnson's own essays, *Clarissa Harlowe*, Joseph Priestley's *Description of a Chart of Biography*, and a play by Edward Young. Of earlier works she uses an occasional phrase from Shakespeare or the Bible; she quotes verse by Dryden, Gay, Pope, and Milton and the essays of Bacon, Leibnitz, and Locke; and she cites *Gulliver's Travels* and Butler's *Hudibras*.[53]

It would be dangerous to leap to specific conclusions from this list; yet one is strongly tempted to speculate about its significance. Certainly the names included suggest that Mary was far better acquainted with English writers than with those of other nations, despite her reading knowledge of French and German. It suggests too that she had read more of *belles lettres* than of philosophy or social criticism, and that she was practically unacquainted with literature before 1600. She shows no knowledge of the classics except for passing references to Cato, Cerberus, Diana, and Argus such as she might have garnered from a child's compendium of classical lore.

Evidently Mary had found time for a good deal of reading quite apart from the books she had read for her reviews in the *Analytical;* she had, it would seem, acquired a good general knowledge of English literature since 1600. It was truly a general knowledge, remarkable rather for its scope than for any apparent specialization. Surprisingly enough, Mary had not immersed herself wholly in the new revolutionary writings of Priestley, Paine, Price, and their coterie. As a result she had gained a rather satisfactory liberal education, an education *truly* "liberal" in that it confined her to no narrow channel of thought but allowed her freedom to think for herself. And the impression given by Mary's reading is confirmed when one assembles her casual remarks on several topics which she treated in the course of her book.

In politics, indeed, Mary showed little originality. She accepted almost wholesale the common radical theories of her era, deploring the evils of "arbitrary power" on the one hand and blind obedience on the other, and declaring her utter confidence that when social equality is attained men will be both virtuous and happy. But to Mary politics was always subservient to religion, and in her religious ideas she shows marked independence. Unlike most of her fellow radicals she was a devout believer, convinced that the perfection attainable in this world was not the ultimate toward which man should strive, but only a pale shadow of the perfection which God had reserved for him in heaven. She still had not forsaken her old belief that earthly life was a preparation (or, as she now said, an "education") for the life to come; and she reaffirmed her belief repeatedly. Ostensibly she subscribed to the doctrines of rational religion—which she defined as "submission to the will of a being so perfectly wise, that all he wills must be directed by the proper motive—must be reasonable."[54] Yet she was never a deist in the usual sense of the word; however much she might trumpet her faith in reason, she remained an intensely spiritual woman, and her religion was always personal and intimate. She could not say too often that God wounds but to heal, that He has put evil into the world for a reason, that in His divine plan (though not in contemporary society) whatever is is right. In fact she could not too often dwell on God's goodness and justice. He is no tyrant, she declares; He demands obedience, yes, but obedience to what is right and reasonable—and His service is perfect freedom. She even attributes benevolence to Him, saying that she cannot believe that He ignores the conduct of men or that He would create women inferior to men. Mary never outgrew her innate piety (which has even been considered to have elements of mysticism[55]); she could not conceive of man without God or of this world without a better. Her "rational religion" was never *merely* rational; it was, as Godwin said, "almost entirely of her own creation."[56]

Mary's independence of thought is reflected also in her statements about ethical problems. In an age of worldly wisdom and conventionality she showed her disdain for both. She deplored the "unmanly, immoral system" of Lord Chesterfield and declined to "cull any of the useful, shrewd remarks which occur in his epistles."[57] Any virtue cultivated because it might prove advantageous to the possessor or because it was socially advisable, she found repulsive and damned emphatically. That attitude is apparent, of course, in her whole treatment of the problems of her sex, but especially in her remarks about sexual morality. She had no use for the double standard of morality; she believed that equality of the sexes could never be achieved so long as separate virtues were inculcated in men and women. And she was especially distressed that so much was made of feminine chastity and so little, of masculine. She pleaded that prostitutes be treated more justly, that fathers of illegitimate children be compelled to support their offspring, and that men as well as women be taught modesty.

In other respects too she showed her freedom from the prejudices of her age. She had much to say about the relationships of parents and children and the need for filial respect rather than blind obedience. And the duties of the teacher she discussed in considerable detail, pleading always that teachers be severe but not tyrannical, and that parents expect of them no more than they can accomplish singlehandedly. Above all she wanted children to learn by experience to think for themselves; she urged that teachers strive above all to perfect their charges' morals rather than their knowledge of Latin and Greek. For Mary's educational philosophy was what has since been termed Jacksonian: she wanted education adapted to the means of the many, not the exceptional few. Firm believer in democracy that she was, she looked to the schools to train good citizens who would love their homes and their country—who would be generous-minded, having learned at home and at school a sound benevolence which they would naturally extend to all mankind—and who would have enjoyed enough freedom of action in their youth to enable them to govern themselves wisely as adults. Moreover, her natural piety made her hope that education not only would train them for this life but would serve as "the first step to form a being advancing gradually towards perfection."[58]

On the question of reason *versus* emotion Mary had much to say. It was an old question for her, one which she had been pondering ever since her arrival in London; and it echoed the conflict between head and heart which her passionate nature had undergone from the moment when she first tried to live by rational principles.

Mary still considered herself a rationalist, of course; she preached rational politics, rational religion, and rational education. She was much concerned, too, about the place of reason in human affections, claiming that love cannot be truly moral unless it is based on reason, and that even sensual love demands an element of reason. Again and again she begged her contemporaries to cultivate reason as a basis for freedom, virtue, and immortality. She sought especially to combat the stylish "sensibility" which too often usurped the place of reason in women; for she naturally deplored the common notion that men had been created to reason and women only to feel. Yet she did not damn all sensibility or feeling. On the contrary she maintained that poetry, art, and music are the products of human beings endowed with the highest degree of sensibility, and she even went so far as to say that it is not always wise to try to regulate the passions. In her desire to avoid sentimentality she did not make the mistake of damning all emotion. What she deplored was "partial feeling," the unreasonable emotion of the fine lady who weeps over an injured bird and yet leaves her coachman shivering in the cold. But given a choice, Mary would prefer sensibility to pure reason, enthusiasm to cynicism. "One reason why men have superior judgment, and more fortitude than women," she declares, "is undoubtedly this, that they give a freer scope to the grand passions."[59] Unreasoning emotion was dangerous, Mary believed; but so was reason when divorced from human feeling. It is a nice problem, and Mary admits it. "Perhaps," she says, "in the education of both sexes, the most difficult task is so to adjust instruction as not to narrow the understanding, whilst the heart is warmed by the generous juices of spring, just raised by the electric fermentation of the season; nor to dry up the feelings by employing the mind in investigations remote from life."[60]

Certainly Mary was not, as often she has been superficially considered, a pure rationalist in *The Rights of Woman,* only to be roused to an awareness of the complexity of the emotions a few months later. She knew that wisdom was a compound of reason and emotion, demanding a delicate balance hard to achieve. And if she appealed for reason in politics, religion, and education, she did so because she found far too little of it in contemporary institutions. If she tried to govern her own life by rational principles, it was because she knew that in the battle between her head and her heart, her head too often yielded. Yet by nature she was a woman of intense feeling—for individuals, for humanity, and for God—and her noisy rationalism was in part only wishful thinking. Reason may have furnished the scaffolding for her grand edifice of the future, but it was founded on love.

In all her thinking, then, Mary shows that though she had borrowed from others she had accepted only those ideas which her experience confirmed. Her religion and ethics, her educational theories, and her philosophy never followed the conventional patterns of her era, nor did they adhere to the theories adopted by the radical group with whom she associated. Mary was unconventional even in her liberalism; she had been truly "liberated" by her education, much as she hoped that other women might be by theirs. "The most perfect education, in my opinion," she wrote in *The Rights of Woman,* "is such an exercise of the understanding as is best calculated to strengthen the body and form the heart. Or, in other words, to enable the individual to attain such habits of virtue as will render it independent."[61] Mary wanted women to develop "the power of generalizing ideas, of drawing comprehensive conclusions from individual observations," which she regarded as "the only acquirement, for an immortal being, that really deserves the name of knowledge."[62] She wanted women to burst the bonds of ignorance, to think for themselves, and to declare their opinions openly. In short she wanted other women to be liberated as she had been liberated, to enjoy the satisfaction which she had found in her personal emancipation. And if at times she seemed overconfident of herself—if she seems a bit pontifical when she declares in *The Rights of Woman* that "as a philosopher" she cannot accept another writer's conclusions—she can be pardoned. The truly great are not modest; and Mary's book was to prove her the most fearlessly intelligent woman of her time—and perhaps the greatest.

CHAPTER VII

Theories on Trial
(1792-1794)

Love is a want of my heart.
—Letter to Imlay.

ONCE Mary had displayed her full powers in *The Rights of Woman,* she could afford more than ever before to relax from the strain of life as a literary hack.[1] She had proved herself able to compete with the foremost men of her time, and her future as an author looked secure. She had not finished with her new subject by any means: she was confidently planning at least one other volume of her latest work. The ramifications of the topic seemed endless, but she hoped to exhaust them in good time. And she had other reasons to be satisfied with life: she was known as *Mrs.* Wollstonecraft now, in recognition of her literary achievements, and she was comfortably settled in a pleasant house on Store Street with a growing circle of admirers. In a letter to her sister Everina dated February 23, 1792, she announced proudly: "Be it known to you that my book &c &c has afforded me an opportunity of settling *very* advantageous in the matrimonial line with a new acquaintance; but entre nous—a handsome house and a proper man did not tempt me; yet I may as well appear before you with the feather stuck in my cap." Soon afterwards she received a letter of extravagant praise from Mary Hays, an intense little woman who had just read *The Rights of Woman* and who begged to be allowed the favor of meeting the author. And when the great Talleyrand visited London in the same year, he called to see the lady who had addressed her latest book to him. Mary received him graciously but, as if to show how little she valued appearances, served him tea and wine from the same glass.[2]

Some of Mary's admirers may have been attracted not by her mind alone but by her growing personal charms. She had re-

marked in *The Rights of Woman* that women are more beautiful
at thirty than at twenty—because they have "more of mind"[3]—
and she herself was living proof of her claim. Now that she wore
her hair in a loose knot at the back of her head, her features seemed
softer and her complexion fresher than when she had let her locks
hang lank to her shoulders. And her new clothes set off her figure
to advantage, for they were designed on the fashionable "classical"
lines so much better adapted to her pocketbook and her theories
of dress than the elaborate décolletages and farthingales of the
'eighties. Her brother Charles, who spent most of the year 1792 at
her house, reported to Eliza Bishop that Mary had "grown quite
handsome," and that "being conscious that she is on the wrong
side of Thirty she now endeavors to set off those charms (she
once despised) to the best advantage."[4] Mary Hays later wrote:
"Her person was above the middle height, and well proportioned;
her form full; her hair and eyes brown; her features pleasing; her
countenance changing and impressive; her voice soft, and, though
without great compass, capable of modulation. When unbending
in familiar and confidential conversation, her manners had a
charm that subdued the heart."[5]

Probably, however, she did not always unbend. Her letters to
Miss Hays certainly suggest that, towards her at least, Mary often
displayed an attitude of generous condescension which reflected
the inordinate self-esteem that had antagonized Godwin when
they met. In her reply to Miss Hays's first letter begging for an
interview, Mary wrote: "I will . . . simply acknowledge the receipt
of your testimony of esteem merely to have an opportunity of telling you that when I return to Town, I shall be glad to see you."[6]
And later, when Miss Hays submitted her literary work to Mary
as Johnson's reader, she retained the same attitude. For example:

I have just cast my eye over your sensible little pamphlet, and found fewer
of the superlatives, exquisite, fascinating, &c, all of the feminine gender,
than I expected. Some of the sentiments, it is true, are rather obscurely expressed; but if you continue to write you will imperceptibly correct this
fault and learn to think with more clearness, and consequently avoid the
errours naturally produced by confusion of thought.[7]

Evidently Mary's self-esteem was fast approaching conceit.

Soon, however, it was to suffer a stunning blow. For though she had refused an offer of marriage, she was not immune to love. This time the object of her interest was no debonair man-of-the-world like Joshua Waterhouse, but the irascible, white-haired artist Henry Fuseli, whom she had known and admired for some time.[8] To most women shy, vain Fuseli, with his thick accent, his trembling hands, and his sarcastic manner, would have been repulsive; but Mary prided herself on her superiority to physical attractions. In *The Rights of Woman* she had expressed disdain for romantic love—"love, such as the glowing pen of genius has traced," but love which "exists not on earth, or only resides in those exalted, fervid imaginations that have sketched such dangerous pictures."[9] But her love was different. It sprang from her respect for Fuseli's mind, his liberal sentiments, his rational piety. It was a love not of bodies but of minds, of souls—a platonic love. And she assured herself that love so noble must be free of the usual hazards. She had perhaps forgotten her statement in *Thoughts on the Education of Daughters*: "Nothing can more tend to destroy peace of mind, than platonic attachments. They are begun in false refinement, and frequently end in sorrow, if not in guilt."[10]

Convinced that her affection was pure, Mary showed little restraint in her letters to Fuseli. She wrote him that she felt for him a "strength of feeling unalloyed by passion"—that she had long refrained from marrying because she "always thought, with some degree of horror, of falling a sacrifice to a passion which may have a mixture of dross in it."[11] Never before, she assured him, had she known a man with "those noble qualities, that grandeur of soul, that quickness of comprehension, and lively sympathy" which she demanded. And to her friends she is supposed to have declared: "I always catch something from the rich torrent of his conversation, worth treasuring up in my memory, to exercise my understanding."

Fuseli seems to have taken Mary's tributes calmly. According to John Knowles, he often kept her letters unopened in his pocket for days. Why he failed to discourage her publicly is hard to explain. Perhaps his natural shyness prevented him from making a scene; or perhaps his vanity was gratified by her attentions. Surely he must have realized from the outset that Mary's love for him was impossible. For though he probably admired her liberal opinions and her achievements, he had been married four years earlier to Sophia Rawlins, whom he genuinely loved.

But Mary probably demanded no encouragement whatsoever from her beloved. Convinced as she was that her affection for him was blameless, she felt no compulsion to conceal it; in fact she so disdained conventions that she may even have gloried in making the first advances rather than waiting to be pursued. Even Fuseli's marriage would hardly have discouraged her, positive as she was that her love was wholly platonic.

And so the luckless affair dragged on. Mary had perhaps tried too long to play the rationalist; now her heart was in revolt—and quite out of control. She seized every opportunity to be near Fuseli. She seems even to have cultivated his wife's acquaintance and to have gone out regularly with them. When Lavater, the physiognomist, an old friend of Fuseli, visited London, the four attended a masquerade together. And by June of 1792 Mary, Joseph Johnson, and the Fuselis were planning to leave early in August for a six weeks' trip to Paris so that they could view the Revolution at first hand.

Meanwhile, whatever Mrs. Fuseli may have been thinking about her husband's new admirer, the world had evidently reached its own conclusions. On June 20 Mary wrote to her sister Everina announcing the proposed trip and adding that she hoped to locate a situation for Eliza while she was in France. But when the news was relayed to Eliza, she was very dubious; and she hinted that she was aware of Mary's infatuation:

> So the author of The Rights of Women is going to France! I dare say, her chief motive is to promote her poor Bess's Comfort! or thine, my girl, or at least I think she will thus reason. Well, in spite of Reason, when Mrs. W reaches the Continent she will be but a woman. I cannot help paint-

ing her in the height of all her wishes, at the very summit of her happiness, for will not ambition fill every chink of her Great Soul? (for such I really think hers) that is not occupied by *Love* . . . .

And you actually have the vanity to imagine that in the National Assembly Personages like M. & F. will bestow a thought on two females whom nature meant to "suck fools and chronicle small beer."

If Mary could have read her sister's letter, she would probably have been disturbed by its malice—but would hardly have allowed it to alter her plans. She was little concerned about her sister's opinion, or the world's; she was looking forward to six weeks in the company of the man on whom she doted, in a land where she could thrill to the sight of men and women released from the chains of tyranny. Joel Barlow had already engaged rooms for the party,[12] and all was ready for their departure.

But for some reason the trip was canceled. Perhaps Fuseli decided that six weeks in Mary's company would be a dubious pleasure. According to Knowles, she was complaining of his "neglect" and (perhaps even worse) had been taking him to task for his vanity. Moreover, she had been talking indiscreetly to friends, maintaining that though Mrs. Fuseli had a right to her husband's person, she herself should hold a place in his heart because "she hoped to unite herself to his mind." When Fuseli remonstrated with her, she countered: "If I thought my passion criminal, I would conquer it, or die in the attempt. For immodesty, in my eyes, is ugliness; my soul turns with disgust from pleasure tricked out in charms which shun the light of heaven." Not only was she growing more possessive in her claims, but she was apparently admitting to herself that her feeling for Fuseli was growing more intense; for she speaks now of her "passion," rather than of her "feeling unalloyed by passion."

Meanwhile Mary's literary work languished. Evidently she could not rouse her efforts to any major project, and she seems to have been content with the workaday tasks of directing her department of the *Analytical* and serving as Johnson's editorial assistant. Her own contributions to the magazine fell off perceptibly. To be sure, she reviewed some forty books for the *Analytical* during the first six months of 1792; but her reviews averaged little more than a page apiece, many consisted largely of excerpts from the books reviewed, and none were leading articles. She treated a great variety of topics and kinds of writing: education, history, music, feminism, natural history, travels, poetry, drama, novels, biography, sermons—all the topics and genres which she had reviewed before, but no new ones. They merit attention only because they show in Mary a growing interest in the French, whom she hoped soon to know better, and a keen concern with the progress of the Revolution. For example, in a review of Madame Sillery Brulat's *Leçons d'une Gouvernante* (January, 1792) she remarked that "they contain some views of the servility of the French character, when debased by the system of intrigue, that was spread by despotism through the whole mass, rendering the private character as mean as the public was infamous." And a few pages later, in a review of *Letters of the Countess du Barré*:

These letters develope, in an interesting manner, the polished villainy of court intrigue, and that fatal system of *profusion* and *oppression,* which, in the latter part of the reign of Louis XV, hurried France to the brink of destruction, and at length brought the affairs of that Kingdom to the crisis which gave birth to the present revolution. The French patriots have been reviled, even to a degree of execration, by the *admirers* of *despotism;* but this collection of letters might alone serve as an apology for National assembly, were any apology necessary for the *glorious* labours of that *patriotic body.*

Mary was proud to count herself a friend of the French Revolution, and willing to exert all her powers of expression to convert others to her way of thinking. Again and again propaganda crept into her reviews. And in one article, a review of *A Letter to the Right Honourable William Pitt on the Subject of a Tax* (May, 1792), she boldly suggested that the revolutionary spirit was not and need not be confined to France: "A spirit is abroad to break the chains that have hitherto eaten into the human soul, which bids fair to mould the body-politic of Europe into a more proportional form, if we may be allowed the phrase, than has yet been seen on earth." To many of Mary's countrymen this statement in its context would have seemed positively seditious.

Meanwhile, though she was neglecting her writing, she was, as usual, busying herself for the benefit of her family. Early in the year she gave up her attempts to find her brother Charles a position in India and accepted Joel Barlow's suggestion that the young man emigrate to America with him and try his hand at farming. On February 23 she wrote hopefully to Everina:

Since I wrote to you last I have seen and heard more of Mr. Barlow, and think Charles' prospect a most promising one indeed. I shrewdly suspect that Mr. B. has some thoughts of keeping him in his own family; but he waits till he sees more of him before he avows his intention. Such a situation would be a most desirable one, for he has a sound understanding with great mildness of temper. I mean rather a regulated temper than natural good humour. The other day he clapped C., in his dry way, on the knee and said—"that as his wife and he could never contrive to make any boys they must try what they could do with one ready brought up to their hands." I am particularly anxious that C. should behave properly for unless he forgets himself I have not the least doubt of his doing *very* well.

So Mary packed her brother off to a farm near Leatherhead, where he could learn the elements of agriculture in preparation for his new career.

But weeks passed, Barlow failed to return from a trip to France when he was expected, and Charles's departure for America was postponed time after time. On June 20 Mary was reporting to Everina that Barlow was still abroad and that Charles was still on the farm—at her expense, of course. Yet she seemed confident that her plans for her brother would eventually be carried out. And she went on to tell Everina that she had been discussing her sisters' welfare with Mrs. Barlow, who had assured her that women of their abilities could easily find comfortable positions—perhaps even husbands—if they emigrated to America. Apparently she had, however, begun to suspect that her new friends were likely to be carried away by their enthusiasm. "Mrs. B.," she wrote,

has a very benevolent, affectionate heart, and a tolerable understanding, a little warped it is true by romance; but she is not the less friendly on that account. Delighted with some of her husband's letters, she has exultingly shewn them to me; and, though I took care not to let her see it, I was almost disgusted with the *tender* passages which afforded her so much satisfaction, because they were turned so prettily that they looked more like the cold ingenuity of the head than the warm overflowings of the heart. However, she did not perceive that the head and the heart were gadding far away, when he calls "her arms his heaven," in search of fame on this same dirty earth—so all was well.

And in the same letter Mary announced that she was still hoping to find a situation for Eliza in France.

Her suspicions proved to be correct. By September 14 she had been unable to "get a decided answer from Mr. Barlow." "He is a worthy man," she wrote, "but devoured by ambition. His thoughts are turned towards France and till the present commotions are over, I am very much mistaken if he do not find some excuse every month to make to *himself* for staying in Europe." And eventually she sent Charles off to America alone, and no more was heard of her sisters' glorious prospects in the new country. She continued, however, to seek a place for Eliza in France. Neither fame nor love had distracted her from her benevolence to her family. Indeed before the end of the year her brother James reappeared ("like an accomplished youth, just arrived from making the *tour* of France," Eliza observed sourly) and asked Mary to outfit him for his new commission in the Royal Navy.

Meanwhile Mary's contributions to the *Analytical* continued to dwindle. During the last six months of 1792 she wrote no leading articles and few of any real consequence. Indeed the only reviews deserving of even passing notice are two, in July, of essays about Dr. Johnson; and they are interesting only because they show how Mary's opinion of Johnson and all that he stood for had altered since the early days of the *Analytical*.[18] Thereafter Mary contributed no article deserving of comment; in fact the magazine contained no review by her in October and only a brief one, filling a third of a page, in November. And it was her last for three and a half years.

By that time her relations with Fuseli had reached a climax. For months she had been sinking ever deeper in her hopeless love for him, and ultimately she decided that she could no longer live apart from her beloved. Still confident of the purity of her intentions, she went to his house, asked to see Mrs. Fuseli, and begged to be accepted as a member of the family. Of course she assured herself—and Mrs. Fuseli—that she had no desire to come between husband and wife; her affection for Fuseli was platonic and would remain so. She frankly admitted, however, that her passion had become so powerful that she could not survive unless she was able to see and converse with her beloved daily. Fortunately for all concerned, Mrs. Fuseli kept her head. Perhaps she was used to unconventional behavior from her husband's friends; or perhaps she knew that she had no cause to be jealous. In any case she merely ordered Mary to leave the house.

It is a preposterous tale, and one in which Mary acts a very shabby part. And it is superfluous to remark that she felt her behavior quite justified. She had obeyed the rules of her own morality, if not the world's. But if she had momentarily lost her head, she regained it quickly and once again set it to its task of controlling her unruly emotions. Common sense told her that she must see no more of Fuseli for the present. The only wise course was to go as far away from him as possible; and since she still longed to see the French Revolution at close quarters, she determined to go to Paris. She must have realized at last that she had not (as Browning makes her say in his poem "Mary Wollstonecraft and Fuseli")

> . . . quickened his pulse one beat,
> Fixed a moment's fancy, bitter or sweet;

for she wrote to him, apologizing for "having disturbed the quiet tenour of your life," and early in December she prepared to set off alone for Paris.

In an undated letter to Everina, written just before her departure, Mary naturally said nothing about the reason for her sudden decision to go to France. Though she complained of sinking spirits, she attributed them to her fear that Joseph Johnson might be seriously ill during her absence. She had nothing to say, either, about her plans for her trip; she seemed to be concerned only about securing Eliza a promising position, of which she had recently heard. As for her little "daughter" Ann, she failed to mention her. Doubtless the child was sent to stay with relatives. And Mary may have had few regrets at parting with her, for the arrangement had not proved altogether satisfactory: it had entailed more of the cares of motherhood than of its joys. As early as October 6, 1791, she had written to George Blood: "When Everina went [to Ireland] I found little Ann, at first, very troublesome; but now I manage her better, she is, as usual, in great spirits—in fact, her spirits sometimes oppress me, though I would not for the world damp them. She is an affectionate, artless child." And on February 23, 1792, she wrote to Everina:

I am sorry to give you a bad account of Ann after my late praise; but a few days ago I discovered that she has been stealing sugar out of my closet constantly, and the artful way she managed it, not to mention the lies, really vexes me. She is undoubtedly very much improved and my visitors think her a fine girl—yet I have long been convinced that she will never be the kind of child I should love with all my heart. She has great *animal* spirits and quick feelings, but I shall be much mistaken if she have any considerable portion of sensibility when she grows up.

Mary was reputedly trying to rear the little girl as a child of nature, and her experiment had evidently proved disappointing. Perhaps Rousseau's theories would succeed only when one could apply them from earliest infancy.—But Mary probably did little speculating about such matters when she set out for Paris; she had weightier problems on her mind. She would have been incredulous, certainly, could she have known that within eighteen months she would have another little girl to experiment with—one whom she could certainly love with all her heart: a daughter of her own.

Her journey to Paris must have been dismal. It was a cheerless time of year, and her thoughts were probably as dreary as the landscape. She who had lately enjoyed such complete self-confidence had suffered thorough humiliation. Did she reflect that, unlike previous sorrows, this sorrow was of her own making? Did she resolve to be more cautious in the future? Or was she philosophic enough to recall the words which she had innocently written in *The Rights of Woman* only a year before, "It is far better to be often deceived than never to trust; to be disappointed in love, than never to love"?[14]

Whatever her thoughts, she could hardly have avoided contrasting her solitary trip through the frosty countryside and across the Channel with the gay party which she and her friends had planned for the preceding summer. Yet she was determined "to lose in public happiness the sense of private misery";[15] the glorious prospect of liberated France would, she hoped, solace her wounded heart. Yet that was rather chill comfort for even the most philosophical of women in love.

She arrived in Paris at a crucial moment. Four months earlier, on August 10, 1792, the moderation which had characterized most of the early years of the Revolution had been discarded with the uprising of the Paris Commune, the imprisonment of the King, and the passing of the law extending suffrage to all male citizens over twenty-one. September had seen the horrible massacre of prisoners in Paris and elsewhere, the formation of the National Convention to take the place of the old Legislative Assembly, and the proclamation of the French Republic. To Mary it doubtless seemed that events were shaping up admirably; she had probably heard reports of the excesses of the Paris mob, but she was prepared to condone them on the ground that eventually good would rise from the present evils. She could hardly have foreseen that even greater evils would follow presently. As yet the moderate Girondins were in control of the National Convention, the King was unharmed, and the Montagnards—Robespierre, Danton, Marat, and their fellow-radicals—were only a threat, though a growing one. But at about the time that Mary reached Paris, the Montagnards practically forced the Girondins to bring the King to trial for his misdeeds. It was a good time to be quitting Paris, hardly an auspicious moment for the arrival of a woman unaccompanied.

Fortunately Mary was not cast entirely adrift in the storm. She had evidently been invited to stop at the home of Madame Aline

Filliettaz, daughter of the Mrs. Bregantz who had kept the school at Putney where Mary's sisters had taught. And once she had arrived, Mary settled down to study French and observe the momentous happenings. She was uncertain how long she would stay in France. She had thought of proceeding to Switzerland to see the Alps. But she intended eventually, when she had driven Fuseli from her mind, to return to London and resume her old life at the house on Store Street. She little knew what joys and sorrows awaited her in Paris.

Though the Filliettaz house provided shelter and a measure of protection, it was hardly a cheerful place. The family was out of town—perhaps to escape the excesses of the Commune—and Mary was left alone in the "immense hotel," as she called it, with only the servants for company. She was obviously out of spirits when she sat down to write to Everina on Christmas Eve. She had caught a cold during her journey across the Channel, and was bothered by a severe cough. Paris had proved disappointing—"the streets are so dirty," she complained, good Englishwoman that she was—and the people seemed affable enough, but decidedly frivolous. She was spending her long overdue vacation in concentrated study, determined to gain a speaking knowledge of French. "I apply so closely to the language, and labour so continually to understand what I hear," she wrote, "that I never go to bed without a headache." Probably she was trying to smother her unhappiness in hard work. She might have succeeded better had she sought companionship; but she was determined not to appear in society until she had mastered the language. And so she continued her solitary existence.

Soon her little worries gave way to genuine fear. On the day after Christmas the King was conducted from the tower of the Temple to defend himself before the Convention; and Mary, who saw him pass her window, forgot her passion for universal liberty in her sympathy for the humiliated monarch. It was one thing to contemplate the birth of freedom from the safe distance of London, but quite another to witness the event at close range. She was terrified. And that evening, as she sat in her room writing to Joseph Johnson, her emotions overflowed in one of her finest and most vivid passages of prose:

About nine o'clock this morning, the king passed by my window, moving silently along (excepting now and then a few strokes on the drum, which rendered the stillness more awful) through empty streets, surrounded by the national guards, who, clustering around the carriage, seemed to deserve their name. The inhabitants flocked to their windows, but the casements were all shut, not a voice was heard, nor did I see any thing like an insulting gesture.—For the first time since I entered France, I bowed to the majesty of the people, and respected the propriety of behaviour so perfectly in unison with my own feelings. I can scarcely tell you why, but an association of ideas made the tears flow insensibly from my eyes, when I saw Louis sitting, with more dignity than I expected from his character, in a hackney coach, going to meet death, where so many of his race have triumphed. My fancy instantly brought Louis XIV before me, entering the capital with all his pomp, after one of the victories most flattering to his pride, only to see the sunshine of prosperity overshadowed by the sublime gloom of misery. I have been alone ever since; and, though my mind is calm, I cannot dismiss the lively images that have filled my imagination all the day.—Nay, do not smile, but pity me; for, once or twice, lifting my eyes from the paper, I have seen eyes glare through a glass-door opposite my chair, and bloody hands shook at me. Not the distant sound of a footstep can I hear. . . . I wish I had even kept the cat with me!—I want to see something alive; death in so many frightful shapes has taken hold of my fancy.—I am going to bed—and, for the first time in my life, I cannot put out the candle.[16]

Surely such an experience would prove far more effective than hard work in banishing Mary's thoughts of Fuseli. In fact the whole affair probably seemed strangely remote to her before many weeks had passed, for she wrote to him only once after her arrival in France.

By the middle of January England was aware of the state of affairs in France, and the trial of the King shocked lukewarm advocates of the Revolution into abandoning the liberal cause altogether. Hatred of Jacobinism burned intense. Loyal Englishmen were venting their wrath against the French rebels on whatever scapegoat they could find. From Wales Eliza Bishop wrote to her sister Everina on January 20 that Tom Paine had been burned in effigy at Pembroke, adding: "Nay, [they] talk of immortalizing Miss Wollstonecraft in the like manner." Mary may well have felt she was safer in Paris than in London; indeed many of her radical friends had left England as anti-Jacobin sentiment grew more and more intense. At all events she stayed on at Paris, doubtless waiting for the excitement to blow over. Then on January 21 the King was beheaded, and on February 1 England declared war on France. Overnight Mary became an enemy alien with no means of support and only a few acquaintances to befriend her. If she had hunted the civilized world over, she could hardly have found a less desirable place for a lone Englishwoman.

To make matters worse, she had apparently concluded by this time that the Revolution had miscarried. She was at work on the first of a series of "Letters on the Present Character of the French Nation," a report on conditions in France, which Johnson was to publish for her. The tone of that letter is significant, for it reveals that for the moment Mary (perhaps partly because of her unhappiness about Fuseli) was disillusioned not only with the Revolution but with all prospects of future perfection. "I would I could first inform you," she wrote,

> that, out of the chaos of vices and follies, prejudices and virtues, rudely jumbled together, I saw the fair form of Liberty slowly rising, and Virtue expanding her wings to shelter all her children! I should then hear the account of the barbarities that have rent the bosom of France patiently, and bless the firm hand that lopt off the rotten limbs. But, if the aristocracy of birth is levelled with the ground, only to make room for that of riches, I am afraid that the morals of the people will not be much improved by the change, or the government rendered less venal. Still it is not just to dwell on the misery produced by the present struggle, without adverting to the standing evils of the old system . . . .
>
> Before I came to France, I cherished, you know, an opinion, that strong virtues might exist with the polished manners produced by the progress of civilization; and I even anticipated the epoch, when, in the course of improvement, men would labour to become virtuous, without being goaded on by misery. But now, the perspective of the golden age, fading before the attentive eye of observation, almost eludes my sight; and, losing thus in part my theory of a more perfect state, start not, my friend, if I bring forward an opinion, which at the first glance seems to be levelled against the existence of God! I am not become an Atheist, I assure you, by residing at Paris: yet I begin to fear that vice, or, if you will, evil, is the grand mobile of action, and that, when the passions are justly poized, we become harmless, and in the same proportion, useless.[17]

The letter, as Godwin published it in Mary's *Posthumous Works,* was dated February 15, 1793, two weeks after England's declaration of war on France. It was the only one of the projected series that Mary ever wrote.

Already she was stranded with no means of support, just when she had concluded that the French Revolution was not all that she had supposed it to be, that "names, not principles, are changed." She was revolted by the sights all around her. Mankind liberated from serfdom did not reveal the nobility which she had expected; instead, "the same pride of office, the same desire of power are still visible; with this aggravation, that, fearing to return to obscurity after having but just acquired a relish for distinction, each hero, or philosopher, for all are dubbed with these new titles, endeavours to make hay while the sun shines; and every petty municipal officer, become the idol, or rather the tyrant of the day, stalks like a cock on a dunghil."[18] It was all thoroughly disillusioning; Mary had not yet given up all hope "that a fairer day is dawning on Europe," but for the present she confessed that "it is the most terrific of all sights, to see men vicious without warmth—to see the order that should be the superscription of virtue, cultivated to give security to crimes which only thoughtlessness could palliate."[19] Yet however much she may have yearned to be back in her comfortable house on Store Street, she had no choice but to remain where she was.

Fortunately she was in no immediate danger because she was known to be a friend of democracy and of the American circle in Paris. As soon as she gained an adequate speaking knowledge of French, she went more into society. She saw much of her old friends the Barlows and the Christies, who were now staying in Paris. She saw also (and "*rather* liked") the intense, unconventional Helen Maria Williams, and renewed her acquaintance with Tom Paine, who had fled from England during the preceding September, when Blake warned him one evening at Joseph Johnson's that his life was in immediate danger. At Paine's lodgings she could meet many kindred spirits—leaders of the Revolution such as Brissot or Roland, and Englishmen and Americans (many of them honorary citizens of the French Republic) who had come over to assist at the birth of French liberty. Mary was soon accepted as a member of this international group; she was friendly with the Swiss Jean Caspard Schweitzer and his vivacious wife Madeleine; with the German Count Gustav von Schlabrendorf, who realized in after years that he had loved Mary dearly;[20] with J. G. Forster, the German-born, Russian- and English-educated Fellow of the Royal Society who had sailed around the world with Captain Cook; with Thomas Cooper of Manchester, the "learned, ingenious, scientific, and talented madcap" (as John Adams later called him) who was in France as a representative of Jacobin clubs in England. They were a stimulating lot of people, thanks to their varied backgrounds and their sociable personalities; and they provided lively companionship, such as Mary doubtless needed.

Yet she must have known moments of sheer terror, wondering how she could support herself in the months ahead. The sum which she had set aside for her vacation must soon have been exhausted, with food growing scarce and prices rising. She could always borrow from her friends, many of whom were well-to-do; but Mary had left debts enough in England, and she must have dreaded the prospect of further borrowing. Where could she turn? Paris offered no occupation for an English literary lady, and the London market was closed to her. She thought of taking refuge in Switzerland, where living would be cheaper. But she could not get a passport.

Then suddenly all her worries were dissolved. One day, probably in April, 1793, while she was visiting the Christies, she met a lean, gawky American named Gilbert Imlay. He was an alert, personable man of liberal opinions who seems to have been cultivating the impression that, more than most Americans, he was an unspoiled child of nature, an incarnation of Rousseau's Emile. He liked to think of himself as "different," to point up the contrast between himself and the average European—always to his own advantage. "We have more of simplicity," he had written,

and you more of art.—We have more of nature, and you more of the world. Nature formed our features and intellects very much alike; but while you have metamorphosed the one, and contaminated the other, we preserve the natural symbols of both. You have more hypocrisy—we are sincere. You are more cunning and adroit, which your laws and habits have rendered part of your natures. We are not so stupid as not to see through the veil; but when an European does us the honour to visit us, we have both too much hospitality and suavity of manners to inform them they have neither sentiments nor religion.[21]

At first Mary disliked Imlay. Though her own self-confidence may have been shaken in recent months, she doubtless still had enough spirit to resent such overweening self-esteem as he displayed. For a while she even avoided meeting him in company. But as time passed and as Imlay showed a growing interest in her, she modified her first impression. Gradually the memory of Fuseli faded from her mind, and Imlay's charms won her heart. And before long she was madly in love with this "natural and unaffected creature," as she later described him.

Actually Imlay had somewhat overstated his claims to be considered a child of nature. He was born in Upper Freehold, Monmouth County, New Jersey, probably in 1754, and served as a lieutenant or captain in the American Revolution.[22] But he preferred to be known not as a soldier or a New Jerseyan but as an explorer of the wilds of Kentucky, where he had spent two years as a surveyor and speculator after the close of the war. In fact he had attracted some little attention in 1792 by his book *A Topographical Description of the Western Territory of North America: Containing a Succinct Account of its Soil, Climate, Natural History, Population, Agriculture, Manners, and Customs*, which was to be published in three English editions, a German translation, and an American reprint. The volume was composed of eleven letters supposedly written to a friend in England (or possibly Ireland) setting forth the factual material announced in the title. Such information was bound to interest contemporary readers because of the general curiosity about the outlying regions of America. But Imlay gave his book a secondary appeal by announcing on his first page that he undertook his task "with the greatest pleasure, as it will afford me an opportunity of contrasting the simple manners, and rational life of the Americans, in these back settlements, with the distorted and unnatural habits of the Europeans: which have flowed no doubt from the universally bad laws which exist on your continent, and from that pernicious system of blending religion with politics, which has been productive of universal depravity." And periodically thereafter (often when there seemed to be no very good reason for doing so) he turned from his factual description of land and people to assail despotic governments or established religion, to dilate on the beauties of the landscape or the joys of freedom, or to anticipate the era of universal perfection. For example:

While the setting sun gilds those extensive plains, the mild breezes of a summer's eve, playing upon the enraptured senses, softens the heart to love and friendship. Unperceived, upon some eminence, you may enjoy the sports of wild animals, which here rove unconcerned lords of the field. Heavens! what charms are there in liberty! Man, born to enslave the subordinate animals, has long since enslaved himself. But reason at length, in radiant smiles, and with graceful pride, illumines both hemispheres; and FREEDOM, in golden plumes, and in her triumphal car, must now resume her lost empire.[23]

Yet this was not the worst of Gilbert Imlay. He incorporated his favorite theory—that "men feeling the spirit of liberty are always superior to slaves"—into a three-volume epistolary novel, *The Emigrants,* which was published soon after he and Mary met. The subject matter of the *Topographical Description* had somewhat restrained his natural ebullience; but in *The Emigrants* he allowed his sentiment and imagination to flow unchecked. The result is one of the most flamboyant examples of the thesis novel ever to appear, even in the ecstatic 1790's. For while Imlay never lost sight of his theories, he constantly dazzled his readers with literary pyrotechnics of a very specious sort. For example, the hero "Arl - - - ton" writes to his friend "Il - - - ray": "Oh my friend!

three days since, when we found Caroline half unzoned, setting
in the *marquee* to receive the cool breezes, which seemed to wanton in her bosom as if enraptured with its sweets, while her conscious thoughts diffused their roseate charms over her heavenly
face, how did my senses beat with the ecstacy of desire?"[24] Elsewhere Arl - - - ton celebrates his beloved thus:

> Oh! how I could for ever her adore,
> By tasting sweets new beauties to explore,
> Then to entangle in her lovely arms,
> And drown ev'ry sense in unrivall'd charms?[25]

The scene of the novel is set at first in the bucolic environs of
Pittsburgh, where Caroline T - - - - n and her impoverished family
have settled, and where she is wooed by Arl - - - ton. Their love
is impeded by obstacles innumerable—from a hateful sister to a
tribe of Indians; but of course such difficulties merely present opportunities for Arl - - - ton to prove his devotion. Eventually all
ends well, with the lovers united, enriched by the generosity of
Caroline's wealthy uncle, and preparing to found a utopian com-
monwealth on the banks of the Ohio River.

To a modern reader *The Emigrants* is preposterous, but to
Mary it would probably have seemed at least inoffensive. After all,
she had written a sentimental novel herself. And she doubtless
was willing to overlook superficial faults in Imlay's books as well
as in his character, once she was convinced that he was "enlightened"—even to the point of urging more freedom and education
for women.

So once again Mary's heart overruled her head. She could
hardly have been won by Imlay's physical appearance: he was
tall and awkward,[26] and she later twitted him on his "poor bare
ribs." His reputation too was hardly attractive. He seems to have
left America in order to avoid his debts, and he had evidently had
previous affairs, one of them perhaps with Helen Maria Williams,
whom Mary had recently met.[27] But such details mattered little.
Mary was ripe for love. She had achieved everything else to which
she aspired, and her disappointment with Fuseli had probably

only sharpened her longing for affection and companionship. Whatever misgivings she might have felt about Imlay could be quickly argued away: theirs would be a union of minds and souls, quite capable of surmounting minor obstacles. Unfortunately, however, the truth was that Imlay was a sensualist utterly incapable of appreciating Mary's nature. He was doubtless flattered by the attentions of so distinguished a woman, and welcomed a passing affair with her. But the enduring sort of love that Mary craved was quite beyond his ken.

The affair advanced rapidly. Soon Mary left Paris for a small cottage near Neuilly, on the Seine three miles from the city. There they could meet secretly, unobserved by any of their acquaintances. There Mary could spend the long summer days in reading or writing, untouched by the havoc which had disrupted life in Paris. During her stay at Neuilly she found time to write two letters to her sister Eliza, to be forwarded through friends in Ireland. On June 13 she reported that she was "at the house of an old Gardener writing a great book; and in better health and spirits than I have ever enjoyed since I came to France." She had at last concluded that it was "next to impossible" to settle Eliza in France for the present, yet she still had not given up hope of aiding her. "Do not despair, my dear girl," she wrote, "once more breathe on the ashes of hope (I mean not to pun on the word), and I will render your fate more tolerable, unless *my* hopes deceive me." On the 24th she wrote again, lest her previous letter should have miscarried. And again she assured Eliza that she had "a plan in my head which promises to render the evening of your life more comfortable." Doubtless she had recalled what Mrs. Barlow had told her of the opportunities which her sisters would find in America; and she was probably planning to send for them after she and Imlay had settled in his own country. Yet she would not reveal the nature of her scheme; for, as she added somewhat ironically, "Knowing how sanguine you are I am almost afraid to set your imagination to work and lead you to rekindle hope with all your might and main, whilst you are talking in heroics of despair."

Meanwhile Imlay was busy in Paris on plans of his own. He was involved in an extraordinary scheme initiated by Brissot, who was eager to weaken the power of Spain in America and enrich France by annexing an area which had remarkable commercial possibilities. The idea dated back to 1788, when he had been in America and had become interested in the plight of the French and American settlers in the Mississippi Valley, then under Spanish control. On January 25, 1793, the French Committee of General Defense had directed Brissot to report on the feasibility of wresting control of Louisiana from Spain; and soon afterwards Thomas Cooper of Manchester had introduced Imlay to Brissot as a man whose knowledge of the Western Territory would make him a valuable adviser—perhaps even leader of an expedition to seize the area. Imlay's part in the affair was perfectly honorable; in fact such patriotic Americans as Joel Barlow, General George Rogers Clark, and Mark Leavenworth were parties to the plot, doubtless feeling that their nation would gain considerably if France, their natural ally, were to occupy the land immediately to the west of them. At first Brissot's scheme moved along rapidly, and Genêt was despatched to Washington to serve as French Ambassador and complete arrangements for the expedition. On April 22, about the time that Imlay and Mary met, Genêt wrote to Lebrun, the French Foreign Minister, urging him to act quickly on the plans already made. But by the time the letter reached France, Brissot and Lebrun had more pressing affairs to occupy their attention. Their position in France had become perilous. Presently they were to be crushed by the rise of the Montagnards, to be among the first of the victims of the Reign of Terror.

During that frightful summer of 1793 Mary was at Neuilly. Once when she went up to Paris she saw the pavement wet with the blood of the guillotine. She came upon the sight unawares and was so shocked that she spontaneously expressed her horror to those who were standing nearby—until she was warned that she must be silent if she did not wish to be arrested. Most of the time, however, she remained in her rural haven, welcoming Imlay whenever he could get away from the city. The old gardener who owned her cottage delighted in pampering her: he brought her gifts of fresh grapes, he performed all sorts of services for her (even making her bed), and he scolded her for her recklessness in walking alone in the nearby forest. Such solicitude was a new experience for Mary. So was the sensation of being loved. That alone must have compensated for all the horrors of those dreadful days. She had no longer to wonder how she could support herself or who would protect her if she were arrested as an enemy alien. She had only to savor the joys of peace and contentment, to bask in the glow of Imlay's love.

To keep herself occupied, she undertook the obvious project: a history of the French Revolution for English readers. Only a few months earlier she had written in the *Analytical* that it was too soon to write a history of the Revolution, that no historian could hope to "consider it as an *abstract question*."[28] But she had evidently changed her mind in the meantime: perhaps she felt that her experience in France had qualified her to judge events there—or she may have argued to herself that she would be able to see the Revolution in proper perspective long before she would be able to publish her book. So she launched on her new task. This time, however, she was not obliged to write against a deadline. She could work at leisure. That too was a new experience. Indeed Mary seems to have created for herself an island of peace in the midst of the Reign of Terror. She could relax completely at Neuilly and enjoy the pleasures of comfort, work, and love as never before in her life.

Doubtless Imlay came out to her cottage frequently. Sometimes when he could not leave the city, they met at the Barrière or toll-gate of the city nearest Neuilly. There evidently their child —the "barrier girl," as Mary later called her—was conceived.

Since Mary and her lover saw each other frequently during these summer months, they wrote few letters. Only two survive. The first is a brief and reserved note from Mary saying that she must forego the "snug dinner" which they had planned, but that she hopes "to find you at my fire-side when I return, about eight o'clock." But the second, written in August, shortly before she went to live with Imlay in Paris, shows no restraint:

You can scarcely imagine with what pleasure I anticipate the day, when we are to begin almost to live together; and you would smile to hear how many plans of employment I have in my head, now that I am confident my heart has found peace in your bosom. Cherish me with that dignified tenderness, which I have only found in you; and your own dear girl will try to keep under a quickness of feeling, that has sometimes given you pain. Yes, I will be *good,* that I may deserve to be happy; and whilst you love me, I cannot again fall into the miserable state which rendered life a burthen almost too heavy to be borne.

There is no reticence, no hesitation here. Mary not only loves Imlay tenderly, but feels so sure of his love for her that she can speak her heart and even admit her shortcomings to him. Her love—and her happiness—have reached their zenith: she feels wholly secure, and addresses her lover not as a mistress but as a wife. And when she closes with affection, she adds: "I like the word affection, because it signifies something habitual; and we are soon to meet to try whether we have mind enough to keep our hearts warm." Mary had not forgotten her theories of love; she still disdained the blind affection which she had encountered when she visited the Gabells three years before. But she hoped—and believed—that her love and Imlay's would be finer and more lasting because it was grounded in reason.

Mary's tenderness was probably intensified by the knowledge that she was pregnant. For that reason, perhaps, she decided now to leave Neuilly and go to live with her lover. Imlay doubtless had more time on his hands now, for after the fall of Brissot in June the Louisiana project had been abandoned. He may already have been involved in a new scheme; at least he seems to have been out of town when Mary next wrote to him. Evidently she was in the process of moving to their new lodgings, for she speaks of hiring a carriage because she has "so many books that I immediately want"—doubtless for her research on her history. But there is a new and ominous note in her letter. "I shall not . . . be content with only a kiss of *duty*," she tells Imlay. "You *must* be glad to see me because you are glad. . . ." Such slight criticism seems negligible, but it is perhaps significant. Already Mary is recognizing flaws in her lover and calling his attention to them. Perfectionist that she was, she could not seem to avoid reminding her dearest friends of their imperfections. She had in the past been troubled by Fanny Blood's timidity, by Fuseli's vanity, and doubtless by Joshua Waterhouse's worldliness. When Godwin had met her in 1791 she had managed to find some fault with every person mentioned in the evening's conversation. And now as her passions impelled her toward Imlay, her intellect withdrew to view him critically and to suggest just how he might be perfected. Her head and her heart were again at cross-purposes.

Common sense seems to have told her that such criticism was fruitless, that men could not be reformed so easily. In the very letter in which she made her first criticism of Imlay, she wrote, after commenting on Mirabeau's principles: "If I had not begun to form a new theory respecting men, I should, in the vanity of my heart, have imagined that I could have made something of his." Did Mary's *men* mean humanity in general or only the male sex? Was she learning more about human nature from her observation of the French Revolutionists or from her experience with Gilbert Imlay? Perhaps she had already discovered that the respect which she had hoped to inspire in Imlay was not strong enough to make him correct his faults. Unfortunately, however, she failed for a long time to learn his worst shortcomings—to discern that he was shallow of mind and of heart, and that his love could be snuffed out by just such criticism as she was making. For it was surely Mary's hypercritical nature as well as Imlay's shallowness and egotism that brought about the eventual debacle.

When Mary settled in Paris with her lover, probably in mid-August of 1793, they no longer sought to conceal their relationship; in fact Imlay registered Mary as his wife in the American Embassy. Probably he took this precaution not because either he or Mary wished to legalize their union but only because he sought to protect her, as the wife of an American citizen, from possible repercussions from the war between England and France.[29] The action proved to be well-advised, for in October, after Lord Hood's seizure of the French fleet at Toulon, all Englishmen living in Paris (even so ardent a revolutionist as Helen Maria Williams) were imprisoned as hostages. But Mary did not regard the certificate of registration as a marriage license. She was not Imlay's wife, and she was proud of the fact. Though she had never openly opposed marriage, she had good reason to know its faults; and she apparently found real satisfaction in flouting it. On April 27, 1794, in a letter to Ruth Barlow, she referred to *"us"* and added: "You perceive that I am acquiring the matrimonial phraseology without having clogged my soul by promising obedience &c &c."[30] Obviously she was exulting in her unconventional status.

The first few weeks after Mary went to live with Imlay were undoubtedly blissful. Now, Godwin later wrote, she "first . . . gave a loose to all the sensibilities of her nature."[31] Though Paris was ablaze with the atrocities of the Reign of Terror, the two lovers could forget all the rest of the world. Indeed their privacy was due in part to the political upheaval: without it Mary could never have been so free from her troublesome family, so delightfully isolated with the man she loved. Doubtless she became tenderer, more vivacious, than ever before in her life. She had never known such happiness. She was looking forward to the birth of her child, and the future seemed cloudless. As soon as Imlay had accumulated £1000, they would emigrate to America, buy a farm, and abandon themselves to the joys of pastoral life. The barren years were past.

But first Imlay had to find a means of accumulating the needed £1000. And since the Louisiana scheme had failed and his books had yielded no very large returns, he was obliged to try another source of income. In keeping with the spirit of the times he had apparently decided that commerce, not conquest, was the best means of achieving prosperity. And soon he found what he wanted. The details of the new scheme are not altogether clear,[32] but ostensibly it began when Imlay met Elias Backman, an exporter, of Gothenburg, Sweden, who visited France in 1792 and 1793. Apparently Imlay and Joel Barlow were seeking to set themselves up as importers, and by establishing certain agreements with Backman, were able to import through him and other Scandinavian agents such badly needed products as ammunition, grain, steel, iron, wooden goods, pitch, and alum. Imlay's share in the arrangement proved very demanding—even nerve-racking. The French customs regulations changed from month to month, and ships approaching France were in constant danger. Because of the exorbitant prices which prevailed in France, he enjoyed an even chance of making a fortune quickly. But it was hardly ideal employment for a man who was just settling down to domestic life.

In fact, not long after Mary had joined him in Paris, he was called to Havre on business. Perhaps one of Backman's vessels was expected to dock there. In any event he was supposed to be gone only a short time, and Mary did not accompany him. She was probably content to remain behind, for she was well along in her pregnancy and might have encountered serious dangers and delays during a coach trip in those fearful autumn days of 1793.

But when Imlay was gone not a few days, but weeks, and when conditions in Paris went from bad to worse, she must have wondered how he could allow her to stay alone in the city. In October Brissot and the twenty-one Deputies were guillotined, and Mary "sunk lifeless on the floor" when she heard the news.[33] In the same month most of her English friends were jailed, and she was spared their fate only because she had been registered as Imlay's wife. Actually she seems to have been listed among those reported imprisoned; for on November 5 her sister Eliza wrote to Everina: "I am half afraid poor Mary is not perfectly secure, for you have undoubtedly read in the papers of her having been arrested; I hope in God she is safe, yet the contrary idea haunts and makes me forget her few faults." But even though Mary was in no immediate danger of imprisonment or guillotine, she had no guarantee, in a nation where law was so flagrantly disregarded, that she was safe. Safety was nonexistent in Paris in the fall of 1793. If the party in power had known that she was writing a history of the Revolution unsympathetic to them, her life would indeed "not have been worth much," as she later told her sister. Soon after Imlay left for Havre, she felt the "first twitches" of the child she was carrying; and her anxiety must have doubled. She was alone and lonely in a world gone mad. Now, if ever, she needed the protection of a man.

Her first letter to Imlay written after his departure shows clearly that her faith in him had been shaken. But it was probably not so much because of his departure as because of some disagreement which they had had before he left Paris. Mary's letters fail to make clear exactly what happened between them, but she refers to Imlay's "want of confidence—and subsequently affection" on one occasion.[34] Though the quarrel may have been slight—and, by Imlay, soon forgotten—it had hurt Mary deeply and prompted her to address her lover coldly:

How are you? I have been following you all along the road this comfortless weather; for, when I am absent from those I love, my imagination is as lively as if my senses had never been gratified by their presence—I was going to say caresses—and why should I not? I have found that I have more mind than you, in one respect; because I can, without any violent effort of reason, find food for love in the same object, much longer than you can. The way to my senses is through my heart; but, forgive me! I think there is sometimes a shorter cut to yours.

With ninety-nine men out of a hundred, a very sufficient dash of folly is necessary to render a woman *piquante,* a soft word for desirable; and, beyond these casual ebullitions of sympathy, few look for enjoyment by fostering a passion in their hearts. One reason, in short, why I wish my whole sex to become wiser, is, that the foolish ones may not, by their pretty folly, rob those whose sensibility keeps down their vanity, of the few roses that afford them some solace in the thorny road of life.

I do not know how I fell into these reflections, excepting one thought produced it—that these continual separations were necessary to warm your affection. Of late we are always separating. Crack! crack! and away you go! This joke wears the sallow cast of thought; for, though I began to write cheerfully, some melancholy tears have found their way into my eyes, that

linger there, whilst a glow of tenderness at my heart whispers that you are
one of the best creatures in the world. Pardon then the vagaries of a mind
that has been almost "crazed by care," as well as "crossed in hapless love,"
and bear with me a *little* longer! When we are settled in the country together, more duties will open before me, and my heart, which now, trembling
into peace, is agitated by every emotion that awakens the remembrance of
old griefs, will learn to rest on yours, with that dignity your character, not
to talk of my own, demands.

It is a pathetic passage. Mary is torn as never before by the battle
between her head and her heart. She feels neglected; and she tries
to blame that neglect on the nature of men or on her own mental
instability. For only a moment does she suggest that it is due to a
flaw in her lover's character. Obviously she wants to respect him,
and she offers her hint of criticism with an apology. Yet she realizes that his love is not as strong as hers. Hence the relapse into
her old depression, the reference to "the thorny road of life" and
being "crazed by care." For the present she attributes her depression to her physical condition and begs her lover to "bear with
me a *little* longer" until the crisis has passed. Had she known Imlay
for what he was, she would have realized that such complaints and
criticisms, however just, would only antagonize him. But she still
loved him too dearly to be able to regard him objectively; and so
she succeeded only in making herself seem like a burdensome
responsibility which a selfish man would gladly shirk.

For several weeks Mary lived on in Paris lonely and uncomfortable. There were moments of real anxiety—as when she
strained herself while lifting a log (doubtless for want of a man
to do the job) and "sat down in an agony, till I felt those said
twitches again." There were interminable hours of waiting—waiting for a letter from her beloved, waiting for the day of his return,
"when you shall read, whilst I mend my stockings," waiting for
that far-off time when they would be settled on their farm in
America. She knew that his trip to Havre was necessary if ever
he was to have the money needed to buy such a farm; yet she resented being separated from him in these crucial months before she
bore his child. Sometimes her resentment of his business intruded

even upon her expressions of tenderness. "Recollection now makes my heart bound to thee," she wrote one day; "but, it is not to thy money-getting face, though I cannot be seriously displeased with the exertion which increases my esteem, or rather is what I should have expected from thy character."

Whenever she received a letter from Imlay assuring her of his devotion, her distress gave way to joy. "Tell me also over and over again," she replied to one of his tender letters, "that your happiness (and you deserve to be happy!) is closely connected with mine, and I will try to dissipate, as they rise, the fumes of former discontent, that have too often clouded the sunshine which you have endeavoured to diffuse through my mind." But though she might sometimes dismiss her worries by laying them to her own melancholia, at other times she found her only consolation in the bitter thought expressed in another letter: "I do not know why, but I have more confidence in your affection, when absent, than present." Again and again the letters show that though Mary loved Imlay to distraction, though she tried to assure herself of his nobility and affection, she never felt positive that his love would endure.

Yet she could do nothing but wait. And meanwhile she was a prey to conflicting whims and emotions. In a single brief letter dated December 29, 1793, she shifted from mood to mood, apparently uncertain how she should treat the subject uppermost in her mind. At first she tried irony: "You seem to have taken up your abode at Havre. Pray sir! when do you think of coming home? or, to write very considerately, when will business permit you?" Next came exasperation: "Well! but, my love, to the old story—am I to see you this week, or this month?" Then she was coy: "I will cork up some of the kind things that were ready to drop from my pen, which has never been dipt in gall when addressing you; or, will only suffer an exclamation—'The creature!' or a kind of look, to escape me, when I pass the slippers, which I could not remove from my *salle* door, though they are not the handsomest of their kind." But she closed with the sober warning: "Be not too anxious to get money! for nothing worth having is to be purchased. God bless you."

Three days later, however, Mary's vacillation was gone. It was the beginning of a new year, Imlay still had not told her when he would return, and her patience had reached the breaking point. This time she made no effort to disguise her feelings:

As I have been, you tell me, three days without writing, I ought not to complain of two; yet, as I expected to receive a letter this afternoon, I am hurt; and why should I, by concealing it, affect the heroism I do not feel?

I hate commerce. How differently must - - -'s head and heart be organized from mine! You will tell me that exertions are necessary: I am weary of them! The face of things, public and private, vexes me. The "peace" and "clemency" which seemed to be dawning a few days ago, disappear again. "I am fallen," as Milton said, "on evil days;" for I really believe that Europe will be in a state of convulsion during half a century at least. Life is but a labour of patience: it is always rolling a great stone up a hill; for, before a person can find a resting-place, imagining it is lodged, down it comes again, and all the work is to be done over anew!

Should I attempt to write any more, I could not change the strain. My head aches, and my heart is heavy. The world appears an "unweeded garden" where "things rank and vile" flourish best.

If you do not return soon—or, which is no such mighty matter, talk of it—I will throw my slippers out at window, and be off—nobody knows where . . . .

Considering the care and anxiety a woman must have about a child before it comes into the world, it seems to me, by a *natural right,* to belong to her. When men get immersed in the world, they seem to lose all sensations, excepting those necessary to continue or produce life! Are these the privileges of reason? Amongst the feathered race, whilst the hen keeps the young warm, her mate stays by to cheer her; but it is sufficient for a man to condescend to get a child, in order to claim it. A man is a tyrant!

You may now tell me, that, if it were not for me, you would be laughing away with some honest fellows in London. The casual exercise of social sympathy would not be sufficient for me—I should not think such an heartless life worth preserving. It is necessary to be in good humour with you, to be pleased with the world.

The blue devils were plaguing her again. The future of Europe and her own future were alike discouraging. Her old resentment of male tyranny had returned. And at the bottom of all the trouble was Gilbert Imlay. It was on his account that she railed against business, against men, against life. Of course she would not rail against him! But her remarks implied criticism of him—and, unfortunately, often implied her superiority to him. It was hardly the way to hasten his return.

But a few days later, after she had received a "kind and rational letter" from him, she repented of her vehemence. After all, she had suffered fits of despondency before, only to find them unjustified. "It is time for me to grow more reasonable," she admitted; "a few more of these caprices of sensibility would destroy me." She blamed her distress on her weakened condition, begged for forgiveness, and revealed as never before how much her happiness depended on Imlay. "Write the moment you receive this," she urged him.

I shall count the minutes. But drop not an angry word. I cannot now bear it. Yet, if you think I deserve a scolding (it does not admit of a question, I grant), wait till you come back, and then, if you are angry one day, I shall be sure of seeing you the next . . . .

God bless you, my love; do not shut your heart against a return of tenderness; and, as I now in fancy cling to you, be more than ever my support.

The tone of her next few letters was equally submissive: she apologized for her "querulous humours," promised to go out more often to restore her health and spirits, and swore that she would never again "begin to encourage 'quick coming fancies,' when we are separated." When Imlay suggested that she come to Havre, she replied that she did not at the moment feel strong enough for the trip, but that she would join him in a fortnight if he had not returned meanwhile. And she consoled herself once again with the picture he had sketched of their future life in America with a family of six gathered about the hearth.

Thus Mary's worries vanished. She had been foolish, she told herself, to question Imlay's love; she never would have done so but for the melancholia which always tormented her when she was in poor health. She explained that she had been "very wretched since the night I was so cruelly hurt by thinking that you had no confidence in me," but that in all her distress she had not for a minute ceased to love him. "One thing you mistake in my character," she wrote, "and imagine that to be coldness, which is just the contrary. For, when I am hurt by the person most dear to me, I must let out a whole torrent of emotions, in which tenderness would be uppermost, or stifle them altogether; and it appears to me almost a duty to stifle them when I imagine *that I am treated with coldness.*" So once again all was serene. But if Imlay was a shrewd man, he must already have begun to realize that (in Virginia Woolf's phrase) while "tickling minnows" he had "hooked a dolphin."[35]

Soon Mary wrote that she was about to set out for Havre to stay with Imlay at the lodgings which he had engaged. Her heart glowed at the thought of seeing him again, and she confessed: "You have, by your tenderness and worth, twisted yourself more artfully round my heart than I supposed possible. Let me indulge the thought that I have thrown out some tendrils to cling to the elm by which I wish to be supported." She added wryly: "This is talking a new language for me!" But she hastened to assure her lover: "Knowing that I am not a parasite-plant, I am willing to receive the proofs of affection, that every pulse replies to, when I think of being once more in the same house with you."

In mid-January of 1794 Mary made the trip to Havre and settled down once again to enjoy the companionship of her lover.[36] Soon she was writing to Ruth Barlow: "My lodgings are pleasantly situated, and I have hired a maid servant, so that I am very comfortably settled, and shall remain so, if the high price of all the necessaries of life, do not ruin us."[37] She was busy, she added, with the manuscript of her book, finishing off the first volume of it, which was to be carried over to London by a Mr. Codman. Though she lamented "the want of my POOR BOOKS," she seemed happy and contented; and doubtless she was so during these last months before her confinement. She had escaped the horrors of life in Paris, her health and spirits had improved, and she was about to bear a child which would presumably bind her more closely to the man she loved. On March 10 she wrote to her sister Everina reporting that she was "safe, through the protection of an American, a most worthy man, who joins to uncommon tenderness of heart and

quickness of feeling, a soundness of understanding, and reason-
ableness of temper, rarely to be met with." And after deploring the
horrors she had witnessed since her arrival in France, she added:

I certainly am glad that I came to France, because I never could have had
else a just opinion of the most extraordinary event that has ever been recorded, and I have met with some uncommon instances of friendship, which
my heart will ever gratefully store up, and call to mind when the remembrance is keen of the anguish it has endured for its fellow-creatures, at large
—for the unfortunate beings cut off around me—and the still more unfortunate survivors.

Moreover, when Imlay was called back to Paris for a few days in
March, Mary wrote to him in a cheerful vein which suggests that
she now felt no doubt of her place in his affection. "I could not
sleep," she complained jokingly. "I turned to your side of the
bed, and tried to make the most of the comfort of the pillow, which
you used to tell me I was churlish about; but all would not do. I
took, nevertheless, my walk before breakfast, though the weather
was not inviting—and here I am, wishing you a finer day, and
seeing you peep over my shoulder, as I write, with one of your
kindest looks—when your eyes glisten, and a suffusion creeps over
your relaxing features." Apparently all was well now in the Imlay
ménage. Mary had doubtless persuaded herself that her uncertainty
of a few months back had been the product of upset nerves. But
now she had extricated herself from the fears that had dogged
her heart, and she would guard herself against lapsing into them
again.

Of course there were minor frictions: Imlay's imperfections
and Mary's passion for perfection must still have brought about
occasional squabbles. The child of nature who had captured
Mary's fancy had grown into a business man, and she could never
quite reconcile herself to his "money-getting face." She resented
his claim that business and love "will not chime together," but as
long as she could enjoy his company when business left him free,
she was reasonably content. Perhaps there was cause to believe that
his commercial venture would soon be completed; for on April 27
she wrote to Ruth Barlow:

I indulge the expectation of success, in which you are included, with great pleasure . . . . Teasing hinderance of one kind or other continually occur to us here . . . . Still we do not despair—Let but the first ground be secured— and in the course of the summer we may, perhaps celebrate our good luck, not forgetting good management, together.[38]

In the same letter Mary reported that she was well, that she had finished her book, and that "it cannot be long before this lively animal pops on us." Seventeen days later, on May 14, 1794, the lively animal popped. It proved to be a "vigorous little girl," who was named after Fanny Blood. Six days after the event Mary was writing again to Ruth Barlow, boasting that "you were so out in your calculation respecting the quantity of brains she was to have, and the skull it would require to contain them, that you made almost all the caps so small that I cannot use them." Childbirth, she remarked as one of the initiate, was "not smooth work," but she was pleased to report that her labor had been "natural" and "easy" and that she was now discommoded only by "an inundation of milk." "I dwell on these circumstances," she explained, "not only as I hope it will give you pleasure; but to prove that this struggle of nature is rendered much more cruel by the ignorance and affectation of women." She herself had disdained to take any advantage of her condition; in fact she had remained in bed only one day after the baby's birth, and a week later she had gone out walking. Her nurse was dumfounded at her resilience and assured her that she "ought to make children for the Republic," since she took the process so casually.

Naturally Mary was overjoyed to be able to announce that Imlay, though "rendered almost impatient" by "continual hinderances" and shifting embargoes, had proved to be a devoted father. Her highest hopes had been confirmed, and she had good reason to feel sure of her future happiness. "The constant tenderness of my most affectionate companion makes me regard a fresh tie as a blessing," she confided to Mrs. Barlow. And in a postscript she added jubilantly: "My little Girl begins to suck so MANFULLY that her father reckons saucily on her writing the second part of the R - - - ts of Woman."[39]

On July 8 she wrote again to Mrs. Barlow; and still her happiness seemed unmarred. She was very well, she announced, and Fanny "not only uncommonly healthy, but already, as sagacious as a child of five or six months old, which I rather attribute to my good, that is natural, manner of nursing her, than to any extraordinary strength of faculties." Imlay was unwell—even feverish—because of "continual disappointments" in his business affairs. Yet Mary seemed to sympathize with him—though she remarked that "the fulfilling of engagements appears to me of more importance than the making of a fortune." Indeed her only trace of unhappiness sprang from distress about the war. "The French will carry all before them," she wrote, "—but, my God, how many victims fall beneath the sword and the guillotine! My blood runs cold, and I sicken at thoughts of a Revolution which costs so much blood and bitter tears."[40]

Yet though Mary might seem wholly contented when writing to a friend, she must still have been haunted by misgivings about Imlay. She was not yet wholly satisfied with the love he gave her; something was missing. And when he went to Paris for a brief stay in August, she wrote him three letters, all of which reflect concern about the course of their love. After describing a visit with a French family, whose "house smelt of commerce from top to toe," she launched into an attack on "the demon of traffic." Then: "But I am philosophizing; nay, perhaps you will call me severe, and bid me let the square-headed money-getters alone. Peace to them! though none of the social sprites (and there are not a few, of different descriptions, who sport about the various inlets to my heart) gave me a twitch to restrain my pen." Probably she was trying to persuade Imlay to give up the business venture at once, to be content with the profit which he had already realized; for she concluded:

Yet, as common life, in my opinion, is scarcely worth having, even with a *gigot* every day, and a pudding added thereunto, I will allow you to cultivate my judgment, if you will permit me to keep alive the sentiments in your heart, which may be termed romantic, because, the offspring of the senses and the imagination, they resemble the mother more than the father, when they produce the suffusion I admire. In spite of icy age, I hope still to see it, if you have not determined only to eat and drink, and be stupidly useful to the stupid.

Two days later she wrote again. And though she assured Imlay that he was "the friend of my bosom, and the prop of my heart" —though she had found that she could not eat dinner alone in "the great room" because she missed him so—she seized upon a remark in his last letter that reason made him seek her happiness. And once again she was on the offensive. "I do not think it false delicacy, or foolish pride," she argued,

> to wish that your attention to my happiness should arise *as much* from love, which is always rather a selfish passion, as reason—that is, I want you to promote my felicity, by seeking your own. For, whatever pleasure it may give me to discover your generosity of soul, I would not be dependent for your affection on the very quality I most admire. No; there are qualities in your heart which demand my affection; but unless the attachment appears to me clearly mutual, I shall labour only to esteem your character instead of cherishing a tenderness for your person.

Such hair-splitting was hardly adapted to increase Imlay's ardor. Neither were the remarks included in the letter which Mary wrote on the following day:

> In *managing* my happiness, you now and then wounded my sensibility, concealing yourself till honest sympathy, giving you to me without disguise, lets me look into a heart, which my half-broken one wishes to creep into, to be revived and cherished. You have frankness of heart, but not often exactly that overflowing (*épanchement de coeur*), which becoming almost childish, appears a weakness only to the weak.

What did the woman want? Imlay must have asked himself. Could she not leave well enough alone? Must she make him over to her own specifications? And who could hope ever to fill those specifications?

Mary certainly did not feel that her affair with Imlay was falling to pieces. Her letters reveal that she still loved him devotedly and that she meant no malice by her criticisms. In fact, she could turn quickly from criticism to affection, or whatever might happen to pop into her mind. For example, her complaints about Imlay's lack of *épanchement de coeur* were introduced into her letter incidentally, apropos of some remarks about Tallien, the French statesman. A moment later she was urging Imlay to "enquire . . . whether, as a member declared in the Convention, Robespierre really maintained a *number* of mistresses"; and presently she was reporting that Fanny, "who has been almost springing out of my arm, . . . looks very like you; but I do not love her the less for that, whether I am angry or pleased with you."

Yet something was wrong: probably Mary was distressed to find that Imlay's love was less absorbing then her own, that to him it was gradually becoming subordinate to other interests. And she was fighting to gain first place in his mind and heart. Of course her complaints were not confined wholly to her letters. Earlier she had told him that she was "more confident of your affection when absent, than present." Now she told him: "When you are from me, I not only wonder how I can find fault with you, but how I can doubt your affection." The two must have had many a miserable hour in their lodgings at Havre. Mary could not hold her tongue, could not realize that Imlay would never understand her kind of love—the kind that could transcend anger or pleasure. Yet she would never quite admit to herself that he did not deserve the love she gave him, though her complaints suggest that she was half aware of the truth. And so she continued to cavil about this or that flaw in his nature—and, as she did so, to goad him ever closer to the point of wishing to be rid of her importunings.

But presently Mary had a new and more urgent matter to worry about: late in the summer Fanny fell ill with smallpox. Mary was naturally terrified—the more so because she had no confidence in the doctors at Havre. But as usual she rose to the occasion. She took the case into her own hands and proceeded to effect her own cure. "I . . . determined to follow the suggestions of my own reason," she later wrote to her sister Everina, "and saved her much pain, probably her life, for she was very full, by putting her twice a day into a warm bath." Fortunately the treatment proved successful, and soon Fanny was on the mend.

Before she was completely recovered, Imlay was called to Lon-

don for two months on business. Since the war between England
and France was at a standstill, Mary might have been able to travel
with him had she wanted to do so. But she remained behind, perhaps because of Fanny's health, perhaps by choice. She soon decided, however, that there was no reason why she should stay at
Havre. Most of her dearest friends were in Paris, and since the
downfall of Robespierre in July, order had prevailed there. Certainly she would be happier there, with her engaging friends, than
at Havre with only Imlay's business acquaintances for companionship. And so as soon as Fanny was able to travel, they set off by
stagecoach for the capital. It was a hectic trip. The coach overturned four times on the way, and Mary feared for her own life and
her child's. But eventually they reached Paris and settled down on
the outskirts of the city to pass the time until Imlay's return.

Meanwhile she had sent to Joseph Johnson the manuscript of
her latest work: *An Historical and Moral View of the Origin and
Progress of the French Revolution; and the Effect It Has Produced
in Europe, Volume the First.*[41] And presently, late in 1794, it was
published in London, where it naturally commanded attention as
the report of one who had seen the horrible effects of the Revolution and who wished to inform her countrymen of her impressions. But anyone who bought the book expecting to find confirmation for his hatred of revolutionary doctrines was disappointed.
Mary's conclusions about the Revolution had changed since the
time when she wrote her "Letter on the Present Character of the
French Nation." No longer did she despair of revolutionary doctrines or the future of mankind; in fact her new book was in a
sense a second "Letter to Edmund Burke," a reaffirmation of the
rights of men.

The eighteenth century reader who took up the book to learn
what new material Mary might have to offer after her observation
of the Revolution at first hand would also have been disappointed,
for she treated only the events up to October 19, 1789, more than
three years before her arrival in France. As the title implies, her
interest was not primarily in events but in their significance; and

though she presented her history chronologically, her real purpose was to prove to her English readers that the excesses of the Revolution were due not to a fallacy in the principles on which it was based, but to the character of the French people, corrupted by years of despotic government. Mary had gone to Paris eager to assist at the birth of liberty in Europe, only to be disappointed at the issue. But in the long run she had not been disillusioned; and she sought now to make others reflect on the events which had taken place, to consider their motivation in the past and their probable outcome in the future. True, the Revolution seemed to have miscarried, but that failure was only to be expected: what was more natural from men unused to thinking for themselves or acting on generous principles? Eventually, Mary argued, these men or their successors would learn to do both and would then establish in France a government which would insure the rights of all citizens.

The book was, therefore, history with a thesis; and the thesis was much more important to Mary than the historical facts which she presented. At times the book became virtually an essay on historical principles; for whether she was glancing back to catalogue the abuses of Louis XIV's reign or describing the grossness of the Revolutionary rabble, she recurred constantly to her fixed belief that the depravity of the French was due to past restraint rather than present liberty. Thus she devoted 522 quarto pages to narrating the events of the first three months of the Revolution; and although she sketched in the events of that period, quoted liberally from records of the Assembly, and discussed its legislation in detail, she did so only to reaffirm her confidence in the principles which had been betrayed.

Mary knew full well that all readers would not agree with her thesis. In her Preface she appealed for a reasonable approach to the facts which she was about to present. Sketching "the rapid changes, the violent, the base, and nefarious assassinations, which have clouded the vivid prospect that began to spread a ray of joy and gladness over the gloomy horizon of oppression" is, she remarked, "a task so arduous and melancholy, that, with a heart trembling to the touches of nature, it becomes necessary to guard against the erroneous inferences of sensibility; and reason beaming on the grand theatre of political changes, can prove the only sure guide to direct us to a favourable or just conclusion."[42] Then, like most reasonable historians of her time, she resorted to a quick survey of political history in order to convince her readers that governments had been corrupt in the past simply because they had been based on passion rather than reason. In pre-Revolutionary France, especially during the reign of Louis XIV, she found everywhere traces of utter depravity relieved only by "a taste for majestic frivolity." It was only natural, therefore, that "politeness took [the] place of humanity" and "almost every thing [was] said and done for stage effect." And as she reviewed the events of the early months of the Revolution, she paused again and again to demonstrate how the sentimentality or frivolity or effeminacy of the "headstrong French" had perverted the principles upon which their noble cause was based. From the very outset, she maintained, Frenchmen had "neither sufficient purity of heart nor maturity of judgment" to carry out a worthy revolution. To make matters worse, they had not digested the principles which underlay their revolt; they were, as Mary expressed it, "a little inebriated" with the doctrines of the liberal writers who had roused them to action. They seldom paused to deliberate on the reasonable course to follow; they acted quickly and precipitately. As a result, Mary declared, "we have seen the french engaged in a business the most sacred to mankind, giving, by their enthusiasm, splendid examples of their fortitude at one moment, and at another, by their want of firmness and deficiency of judgment, affording the most glaring and fatal proofs of the just estimate, which all nations have formed of their character."[43] Thus they were bound to err: the handicap of the past was too strong to be suddenly overcome. And at every step in the Revolution that handicap betrayed them. Because the Assembly was composed of men "totally destitute of experience in political science," it acted slowly and inefficiently.

Because the citizens had never learned what justice was, they failed to exercise "the moderation and reciprocity" needed for a working compromise. Again and again Mary repeated: the present anarchy in France was only the logical result of too abrupt a change after long years of tyranny. The Reign of Terror was not a natural consequence of revolutionary principles; rather, it resulted from a misunderstanding and perversion of those principles. The Revolution failed, and the ghastly excesses followed, Mary insisted, when the French "began to look for a degree of freedom in their government, incompatible with the present state of their manners; and of which they had no perfect idea."[44]

Yet Mary had not despaired of the cause of democracy, or even of the French Revolution itself. In her Preface she remarked that "the revolution was neither produced by the abilities or intrigues of a few individuals; nor was the effect of sudden and short-lived enthusiasm; but the natural consequence of intellectual improvement, gradually proceeding to perfection in the advancement of communities, from a state of barbarism to that of polished society."[45] And though the Revolution had miscarried momentarily, Mary believed that eventually its excesses would end, and good would come of evil. Her conclusions were consistent, of course, with all that had gone before; she had claimed that the Revolution failed because of the weaknesses of the French character, not the weaknesses of human character—or, in her phraseology, because of "moral depravity" rather than "innate turpitude." Thus she could legitimately hope for an improvement in the character of the French as their environment improved. "As a change also of the system of education and domestic manners will be a natural consequence of the revolution," she wrote, "the french will insensibly rise to a dignity of character far above that of the present race; and then the fruit of their liberty, ripening gradually, will have a relish not to be expected during it's crude and forced state."[46]

Wherever she looked, Mary saw evidence of the grand march of civilization toward perfection. To her, France was the first of the European nations to "throw off the yoke of old prejudices" simply because it was the most highly civilized; to her, reason was gaining sway, government was improving, and progress continued despite men's vanity and weakness. She could "contemplate with complacent serenity the approximation of the glorious era, when the appellations of fool and tyrant will be synonymous," when wars will be extinct (because free men are unconquerable), and when splendid cities like Paris will "rapidly crumble into decay" as men learn to disdain superficial splendor. It would, of course, take many years for the French to develop a satisfactory government, and many more for mankind to develop a satisfactory civilization. But in such matters Mary was as patient as she was optimistic.

There can be no argument with Mary's reasoning processes, but many readers would question her first principles. To her these were incontrovertible; they sprang from deep-rooted convictions, and she felt no call to substantiate them. Though her account of the Revolution itself was often rich in concrete detail, she offered little evidence to justify her interpretation of French character and her belief that the faults of the French issued directly from their despotic government. Indeed the effect of her book throughout was generalized rather than specific: she was writing about a system; and when she treated individuals, she considered them only as typical products of that system. Her old belief that character is the product of environment underlay her whole argument —so much so as almost to impel her to sympathize with Louis XVI and Marie Antoinette. Of the King she said: "The education of the heir apparent of a crown must necessarily destroy the common sagacity and feelings of a man; and the education of this monarch, like that of Louis XV, only tended to make him a sensual bigot."[47] And of the Queen she asked: "In such a voluptuous atmosphere, how could she escape contagion?"[48]

Like Mary's previous books, the *French Revolution* suffers from weakness of organization. Superficially it seems to have a clearer structure than her other works, but that is only because she had a chronological scheme to follow. However, since her purpose was not primarily historical, her adherence to chronology merely confuses her issues. The reader is led to believe that the events are more important than they were in Mary's mind. In fact only in her Preface and in her final chapter are the events properly subordinated to her apology for the Revolution.

But in some respects this book is superior to its predecessors. Certainly it is more unified. Mary did not diverge constantly from her announced subject to air her views on religion or education or female emancipation or any of the other topics which had so often distracted her from her central purpose. The book is more reasonable too—less dominated by personal feeling than Mary's other books. And in matters demanding incisive penetration, she showed marked improvement. She had seen more of life since she had been living in the midst of chaos; she knew men better, and she had greater confidence in the validity of her own observations on life. Thus her analyses of human behavior were more penetrating than hitherto; she was, as we say today, more "realistic." She was more expert, too, at discerning distinctions and at expressing herself exactly. For example, in distinguishing between the philosopher and the politician, she remarked that the philosopher "dedicates his exertions to promote the welfare, and perfection of mankind, carrying his views beyond any time he chooses to mark," while the politician has as his duty "to attend to the improvement and interest of the time in which he lives, and not sacrifice any present comfort to a prospect of future perfection or happiness."[49]

The style of the book is sometimes (as in the lines just quoted) clear and trenchant, and at other times, as in the following, richly rhetorical:

How silent is now Versailles!—The solitary foot, that mounts the sumptuous stair-case, rests on each landing-place, whilst the eye traverses the void, almost expecting to see the strong images of fancy burst into life.—The train of the Louises, like the posterity of the Banquoes, pass in solemn sadness, pointing at the nothingness of grandeur, fading away on the cold canvas,

which covers the nakedness of the spacious walls—whilst the gloominess of
the atmosphere gives a deeper shade to the gigantic figures, that seem to be
sinking into the embraces of death.[50]

But sooner or later Mary becomes too enamored of her "nervous"
style, and in trying to maintain its richness she slips into bathos.
Her description of Versailles, for example, reaches the nadir in a
cacophonous account of the "lascivious pictures, in which grace
varnishes voluptuousness, no longer seductive," and which "strike
continually home to the bosom the melancholy moral, that antic-
ipates the frozen lesson of experience."

Though the longest of her later works, Mary's *French Revolution* has least interest for a modern reader. Because she rarely de-
parted from her announced topic, it contained practically no indication of the progress of her thinking about religion, philosophy,
or education. And because she wrote about events which happened
long before her arrival in France, it is devoid of autobiographical
interest. Indeed, apart from her thesis, the book is negligible. It is
the result of historical research performed before adequate materials were available—a compound of various earlier accounts of
the first months of the Revolution expanded by quotations from
the *Journal des Débats et des Décrets* of the National Assembly,[51]
and by occasional references to such commentators as Mirabeau,
Rabaut St. Etienne, and Lally-Tolendal. There is even reason to
believe that for some of her factual material Mary was content
to carry her researches no further than the *New Annual Register*
for 1791. If so, she would certainly have defended herself by claiming, as was quite true, that facts were of only secondary importance
to her; what mattered was that the interpretation of those facts be
reasonable and just. Mary's talents and judgment had matured in
the four years since she had published her *Vindication of the
Rights of Men*; but she was still a propagandist.

Like most propaganda, the book soon outlived its popularity.
Yet it was reasonably well received at first. Johnson brought out a
second edition in 1795, and in the same year another edition,
doubtless pirated, was issued in Dublin. John Adams read the book

with interest and made frequent observations in the margins of his copy.[52] And another reader, John Henry Colls, was inspired to address a "poetical epistle" to Mary on her achievements in this book and her *Rights of Woman.*

The reviewers lined up much as one might expect. The *Analytical* was favorable, and so was the liberal *Monthly Review,* which praised particularly the author's philosophical point of view and "the metaphorical cast of her language." The *Critical Review* was naturally much less enthusiastic: its critic damned Mary's contempt for the Crown and maintained, with some justification, that she should have confined herself either to history of the Revolution or to reflections on its significance. Much more damaging, however, was the review in the *British Critic,* which presented five parallel passages from Mary's book and the *New Annual Register* to prove that she had borrowed too generously. The reviewer continued. "This work . . . is now to be considered as an abridgement of the history of the French revolution given in the New Annual Register, with moral, political, and miscellaneous reflections"; and he proceeded to flay Mary's morality, her political ideas, and her style, with special attention to her tendency to mix her metaphors.[53] She might have profited a good deal by reading the latter part of the review.

But she was too far away to see or be disturbed by the claims of the *British Critic.* And if she had read the article, she would probably have been much less disturbed by it than by earlier criticisms of her work. She had new interests now, interests to which her writing took a second place. She had a lover—whom she considered a husband—and a daughter. She had created a whole new life for herself in France—a private world into which critics could not penetrate.

Back in England, her sisters, able to hear from her only rarely, were puzzled. Mary had written in March, 1794, that she was "safe, through the protection of an American." Then in August came news from Joseph Johnson and from their brother Charles in

America that Mary was married. It was incredible, and Eliza could only "doubt my senses" when she heard the report. And even as she sought to reconcile herself to the thought, as she discussed it in a letter to Everina, she exclaimed, "Yet Mary cannot be *Married!!*"

Eliza was right. Mary was not married; she was indeed in a precarious position, subject to the whims of an irresponsible lover. Her future happiness depended altogether on his constancy. And of that she had already suffered momentary doubts.

CHAPTER VIII

Frustration and Despair
(1794-1796)

My friend, I have dearly paid for one conviction.
—Letter to Imlay.

FOR SOME time after Imlay's departure for London, Mary had no reason to suppose that they would never again live together. Her letters continued much as before, with occasional complaints or criticisms apparently thrown in without a hint of malice.[1] "Shall I talk about alum or soap?" she asked in her first letter. "There is nothing picturesque in your present pursuits; my imagination, then, rather chooses to ramble back to the barrier with you, or to see you coming to meet me, and my basket of grapes." Then, after a paragraph in praise of the imagination (for which Imlay had evidently expressed scant respect) she added:

If you call these observations romantic, a phrase in this place which would be tantamount to nonsensical, I shall be apt to retort, that you are embruted by trade and the vulgar enjoyments of life. Bring me back then your barrier-face, or you shall have nothing to say to my barrier-girl; and I shall fly from you, to cherish the remembrances that will ever be dear to me, for I am yours truly . . . .

Always she blamed business for his coolness; as yet she had not once accused him of faithlessness. And she continued to live in the delusion that his preoccupation when they were together and his neglect when they were apart were only temporary.

On her side love was intensified every day by her growing affection for her lively baby daughter, the "little Hercules." Fanny soon recovered from her attack of smallpox and was a constant delight to her mother, who reported that the baby was "a little affectionate, intelligent creature, with as much vivacity, I should think, as you could wish for." At times, of course, she was a nuisance: she had an annoying habit of waking too early in the morning and cutting short her mother's rest. To make matters

worse, the nurse who had accompanied them from Havre to
Paris now proved to be pregnant and was of so little assistance that
Mary soon discharged her. There were other vexations: all the
little details that can plague a woman living without her husband. But Fanny could chase the memory of them all quite away.
Her mother was surprised and fascinated to trace in herself the
development of maternal affection. "I once told you," she wrote
to Imlay, "that the sensations before she was born, and when she
was sucking, were pleasant; but they do not deserve to be compared to the emotions I feel, when she stops to smile upon me,
or laughs outright on meeting me unexpectedly in the street, or
after a short absence." And the warmth of Mary's affection for
the baby restrained her criticism of the father. In describing the
growing resemblance between the two, she was careful to remark
that Fanny recalled to her Imlay's "best looks," adding, "for I do
not admire your commercial face." But she soon forgot the sarcasm
and confessed in the same letter that she "began to think that
there was something in the assertion of man and wife being one—
for you seemed to pervade my whole frame, quickening the beat
of my heart, and lending me the sympathetic tears you excited."
And as time passed, Mary frequently observed that any harsh
remarks which she had been about to make had been driven away
by the tenderness she felt at a smile or embrace from the baby.
Eventually, in fact, she confessed that her unhappiness about
Imlay's preoccupation with business was "much more lively soon
after you went away, than at present."

Despite her occasional complaints Mary was probably happy
and contented during these first two months at Paris. She was
among friends again, in a city which was rousing itself with
relief after the nightmare of the Reign of Terror. On October 26
she wrote one of the sprightliest of all her letters to Imlay. She
had hired two good nurses to care for Fanny, she reported, and
had been able to spare time to study her French again and apparently to go more often into society. Her new-found liberty had
cheered her considerably. She deliberately played the coquette,

telling her lover that she had "almost *charmed* a judge of the tribunal" and that she soon would be "half in love" with Rouget de Lisle, author of "La Marseillaise," whom she had recently met. She concluded, though, in the most affectionate terms:

My heart longs for your return, my love, and only looks for, and seeks happiness with you; yet do not imagine that I childishly wish you to come back before you have arranged things in such a manner that it will not be necessary for you to leave us soon again, or to make exertions which injure your constitution.

There is not a hint of complaint or criticism in the letter. For the time being, at least, Mary was free of all her doubts and worries. She was looking forward to Imlay's early return, she had Fanny to cheer her solitary hours, and she was among friends whose company she enjoyed.

Two of those friends have left impressions of Mary at this period which confirm the belief that she was enjoying herself during her stay in Paris. The Swiss Madeleine Schweitzer wrote:

I passed one evening with her in the country. The blending of the varying tints of colour in the sky were of a marvellous poetical beauty. Mary was sitting with the B[aron] de W[alzogen?] beneath a tree gilded by the rays of the setting sun. I was opposite them, and was so enraptured by the scene that I said to [her]: "Come, Mary,—come, nature lover,—and enjoy this wonderful spectacle—this constant transition from colour to colour!" But, to my great surprise, Mary was so indifferent that she never turned her eyes from him by whom she was at the moment captivated.[2]

And Archibald Hamilton Rowan, the mercurial Irish rebel in exile, who met her at about this time, seemed to find her in excellent spirits. He wrote in a letter to his wife some time afterwards:

On the day of the celebration of one of the numerous feasts with which this country has abounded . . . Mr. B[ingham] who was with me, joined a lady who spoke English, and who was followed by her maid with an infant in her arms, which I found belonged to the lady. Her manners were interesting and her conversation spirited, yet not out of her sex. B[ingham] whispered me that she was the author of the *Rights of Woman*. I started! "What!" said I within myself, "this is Miss Mary Wollstonecraft, parading about with a child at her heels, with as little ceremony as if it were a watch she had just bought at the jeweler's. So much for the rights of women," thought I . . . . My society, which before that time, was wholly male, was now most agreeably increased, and I got a dish of tea, and an hour's rational conversation whenever I called on her.[3]

By the end of November Imlay's two months in London had elapsed, and he was scheduled to return to Paris shortly. From London he wrote a very formal letter to Eliza Bishop, referring to Mary as "Mrs. Imlay," assuring Eliza that "whenever she has it in her power" her sister would "apply some specific aid to promote your happiness," and announcing that he expected to leave for Paris at the beginning of the following week.[4] According to Godwin[5] Imlay left London but, after getting as far as Ramsgate, was recalled. Of course he could not notify Mary promptly of the change in his plans, and because there had been storms at sea, she was "tormented by fears" until she heard from him. When she wrote to him on December 26, her affectionate tone of two months earlier was only intensified by the anxiety which she had undergone. Yet beneath it was a new note of foreboding. "I want to be sure that you are safe," she wrote,

and not separated from me by a sea that must be passed. For, feeling that I am happier than I ever was, do you wonder at my sometimes dreading that fate has not done persecuting me? Come to me, my dearest friend, husband, father of my child! All these fond ties glow at my heart this moment, and dim my eyes. With you an independence is desirable; and it is always within our reach, if affluence escapes us—without you the world again appears empty to me.

Two days later, when she wrote again, the note of foreboding was even stronger. A month had passed since the time set for Imlay's return, and now his partner in Paris was urging further delays.[6] "I wish then, to counteract, in some measure, what he has doubtless recommended most warmly," she wrote. She insisted that she had no desire to amass a large fortune, that for reasonable people like themselves business should always remain "a secondary object," that she would be "hurt, rather than made angry," by further delays. "It appears to me absurd to waste life in preparing to live," she declared. And then, as if in apology for her tiresome insistence: "Having suffered so much in life, do not be surprised if I sometimes, when left to myself, grow gloomy, and suppose that it was all a dream, and that my happiness is not to last." Obviously Mary was worried again. Imlay's partner was urging

him to remain in London, and she longed to have him return.
Would his decision reveal where his keenest interests lay? Would
she learn presently whether it was herself or his business which
was the "secondary object" in his mind? Apparently she feared so;
and her attempt to hold him was only thinly disguised by playfulness. *"I do not consent* to your taking any other journey," she
stated emphatically, "or the little woman and I will be off, the
Lord knows where."

The next day she continued her appeal, this time with much
less playfulness. She was, she assured him, "really tormented by
the desire which --- manifests to have you remain where you are."
And she exclaimed:

How I hate this crooked business! This intercourse with the world, which
obliges one to see the worst side of human nature! Why cannot you be
content with the object you had first in view when you entered into this
wearisome labyrinth? I know very well that you have been imperceptibly
drawn on; yet why does one project, successful or abortive, only give place
to two others? Is it not sufficient to avoid poverty? I am contented to do my
part; and, even here, sufficient to escape from wretchedness is not difficult
to obtain. And, let me tell you, I have my project also, and, if you do not
soon return, the little girl and I will take care of ourselves; we will not
accept any of your cold kindness—your distant civilities—no; not we.

She went on to say that "this is but half jesting," and in truth it
seems considerably less than that; for presently she described a
poor German woman whom she pitied for her poverty but envied
for her devoted husband. And in conclusion she showed that she
had faced the possibility of a permanent separation from Imlay
when she wrote: "It is your own maxim to 'live in the present
moment.' *If you do,* stay, for God's sake; but tell me the truth—if
not, tell me when I may expect to see you, and let me not be
always vainly looking for you, till I grow sick at heart."

The next day Mary announced in a letter that she was determined to earn some money in order to prove that she and Fanny
could, if necessary, be independent. She apologized for repeating
her threat by saying that she feared that only one out of three of
her letters would ever reach him in England. She insisted once
again that she was "not of --- 's opinion, who talks till he makes

me angry, of the necessity of your staying two or three months longer." And in her anger she resorted to her old theories: men, she declared, are "systematic tyrants," and "if they debauch their hearts, and prostitute their persons, following perhaps a gust of inebriation, they suppose the wife, slave rather, whom they maintain, has no right to complain, and ought to receive the sultan, whenever he deigns to return, with open arms, though his have been polluted by half an hundred promiscuous amours during his absence." Then she disclosed the fear that was haunting her mind: "If a wandering of the heart, or even a caprice of the imagination detains you, there is an end of all my hopes of happiness. I could not forgive you if I would." And from the depths of her despair: "Say but one word, and you shall never hear of me more."

Ten days later, on January 9, 1795, Mary wrote again in despair. She was lonely, she said, and found little consolation in the hasty notes which Imlay sent her. She had no servant and, for want of wood to build a fire, had caught "the most violent cold I ever had." Again she complained of Imlay's business: "I should have been content, and still wish, to retire with you to a farm. My God! anything but these continual anxieties, anything but commerce, which debases the mind, and roots out affection from the heart." Again she threatened that she and Fanny would run away if he did not return soon. But this time she did not pretend to be "half jesting"; on the contrary she warned: "This is not a caprice of the moment, for your absence has given new weight to some conclusions that I was very reluctantly forming before you left me. I do not choose to be a secondary object. If your feelings were in unison with mine, you would not sacrifice so much to visionary prospects of future advantage."

Never for a moment did she suggest that her own love had cooled. In fact, on January 15, after she had received two letters from Imlay, her "anger died away," and she abandoned complaints to describe Fanny's first two teeth, her squirrel-like liveliness, and her bouncing good health. And on the 30th, though exasperated at his delays, she refused to rehearse her complaints. "It is useless," she wrote, "for me to say any more on the subject. I have done with it for ever . . . ." Yet on February 9 she was more despondent than ever before. Imlay had written that he had decided to stay on in London for a while, and she interpreted the news as evidence that she had lost her battle to wrest his mind from business. He had, to be sure, suggested that she join him in London—only to intimate that he might, after all, return to Paris presently.

Mary's mind was utterly confused. Should she go to England or remain where she was? Could he possibly be hoping to avoid a reunion? And if so, should she not make a clean break at once? She wrote:

> The melancholy presentiment has for some time hung on my spirits, that we were parted for ever; and the letters I received this day, by Mr. - - -, convince me that it was not without foundation . . . .
> When I determined to live with you, I was only governed by affection. I would share poverty with you, but I turn with affright from the sea of troubles on which you are entering. I have certain principles of action; I know what I look for to found my happiness on. It is not money. With you I wished for sufficient to procure the comforts of life, as it is, less will do. I can still exert myself to obtain the necessaries of life for my child, and she does not want more at present. I have two or three plans in my head to earn our subsistence; for do not suppose that, neglected by you, I will lie under obligations of a pecuniary kind to you! No; I would sooner submit to menial service . . . .
> Perhaps this is the last letter you will ever receive from me.

It would have been well for Mary if this had been her last letter to Imlay. But though he had doubtless tired of her, he realized that his conduct was contemptible. For months he waited for her to say what he was too cowardly to say: that their affair was ended. Meanwhile Mary suffered in mind and body. All the nervousness and debility of former years returned to torment her, and her letters were weighed down by her oppression of mind and body. On February 10 she believed herself to be in "a galloping consumption"; she was suffering nightly fevers again and making plans for Fanny's future in the event of her own death. Again she berated Imlay for his materialism, prophesying: "For a year or two

you may procure yourself what you call pleasure; but, in the solitude of declining life, I shall be remembered with regret—I was
going to say with remorse, but checked my pen." She had come
full circle now—back to the morbid depression of her year in Ireland. Meanwhile Imlay was doubtless coming more and more to
the conclusion that her melancholy was constitutional, and that he
had been foolhardy to let himself become involved in her affairs.

By February 19 she was calmer; but as she herself said, "The
more I think, the sadder I grow." Imlay, now alarmed by the
increasing despondency of her letters, was urging that she might
cross over to England; yet she was loath to do so. She felt, she told
him, "a repugnance that almost amounts to horror" at the thought
of living in England again. She probably knew that, though in
republican France her relations with Imlay were accepted as evidence of freedom from tiresome conventions, in England she
would be branded as a kept woman. Yet evidently anything was
better than the separation which she herself had first threatened,
for by April 7 she was at Havre again en route to London. Her
dying hopes had been sparked by a letter from Imlay saying,
"Business alone has kept me from you.—Come to any port, and
I will fly down to my two dear girls with a heart all their own."[7]
Yet she still was not sure that her troubles had ended. "I sit, lost in
thought, looking at the sea," she wrote from Havre; "and tears
rush into my eyes when I find that I am cherishing any fond
expectations." She was torn by warring emotions, for she dared
not "indulge the very affectionate tenderness which glows in my
bosom, without trembling, till I see, by your eyes, that it is mutual."

Two days later she was hurried off, with Fanny and her nurse
Marguerite, to her ship at an hour's notice. But the pilot ran the
vessel aground, and she was forced to return to her house in
Havre and wait impatiently for her departure.[8] Presently she was
called again to the ship, and on April 11 she was at Brighthelm-
stone (Brighton) writing to Imlay that she would meet him at
his hotel in London. Of the problem which had so long been pend-

ing and which was soon to be settled, she wrote only, "What does your heart say?"

The reunion on the following day only strengthened her fears. Imlay was preoccupied and ill at ease. Again he begged the pressure of business. And as time passed, Mary realized that his affection for her had died. Still, however, she struggled to revive it; she who had threatened to leave him a few weeks before could not bear the thought of a separation, now that she had seen him again. But once more she chose the wrong course to win his heart: she argued, she demanded rational explanations for his behavior —and she only repulsed him whom she yearned to retain. The constant arguments and explanations, designed to convince a thoroughly rational man, failed to move the sensualist Imlay. In his calmer days he might have heeded her appeals; but no more. He had presumably become infatuated with a young actress, and no appeal from Mary could reach him. But still he lacked the courage to tell her outright that he no longer loved her. Instead he postponed making any final decision and settled her and Fanny in a furnished house at 26 Charlotte Street, Rathbone Place. But the arrangement could not last long; for obviously Imlay was trying to salve his conscience—trying to do his duty and no more. And Mary was not the woman to be satisfied with mere dutiful treatment.

But though she must soon have despaired of regaining his affection, pride made her conceal her suffering from others. Late in April she wrote to her sister Eliza enclosing a small sum of money and bravely promising more. "When Mr. Imlay and I united our fate together, he was without fortune," she explained;

since that, there is a prospect of his obtaining a considerable one; but though the hope appears to be well founded, I cannot yet act as if it were a certainty. He is the most generous creature in the world, and if he succeed, as I have the greatest reason to think he will, he will, in proportion to his acquirement of property, enable me to be useful to you and Everina. I wish you and her could adopt any plan in which five or six hundred pounds could be of use.

Then, because she had surmised that Eliza had hopes of settling with her and Imlay, Mary added:

> I know you will think me unkind—and it was this reflection that has prevented my writing to you sooner, not to invite you to come and live with me. But, Eliza, it is my opinion, not a readily formed one, the presence of a third person interrupts or destroys domestic happiness. Excepting this sacrifice, there is nothing I would not do to promote your comfort. I am hurt at being obliged to be thus explicit and do indeed feel severely for the disappointments which you have met with in Life.

Mary's pretense is obvious enough to anyone who knows her situation: she could not bear the thought of revealing her troubles to her sisters. Eliza, however, interpreted the letter as a gross insult. The poor woman, whose nerves were never steady, had been feeding on hopes for months. Mary had promised to find her a situation in France; Charles had asked her to join him in America; James had suggested that she settle with him in France—and all had come to nothing. Lately she had been buoyed up by the news that Imlay had made a fortune of £100,000; and now came Mary's small remittance and her clear statement that Eliza must not plan to take refuge at her house. It was too much! All the resentment against the world stored up during her four hateful years in Wales was released. "Good God, what a letter!" she wrote to Everina.

> How have I merited such pointed cruelty? I may say *insolence*. When did I wish to live with her? At what time wish, for a moment, to interrupt their *Domestic* happiness? Was ever a present offered in so humiliating a style? Ought the poorest domestick to be thus insulted? . . . This letter has so strongly agitated me that I know not what I say; but . . . I am positive I will never torment our amiable friend in CHARLOTTE Street.

Earlier Mary would have been deeply hurt by Eliza's resentment, but now it must have seemed relatively unimportant. She had been so deeply wounded that she was doubtless impervious to lesser injuries.[9]

At last, sometime in May, Mary's grief became intolerable. Her old confidence in herself was now completely dissipated. Hitherto whenever she had mentioned the possibility of her death, she had worried about what might happen to Fanny. But now even that problem failed to deter her. She was convinced that she could not go on. She was desperate, and she could think of only one possible escape from her misery: suicide. No one knows what means she chose or how far she carried out her plan. Somehow Imlay learned of it and managed to intercept it. And so Mary was unwillingly obliged to abandon the attempt, to grapple again with the problem which she longed to evade. Now, more than ever before, Imlay must have realized how grave a situation he was facing. For though he may have sought to reassure Mary in one way or other, he probably loved her only the less for her desperate action. Naturally he wanted their affair to end in no such scandal. He must, then, find a means of keeping her reasonably calm until such time as she herself would agree that their love had burned itself out.

And so he suggested that she go abroad. His affairs in the Scandinavian countries needed attention, and he himself could not spare the time for an extended trip. On May 19, 1795, he executed a document empowering "Mary Imlay, my best friend and wife," to serve as his agent in "all my affairs and business which I had placed in the hands of Mr Elias Backman, negociant, Gottenburg, or in those of Messrs Myburg & Co., Copenhagen," and to collect whatever sum might be awarded him in his suit against one Peter Ellisson for violation of trust.[10] Doubtless Imlay congratulated himself on having found an ideal solution for his difficulties. If Mary were away from London, life would certainly be a good deal simpler for him. Perhaps a change of scene would settle her nerves too and enable her to resign herself to the only possible course for them. At least it would postpone the disagreeable decision which he was expected to make. As for Mary, she must have agreed to the scheme with only faint enthusiasm; the despondency which had carried her to the point of suicide had certainly not yet left her. There was, to be sure, one incentive: Imlay had promised to meet her in Switzerland for a holiday after she had completed her business in the North. And she doubtless found a melancholy pleasure, as Godwin suggests, in serving the man who had injured her.

Of course she made her plans for the trip with a heavy heart. On May 22, in answer to an "affectionate letter" from Imlay, she wrote:

I have laboured to calm my mind since you left me. Still I find that tranquillity is not to be obtained by exertion; it is a feeling so different from the resignation of despair! I am, however, no longer angry with you, nor will I ever utter another complaint; there are arguments which convince the reason, whilst they carry death to the heart. We have had too many cruel explanations, that not only cloud every future prospect, but embitter the remembrances which alone give life to affection. Let the subject never be revived!

The truth was, however, that Mary could not help reviving the subject; she could not resign herself to failure, and she still hoped for a happy outcome to all her sorrow. "My friend—my dear friend—," she begged, "examine yourself well. I am out of the question; for, alas! I am nothing, and discover what you wish to do—what will render you most comfortable—or, to be more explicit, whether you desire to live with me, or part for ever! When you can once ascertain it, tell me frankly, I conjure you! for, believe me, I have very involuntarily interrupted your peace." But she begged in vain. Imlay still refused to reach a decision, and he apparently allowed her just enough of his company to keep her constantly distraught. And after all her begging, she closed with the pathetic promise that she would try to "assume a cheerful face" to greet him when he came to dine with her on the following Monday.

On or about Tuesday, June 9, Mary set out by mail-coach for Hull with Fanny and her French nursemaid Marguerite.[11] Doubtless worn out before she started, Mary found the trip exhausting. But Fanny enjoyed every minute of it and amused herself by imitating the sound of the mail-horn. At night, however, she refused to be separated from her mother, and Mary had little sleep. To add to her discomfort, they were forced to lodge, on their arrival at Hull, in a "comfortless, damp room, in a sort of tomb-like house" in the "frightful, dirty, *brick-housey,* tradesmanlike, rich, vulgar" town which Dorothy Wordsworth was later to find so obnoxious, and which was scarcely designed to please Mary in her depressed state of mind. She felt homesick—or rather, sick for want of a home. Once again she was tearing up roots; she was wrenching herself from everything that suggested permanence, setting off on a trip which might well end in bitter disappointment. "Imlay,—dear Imlay," she wrote,

am I always to be tossed about thus? shall I never find an asylum to rest *contented* in? How can you love to fly about continually, dropping down, as it were, in a new world—cold and strange—every other day! Why do you not attach those tender emotions round the idea of home, which even now dim my eyes? This alone is affection—every thing else is only humanity, electrified by sympathy.

Thanks to a friend who had given her a letter of introduction to a physician at Hull, Mary was not left entirely alone during her tiresome wait for favorable winds. The day after her arrival the physician's wife drove her to nearby Beverley, where she had lived as a girl, and Mary had a chance to observe the changes which time had wrought—in herself, if not in the town. "I ran over my favourite walks with a vivacity that would have astonished you," she wrote to Imlay. "The town did not please me quite so well as formerly. It appeared so diminutive; and when I found that many of the inhabitants had lived in the same houses ever since I left it, I could not help wondering how they could thus have vegetated, whilst I was running over a world of sorrow, snatching at pleasure, and throwing off prejudices." She visited in the physician's home too, and found him to be "an intelligent and rather interesting man," and his wife a charming woman. "I can admire, you know, a pretty woman, when I am alone," she added parenthetically. And she remarked that "poor Fanny was never so happy in her life as amongst their young brood."

But most of the time during the eleven days which Mary spent in waiting for her ship to sail was doubtless devoted to anxious wondering about her fate. She wrote to Imlay almost every day. She was despondent, of course, and complained of violent fits of trembling when she awoke in the morning. She described how she "looked at the sea, and at my child, hardly daring to own to myself the secret wish, that it might become our tomb." And she tried, by every means at her command, to regain the affection of her lover. Now she was preaching to him:

Ah! my friend, you know not the ineffable delight, the exquisite pleasure, which arises from an unison of affection and desire, when the whole soul and senses are abandoned to a lively imagination, that renders every emotion delicate and rapturous. Yes; these are emotions, over which satiety has no power, and the recollection of which, even disappointment cannot disenchant; but they do not exist without self-denial. These emotions, more or less strong, appear to me to be the distinctive characteristic of genius, the foundation of taste, and of that exquisite relish for the beauties of nature, of which the common herd of eaters and drinkers and *child-begetters* certainly have no idea.

Now she was appealing to his better nature:

I cannot indeed, without agony, think of your bosom's being continually contaminated; and bitter are the tears which exhaust my eyes, when I recollect why my child and I are forced to stray from the asylum, in which, after so many storms, I had hoped to rest, smiling at angry fate. These are not common sorrows; nor can you perhaps conceive how much active fortitude it requires to labour perpetually to blunt the shafts of disappointment.

Sometimes she pleaded:

Do write by every occasion! I am anxious to hear how your affairs go on; and, still more, to be convinced that you are not separating yourself from us. For my little darling is calling papa, and adding her parrot word— Come, Come! And will you not come, and let us exert ourselves?

Sometimes she lapsed into transparent rhetorical devices:

Accuse me not of pride—yet sometimes, when nature has opened my heart to its author, I have wondered that you did not set a higher value on my heart.

Receive a kiss from Fanny, I was going to add, if you will not take one from me . . . .

And at times she tried to describe the torments she was suffering on his account:

My spirits are agitated, I scarcely know why . . . . A thousand weak forebodings assault my soul, and the state of my health renders me sensible to everything. It is surprising that in London, in a continual conflict of mind,

I was growing still better, whilst here, bowed down by the despotic hand of fate, forced into resignation by despair, I seem to be fading away—perishing beneath a cruel blight, that withers up all my faculties.

And still she waited. The days dragged along interminably.

Finally, on the afternoon of Tuesday, June 16, she was summoned to the harbor. The wind had shifted, and the ship was to depart at once for Helsingör (Elsinore). But before nightfall the wind had veered back, leaving the vessel to drift slowly with the tide. So once again Mary waited.

At first she seemed to be better pleased with her surroundings on shipboard than when she had been in Hull. She found the captain to be "a civil, open-hearted, kind of man," and she took comfort in her solitary hours of reading and writing in the cabin. But her mind was still far from calm; she was, as she said, "in every mood," and her letters to Imlay often verge on utter distraction. For example:

My dear friend, my heart sinks within me! Why am I forced thus to struggle continually with my affections and feelings? Ah, why are those affections and feelings the source of so much misery, when they seem to have been given to vivify my heart and extend my usefulness! But I must not dwell on this subject. Will you not endeavour to cherish all the affection you can for me? What am I saying? Rather, forget me, if you can—if other gratifications are dearer to you. How is every remembrance of mine embittered by disappointment? What a world is this! They only seem happy who never look beyond sensual or artificial enjoyments. Adieu!

Soon solitude and the novelty of being on shipboard palled on her. "In spite of the commodiousness of the vessel," she wrote, "everything here would disgust my senses, had I nothing else to think of." She shivered constantly from "the Northeast *chillers*"; and the "disagreeable smells" of the ship robbed her of her appetite. When Marguerite, the nursemaid, fell seasick from the constant rocking of the boat, Mary was obliged to take full charge of the baby, who was teething. "These are, however, trifling inconveniences," Mary wrote, "compared with anguish of mind, compared with the sinking of a broken heart. To tell you the truth, I never suffered in my life so much from depression of spirits, from despair. I do not sleep, or if I close my eyes, it is to have the most terrifying dreams, in which I often meet you with different casts of countenance." Her only relief came from the occasional letters of the man responsible for her misery.

On the fifth day of confinement aboard the ship Mary and her baby went ashore with the captain to buy some provisions and spend the night in Hull. The next morning (Sunday, June 21) they were called back to the ship. The wind had at last shifted, and the long wait had ended. Naturally Mary welcomed the chance to be off; she had sickened of her "lingering adieu" and had lost all her reluctance to leave England again.

Yet the voyage itself was hardly more agreeable than the long wait which had preceded it. The weather was rough, the food served on the ship was revolting, and Marguerite continued to be seasick. Mary fought constantly against fatigue but could find no rest; again she looked out over the water and longed to drown herself and her misery.

On the morning of Friday, the 26th, she awoke to learn that the ship had passed both Arendal, Norway, and Gothenburg during the night. Mary, who had arranged to be put down at either port, found herself sailing on toward Helsingör. Fortunately, however, the ship was becalmed a few miles beyond Gothenburg, and the captain headed toward a lighthouse on a nearby island to signal for a pilot to take his passengers ashore. For two hours they watched in vain for a boat to appear. Then the captain explained that Swedish pilots were so poorly paid that they seldom performed more than the minimum duty exacted of them. Mary was moved to pertinent reflections on the effects of despotism; but she was at a loss to think how she could get ashore.

She was not long stalemated. She argued with (and bribed) the captain to allow her to be taken to the lighthouse in the ship's boat. For a long time he refused ("Common minds seldom break through general rules," Mary observed in describing the transaction); but at last he consented, and Mary set off at once toward the lighthouse with Marguerite, Fanny, and a few sailors. She had no notion what adventures she might encounter, but she was, as usual, dauntless.

At the lighthouse they found only two old men who had no boat and could therefore be of no help to her. They directed her to the house of a pilot eight or ten miles away, on the other side of the island, and Mary bribed the sailors to row her to it. Two hours later—after traveling along a picturesque but, even to Mary, rather formidable coast—they reached the pilot's hut, only to be directed to the house of a superior officer, a retired lieutenant who spoke English. Again they pushed off in their little boat, now headed for the lieutenant's cottage; but presently they met the lieutenant himself, come to investigate the new arrivals. Mary discharged her sailors at once and, much to Marguerite's consternation, transferred immediately to the strange lieutenant's boat. Her confidence proved to be justified; for he rowed them at once to a neat cottage, where his wife served them lunch.

That afternoon Mary insisted on climbing to a nearby cliff to make sure that the sailors had succeeded in reaching their ship again. Then she went with her host to call on a neighboring family and afterwards engaged a "car with post-horses" to carry her the twenty-odd miles to Gothenburg on the following day.

But her troubles were not yet over. While she was walking to the car next morning, she fell suddenly on the rocks. Evidently the griefs and exertions of the past weeks had at last overpowered her. But though she remained unconscious for fifteen minutes, she soon mastered herself and set off on her journey—a cheerless one, thanks to rain, and a rather terrifying one, thanks to the "sudden acclivities and descents" of the road. At least Marguerite found the trip terrifying; Mary's courage, as usual, sustained her. Once again she was obliged to take full charge of the baby while the nursemaid indulged her fears.

At Gothenburg they were forced to put up at an uncomfortable inn, where they could obtain neither fire nor warm food to cheer them after their strenuous trip. When Mary wrote that evening to Imlay to announce her arrival and give him some notion of the hardships of the trip which she had undertaken for his sake, she concluded with the agonized plea: "For God's sake, let me hear from you immediately, my friend! I am not well, and yet you see I cannot die."

After hunting in vain for better lodgings, Mary was "forced to accept" the hospitality of one of Imlay's business associates, probably Elias Backman. Soon she was "overwhelmed with civilities on all sides"; the best merchant families were of course eager to entertain such a distinguished visitor. But their efforts merely fatigued her; she cared little for them or for the material success which they represented, and she struggled against weakness induced by nightly fevers. " 'How flat, dull, and unprofitable' appears to me all the bustle into which I see people here so eagerly enter," she complained in a letter to Imlay. "I long every night to go to bed, to hide my melancholy face in my pillow; but there is a canker-worm in my bosom that never sleeps." And again she begged him to decide about their future. Are they ever to live together again? If so, let him set the date when they are to meet in Switzerland. If not, let him tell her so at once so that she can plan for the future—"for we must either live together, or I will be entirely independent."

Gradually, however, she grew calmer. Her health improved during her stay in Gothenburg, and soon she was able to report that she was "more alive than you have seen me for a long, long time." She was, she wrote, "endeavouring to recover" herself, and she had achieved "a degree of vivacity, even in my grief, which is preferable to the benumbing stupor that, for the last year, has frozen all my faculties." Consequently she was able, in one of her letters, to discuss the effect of her relations with Imlay more dispassionately than ever before. "My friend," she wrote,

I have dearly paid for one conviction. Love, in some minds, is an affair of sentiment, arising from the same delicacy of perception (or taste) as renders them alive to the beauties of nature, poetry, &c., alive to the charms of those evanescent graces that are, as it were, impalpable—they must be felt, they cannot be described.

Love is a want of my heart. I have examined myself lately with more care than formerly, and find that to deaden is not to calm the mind. Aiming at tranquillity, I have almost destroyed all the energy of my soul—almost rooted out what renders it estimable. Yes, I have damped that enthusiasm of character, which converts the grossest materials into a fuel that imperceptibly feeds hopes, which aspire above common enjoyment. Despair, since the birth of my child, has rendered me stupid; soul and body seemed to be fading away before the withering touch of disappointment.

For the moment she was determined to revive her dormant spirits. "With what a cruel sigh have I recollected that I had forgotten to hope!" she wrote. And with a new air of confidence: "Do not tell me that you are happier without us. Will you not come to us in Switzerland?" Imlay must needs have a callous heart to resist entreaties expressed in such a tone.

Unfortunately Mary failed to continue in this new strain. In fact she soon lapsed into the kind of criticism which had, perhaps, first repulsed Imlay. "Ah, why do you not love us with more sentiment?" she asked in her next letter,

—why are you a creature of such sympathy, that the warmth of your feelings, or rather quickness of your senses, hardens your heart? It is my misfortune that my imagination is perpetually shading your defects, and lending you charms, whilst the grossness of your senses makes you (call me not vain) overlook graces in me, that only dignity of mind and the sensibility of an expanded heart can give.

This was no way to recapture an errant lover! Mary could not seem to learn that comparisons are odious.

Of course her improvement in spirits was only temporary. Three days later, disappointed not to have received a letter from her beloved, she was again beside herself. "There are," she declared,

misfortunes so great as to silence the usual expressions of sorrow. Believe me there is such a thing as a broken heart! There are characters whose very energy preys upon them; and who, ever inclined to cherish by reflection some passion, cannot rest satisfied with the common comforts of life. I have endeavoured to fly from myself, and launched into all the dissipation possible here, only to feel keener anguish, when alone with my child.

And presently she added, despondent as ever: "Am I ever to feel alive only to painful sensations? But it cannot—it shall not last long."

On or about July 10, after a fortnight in Gothenburg, Mary set off toward the north for Strömstad en route to Tönsberg, Norway, where she was to transact further business for Imlay. Because Fanny was teething again, Mary left her in Gothenburg in Marguerite's care; and she traveled north by coach in the company of two Germans and their coachman. As usual Mary was alert to all the details of the life and the country around her: she was pleasantly surprised with the accommodations offered her, but oppressed at having to sleep "between two down beds"; she thrilled to the "wild beauties" of the landscape, but was saddened by the poverty of the Swedish peasants.

On the third day after their departure from Gothenburg they reached Strömstad, and Mary spent the night at the home of a prosperous merchant, "the little sovereign of the place, because he was by far the richest." The next day high winds prevented her from crossing the Skagerrak to Laurvik, Norway, and her two German friends persuaded her to accompany them on a brief trip across the Norwegian border to Frederikshald (Halden), which was only eighteen miles from Strömstad. The trip was delightful; they passed over steep mountains and ferried across the scenic Tiste River, but they were served so slowly at every stop that they could only take a fleeting glimpse of Frederikshald and hurry back toward Strömstad. Even so, they were obliged to travel all night— lighted by a brilliant moon and by the sun "loitering just below the horizon"—and they reached Strömstad at five o'clock in the morning. Mary had barely time to swallow a cup of coffee and change her clothes, before she embarked westward across the Skagerrak toward Laurvik.

The sea was rough, but the wind was favorable and drove the boat rapidly toward its destination. Because she had spent most of the night awake in the carriage with her bosom "opened . . . to the embraces of nature" while her companions slept, Mary lay down on a pile of sails to rest. But a "discourteous wave" roused her and forced her to be more attentive thereafter.

Mary had arranged in advance for a carriage to meet her at Laurvik and carry her immediately to Tönsberg. But she failed to find the carriage, and she was obliged to wait "whilst the good people of the inn sent round to all their acquaintance to search for a vehicle." Meanwhile she wrote to Imlay telling him how sorely she missed her baby and deploring his failure to write to her. "I will not complain," she told him; "but from the soundness of your understanding, I am convinced, if you give yourself leave to reflect, you will also feel that your conduct to me, so far from being generous, has not been just. I mean not to allude to factitious principles of morality; but to the simple basis of all rectitude. However, I did not intend to argue." She compared herself to King Lear; like him she had been forced to bare her breast to the pitiless storm, and had learned that "the war of the elements" was nothing compared to "the pangs of disappointed affection, and the horror arising from a discovery of a breach of confidence that snaps every social tie."

When at last she learned that a vehicle had been engaged for her, she went out to find "a rude sort of *cabriole*," which she was to share with a Danish sailor. The equipage itself was grotesque enough, but it was rendered more so by the presence of a half-drunken driver and a sea captain who accompanied them on horseback. She was mortified to find a "gentlemanlike man," obviously amused, among the onlookers as they prepared to set out; and she tried to avoid his gaze. But presently he caught her eye, her embarrassment changed to mirth, and they both burst into a laugh as the cabriole dashed away. Mary's sense of humor had not entirely abandoned her, for all her troubles. It was unfortunate that she could not use it to leaven her letters to Imlay.

After a journey northeast through a fertile and well-cultivated countryside, Mary reached Tönsberg, on Christiana Fjord, late in the evening of July 16. She put up at a pleasant inn and on the following morning called on the mayor of the town, with whom she was to transact her business. To her dismay she learned that she could not hope to terminate her affairs there for three weeks or a month, and she was forced to bide her time. She bitterly regretted having left Fanny in Gothenburg, but otherwise she could not complain. Tönsberg, one of the most ancient towns in Norway, had some interesting old buildings and a superb location—between forests and sea—to recommend it; and the inn was clean and quiet.

Mary soon became reconciled to her enforced vacation and proceeded to make the most of it. She deliberately cultivated solitude. Occasionally she ventured into local society: she dined at the mayor's house and spent a day at the home of one of the richest merchants, where she was pleased by the guests' "artless kindness," but depressed by their tendency to overeat and their bondage to custom. Most of the time, however, she preferred her own company. And since no one at the inn spoke English or French, she was left alone except for two visits each day from a young woman who served as her interpreter. She dined by herself later than the usual dinner hour in the North, which she had found inconvenient ever since her arrival; and she gave up most of the day to enjoyment of the balmy summer weather. She found haunts in the woods where she could go to rest and reflect. Sometimes she walked or rode on horseback to a ruined fort on a nearby mountain, which commanded a fine view of the harbor; sometimes she strolled out to drink from a clear brook which tasted of iron. She went bathing, too, and in order to reach a suitable beach on the fjord, learned to row a boat. All in all, she managed to work out for herself a routine ideally adapted to strengthening her body and calming her nerves.

Her new regimen soon bore results. Her strength returned, her weight increased, and her nightly fevers disappeared. "I have seldom been in better health," she reported to Imlay on August 5;

and my mind, though trembling to the touch of anguish, is calmer—yet still the same. I have, it is true, enjoyed some tranquillity, and more happiness here, than for a long, long time past. (I say happiness, for I can give no other appellation to the exquisite delight this wild country and fine summer have afforded me.)

She had not, of course, forgotten her sorrow; but she had determined that henceforth she would not allow it to overwhelm her.

For Fanny's sake she wanted to return to Imlay, whatever the cost; but she was resolved not to be a burden to him. "When we meet again," she had written six days earlier, "you shall be convinced that I have more resolution than you give me credit for. I will not torment you. If I am destined always to be disappointed and unhappy, I will conceal the anguish I cannot dissipate; and the tightened cord of life or reason will at last snap, and set me free."

Yet her plans depended necessarily on Imlay's willingness to live with her again. And his occasional letters remained noncommittal. She was perfectly willing to demean herself to win her point; and in a letter written August 5 she revealed that she was willing to sacrifice all pride for the sake of being near him:

This state of suspense, my friend, is intolerable; we must determine on something, and soon; we must meet shortly, or part for ever. I am sensible that I acted foolishly, but I was wretched when we were together. Expecting too much, I let the pleasure I might have caught slip from me. I cannot live with you, I ought not—if you form another attachment. But I promise you, mine shall not be intruded on you.

She begged him to take her back for their child's sake. But above all she begged for a decision. "You must determine—examine yourself," she wrote. "But for God's sake! spare me the anxiety of uncertainty! I may sink under the trial; but I will not complain." Yet by August 9, when she had received five letters from him, forwarded from Strömstad, she again despaired:

One, dated the 14th of July, was written in a style which I may have merited, but did not expect from you. However this is not a time to reply to it, except to assure you that you shall not be tormented with any more complaints. I am disgusted with myself for having so long importuned you with my affection.

And she wrote no more until her return to Gothenburg seventeen days later.

Presently Mary left Tönsberg for a short trip south. She traveled back through Laurvik and then on to Helgeraa, from which she embarked one evening at sunset to sail southwest through rocky islands toward Österrisöer. Because of rain and falling darkness she was forced to stop overnight at Portöer, a charmingly primitive settlement of "some half dozen houses scattered under the curve of a rock." The next day she went on to Österrisöer, which she found most depressing. "Talk not of bastilles!" she wrote of it. "To be born here, was to be bastilled by nature—shut out from all that opens the understanding, or enlarges the heart. Huddled one behind another, not more than a quarter of the [two hundred] dwellings even had a prospect of the sea. A few planks formed passages from house to house, which you must often scale, mounting steps like a ladder, to enter."[12]

Here Mary was obliged to spend three or four depressing days. She was confined to her room and, in the absence of books, to writing as a pastime. If she wished to take a bit of exercise, she must climb two hundred steps to a level spot about one hundred yards wide, where she could only pace back and forth in the burning sunshine or stare out over the barren expanse of water. She felt stifled, and though she maintained that she "found solitude desirable," she seems to have welcomed an invitation to dine at the home of the English vice-consul, where she could feel "more at large." A day or two afterward she left Österrisöer with few regrets, having been inspired to dilate on the confining effects of life remote from the centers of civilization.

Her return to Tönsberg only reminded her of her loneliness; it was "something like a home—yet I was to enter without lighting-up pleasure in any eye—I dreaded the solitariness of my apartment, and wished for night to hide the starting tears, or to shed them on my pillow, and close my eyes on a world where I was destined to wander alone." "I reasoned and reasoned," she wrote; "but my heart was too full to allow me to remain in the house, and I walked, till I was wearied out, to purchase rest—or rather forgetfulness."[13]

After stopping over only one day to complete her affairs, Mary set out again from Tönsberg, this time traveling to the northeast via Moss to Christiania (now Oslo). Although the country was less picturesque than that which she had seen elsewhere in Norway, she rejoiced to find it dotted with prosperous farms and comfortable cottages which suggested independence.

At Christiania she was well received. But though she admired the cleanliness and the pleasant situation of the city, she cared little for it otherwise: its ugly buildings, its reminders of the baneful effects of commerce, and the sight of slaves in chains damped Mary's spirits. "I can scarcely say why . . . ," she wrote, "but in this city, thoughtfulness seemed to be sliding into melancholy, or rather dullness.—The fire of fancy, which had been kept alive in the country, was almost extinguished by reflections on the ills that harass such a large portion of mankind.—I felt like a bird fluttering on the ground unable to mount; yet unwilling to crawl tranquilly like a reptile, whilst still conscious it had wings."[14] The temporary blow which she had enjoyed at Tönsberg was wearing off; after all, it had risen from physical relaxation rather than from any real mental well-being.

From Christiania Mary traveled southeast to Frederikstad and Strömstad en route to Gothenburg again. At last, on August 25, she reached her destination and "once more pressed my babe to my heart." But her joy was blighted when she sat down to read the packet of letters from Imlay awaiting her.

"You tell me that my letters torture you," she wrote in reply;

I will not describe the effect yours have on me. I received three this morning, the last dated the 7th of this month. I mean not to give vent to the emotions they produced. Certainly you are right; our minds are not congenial. I have lived in an ideal world, and fostered sentiments that you do not comprehend, or you would not treat me thus. I am not, I will not be, merely an object of compassion—a clog, however light, to teaze you. Forget that I exist: I will never remind you. . . . You need not continually tell me that our fortune is inseparable, *that you will try to cherish tenderness* for me. Do no violence to yourself! When we are separated, our interest, since you give so much weight to pecuniary considerations, will be entirely divided. I want not protection without affection; and support I need not, whilst my faculties are undisturbed.

At last Mary was persuaded that she and Imlay would never be reunited, that she must reconcile herself to her fate. And, having faced the inevitable, she showed surprising command of her emotions. She told her lover that her "lips tremble, as if shook by cold" and her "whole frame is convulsed"; but in spite of all, she seemed able to recognize the grim truth. She had even achieved a degree of resignation. "As for peace," she wrote, "we will not talk of it. I was not made, perhaps, to enjoy the calm contentment so termed."

She continued her trip as scheduled. Before she left Gothenburg she made a two-day journey to Trollhättan to see the cascade and canal there. Then she headed south via Falkenberg and Helsingör (Elsinore) to Copenhagen. On her arrival she found a quarter of the city in ruins as a result of a recent fire, and survivors living in tents outside the city. And from that point onward she cared little for what she saw of the city. It lacked the elegance and grandeur which she had been led to expect; indeed the Danes seemed to be, of all Scandinavians, "the people who have made the fewest sacrifices to the graces." She had letters of introduction to families who proved hospitable; she was presented to the Prime Minister, Count Bernstorff; she dutifully visited the public library, the royal museum, and the Rosenborg Palace. But she was usually content to remain in her room; and she found little to interest her beyond it—perhaps, she admitted, because she viewed all things "with the jaundiced eye of melancholy."

On September 6 she wrote again to Imlay, having determined not to send him an earlier letter into which some of her "bitterness of soul" had "imperceptibly slipt." After all, she implied, her complaints would be wasted on him: "I am not sufficiently vain to imagine that I can, for more than a moment, cloud your enjoyment of life. . . ." Yet she could not stifle all her resentment, could not forget all that Imlay had made her suffer. "I have not," she wrote, "that happy substitute for wisdom, insensibility—and the lively sympathies which bind me to my fellow creatures, are all of a painful kind. They are the agonies of a broken heart; pleasure and I have shaken hands." Yet despite the apparent finality of all that she had written, Mary presently reverted to her old question: "I cannot endure this suspense. Decide. Do you fear to strike another blow? We live together, or eternally apart! I shall not write to you again, till I receive an answer to this." She had still not quite despaired of a reconciliation!

Soon she was off on her journey again. This time her route took her southwest to Korsor, where she crossed the Great Belt by barge in the company of two congenial Germans. She continued with them across the Island of Fyn and then embarked on the Little Belt. There the wind failed them, and for ten hours they were becalmed. Unfortunately, Mary, misled by the name "*Little* Belt," had failed to carry along a reserve of food for an emergency; and when Fanny grew hungry and cried for food, her mother's raw nerves were grated to the quick. "Fancy conjured up before me the wretched Ugolino, with his famished children," she wrote, in her *Letters Written during a Short Residence in Sweden, Norway, and Denmark;* "and I, literally speaking, enveloped myself in sympathetic horrours, augmented by every tear my babe shed."[15]

At last, however, they reached the shore, found something to eat, and soon were riding along the Baltic toward Hamburg, the last stop on their journey. Mary found the countryside monotonous but the towns clean and sightly and the inhabitants more alert than the Swedes or Danes. She visited the castle of Prince Charles of Hesse-Cassel and reflected on "the unpleasing ideas of german despotism," but she was forced to admit that she was "agreeably surprised" to find the people she encountered so industrious, comfortable, and cheerful, though enslaved by a tyrannous government.

Hamburg was crowded, and Mary had difficulty in locating even miserable quarters. But after one night in a wretched room she learned that a man whom she had met at Copenhagen had engaged rooms for her in nearby Altona. She was comfortable there and enjoyed the company of Imlay's friend "St. John de Crèvecoeur," author of *Letters from an American Farmer;* but she was distressed at the high cost of living and eager to set out for England. Of course Imlay showed no sign of joining her for a trip to Switzerland.

Mary's stay in Hamburg was naturally disagreeable to her. She seemed unable to enjoy anything that she saw. She visited the country houses of local merchants, only to be repelled by their conversation "ever flowing in the muddy channels of business." Indeed she encountered in Hamburg, more markedly than ever before, the hateful effects of commerce, which she so abhorred; and in her *Letters Written ... in Sweden* she inveighed against the vulgarity and selfishness of the newly-rich merchants (and, incidentally, berated Imlay again for his preoccupation with business). She complained that the gates of Hamburg were closed at seven o'clock every evening so that anyone who did business there would be obliged to lodge (and spend money) in the city; she complained that the smell from a glue factory marred her enjoyment of a fine view of the Elbe; she complained that rope makers monopolized the shady walks where she liked to stroll. Even the French aristocrats in exile in Hamburg and Altona were more sympathetic to her than the gross merchants; for despite her approval of the French Revolution Mary could not help pitying those who had suffered from it—at least those who had been able to rise above their suffering. She felt genuine admiration for Madame de La Fayette, who had been living without servants in a third-floor apartment; for a duke who had gone into business with his former cook; for an ex-president of the assembly who was keeping an ordinary. Such people had real courage; dignity and good breeding had sustained them in disaster. But the merchants lacked these redeeming qualities. "The tyranny of wealth" was indeed "more galling and debasing than that of rank," and "sentiments of honour and delicacy appear the offspring of greatness of soul, when compared with the grovelling views of the sordid accumulators of *cent. per cent.*"[16]

From Hamburg Mary wrote to Imlay on September 25 complaining of his silence, which she termed "a refinement on cruelty." This time she did not bother to indulge in the rhetorical flourishes which had marred so many of her letters. "I have repeatedly written to you fully," she told him angrily. "Do you do the same, and quickly." She was obviously at her wits' end. And when she wrote again two days later, after she had received a chilling letter from him, she was no calmer. Evidently he had refused to make the decision which she had begged him to reach; in fact he seems to have made light of the matter and told her that the decision was for her alone. She replied:

By what criterion of principle or affection you term my questions extraordinary and unnecessary, I cannot determine. You desire me to decide. I had decided. You must have had long ago two letters of mine, to the same purpose, to consider. In these, God knows! there was but too much affection, and the agonies of a distracted mind were but too faithfully pourtrayed! What more then had I to say? The negative was to come from you. You had perpetually recurred to your promise of meeting me in the autumn. Was it extraordinary that I should demand a yes, or no? Your letter is written with extreme harshness, coldness I am accustomed to, in it I find not a trace of the tenderness of humanity, much less of friendship. I only see a desire to heave a load off your shoulders.

Then she lapsed again into her attitude of injured nobility:

The tremendous power who formed this heart, must have foreseen that, in a world in which self-interest, in various shapes, is the principal mobile, I had little chance of escaping misery. To the fiat of fate I submit. I am content to be wretched; but I will not be contemptible. Of me you have no cause to complain, but for having had too much regard for you—for having expected a degree of permanent happiness when you only sought for a momentary gratification.

I am strangely deficient in sagacity. Uniting myself to you, your tenderness seemed to make me amends for all my former misfortunes. On this tenderness and affection with what confidence did I rest!—but I leaned on a spear that has pierced me to the heart. You have thrown off a faithful friend, to pursue the caprices of the moment. We certainly are differently organized; for even now, when conviction has been stamped on my soul by sorrow, I can scarcely believe it possible. It depends at present on you, whether you will see me or not. I shall take no step, till I see or hear from you.

She was, she told him, proceeding with her own plans. She would return to London at once—would, in fact, be in England or approaching it when he received her letter. Unless his next letter contained unexpected encouragement for her, she would arrange with Joseph Johnson to find lodgings for her without announcing her return to anyone. Then she would settle down to earn enough money to enable her to move with Fanny to France, there to spend the rest of her life in educating her child and making her future secure.

A week later, on Sunday, October 4, she was writing from Dover, having left her ship there because she had no place to stay in London. Again she was distraught; she had felt "extreme anguish. . . at landing without having any friend to receive me"; and worse: she had sensed "from the tenour of your last letter . . . that you have formed some new attachment." Yet she begged him to see her once more:

> I now most earnestly entreat you to write to me, without fail, by the return of the post. Direct your letter to be left at the post-office, and tell me whether you will come to me here, or where you will meet me. . . .
> Do not keep me in suspense. I expect nothing from you, or any human being; my die is cast! I have fortitude enough to determine to do my duty; yet I cannot raise my depressed spirits, or calm my trembling heart. That being who moulded it thus, knows that I am unable to tear up by the roots the propensity to affection which has been the torment of my life—but life will have an end!

Imlay consented to see her, and again established her and their child in lodgings. She must have thought he was sincere in his desire for a reconciliation, else she would never have consented to the arrangement. But she was not long contented; she had said over and over again that she disdained such attention as he felt in duty bound to give her. And soon she was chafing again under his neglect.

Then her suspicions that he had "formed a new attachment" grew stronger. At first she could find no evidence to confirm her suspicions, but eventually she wormed the truth from her cook. She learned also the address of the house where he had installed his new love; and regardless of appearances she rushed there, found Imlay, and confronted him with his duplicity. According to one version of the story he silenced her by claiming that the woman was his wife by a marriage previous to his affair with Mary.[17] But whatever his defense, Mary had no recourse but to drag miserably back to her own quarters.

After a wretched night there she rose with a fixed purpose. In her frenzy she had again forgotten even her responsibility to her child. She could think of only one course of action.

First she wrote Imlay a letter of farewell:

> I write you now on my knees; imploring you to send my child and the maid with - - - to Paris, to be consigned to the care of Madame - - -, Rue - - -, Section de - - -. Should they be removed, - - - can give their direction.
>
> Let the maid have all my clothes without distinction.
>
> Pray pay the cook her wages, and do not mention the confession which I forced from her; a little sooner or later is of no consequence. Nothing but my extreme stupidity could have rendered me blind so long. Yet, whilst you assured me that you had no attachment, I thought we might still have lived together.
>
> I shall make no comments on your conduct, or any appeal to the world. Let my wrongs sleep with me! Soon, very soon, I shall be at peace. When you receive this, my burning head will be cold.
>
> I would encounter a thousand deaths, rather than a night like the last. Your treatment has thrown my mind into a state of chaos; yet I am serene. I go to find comfort, and my only fear is, that my poor body will be insulted by an endeavour to recall my hated existence. But I shall plunge into the Thames where there is least chance of my being snatched from the death I seek.
>
> God bless you! May you never know by experience what you have made me endure. Should your sensibility ever awake, remorse will find its way to your heart; and, in the midst of business and sensual pleasure, I shall appear before you, the victim of your deviation from rectitude.

Then she went out to the Battersea Bridge. Finding it too much frequented, she took a boat up the Thames to Putney. It was after dark when she arrived there, and rain was falling steadily. For half an hour she paced back and forth on the bridge so that her clothes would become too thoroughly drenched to be buoyant. In all that time no one had passed, and so she concluded that she had found the ideal spot for her purpose. Then, anticipating at last the end of her agony, she climbed to the top of the bridge and hurled herself into the river.—But despite her precautions, her skirts buoyed her up. She struggled to press them close to her body. She tried to swallow mouthfuls of water.—Then she lost consciousness.

But once again she failed to escape. It seemed that she could not die. A passer-by saw her body floating in the river and rescued her, and presently she was revived. All the horror of the experience had been in vain. Imlay was notified of her plight and sent a physician to attend her. And soon she was carried back to London and taken to the Christies' house in Finsbury Square.

Then again she was forced to face the reality which she was striving so painfully to avoid. She did not regret her folly; she regretted only her failure—and intimated that she might well make another attempt on her life. "I have only to lament," she wrote to Imlay, "that, when the bitterness of death was past, I was inhumanly brought back to life and misery. But a fixed determination is not to be baffled by disappointment; nor will I allow that to be a frantic attempt which was one of the calmest acts of reason."

This time Imlay did not rush back to her; in fact he was doubtless regretting more than ever before that he had allowed himself to become entangled with so erratic a creature. He could offer no helpful suggestions; and he contented himself with saying that he knew not "how to extricate ourselves out of the wretchedness into which we have been plunged."[18] He even refused to visit Mary while she was confined to her room, claiming that it would be "indelicate" for him to do so. Of course she was outraged at the thought. "It appears to me that you lay more stress on delicacy than on principle," she wrote to him; "for I am unable to discover what sentiment of delicacy would have been violated by your visiting a wretched friend, if indeed you have any friendship for me. But since your new attachment is the only sacred thing in your eyes, I am silent—Be happy! My complaints shall never more damp your enjoyment; perhaps I am mistaken in supposing that even my death could, for more than a moment." She refused to accept further support from him; she wanted no "such vulgar comfort" and would "consider any direct or indirect attempt to supply my necessities, as an insult which I have not merited, and as rather done out of tenderness for your reputation, than for me." In her distraction she was callous even in regard to Fanny's future, dismissing what had hitherto been one of her foremost worries with the words: "When I am dead, respect for yourself will make you take care of the child."

Imlay continued, however, to write to her from time to time or to inquire about her health from mutual friends. When he asked in a letter if she was "well or tranquil," she replied acidly: "They who think me so, must want a heart to estimate my feelings by." And when he called to see her, she was convinced that he did so "to oblige other people, and not to soothe my distracted mind." But while she might be venomous in one letter and almost objective in the next, she still had not given up all hope of a reconciliation. In a weak moment Imlay had assured her that his present affair was only temporary; and Mary took him at his word and suggested that she and Fanny go to live with him and his mistress. In an even weaker moment he had consented to the crazy scheme, and he took her to inspect a house which he was planning to hire for his curious ménage. But of course he thought better of the scheme presently and moved into the house without Mary. Then again she wrote in doubt and despair. His removal to the new house was in her eyes, she told him, "an open avowal" that he had abandoned her. Yet she was not content with even such convincing evidence, and she implored: "But let me see, written by yourself—for I will not receive it through any other medium—that the affair is finished."

Yet she knew herself defeated, and she compensated for her loss by morbid attempts to make herself even more wretched. She was perfectly willing, she wrote to Imlay, to bear alone the "obloquy" which would fall upon her when the world learned the true nature of their relations. "And, whatever I may think and feel," she assured him, "you need not fear that I shall publicly complain. ... I shall be silent as the grave in which I long to forget myself." As soon as possible she would remove herself "where it will not be necessary for you to talk—of course, not to think of me." And when she was disappointed in her first attempt to "obtain a temporary supply" of money, she observed lugubriously:

"But this even pleases me; an accumulation of disappointments and misfortunes seems to suit the habit of my mind."

But the nervous energy which had so often sustained her in the past soon roused her to action. Before the end of November she took lodgings of her own in Finsbury Place and steeled herself to clear up the wreckage of the past. She asked Imlay to return all her letters (perhaps to aid her in revising *Letters Written . . . in Sweden*) and even sent a similar request to Fuseli, scolding him for not having returned a call which she paid on him before her departure on her Scandinavian trip. Apparently she was no longer trying to conceal her misfortunes from the world, for she wrote:

I have long ceased to expect kindness or affection from any human creature, and would fain tear from my heart its treacherous sympathies. I am alone. The injustice, without alluding to hopes blasted in the bud, which I have endured, wounding my bosom, have set my thoughts adrift into an ocean of painful conjectures. I ask impatiently what—and where is truth? I have been treated brutally; but I daily labour to remember that I still have the duty of a mother to fulfil.[19]

Fuseli ignored Mary's request for her letters, but Imlay wrapped up all her correspondence and sent it off to her with a note announcing his departure for Paris.

Mary's letter of November 27 acknowledging receipt of her "register of sorrow," as she called the packet of letters, shows that she was still despondent, but struggling to master her grief. "My mind is injured," she told him. "I scarcely know where I am or what I do. The grief I cannot conquer (for some cruel recollections never quit me, banishing almost every other), I labour to conceal in total solitude. My life therefore is but an exercise of fortitude, continually on the stretch, and hope never gleams in this tomb, where I am buried alive." Yet she could still reason with him, still try to revive his better self. To his claims that his conduct had been always "exalted" and "most refined" she countered:

You tell me "that I shall judge more coolly of your mode of acting some time hence." But is it not possible that *passion* clouds your reason as much as it does mine? And ought you not to doubt whether those principles are so "exalted," as you term them, which only lead to your own gratification? In other words, whether it would be just to have no principle of action but that of following your inclination, trampling on the affection you have fostered, and the expectations you have excited?

My affection for you is rooted in my heart. I know you are not what you now seem, nor will you always act or feel as you now do, though I may never be comforted by the change. Even at Paris, my image will haunt you. You will see my pale face, and sometimes the tears of anguish will drop on your heart, which you have forced from mine.

She could even, in a last desperate attempt to regain his affections, try to argue him into adhering to a more conventional code of morality:

You seem to me only to have been anxious to shake me off—regardless whether you dashed me to atoms by the fall. In truth, I have been rudely handled. *Do you judge coolly,* and I trust you will not continue to call those capricious feelings "the most refined," which would undermine not only the most sacred principles, but the affections which unite mankind. You would render mothers unnatural—and there would be no such thing as a father! If your theory of morals is the most "exalted," it is certainly the most easy. It does not require much magnanimity to determine to please ourselves for the moment, let others suffer what they will.

But her efforts to control herself gradually became more effective, and by December 8, when she wrote to Imlay in Paris, she was calmer. "Resentment, and even anger," she told him, "are momentary emotions with me, and I wish to tell you so, that if you ever think of me, it may not be in the light of an enemy." And though she was, she said, "stunned" by his conduct and could not hold back the tears as she wrote, she admitted that her hope of regaining his love "every day grows fainter and fainter." She seemed, in fact, to be once more resigned to her fate, for she wrote:

Yet you will not always forget me. You will feel something like remorse for having lived only for yourself, and sacrificed my peace to inferior gratifications. In a comfortless old age, you will remember that you had one disinterested friend, whose heart you wounded to the quick. The hour of recollection will come, and you will not be satisfied to act the part of a boy, till you fall into that of a dotard. I know that your mind, your heart, and your principles of action are all superior to your present conduct. You do, you must, respect me—and you will be sorry to forfeit my esteem.

This time Mary's method of reconciling herself to the inevitable was a strange combination of despair, recrimination, and hope.

It is significant, of course, that she still refused to acknowledge that Imlay was the man he seemed to be. To the very end, she loved him for what he had been when first they met.

During the last months of 1795, while Mary was undergoing this tense emotional crisis, she was also trying her hand once more at writing. She had told Imlay repeatedly that she would accept no "pecuniary assistance" from him, and so she was obliged to bestir herself immediately to gain support for herself and her child. In January, 1796, she finished the preliminary sketch of a comedy, the serious scenes of which were based on her own history.[20] At about the same time Joseph Johnson published her *Letters Written during a Short Residence in Sweden, Norway, and Denmark*.[21]

In the Advertisement to her book Mary states that, although these letters were "designed for publication," she deliberately chose the form of personal letters because it allowed her "remarks and reflections" to "flow unrestrained."[22] It also allowed her to assume an intimate and direct approach to her reader, to say whatever happened to occur to her at any given moment. As a result her book was no Baedeker; she saw only a small part of each of the countries she visited, and she made no pretense at thoroughness. Instead she wrote what amounted to twenty-five personal essays. They were held together by the narrative of her travels, from the time her ship arrived off the coast of Sweden until the day she reached Dover on her way back to London. Yet each letter contained disgressions into the endless number of subjects which occupied her fertile mind. Her purpose, she said, was "to endeavour to give a just view of the present state of the countries I have passed through," and she tried conscientiously to describe and evaluate the inhabitants, social institutions, manners, and scenery of each country. But her mind was quick to make comparisons, and it always leapt easily from particulars to generalizations. Thus a visit to a Swedish garden calls forth a little essay on gardening in general; remarks on her loneliness for Fanny during their separation evoke observations on the plight of women;

and an account of the Swedes' abuse of their servants leads her to compare the treatment of servants in England and then to describe how servants should be treated. The book shows Mary at her best, for her talent lent itself to expanding rather than pruning. Moreover, her usual lack of organization did not mar the effect of the book, and her relaxed personal style allowed her to reveal, as never before, her vibrant personality.

The *Letters* is, however, more than a loose collection of facts and interpretation. Mary had written in an *Analytical Review* article that any book of travels should be unified by a "grand object of pursuit";[23] and, true to her theory, she provided her book with such a unifying agent. It is, as one might expect, a far-reaching one—Mary did not usually waste time on trifles. She could almost have said, as Shelley said of "Queen Mab," that "the vast and comprehensive subject" was "the past, the present, and the future," for her book centered about her "favourite subject of contemplation, the future improvement of the world," not neglecting to comment incidentally on its past progress and present imperfections. Thus Mary was interested in describing the countries she visited not because she wished to regale her reader with odds and ends of curious information about foreign lands, but because she sought evidence of their place in the endless march of civilization. And since she had traveled considerably more than most people of her time, she could make ready comparisons to reveal just how the Swedes, Norwegians, Danes, or Germans ranked not only one with another but also with the people of other lands—England, Portugal, Ireland, and France—where she had lived or visited. Occasionally too she made use of hearsay or her reading for further comparisons—especially with America, of which she had learned much from Imlay.

Mary took pains, during her travels, to meet with people of all classes in the countries which she visited; and her observations led her to believe that the Swedes and Danes were less advanced than either the Norwegians or the Germans. The Swedes she found to be sluggish from excessive eating and drinking; they were superficially well bred, but in an abject, servile manner which she attributed to their lack of liberty. The Danes were much like them: indolent and usually lacking in refinement of mind or feelings. The Norwegians seemed much sprightlier and more industrious, thanks to their greater degree of independence, but were not yet sufficiently advanced to be liberated from convention or to have developed any appreciable amount of public spirit. The Germans she considered more capable of improvement; they had a vivacity, an independence of spirit, and a general intelligence which gratified her (though she found these qualities hard to reconcile with her theories about despotism). But regardless of all advantages or drawbacks, Mary had hopes for all four countries. She rejected the notion that any people could be so stupid or brutish by nature as to resist improvement; and she believed that so-called "natural differences" between nations would, upon examination, "be found to consist merely in the degree of vivacity or thoughtfulness, pleasure or pain, inspired by the climate, whilst the varieties which the forms of government, including religion, produce, are much more numerous and unstable." She insisted that "the virtues of a nation . . . bear an exact proportion to their scientific improvements," and she pointed out, whenever possible, evidence of "the first steps of the improvement which I am persuaded will make a very obvious progress in the course of half a century."

Mary was still, then, a believer in human progress. She was too much of a realist to share Rousseau's admiration for society in its primitive state. "The primitive times . . . ," she observed, "probably never existed with such a golden lustre as the animated imagination lends, when only able to seize the prominent features."[24] She exulted in the rugged natural scenery which she saw, but she had no desire to spend her life among the rude inhabitants of such regions. "I begin to think that I should not like to live continually in the country," she wrote, "with people whose minds have such a narrow range. My heart would frequently be interested; but my mind would languish for more companionable society."[25] If obliged to live in the country, she would choose to live by herself. "I am . . . ," she declared, "more and more convinced, that a metropolis, or an abode absolutely solitary, is the best calculated for the improvement of the heart, as well as the understanding; whether we desire to become acquainted with man, nature, or ourselves."[26] Elsewhere she said succinctly: "Nothing so soon wearies out the feelings as unmarked simplicity."[27]

No, Mary had no desire to escape from the world to nature. Though she may at times have been tempted to flee from mankind, common sense soon persuaded her to resist the urge. After describing the idyllic state of northern Norway (which she had not visited), she remarked: "My imagination hurries me forward to seek an asylum in such a retreat from all the disappointments I am threatened with; but reason draws me back, whispering that the world is still the world, and man the same compound of weakness and folly, who must occasionally excite love and disgust, admiration and contempt."[28] She was convinced that she "could not live very comfortable exiled from the countries where mankind are so much further advanced in knowledge, imperfect as it is, and unsatisfactory to the thinking mind." And she maintained: "The more I see of the world, the more I am convinced that civilization is a blessing not sufficiently estimated by those who have not traced its progress."[29]

Yet though civilization is a blessing, though she believed implicitly in the values of progress, she was no longer convinced, as she was in *The Rights of Woman,* that "all will *be* right" on earth eventually. In rejecting the notion of escaping from civilization to an idyllic haven, she declared that she did so because "the world is still the world, and man the same compound of weakness and folly, who must occasionally excite love and disgust, admiration and contempt." And her words implied that man and the world were not likely to undergo any fundamental change. To a realistic reader this may well seem like sound doctrine; and it perhaps is. But it is not the doctrine which Mary had been preaching even so recently as her *French Revolution.* There she assumed that freedom would perfect men; but now in the *Letters* she seems doubtful—

perhaps because she has learned to her cost that a free man can behave abominably. At one point in the *Letters* Mary allowed herself to contemplate the distant era when the world would be so densely populated that it could no longer support mankind. "Where was he to fly to from universal famine?" she asked. "Do not smile: I really became distressed for these fellow creatures, yet unborn. The images fastened on me, and the world appeared a vast prison."[30] Surely this is not perfection! And since Mary frequently hailed God as the source of all perfection and spoke of the fusion of man's soul with godhead as its ultimate objective, it is probable that she had given up the quest for perfection on earth, concluding—as she had believed in earlier years—that the only true perfection could be achieved in heaven.

Nor was this her only departure from conventional eighteenth century rationalistic principle. Indeed the *Letters* reveals a side of Mary's nature which she had often sought to conceal. Experience had confirmed what she had long felt: that it was futile to ignore the claims of the heart; and in this book the heart had its say. In the first place Mary's disappointment in love echoed throughout the book. The letters were obviously addressed to the beloved (though Mary never supplied his name); and she mentioned her melancholy state in the first sentence and recurred to it constantly —becoming ever more specific until the reader could have no doubt as to the cause of her grief. Naturally his curiosity would be aroused and his sympathy enlisted in behalf of the suffering author. As a result the book has a secondary "object of pursuit"; it is held together not only by Mary's remarks on the progress of society, but also by her revelation of the progress of her sorrows. Unfortunately, however, she often lapsed into morbid sentimentality, for in this book, as in her letters to Imlay, Mary seemed to derive an unhealthy satisfaction from probing her wounded heart. She seemed to enjoy comparing herself with Lear, another wanderer of the wasteland, or quoting Hamlet, another baffled idealist. In fact she often paraded her woe with a flourish which recalls Young Werther and his fellow-Romantics.

Moreover, throughout the book Mary showed intense interest in the emotions; she went so far as to say that "whatever excites emotion has charms for me." And her emotions were frequently excited during her journey. Sometimes, of course, she descended to sheer sentimentality—but not always. Her attitude toward nature was usually free of any sentimental taint. She herself remarked, "The beauties of nature appear to me now even more alluring than in my youth, because my intercourse with the world has formed, without vitiating my taste."[31] And she looked upon nature not merely as "the nurse of sentiment," but also as a medium for transcending mortal experience and uniting the soul with God. At times she approached a state of mystical ecstasy as she described the beauty of the mountain country. For example, on her moonlight ride from Frederikshald to Strömstad: "A vague pleasurable sentiment absorbed me, as I opened my bosom to the embraces of nature; and my soul rose to its author, with the chirping of the solitary birds, which began to feel, rather than see, the advancing day."[32] Furthermore she derived joy from nature not only during the moment of immediate contact, but long afterward. "I cannot," she wrote, "without a thrill of delight, recollect views I have seen, which are not to be forgotten."[33] Critics have frequently remarked that in one paragraph of the *Letters*[34] Mary anticipated the doctrine which Tennyson expressed in the lines from *In Memoriam*:

> So careful of the type she [Nature] seems,
> So careless of the single life.

But as yet no one has pointed out that in many respects Mary's treatment of nature quite strikingly foreshadowed Wordsworth's.

Certainly Mary was aware of the changing fashions of thought in these last years of the eighteenth century. It is doubtless significant that she no longer used the words "romantic" or "Gothic" disdainfully, that indeed she delighted in the "sublimity" of Gothic architecture and contemplated Gothic ruins with enthusiasm. It is significant too that young Robert Southey wrote to his friend Joseph Cottle on March 13, 1797: "Have you ever met with Mary Wollstonecraft's Letters from Sweden and Norway? She has made me in love with a cold climate, and frost and snow, with a northern moonlight."[35] Much of the spirit of the *Letters* was, indeed, close to that of the Romantic Revival. Mary may have been influenced to some extent by contemporary precursors of Romanticism, but it is more than likely that she was writing now primarily from her own heart. She had doubtless learned from others all her rational talk about civilization and perfection; but her sensitivity to nature and her interest in the emotions were almost certainly innate.

The *Letters* should not, however, be put down simply as a Pre-Romantic document. It defies such labels: it is a blend of rationalism and romanticism—yes, and realism too—as they are blended in any normal mature human being. And despite its obvious flaws it is Mary's most mature and most delightful book. Here as nowhere else she could forget her theories and be herself. She no longer felt compelled to play the rationalist, and the brashness of the days of her first success was completely gone. She disclosed her sense of humor, her hard-won knowledge of man and the world, her new tolerance, and her wisdom, as never before. In fact Mary made capital in this book of what she had hitherto sought to conceal: her own personality. "What a long time it requires to know ourselves," she observed at one point in the *Letters;* and the reader feels that it has taken Mary a long time not only to know herself but to realize how truly charming she could be when relaxed. To know Mary Wollstonecraft one must read these letters; they reveal the whole woman—in all her complexity. It is a pity that she wrote only one volume of the kind.

Because Mary's heretical views appeared less in the *Letters* than in all her other books since *The Rights of Men*, it was kindly received by most critics. The *Monthly Magazine,* the *Analytical,* the *Critical Review,* the *New Annual Register,* and the *Monthly Review* were all favorable. Even the *British Critic,* which had handled Mary's *French Revolution* so roughly, was well disposed toward her new book; and though it deprecated her liberal notions, remarked that marriage and motherhood seemed to have softened her. Moreover, excerpts from the book were reprinted in the *Universal Magazine,* the *Scots Magazine,* and the *New York Magazine.*[36] And it was widely read. Johnson published a second edition in 1802, and it was reissued in Cassell's National Library in 1889. Meanwhile an American edition was published at Wilmington, Delaware, in 1796;[37] a Dutch translation, at Haarlem in 1799; a Portuguese translation of selections, at Lisbon in 1806; and two German translations, one at Hamburg, undated, and one at Leipzig in 1893. One reader, Thomas Brown, Professor of Moral Philosophy at the University of Edinburgh, was moved to address Mary in a long poem entitled "The Wanderer in Norway," lauding her courage but bewailing her failure to marry—and describing her aptly as "the wretch of others' folly, and her own."

The most significant reaction, however, was that of William Godwin, who had cared little for Mary's earlier work or for her personality. "If ever there was a book calculated to make a man in love with its author," he wrote in his *Memoirs* of Mary, "this appears to me to be the book."[38] Mary had published the *Letters* in an attempt to solve her most immediate problem: how to support herself and her child. But if Godwin's statement truly reflects his first impressions of the *Letters,* the book went a long way toward solving all Mary's problems.

CHAPTER IX

Fulfillment
(1796-1797)

*On examining my heart, I find that it is so con-
stituted, I cannot live without some particular affection—I am afraid not without a passion. . . .*
—*Letter to Imlay.*

WHEN Mary and Godwin met again in the beginning
of the year 1796, she had abandoned almost all hope
of ever realizing happiness and was devoting herself
to "writing for independence."[1] Apparently she still believed
that she would not live long; for in a letter to Archibald Hamilton Rowan written on January 26 she announced that she was
planning to settle in France "because I wish to leave my little
girl there." And although she admitted that she had not written
to her brother Charles because she "hated to explain" herself,
she found some satisfaction in rehearsing her woes for the benefit of a friend who was likely to sympathize. "I am unhappy," she
wrote.

I have been treated with unkindness—and even cruelty, by the person from
whom I had every reason to expect affection. I write to you with an agitated hand—I cannot be more explicit. I value your good opinion—and you
know how to feel for me. I looked for something like happiness—happiness! in the discharge of my relative duties—and the heart on which I leaned
has pierced mine to the quick. I have not been used well—and I live, but
for my child—for [I] am weary of myself.[2]

Though she spent most of her time in her own rooms, she
occasionally went to the houses of her closest friends. And so it
was that, sometime in January, she accepted an invitation from
Mary Hays, the impulsive little creature who had so admired *The
Rights of Woman,* to join a party at her lodgings in Hatton Gardens. Miss Hays, who was a determined lion-hunter, had snared
a new lion during Mary's absence in France: in 1795 she had bold-

ly written to William Godwin asking him to lend her a copy of *Political Justice,* and she had received in reply not only a copy of the book but a call from the great man himself and, as she expressed it, an invitation to a "free disclosure of my opinions in the epistolary mode." The friendship ripened quickly. Miss Hays wrote at great length, disclosing to her new confidant all the most intimate details of her latest disappointment in love. Presently she was to record the course of this love in her novel *Emma Courtney* and to publish in it many of her letters to Godwin,[3] and later she was to be immortalized as Bridgetina Botherim in Elizabeth Hamilton's *Memoirs of Modern Philosophers.* But for the moment she was only a rather obscure lion-hunter, and she doubtless felt that if she could bring Godwin and Mary together at her house, she would achieve a minor social triumph. She had heard that they had met before and that they had been unfavorably impressed with each other. Accordingly she invited Godwin cautiously, intimating that she knew that he cared little for the distinguished lady who was to be present. His reply was typical:

I will do myself the pleasure of waiting on you on Friday, and shall be happy to meet Mrs. Wollstonecraft, of whom I know not that I ever said a word of harm, and who has frequently amused herself with depreciating me. But I trust you acknowledge in me the reality of a habit upon which I pique myself, that I speak of the qualities of others uninfluenced by personal considerations, and am as prompt to do justice to an enemy as to a friend.[4]

Benign William Godwin! If ever a man was sure of himself, it was he. Much had happened since last he saw Mary in 1791. In 1793 he had published his *Enquiry concerning Political Justice,* the most radical book yet to issue from the London press; in 1794 he had published the daring (and thrilling) novel *Caleb Williams* and had taken the leading part in the defense of the radicals Holcroft, Horne Tooke, Thelwall, and Hardy in the State Trials. Thus he was no longer a hack writer of revolutionary sympathies; he was the leading radical in London, and he was more sure of himself than ever before or afterwards—sure of himself and of his extraordinary theories. He little knew that he was destined for a fall.

Godwin "had for many years regarded marriage with . . . well-grounded . . . apprehension";[5] in fact, in *Political Justice* he had described it as a "law, and the worst of all laws," as "an affair of property, and the worst of all properties."[6] To be sure, when he was twenty-eight, back in June, 1784, he had asked his sister Hannah to choose a proper wife for him, and she had recommended a Miss Gay, who was endowed with "a pleasing voice," "an easy politeness," "good sense without vanity," "a penetrating judgment without a disposition to satire," "good nature and humility," and "about as much religion as my William likes."[7] Several months later he had bestirred himself to inquire about Miss Gay's age and opinions, and after two more months he had paid her a call. The interview was disappointing: he was "not struck" with the lady, though he thought it "not impossible" that he might "like her well enough to make certain proposals after a time."[8] And there the matter ended.

But more recently, since he had reached forty and had emerged as a man of prominence, he seems to have been considering once again the possibility of finding a proper mate. He was undoubtedly attracted to Maria Reveley, who was beautiful and talented—and one of his eagerest disciples; but unfortunately she was already married. And he had certainly flirted with Elizabeth Inchbald, the comely actress turned playwright and novelist. She would have been an excellent catch; for though her writing yielded her a good income, she lived frugally on twenty-five shillings per week and invested the rest. Unfortunately, however, she cherished her widowhood as well as her investments, and she was impervious to offers of marriage. None the less she was offended when Godwin began paying court to Amelia Alderson, the talented and pretty girl from Norwich who had marched across the courtroom and kissed Horne Tooke when he was acquitted in the State Trials. "Now you are come," Mrs. Inchbald complained to Amelia, "Mr. Godwin does not come near me." And to counteract Amelia's charms, she told Godwin that whenever she praised him, Amelia praised his friend Holcroft. Yet though Godwin was obviously charmed by Amelia, she was only amused by him and his ungainly courting. "Godwin drank tea and supt here last night," she wrote to her friend Mrs. Taylor;

a leave-taking visit, as he goes to-morrow to spend a fortnight at Dr. Parr's. It would have entertained you highly to have seen him bid me farewell. He wished to salute me, but his courage failed him . . . . "Will you give me nothing to keep for your sake, and console me during my absence," murmured out the philosopher, "not even your slipper? I had it in my possession once, and need not have returned it!" This was true; my shoe had come off, and he had put it in his pocket for some time. You have no idea how gallant he is become; but indeed, he is much more amiable than ever he was.[9]

Godwin was doubtless gallant and amiable again when he went to Miss Hays's lodgings at 30 Kirby Street, Hatton Gardens, to meet "Mrs. Wollstonecraft"—or Mrs. Imlay, as she was more commonly called these days. Mary too was doubtless more amiable than she had been at their last meeting. She had been chastened and subdued since the days of her first success, and she now fancied herself not as a thinker but as a sufferer. The new role was more becoming and much more likely to please a man. And Godwin was, after all, a man. Neither he nor she fell in love during the party at Mary Hays's, yet they both must have gone away better disposed toward each other. "Sympathy in her anguish," Godwin later wrote, "added in my mind to the respect I had always entertained for her talents."[10]

Yet though Mary doubtless sought to enlist sympathy wherever she went, she was not looking for a husband. She had not yet quite despaired of winning Imlay back. And when he returned from Paris she wrote to him: "As the parting from you for ever is the most serious event of my life, I will once more expostulate with you, and call not the language of truth and feeling ingenuity." Then once again she rehearsed the old arguments: Imlay's better self will eventually assert itself, he knows that he has wronged her, he will some day repent. "But for God's sake," she concluded, still unwilling to face the dreaded truth, "keep me no longer in suspense." And her love flared forth again in the last line: "Let me see you once more."[11]

Imlay replied curtly that he would not see her. But one day shortly afterwards Mary happened in at the Christies' house on Finsbury Square while Imlay was visiting them. Mrs. Christie begged her not to enter the dining room, where Imlay was chatting with some other men. But Mary refused to be dissuaded; she had done nothing shameful, she insisted, and she disdained to slink away. So she strode into the dining room, holding Fanny by the hand, and confronted her lover. And this time he could not avoid allowing her an interview. Reluctantly, no doubt, he went with her to another room, where they could talk privately. There they struggled once again through the old agonized explanations. And once again Imlay, who could be resolute only when far away, agreed to see her later—probably, in fact, to dine at her rooms on the following day.

When they met, he seemed more friendly than he had been for some time, and Mary took heart. Perhaps, after all, their difficulties could still be straightened out. At least she could hope. The day after their meeting she left London for a visit with an old friend named Mrs. Cotton at the village of Sonning, near Reading, in Berkshire. While there she received from Imlay a letter which was as callous as ever. Apparently he claimed that he had already shown forbearance in his relations with her—and that his innate delicacy prevented him from remaining faithful to any one woman. Then at last Mary knew that she had no hope of regaining his affection.

Yet she could not be satisfied until she had written a final letter of farewell. But this time she dispensed with arguments and explanations. "It is now finished," she wrote. "Convinced that you have neither regard nor friendship, I disdain to utter a reproach, though I have had reason to think that the 'forbearance' talked of has not been very delicate. It is, however, of no consequence. I am glad you are satisfied with your own conduct."

She still resorted to her misguided attitude of superiority:

Your understanding or mine must be strangely warped, for what you term "delicacy," appears to me to be exactly the contrary. I have no criterion for morality, and have thought in vain, if the sensations which lead you to follow an ancle or step, be the sacred foundation of principle and affection. Mine has been of a very different nature, or it would not have stood the brunt of your sarcasms.[12]

She still refused to believe that he was displaying his true nature; she still speculated as to when he would return to himself. But her last sentence—"I part with you in peace"—was this time final. She had at last passed the crisis of her emotional upheaval. She was still sad, but no longer half crazed by grief.

Reconciling herself to this final disappointment was relatively easy. In her heart she had long since known that Imlay was lost to her; and if she periodically seized at slender threads of hope, she doubtless did so only for the sake of her child—or perhaps for the sake of her own pride. She could hardly have had any firm confidence that he would ever be truly hers again. In the time left of her stay at Mrs. Cotton's house—Mary spent most of March there—she gave herself up completely to distractions which would aid her to banish Imlay from her mind. Mrs. Cotton and her neighbors, the family of Sir William East, of Hall Place, did all in their power to calm and amuse her, and she beguiled much of the time by taking long walks through the open fields, where she could watch for the first signs of spring. Then toward the end of the month she returned to London, determined to begin her new life of hard work and little pleasure, devoting all her efforts to the task of providing for Fanny's future. Soon after her return Miss Hays wrote to Godwin: "Mrs. Imlay is returned. . . . I am sorry to add, her health appears in a still more declining state. It does not signify what is the cause, but her heart, I think, is broken."[13]

Mary settled now not in the rooms which she had been occupying on Finsbury Place but at 1 Cumming Street, Pentonville, not far from Somers Town, where Godwin lived. Because she planned to stay only briefly in London, she again took furnished lodgings and settled down to serious writing, so that she would soon be able to leave for the Continent—for Italy or Switzerland, she now thought, rather than France. But on April 14, when she had been in her new quarters only about two weeks, she did a surprising thing: she called on William Godwin. It was most unconventional procedure, and Mary must have realized it. Certainly Godwin realized it, and he later felt obliged to apologize for Mary.[14] She would have defended herself, of course, by saying once again that she disdained meaningless formality, that she felt free to call on anyone whom she truly admired. And Godwin, another believer in Perfect Sincerity, was in duty bound to approve of her conduct. Perhaps, indeed, he was a bit flattered at receiving unsought the attentions of so charming and distinguished a woman. Since their evening at Miss Hays's he had read the *Letters Written . . . in Sweden, Norway and Denmark,* and his opinion of Mary had risen considerably.

At all events he invited her to dinner at his house eight days later. It was a gala affair: Mr. and Mrs. James Mackintosh, Thomas Holcroft, Mrs. Inchbald, and Dr. Samuel Parr and his two daughters were present.[15] And Godwin must have been pleased with Mary's behavior, for from that time forth their friendship increased steadily.

Did Mary take the initiative? Was she consciously hunting for a successor to Imlay? A few months before, she had written that she could not live without "some particular affection," and she may well have been attracted to Godwin by the knowledge that he was the very reverse of the man who had betrayed her. After their marriage Godwin wrote in one of his letters to her: "I found a wounded heart, & . . . that heart cast itself upon me." And in the *Memoirs* he protests, it seems, a bit too strongly that their love "grew with equal advances in the mind of each," that "it would have been impossible for the most minute observer to have said who was before, and who was after." "One sex," he adds, "did not take the priority which long-established custom has awarded it, nor did the other overstep that delicacy which is so severely imposed."[16] But whatever the circumstances of the affair, Godwin must have known from the outset that he was a lucky man. Mary had faults, to be sure; at times she was exasperating. But she had a fine mind, a charming appearance, and deep resources of affection. Mary was lucky too: she wanted peace and a home and a companion of her own age whom she could respect and look to for support. And of all the single men in her circle of friends, Godwin could best fill the qualifications.

It should be said in her defense, if defense is needed, that she did not snatch at the first man who displayed any interest in her. After she had married Godwin she told Amelia Alderson that she had "had it in my power, more than once, to marry very advantageously."[17] And it was doubtless at about this time that a friend of Joseph Johnson approached her in behalf of another man who was eager to offer her the "security" of marriage.[18] Mary was hotly indignant at the suggestion, and she wrote to Johnson's friend that she was insulted by his implication that she would "prostitute" herself for "a maintenance." She added that she wanted him to understand how she felt so that she would not be obliged to force a smile when next they met.

After Mary had settled at the lodgings on Cumming Street near Godwin's house, their "intimacy increased by regular, but almost imperceptible degrees."[19] By July 1 Godwin had evidently addressed a tribute in verse to her, and she was replying rather wryly:

> I want ... to remind you, when you write to me in *verse,* not to choose the easiest task, my perfections, but to dwell on your own feelings—that is to say, give me a bird's eye view of your heart. Do not make me a "desk to write upon," I humbly pray—unless you honestly acknowledge yourself *bewitched.*
>
> Of that I shall judge by the style in which the eulogiums flow, for I think I have observed that you compliment without rhyme or reason, when you are almost at a loss what to say.[20]

At the same time she sent him the last volume of *La Nouvelle Héloïse,* and placidly informed him: "I do not give you credit for as much philosophy as our friend [Rousseau]."

Obviously Mary felt little or no tenderness for her new suitor. If she thought about the matter at all, she must have felt that she could never love him as she had loved Imlay. In sober truth Godwin was a much less lovable person—in appearance at least. Most people found him quite absurd, with his grave demeanor, which recalled the Dissenting parson, with his massive head and his "most abominable" nose, which Southey longed to cut off whenever he saw it.[21] But Mary had written some time since that esteem was a better basis for marriage than passion;[22] and experience had perhaps confirmed her theory. Thus she was doubtless willing to overlook Godwin's appearance—and even his tiresome conversation, his affectations, and his clumsy attempts at affability. She certainly believed that passion had died in her when she had lost Imlay. What mattered now was that she find a "particular affection" to relieve her loneliness and to forestall her old fits of depression and anguish. She wanted a friend whom she could respect, one who was honest in mind and heart. And Godwin was such a man. Perhaps she mused that in time she would be able to correct his superficial faults.

During the month of July Godwin went down to Norfolk to visit his mother; and he discovered, when deprived of Mary's company, that he missed her a good deal. On July 13, a week before his return to town, he wrote her a letter which was little short of coy:

By way of discharging a debt, an obligation, what shall I say, I take up the pen.

Oh No! exclaimeth Mary, tant soit peu piqué, it is a mere task then, is it?

Now, I take all my Gods to witness—do you know how many they are? —but I obtest & obsecrate them all—that your company infinitely delights me, that I love your imagination, your delicate epicurism, the malicious leer of your eye, in short, every thing that constitutes the bewitching tout ensemble of the celebrated Mary. But to write!

Alas, I have no talent, for I have no subject. Shall I write a love letter? May Lucifer fly away with me, if I do! No, when I make love, it shall be with the eloquent tones of my voice, with dying accents, with speaking glances (through the glass of my spectacles), with all the witching of that irresistible, universal passion. Curse on the mechanical, icy medium of pen & paper. When I make love, it shall be in a storm, as Jupiter made love to Semele, & turned her at once to a cinder. Do not these menaces terrify you?

Well then, what shall be my subject. Shall I send you an eulogium of your beauty, your talents & your virtues? Ah! that is an old subject: beside, if I were to begin, instead of a sheet of paper, I should want a ream.

Shall I write to citizenness Wolstencraft a congratulatory epistle upon the victories of Buonaparti? That I may rejoice the cockles of her heart, shall I cause once more to pass in review before her the Saint Jerome, the Santa Cecilia, & the other inestimable treasures, of which that ferocious freebooter has robbed the classical & delicious cities of Italy?

Invent me a subject against my return, &, the next time I go into the country, I will write you such a letter!

Cause Margaret to drop a line into my letter box, signifying to the janitor, or jailor, Mr. Marshal, that I expect to arrive on this day sevennight at seven o'clock in the morning, to depart no more.

And he signed himself: "Your admirer, W. Godwin."

Back in London Mary was busy settling herself and Fanny in new quarters at 16 Judd Place West, on the edge of Somers Town. "Probably without exactly knowing why," Godwin later observed,[23] she had given up the idea of moving to the Continent. Instead she had decided to remain in London, and she had taken out of storage the furniture which had lain idle ever since her departure for Paris in 1792.

The day after Godwin's return to town she wrote to him:

Had you called upon me yesterday I should have thanked you for your letter—and—perhaps, have told you that the sentence I *liked* best was the concluding one, where you tell me, that you were coming home, to depart *no more*. But now I am out of humour I mean to bottle up my kindness, unless something in your countenance, when I do see you, should make the cork fly out—whether I will or not,

With such encouragement Godwin probably did not delay long in paying her a call. "We met," he says, "with new pleasure, and, I may add, with a more decisive preference for each other."[24] In fact six days after Godwin's arrival in London Mary was writing: "The weather not allowing me to go out about business to day, as I intended, if you are disengaged, I and my *habit* are at your service, in spite of wind or weather." And by August 2 she was even more forward. "I suppose you mean to drink tea with me, *one* of these days," she wrote. "How can you find in your heart to let me pass so many evenings alone? You may saucily ask, why I do not send for Mr. Twiss—but I shall reply with dignity—No; there will be more dignity in silence—so mum."

But Mary was still not absolutely sure of her ground, it would seem, and she apparently felt that she must clear the field of rivals. She chose to do so by laughing them out of the fray—and her method proved effective. In her note of August 2 she was almost certainly referring to Mrs. Inchbald (whom she never liked) when she wrote ironically: "I did not wish to see you this evening, because you have been dining, I suppose, with Mrs. Perfection, and comparisons are odious." And two days later she turned her attention to Godwin's flirtation with Amelia Alderson—and incidentally revealed that Amelia had been mocking him. "I spent the evening with Mademoiselle Alderson," she wrote. "You, I'm told, were ready to devour her—in your little parlour." Then on August 6, when she knew that he was going to call on Amelia, she sent him a note addressed to "Willm. Godwin Philosopher," with the directions: "Not to be opened 'till the Philosopher has been an hour, at least, in Miss Alderson's company, cheek by jowl." The note itself read: "Miss Alderson was wondering, this morning, whether you *ever* kissed a maiden fair. As you do not like to solve problems, *on paper,* TELL her *before* you part. She will tell *me* next—year."

Was this the woman who, only five months earlier, had written her last agonized letter to the man who had forsaken her? Had she forgotten so soon the suffering of the past two years? Hardly so. But Mary's common sense was in control now: she was deliberately routing all thought of the past from her mind. For the moment she was detached—even playful—though she seems to have had her mind fixed on a particular objective. But before long she abandoned her attitude of detachment. She discovered, doubtless to her surprise, that the man whom she had approached so casually had beneath his cold exterior deep resources of affection—even passion. And if Mary succeeded astonishingly well in routing her old passion, it was because she found a new one to take its place. Thus the old story was repeated. She who had found relief from her love for Fuseli by falling in love with

Imlay now found relief from her love for Imlay by falling in love with Godwin.

Only three weeks after Godwin's return from Norfolk he became her lover. "There was," he claims, ". . . no period of throes and resolute explanation attendant on the tale. It was friendship melting into love."[25] Yet the letters which passed between the two on August 17 suggest that Mary did not surrender herself without any qualms. Probably she feared Godwin would be outraged at her becoming his mistress so soon after the end of her affair with Imlay. "I have not lately passed so painful a night as the last," she wrote to him.

I feel that I cannot speak clearly on the subject to you, let me then briefly explain myself now I am alone. Yet, struggling as I have been a long time to attain peace of mind (or apathy) I am afraid to trace emotions to their source, which border on agony.

Is it not sufficient to tell you that I am thoroughly out of humour with myself? Mortified and humbled, I scarcely know why—still, despising false delicacy I almost fear that I have lost sight of the true. Could a wish have transported me to France or Italy, last night, I should have caught up my Fanny and been off in a twinkle, though convinced that it is my mind, not the place, which requires changing. My imagination is for ever betraying me into fresh misery, and I perceive I shall be a child to the end of the chapter. You talk of the roses which grow profusely in every path of life—I catch at them; but only encounter the thorns.

I would not be unjust for the world. I can only say that you appear to me to have acted injudiciously; and that full of your own feelings, little as I comprehend them, you forgot mine—or do not understand my character. It is my turn to have a fever to day. I am not well—I am hurt—But I mean not to hurt you. Consider what has past as a fever of your imagination; one of the slight mortal shakes to which you are liable—and I—will become again a *Solitary Walker*. Adieu! I was going to add God bless you!

Godwin, quick to sense the reason for her remorse, was as quick to reassure her. "How shall I answer you?" he wrote as soon as he had received her letter.

In one point we sympathize; I had rather at this moment talk to you on paper than in any other mode. I should feel ashamed in seeing you.

You do not know how honest I am. I swear to you that I told you nothing but the strict & literal truth, when I described to you the manner in which you set my imagination on fire on Saturday. For six & thirty hours I could think of nothing else. I longed inexpressibly to have you in my arms. Why did I not come to you? I am a fool. I feared still that I might be deceiving myself as to your feelings, & that I was feeding my mind with groundless presumptions. I determined to suffer the point to arrive at its own denouement. I was not aware that the fervour of my imagination was exhausting itself. Yet this, I believe, is no uncommon case.

Like any other man, I can speak only of what I know. But this I can boldly affirm, that nothing that I have seen in you would in the slightest degree authorise the opinion, that, *in despising the false delicacy, you have lost sight of the true.* I see nothing in you but what I respect & adore.

I know the acuteness of your feelings, & there is perhaps nothing upon earth that would give me so pungent a remorse, as to add to your unhappiness.

Do not hate me. Indeed I do not deserve it. Do not cast me off. Do not become again a *solitary walker.* Be just to me, & then, though you will discover in me much that is foolish and censurable, yet a woman of your understanding will still regard me with some partiality.

Upon consideration I find in you one fault, & but one. You have the feelings of nature, & you have the honesty to avow them. In all this you do well. I am sure you do. But do not let them tyrannise over you. Estimate every thing at its just value. It is best that we should be friends in every sense of the word; but in the mean time let us be friends.

Suffer me to see you. Let us leave every thing else to its own course. My imagination is not dead, I suppose, though it sleeps. But, be it as it will, I will torment you no more. I will be your friend, the friend of your mind, the admirer of your excellencies. All else I commit to the disposition of futurity, glad, if completely happy; passive & silent in this respect, while I am not so.

Be happy. Resolve to be happy. You deserve to be so. Every thing that interferes with it, is weakness & wandering; & a woman, like you, can, must, shall, shake it off. Afford, for instance, no food for the morbid madness, & no triumph to the misanthropical gloom, of your afternoon visitor. Call up, with firmness, the energies, which, I am sure, you so eminently possess.

Send me word that I may call on you in a day or two. Do you not see, while I exhort you to be a philosopher, how painfully acute are my own feelings? I need some soothing, though I cannot ask it from you.

And by two o'clock the same afternoon, Mary, now completely reassured, was writing back:

I like your last—may I call it *love* letter?—better than the first—and can I give you a higher proof of my esteem than to tell you (the style of my letter will whether I will or no) that it has calmed my mind—a mind that had been painfully active all the morning, haunted by old sorrows that seemed to come forward with new force to sharpen the present anguish. Well! well—it is almost gone—I mean all my unreasonable fears—and a whole train of tormentors, which you have routed. I can scarcely describe to you their ugly shapes so quickly do they vanish. And let them go, we will not bring them back by talking of them. You may see me when you please. I shall take this letter, just before dinner time, to ask you to come and dine with me, and Fanny, whom I have shut out to day. Should you be engaged come in the evening. Miss H[ays] seldom stays late, never to supper—or to-morrow—as you wish—I shall be content. You say you want soothing. Will it soothe you to tell you the truth? I cannot hate you— I do not think you deserve it. Nay, more—I cannot withhold my friendship from you, and will try to merit yours, that *necessity* may bind you to me. . . .

Now will you not be a good boy, and smile upon me? I dine at half past four. You ought to come and give me an appetite for my dinner, as you deprived me of one for my breakfast.

The contrast between Mary's two letters is startling. It only proves how volatile her nature was, how much a creature of feeling she could be. And it confirms the theory that the tone of her letters is never a sure index to her feelings at any given period of her life. Mary's feelings were never constant for very long at a time; she could be despondent at breakfast (when she feared that she had antagonized a friend) and jubilant at dinner (when assured that she retained his affection).

The new lovers scarcely considered marriage. Godwin had long since declared himself on that subject, and now that he had fallen in love with a woman who had already flouted wedlock, there seemed to be no good reason for being faithless to his theories. There was also, according to Godwin, a more practical reason for their not marrying: Mary was, as usual, deep in debt, and she was reluctant to involve him in her responsibilities. And so they decided to keep their affair absolutely secret. Godwin continued to squire Mrs. Inchbald about town (Miss Alderson having returned to Norwich), and Mary saw much of the artist John Opie. On November 11, 1796, Joseph Farington recorded in his diary the rumor that Mary and Opie were about to be married.[26] And on December 18 Amelia Alderson, herself destined to marry Opie in 1798, wrote to Mary: "I hear in a letter just received from Town, that you are to marry Opie, I mean *Law Willing*. That he would be most happy to marry you, I firmly believe; but I doubt yr willingness to marry *him*. I wish I did *not* for many reasons, all of which, if I explained them, you would find affectionate towards you."[27] But though Mary was undoubtedly seeing Opie regularly, she had no notion of becoming his wife. "Opie called this morning," she wrote to Godwin on November 3. "But you are the man."

Meanwhile the affection between Godwin and Mary grew steadily tenderer. There were petty differences, to be sure, but never the slightest suggestion that the love of either had diminished. Unlike Imlay, Godwin did not resent Mary's occasional criticism; he was not, he proved, an egotist whose self-love was stronger than his affection for any woman. On August 19, soon after she had become his mistress, Mary sent him, without comment, a fable about a sycamore tree which had been frost-bitten because it was too eager to put out its leaves when spring approached. Godwin wrote back promptly that he did not understand how she wished him to apply the allegory, and added:

Your fable of to day puts an end to all my hopes. I needed soothing, & you threaten me. Oppressed with a diffidence & uncertainty which I hate, you join the oppressors, & annihilate me. Use your pleasure. For every pain I have undesignedly given you, I am most sincerely grieved; for the good qualities I discern in you, you shall live for ever embalmed in my memory.

This was talking Mary's own language! Godwin could hardly have chosen a better way to respond to her "uncommonly ingenious" fable, as he called it. He was, in effect, demonstrating that he not only loved her but respected her as well—that he was truly a suitor. And Mary's heart must have been warmed by the knowledge that this new love was shared completely—that she received as much as she gave of affection.

The result was that though Mary flared up at times, she was quick to forget her anger. She was no longer on the defensive, as she had so often been in her affair with Imlay. Since she never felt neglected, she no longer sought to prove herself somehow superior to her beloved. Indeed Godwin was always eager to assure her of her superior qualities. When Mary wrote to him on August 22: "I am sometimes painfully humble. Write me, but a line just to assure me, that you have been thinking of me with affection, now and then—since we parted," Godwin replied before the day was out: "Humble! for heaven's sake, be proud, be arrogant! You are—but I cannot tell what you are. I cannot yet find the circumstance about you that allies you to the frailty of our nature. I will hunt it out." This was genuine devotion, and to Mary it must have been like balm to her undermined self-confidence. It made her long to see more of her lover. On August 26 she wrote to him: "Say when—or where, I am to see you, Godwin." And on the following day:

Should the weather continue uncertain *suppose* you were to bring your tragedy here—and we shall be so snug. Yet, you are such a kind creature, that I am afraid to express a preference, lest you should think of pleasing me rather than yourself—and is it not the same thing?—for I am never so well pleased with myself, as when I please you.

Surely she could not mourn for Imlay, now that she had found such a lover. Surely she had succeeded now in routing all thoughts of the old affair; in fact she succeeded so well that, according to Godwin, she never spoke bitterly of Imlay and was distressed when others did. And when she met him one day while she was walking along the New Road, she remained entirely composed. She even walked and talked with him, when he alighted from his horse. And she remained calm, treating him as a friend whom she had not seen for some time. For her the past was dead. Not that she tried to conceal it; on the contrary, she admitted freely that she had never been married to Imlay, and even made a point of telling one man so because she felt sure that he would pass the information along to others.

Yet Mary's new love did not monopolize all her time. Though Godwin seems to have accomplished less than usual after their affair began, she kept constantly busy. By August of 1796 she had already set to work on her novel *The Wrongs of Woman; or, Maria*, which, as Edward Dowden suggested,[28] was doubtless intended to show the faults of the system which Mary had attacked in *The Rights of Woman*, much as *Caleb Williams* had shown the faults of the system which Godwin had attacked in *Political Justice*. She was reviewing regularly for the *Analytical* too,[29] and serving again as Johnson's editorial assistant.[30] And of course her duties as a mother and the mistress of a household went on as usual. She even found time to play the wife on occasion. When Godwin fell ill, she acted as his nurse. But in reporting the matter to Mary Hays, she took pains to seem quite casual. "Mr. Godwin has been ill," she wrote, "and as I am a tolerable nurse, and he in a little want of one, I have frequently been with him, as well to amuse as to see that the things proper for him were got."[31]

Gradually Mary's life became calmer and more satisfying. She had now not only the satisfactions of love and work to inspirit her, but also the friendship of several women—many of them women of talent like Mrs. Siddons, the celebrated "Tragic Muse," and the beautiful Mary Robinson, once an actress and mistress of the Prince of Wales, but now a novelist and playwright. Mary Hays was still a devoted admirer, and Amelia Alderson, though living in Norwich, was bidding fair to outdo her in admiration. In reply to a postscript which Mary scribbled at the end of one of Godwin's letters, Amelia wrote ecstatically on August 28, 1796:

I derive so much pleasure from thinking of you, that I was delighted to find, you *wish* to retain a place in my remembrance.

Will you help me to account for the strong desire I always feel when with you, to say affectionate things to you? Perhaps it is because you, like *Julie,* appear so capable of feeling affection that you cannot fail to excite it.

I remember the time when my desire of seeing you was repress'd by fear—but as soon as I read your letters from Norway, the cold awe which the philosopher had excited, was lost in the tender sympathy call'd forth by the *woman.* I saw nothing but the interesting creature of feeling & imagination, & I resolved if possible, to become acquainted with one who had alternately awakened my sensibility & gratified my judgement. I *saw* you, & you are one of the few objects of my curiosity who in gratifying have not disappointed it also—You & the *Lakes of Cumberland* have exceeded my expectations.[32]

Soon Amelia was writing regularly to Mary, and in her letters to Godwin she often repeated the extravagant praise of "Mrs. Imlay" which she had heard from her liberal friends in Norwich. Then on November 18 she wrote that "a richish oldish bachelor" of her acquaintance had heard that Mary was in financial straits and wanted to convey an anonymous gift of five guineas to her as evidence of his esteem. Mary was only amused at the suggestion, and she and Godwin made light of it—much to the consternation of Amelia, who hastened to assure them that the gentleman's attentions were wholly disinterested. Yet however Mary might laugh at such attentions, they must have been gratifying and must have helped to bolster up her self-esteem.

But the attention of strangers and the admiration of friends were as nothing compared to the satisfaction which she had found in her new love. On September 12 Mary wrote to Archibald Hamilton Rowan that her mind was calmer than when she had last written to him, and that "self-respect seems to promise me that internal satisfaction on which alone true happiness is built."[33] And since Rowan was far away in America, she dared to drop a hint of the reason for her revived spirits by referring incidentally to "an intimate friend of mine, Mr. Godwin."

Yet only nine days before, her "intimate friend" had had the temerity to speak very frankly to her—in fact to criticize her writing rather sharply. And for once Mary was placed on the defensive in her relationship with Godwin, and was plunged into a profound depression—probably the more profound because she discerned a grain of truth in Godwin's criticism. On the following morning she wrote to him:

Labouring all the morning, in vain, to overcome an oppression of spirits, which some things you uttered yesterday, produced; I will try if I can shake it off by describing to you the nature of the feelings you excited.

I allude to what you remarked, relative to my manner of writing—that there was a radical defect in it—a worm in the bud—&c. What is to be done? I must either disregard your opinion, think it unjust, or throw down my pen in despair; and that would be tantamount to resigning existence; for at fifteen I resolved never to marry for interested motives, or to endure a life of dependence. You know not how painfully my sensibility, call it false if you will, has been wounded by some of the steps I have been obliged to take for others. I have even now plans at heart which depend on my exertions; and my entire confidence in Mr. Imlay plunged me into some difficulties, since we parted, that I could scarcely away with. I know that many of my cares have been the natural consequence of what nine out of ten would have termed folly—yet I cannot coincide in the opinion, without feeling a contempt for mankind. In short, I must reckon on doing some good, and getting the money I want, by my writings, or go to sleep for ever. I shall not be content merely to keep body and soul together. By what I have already written Johnson, I am sure, has been a gainer. And, for I would wish you to see my heart and mind just as it appears to myself, without drawing any veil of affected humility over it, though this whole letter is a proof of painful diffidence, I am compelled to think that there is some thing in my writings more valuable, than in the productions of some people on whom you bestow warm elogiums—I mean more mind—denominate it as you will—more of the observations of my own senses, more of the combining of my own imagination—the effusions of my own feelings and passions than the cold workings of the brain on the materials procured by the senses and imagination of other writers.

I am more out of patience with myself than you can form any idea of, when I tell you that I have scarcely written a line to please myself (and very little with respect to quantity) since you saw my MS. I have been endeavouring all this morning; and with such dissatisfied sensations I am almost afraid to go into company. But these are idle complaints to which I ought not to give utterance, even to you. I must then have done.

The letter could stand as Mary's *apologia pro vita sua*—such an apology as she could have written to no one but Godwin. For all her depression, she felt no resentment toward him; she could accept his criticism, knowing, as she did, that it was entirely honest and without a trace of malice—and knowing, too, that he loved her. Hence the affectionate close of the letter—and hence too the affectionate note which she wrote to him that same evening: "I only write now to bid you Good Night!—I shall be asleep before you—and I would leave you a God bless you did you care for it; but, alas! you do not, though Sterne says that it is equivalent to a—kiss." By September 13 she was expressing not only tenderness but passion:

Now by these presents let me assure you that you are not only in my heart, but my veins, this morning. I turn from you half abashed—yet you haunt me, and some look, word or touch thrills through my whole frame—yes, at the very moment when I am labouring to think of something, if not somebody, else. Get ye gone, Intruder! though I am forced to add dear—which is a call back.

When the heart and reason accord there is no flying from voluptuous sensations, I find, do what a woman can. Can a philosopher do more?

And two days later she was docilely taking lessons in English grammar from the man on whom her heart and reason had at last accorded. "You are to give me a lesson this evening," she wrote.

And, a word in your ear, I shall not be very angry if you sweeten grammatical disquisitions after the Miltonic mode. Fancy, at this moment, has turned a conjunction into a kiss; and the sensation steals o'er my senses. N'oublierez pas, I pray thee, the graceful pauses, I am alluding to; nay, anticipating—yet now you have led me to discover that I write worse than I thought I did, there is no stopping short. I must improve, or be dissatisfied with myself.

The strange courtship progressed pleasantly, with its odd compound of love, good conversation, and lessons in grammar. To many it would have seemed ridiculous, but it satisfied both Godwin and Mary mightily. He seems to have known instinctively how to rouse her from her moods of profound depression. One day she wrote:

Though I am not quite satisfied with myself, for acting like such a mere Girl, yesterday—yet I am better. What did you do to me? . . . Say only that we are friends; and, within an hour or two, the hour when I expect to see you—I shall be wise and demure—never fear—and you must not leave the philosopher behind.

And Godwin quickly replied: "Friends? Why not? If I thought otherwise, I should be miserable. In the evening expect me at nine, or a little before." And a few days later, in an outburst of his clumsy French: *"Adorable maitresse! J'éspère que vous étes plus gai ce matin! Prenez garde à vous!"* And if Godwin knew how to support and cheer her thus, it was primarily because he loved her wholeheartedly.

Soon Mary was asking for a key to his house so that she could stop in there and wait for him when she was in the mood to see him. And in the same letter she wrote:

If you go out, at two, you will perhaps call and tell me that you thought as kindly of me last night, as I did of you; for I am glad to discover great powers of mind in you, even at my own expence. One reason, I believe, why I wish you to have a good opinion of me is a conviction that the strongest affection is the most involuntary—yet I should not like you to love, you could not tell what, though it be a french compliment of the first class, without my explanation of it: the being enamoured of some fugitive charm, that seeking somewhere, you find every where. Yes; I would fain live in your heart and employ your imagination. Am I not very reasonable?

Here there was no self-defense, no rivalry for the upper hand.

Mary rejoiced now in the love of a man whom she respected thoroughly and who, she knew, felt equal respect for her. On October 4 she wrote to him with more genuine affection than she had ever felt for Imlay:

I should have liked to have dined with you to day, after finishing your essays—that my eyes, and lips, I do not exactly mean my voice, might have told you that they had raised you in my *esteem*. What a cold word! I would say love, if you will promise not to dispute about its propriety, when I want to express an increasing affection, founded on a more intimate acquaintance with your heart and understanding.

I shall cork up all my kindness—yet the fine volatile essence may fly off in my walk. You know not how much tenderness for you may escape in a voluptuous sigh, should the air, as is often the case, give a pleasurable movement to the sensations, that have been clustering round my heart, as I read this morning—reminding myself, every now and then, that the writer *loved me*. Voluptuous is often expressive of a meaning I do not now intend to give. I would describe one of those moments, when the senses are exactly tuned by the rising tenderness of the heart, and according reason entices you to live in the present moment, regardless of the past or future. It is not rapture.—It is a sublime tranquillity. I have felt it in your arms. Hush! Let not the light see, I was going to say hear it. These confessions should only be uttered—you know where, when the curtains are up—and all the world shut out.

Ah me! What shall I do to day? I anticipate the unpleasing task of re-pressing kindness—and I am overflowing with the kindest sympathy. I wish I may find you at home when I carry this letter to drop it in the box,—that I may drop a kiss with it into your heart, to be embalmed, till we meet, *closer*.

And Mary drew a line, lightly, through the word *closer*—and added: "Don't read the last word—I charge you!"

Surely Imlay was now a dead issue. Surely Godwin had driven away all Mary's regrets on that score. And oddly enough he whom she had sought as a refuge in her sorrow had brought her real happiness. Though she had doubtless expected to feel for him only an affection based on esteem, she found that she loved him passionately—even yearned for him physically. When in October her good friend Mrs. Cotton came up to the city to visit her for a few days—Mrs. Cotton who, in March, had helped to assuage Mary's wounded spirits—Godwin received a brief note of warning from his beloved: "Mrs. Cotton comes to morrow, should it prove fine, or saturday. She talks of a *few* days. Mon Dieu! Heaven and Earth!"

By November 10 their intimacy had almost reached the point of domesticity; at least Mary seems to have been doing Godwin's mending. And when she sent it back to him, she enclosed a note hinting that she might relish a more permanent sort of domesticity. "I send you your household linen," she wrote.

I am not sure that I did not feel a sensation of pleasure at thus acting the part of a wife, though you have so little respect for the character. There is such a magic in affection that I have been more gratified by your clasping your hands round my arm, in company, than I could have been by all the admiration in the world, tho' I am a woman—and to mount a step higher in the scale of vanity, an author.

And on the following Sunday:

If the felicity of last night has had the same effect on your health as on my countenance, you have no cause to lament your failure of resolution: for I have seldom seen so much live fire running about my features as this morning when recollections—very dear, called forth the blush of pleasure, as I adjusted my hair. . . .

Return me a line—and I pray thee put this note under lock and key— and, unless you love me *very much* do not read it again.

Notes like this must have given Godwin such pleasure as he had never before dreamed of. His new experience by no means substantiated his old theories: co-operation had yielded a measure of joy quite unexpected by this most thoroughgoing of all individualists. But what of that? Why fret about theories? As he wrote naïvely in the *Memoirs*: "I had never loved till now; or, at least, had never nourished a passion to the same growth, or met with an object so consummately worthy."[34] "There are other pleasures in the world, you perceive," Mary remarked in one of her notes, "beside those known to your philosophy."

Of course two people of such markedly different natures could not live always in unbroken harmony. Occasionally their temperaments clashed. Mary was bothered especially by Godwin's natural gravity, which caused him to take her light remarks too seriously. For example, on November 18, she wrote:

How do you do this morning—are you alive? It is not *wise* to be cold during
such a domesticating season. I mean then to dismiss all my frigid airs before
I draw near your door this evening, and should you, in your way from Mr.
Carlisle's, *think* of inquiring for the fourth act of Mrs. Inc's comedy—why
it would be a pretty mark of attention.—And—entre nous, *little* marks of
attention are incumbent on you at present. But—don't mistake me—I do
not wish to put you on your mettle. No; I only want to secure a play of
some kind or other, to rouse my torpid spirits, chez vous.

Godwin replied icily: "Yes, I am alive. Perhaps I am better. I am
glad to hear how enchanting & divine you will appear this evening.—You spoil little attentions by anticipating them." Then
Mary hastened to explain that she had not meant her words un-
kindly:

I wish . . . that you could distinguish between jest and earnest, to express
myself elegantly. To give you a criterion, I never play with edged-tools (I
believe) for when I am really hurt or angry I am dreadfully serious. Still
allow me a little more tether than is necessary for the purpose of feeding,
to keep soul and body together. Let me, I pray thee! have a sort of *comparative* freedom, as you are a profound Grammarian, to run round, as good,
better, best; cheerful, gay, playful; nay even frolicksome, once a year—or
so, when the whim seizes me of skipping out of bounds. Send me a *bill of
rights*—to this purport, under your hand and seal, with a *Bulletin* of health.

But Godwin replied brusquely:

I can send you a bill of rights & a bill of health: the former *carte blanche;*
the latter, much better (as I think). But to fulfil the terms of your note,
you must send me a bill of understanding. How can I always distinguish
between your jest and earnest, & know when your satire means nothing?
But I will try.

Soon the misunderstanding was cleared up, and Mary was writing:
"I do believe you love me better than you imagined you should.
As for me—judge for yourself." Yet Godwin's criticism of her
rankled in her mind, and on November 28, when she was feeling
low in spirits, she wrote:

You tell me that "I spoil little attentions, by anticipation." Yet to have
attention, I find, that it is necessary to demand it. My faults are very
inveterate—for I *did* expect you last night—But, *never mind it.* Your coming would not have been worth any thing, if it must be requested. . . .
    I insist on my not preventing you from going this evening to see Mil-
wood. I am not such a child as I thought myself.

Yet in the long run Mary's new happiness had brought her new wisdom. On December 6 she wrote: "I am not well, to day, yet I scarcely know what to complain of, excepting extreme lowness of spirits." But she added: "I will strive against it instead of talking of it." That same night she went with a friend to the theater, where they occupied very poor seats which Godwin had engaged. To add to her discomfort she knew that her beloved was enjoying himself in the company of Mrs. Inchbald, and she decided that she was a fool not to have asked Opie to escort her to the theater. But when she wrote to Godwin on the following morning, she mocked her own complaints. "If you will call on me this morning," she wrote, "and allow me to spend my spite I will admit you after the play to night." Mary had learned not to demand perfection in others and was at least beginning to see the futility of her own exasperation over small matters. And once again it was through Godwin's love that she was learning these lessons in the art of contented living.

As December wore on, however, she seemed increasingly irritable, and Godwin was obviously perturbed by her treatment of him. On the evening of the 12th, after they had spent an evening together in the company of others, Mary evidently told him that he need not accompany her home, and he took her at her word. The following morning she wrote to complain of his apparent indifference, and he replied: "I own I had the premeditated malice of making you part with me last night unwillingly. I feared Cupid had taken his final farewell." And on the 31st, after an outburst from Mary, he wrote to her:

You treated me last night with extreme unkindness: the more so, because it was calm, melancholy, equable unkindness. You wished we had never met; you wished you could cancel all that had passed between us. Is this—ask your own heart,—Is this compatible with the passion of love? Or, is it not the language of frigid, unalterable indifference?
You wished all the kind things you had ever written me destroyed.

But there was a reason for Mary's irritability. She hinted at it as early as December 20. After saying that Fanny had remarked that *perhaps* Godwin would call on them, she added: "As to other perhaps—they must rest in the womb of time." Then on the 23rd she wrote: "Of myself I am still at a loss what to say." But by the 31st she evidently was positive of her pregnancy. And after receiving Godwin's note charging her with "calm, melancholy, equable unkindness," she replied coldly:

This does not appear to me just the moment to have written me such a note as I have been perusing.

I am, however, prepared for any thing. I can abide by the consequence of my own conduct, and do not wish to envolve any one in my difficulties.

But after all, Godwin's note had doubtless told her what she wished to know: that he would stand by her if she must face the taunts of the world. And thereafter the bond between them was drawn only tighter by the knowledge that they would soon have a child of their own.

During the month of January Mary sent off notes to her lover every few days to inform him of the state of her health or to make appointments for meetings at her house or his. On the 5th she told him: "I was very glad that you were not with me last night, for I could not rouse myself. To say the truth, I was unwell —and out of spirits. I am better to day." On the 12th she was feeling well but feared that the heavy snowfall would prevent her from going to Godwin's house that evening. "What say you?" she asked. "But you have no petticoats to dangle in the snow. Poor Women—how they are beset with plagues—within—and without." And the next day she wrote to apologize for having teased him when they met. "I have been asking myself why it so happened," she mused. "Faith and troth, it was because there was nobody else worth attacking, or who could converse. . . . But, be assured, when I find a man that has anything in him, I shall let my every day dish alone."

Indeed Godwin had become by this time Mary's "every day dish," and their affair gradually took on a snug intimacy that was but one step from domesticity. In the notes which Mary wrote during February and March there is not a word of complaint. On February 3 she was planning to call on Dr. Fordyce but announced that she would not stop off at Godwin's because she seemed "inclined to be industrious." "I believe I feel affectionate to you in proportion as I am in spirits," she added; "still I must not dally with you when I can do any thing else. There is a civil speech for you to chew." On the 17th she asked, "Did I not see you, friend Godwin, at the theatre last night? I thought I met a smile; but you went out without looking round." And on the 22nd, although her sister Everina was visiting her and she was obliged to be cautious about her appointments with Godwin—although Fanny's cat had had fits and "flew up my chimney"—she seemed unperturbed. At times she was deliberately playful; she addressed Godwin as "you goose" and cajoled him with a "there is a good boy" when she asked a favor of him. To be sure, Godwin did not always reply in kind. He was as restrained and terse as ever when he wrote in March: "I will have the honour to dine with you.—You ask me whether I think I can get four orders. I do not know, but I do not think the thing impossible.—How do you do?" Yet by this time Mary had learned to take Godwin more or less as he was. She had jolted him out of some of his stiff sobriety, and she perhaps assured herself that she would eventually be able to enliven his literary style.

But she had learned much from her affair with Godwin. She was more tolerant now than ever before in her life—and more mature. She had learned not to let small matters mar her happiness. If her lover was not perfect, she was willing to bear with him and to help him correct his faults gradually and patiently. She was willing even to try to correct her own faults with his aid. She could relax now in the joyful sensation of being loved and anticipate serenely the birth of a son—whose name, of course, would be William. She was, all in all, wiser and more lovable than ever in her life before—and richer in truly womanly charm. She had found at last what she had been seeking for years, and now she could forget the frantic struggles which had overworked her energies and strained her temper. And her new maturity and wisdom are reflected in the letter signed "W. Q.," which she published in the *Monthly Magazine* for April, 1797 (it was her first contribution to a magazine other than the *Analytical Review*), and which Godwin later reprinted, with slight emendations, in Mary's *Posthumous Works* with the title "On Poetry and Our Relish for the Beauties of Nature."

Like the *Letters Written ... in Sweden, Norway, and Denmark* this essay reveals Mary as an enthusiastic nature-lover. She speaks of "brushing the dew away" on one of her "solitary rambles"; and her primary purpose is to answer the questions: Why is people's love of nature so often insincere? Why do they exclaim at natural beauties but seldom go outdoors to enjoy them? She concludes that it is primarily because most human beings lack imagination and fail to discern beauty until it is pointed out to them. Incidentally, however, she asks herself why poetry "written in the infancy of society" is more natural than that written in more civilized eras. She answers her own question by claiming that the poetry of primitive times

is the transcript of immediate sensations, in all their native wildness and simplicity, when fancy, awakened by the sight of interesting objects, was most actively at work. At such moments, sensibility quickly furnishes similes, and the sublimated spirits combine images, which rising spontaneously, it is not necessary coldly to ransack the understanding or memory, till the laborious efforts of judgment exclude present sensations, and damp the fire of enthusiasm.[35]

She goes on to say that in more advanced states of civilization the poet is a creature of art, not nature: "The silken wings of fancy are shrivelled by rules; and a desire of attaining elegance of diction, occasions an attention to words, incompatible with sublime, impassioned thoughts."[36] And to illustrate her point, she remarks that a schoolboy can be taught to write *pretty* verses but that he leaves his reader cold. "But," she adds, "though it should be allowed that books may produce some poets, I fear they will never be the poets who charm our cares to sleep, or extort admiration. They may diffuse taste, and polish the language; but I am inclined to conclude that they will seldom rouse the passions, or amend the heart."[37] And she disagrees with Dr. Johnson's claim that genius is "a strong mind, accidentally led to some particular study"; she insists, rather, that nature must "discover a bent" before genius flowers.

This is, of course, good Romantic doctrine. Mary, who had admired Rousseau when first she arrived in London, who had recently told Godwin that he was not Rousseau's equal as a philosopher, had turned almost completely away from eighteenth century rationalism. Her preference for "natural poetry," her confidence in the heart and the passions, her belief in innate genius (in sharp contrast to her old faith in education as the panacea for all the ills of society)—all these ideas implicit in her new essay veer markedly from the path which she had tried to follow through most of her adult life. And she gives these ideas more than mere lip-service: in fact she virtually calls for a romantic revival in poetry when she writes in the conclusion of her essay: "In the present state of society, the understanding must bring back the feelings to nature, or the sensibility must have such native strength, as rather to be whetted than destroyed by the strong exercise of passion."[38] Once again Mary reveals herself to be in the very vanguard of contemporary thought; and once again she is doubtless following the dictates of her own heart rather than echoing what she has heard from others. It was no accident that young men like Hazlitt and Coleridge and Southey sought her company. They saw in her a woman of kindred spirit, a person of imagination and sensitivity such as they prized highly. They were delighted by her conversation. Hazlitt later wrote in "My First Acquaintance with Poets":

[Coleridge] asked me if I had ever seen Mary Wolstonecraft, and I said, I had once for a few moments, and that she seemed to me to turn off Godwin's objections to something she advanced with quite a playful, easy air. He replied, that "this was only one instance of the ascendancy which people of imagination exercised over those of mere intellect." . . . He had a great idea of Mrs. Wolstonecraft's powers of conversation, none at all of her talent for book-making.[39]

And they were charmed by her appearance. Southey wrote to his friend Joseph Cottle in March, 1797:

Perhaps you will be surprised to hear that, of all the lions or *literati* that I have seen there is not one whose countenance has not some unpleasant trait. Mary Imlay's is the best, infinitely the best; the only fault in it is an expression . . . indicating superiority; not haughtiness, not sarcasm in Mary Imlay, but still it is unpleasant. Her eyes are light brown, and, though the lid of one of them is affected by a little paralysis, they are the most meaning I ever saw.[40]

If the eyes were "the most meaning," it was because they had seen so much—of both joy and sorrow—in thirty-eight years. If her expression suggested a sense of superiority, it was because she knew that few people had as much true wisdom as she had gained for herself. In all humility she could not fail to realize that she was the ablest woman in England; in all honesty she could not conceal her complacency. Yet it was a mellowed sort of complacency and no longer offensive to others. As Southey wrote to his brother in April: "She is a first-rate woman, sensible of her own worth, but without arrogance or affectation."[41] But in the portrait which Opie was soon to paint of her, after she had been married to one of the ablest men in England, she shows not complacency, but serenity.

The idea of marriage almost certainly originated with Mary. Even before her pregnancy she had hinted in her letters to Godwin that she was not averse to the idea. She was positive that their love would endure and that the marriage bond would never prove onerous to either of them. And as her confinement approached, she could not help seeing obvious practical reasons for marrying. Indeed who could have known them better? Godwin implies in the *Memoirs* that Mary urged him to marry because "she was unwilling, and perhaps with reason, to incur that exclusion from the society of many valuable and excellent individuals, which custom awards in cases of this sort."[42] Undoubtedly Mary was anxious, too, to safeguard her unborn child from such embarrassment as Fanny faced. As for Godwin, he was of course disconcerted at his own failure to live by his theories, and he did his best to ignore the ceremony. He and Mary went quietly to Old St. Pancras Church on March 29 and were married in the presence of only two witnesses: the parish clerk and Godwin's old friend James Marshal.

On or about April 6 the couple moved into a house at 29 The Polygon (a large and many-sided block of attached houses) in Somers Town, and proceeded to notify their friends of their new status. Mary's reasons for marrying were easy enough to explain. Signing herself "Mary Wollstonecraft, femme Godwin," she wrote to Amelia Alderson:

> The wound my unsuspecting heart formerly received is not healed. I found my evenings solitary, and I wished, while fulfilling the duty of a mother, to have some person with similar pursuits, bound to me by affection; and beside, I earnestly desired to resign a name which seemed to disgrace me.[43]

Godwin, however, felt obliged to do more explaining. When he notified Mary Hays, he seemed only slightly embarrassed:

> My fair neighbour desires me to announce to you a piece of news, which it is consonant to the regard that she and I entertain for you, you should rather learn from us than from any other quarter. She bids me remind you of the earnest way in which you pressed me to prevail upon her to change her name, and she directs me to add, that it has happened to me, like many other disputants, to be entrapped in my own toils: in short, that we found there was no way so obvious for her to drop the name of Imlay, as to assume the name of Godwin. Mrs. Godwin—who the devil is that?—will be glad to see you at No. 29, Polygon, Somers Town, whenever you are inclined to favour her with a call.[44]

But when he wrote to Thomas Wedgwood, from whom he had recently borrowed £50 to help settle Mary's debts, he tried manfully to reconcile his theories and his practice:

> Some persons have found an inconsistency between my practice in this instance and my doctrines. But I cannot see it. The doctrine of my 'Political Justice' is, that an attachment in some degree permanent, between two persons of opposite sexes is right, but that marriage, as practised in European countries, is wrong. I still adhere to that opinion. Nothing but a regard for the happiness of the individual, which I had no right to injure, could have induced me to submit to an institution which I wish to see abolished, and which I would recommend to my fellow-men, never to practise, but with the greatest caution.[45]

Soon letters of congratulation arrived from their friends. Holcroft, to whom Godwin had neglected to mention the name of his

new wife, was "a little pained" at his secrecy but otherwise ecstatic.
"From my very heart and soul I give you joy," he wrote. "I think
you the most extraordinary married pair in existence. May your
happiness be as pure as I firmly persuade myself it must be."[46]
Godwin's pious mother took quite a different approach when she
wrote to bless the new union:

Your broken resolution in regard to mattrimony incourages me to hope
that you will ere long embrace the Gospel, that sure word of promise to all
believers, and not only you, but your other half, whose souls should be both
one, as Watts says of his friend Gunston, the sooner the better. . . . You
might have been so good as told me a few more particulars about your
conjugal state, as when you were married, as being a father as well as a
husband; hope you will fill up your place with propriety in both relations;
you are certainly transformed in a moral sense, why is it impossable in a
spiritual sense, which last will make you shine with the radiance of the
sun for ever.

And the good old woman wished them joy, sent them a box of
eggs, offered them a small feather bed, and advised them not to
"make invitations and entertainments."[47]

Not all their acquaintances were so charitable. Mrs. Inchbald,
who had invited Godwin to a theater party, was clearly put out
at the news, for she wrote:

I most sincerely wish you and Mrs. Godwin joy. But, assured that your
joyfulness would obliterate from your memory every trifling engagement,
I have entreated another person to supply your place, and perform your
office, in securing a box on Reynold's night. If I have done wrong, when
you next marry, I will act differently.[48]

The slight to Mary was obvious, and it led to a breach in their
friendship. Undoubtedly Mrs. Inchbald was angry to discover that
Godwin had been carrying on an affair with Mary while she
herself had been regularly going to the theater or to private parties
with him. She claimed, however, that she could not afford to
compromise herself by appearing in Mary's company now that
Mary had, in effect, acknowledged publicly that she had never
been married to Imlay.[49] Mrs. Siddons and her sister Mrs. Twiss,
both of whom had become close friends of Mary's since her return
from her Scandinavian trip, took the same attitude, and broke immediately with her.

But of course the general attitude was one of amusement. Fuseli wryly observed that "the assertrix of female rights has given her hand to the *balancier* of political justice."[50] Joseph Ritson wrote to his nephew: "You have heard, by the way, that [Godwin] is lately married to Mary (alias Mistress) Wolstonecraft, according to the rites and ceremonies of the Church of England, which he was supposed to hold in the utmost detestation or contempt. His *cara sposa,* it seems, had been deceived by trusting to the honour of philosophy of one hackney author already."[51] Mrs. Barbauld wrote to a friend named Mrs. Beecroft: "I suppose you have seen it in the papers the marriage of Mr. Godwin and Mrs. Imlay alias Miss Woolstonecraft. A very suitable match, but numberless are the squibs that are thrown out at Mr. Godwin on the occasion, and he winces not a little on receiving the usual congratulations."[52] And Amelia Alderson wrote to her friend Mrs. Taylor: "Heigho! what charming things would sublime theories be, if one could make one's practice keep up with them; but I am convinced it is impossible, and am resolved to make the best of every-day nature."[53]

Of course the married life of the Godwins was far from conventional. "We do not entirely cohabit," Godwin had written to Thomas Wedgwood. And the truth was that he had taken rooms for himself in the Evesham Buildings, about twenty doors from their house in the Polygon. He went to his office each morning after breakfast, and there he stayed until noon at least, and often until dinnertime in the late afternoon. He and Mary seldom went out in company together; rather, they sought occasions to go out separately, for theirs was to be a marriage without monopoly on either side. "I still mean to be independent," Mary wrote to Amelia Alderson, "even to the cultivating sentiments and principles in my children's minds, (should I have more,) which he disavows."[54] But the world looked on skeptically. Mrs. Barbauld told Mrs. Beecroft:

In order to give the connection as little as possible the appearance of such a vulgar and debasing tie as matrimony, the parties have established separate establishments, and the husband only visits his mistress like a lover when each is dressed, rooms in order, &c. And this may possibly last till they have a family, then they will probably join quietly in one menage, like other folks.[55]

Godwin and Mary must have realized that they would be the butt of such jests. But they cared not; they were both busy, and they were happy. Mary was still laboring over *The Wrongs of Woman* and, perhaps in a special effort to discharge her debts, reviewing three novels and a book of travels for the May *Analytical*.[56] As time passed, the attacks of her old melancholia ceased almost completely, and she took real satisfaction in her new role of wife. When on April 8 she wrote to Godwin that she wished he would call on Joseph Johnson, she added: "But when I press any thing it is always with a true *wifish* submission to your judgment and inclination."

Every now and again, to be sure, she had a day when the details of ordinary living oppressed her. On April 11 she complained that the sink was not functioning properly and that Godwin "plagued me (a little) by not speaking more determinately to the Landlord." And later in the day, when she had some difficulty with a tradesman, she asked Godwin to send Marshal around to help her settle the matter. "Mr. Johnson, or somebody, has always taken the disagreeable business of settling with tradespeople off my hands," she remarked. And she added defiantly:

I am perhaps as unfit as yourself to do it—and my time appears to me as valuable as that of other persons accustomed to employ themselves. Things of this kind are easily settled with money, I know; but I am tormented by the want of money—and feel, to say the truth, as if I was not treated with respect, owing to your desire not to be disturbed.

Then on the 20th they had a real quarrel. Evidently Mary had again charged Godwin with lack of consideration for her. He replied:

I am pained by the recollection of our conversation last night. The sole principle of conduct of which I am conscious in my behaviour to you, has been in every thing to study your happiness. I found a wounded heart, &, as that heart cast itself upon me, it was my ambition to heal it. Do not let me be wholly disappointed.

> Let me have the relief of seeing you this morning. If I do not call before you go out, call on me.

Yet the trouble was soon forgotten, and Mary replied promptly: "I shall probably knock at your door in my way to Opie's; but should I not find you, let me request you not to be too late this evening." And in the fragmentary autobiography which Godwin left after his death he recorded his seasoned comment on the difficulties and satisfactions of life with Mary:

> The partner of my life was too quick in conceiving resentments; but they were dignified and restrained; they left no hateful and humiliating remembrances behind them, and we were as happy as is permitted to human beings.[57]

Mary enjoyed her new home thoroughly. She and Godwin probably lived well despite their financial obligations; they were not too poor to afford an occasional dinner party. And though she had lost a few of her old friends because of her marriage, she doubtless made new ones quickly. One evening she and Godwin entertained a dazzling group—Fuseli, Horne Tooke, Henry Grattan, and John Philpot Curran—and the conversation was so overpowering that Fuseli left in a pet.[58] She went into society frequently: Southey saw her three or four times at parties and was invited to her house once.[59] But as her pregnancy advanced, Mary must have been content usually to stay at home. She still had her reading and writing to occupy her when she had time free from household duties or caring for Fanny. She had her appointments with Opie, who was busy now on her portrait. She had friends in to tea now and then—Mary Hays or Mrs. Robinson or Mrs. Reveley or Mrs. Fenwick, the impulsive author of the novel *Secrecy*. And she must have enjoyed quiet evenings at home, relishing the sight of Godwin's growing love for Fanny and his growing anxiety about the arrival of "William," as they always called the baby soon to be born. Thus passed the months of April and May.

On Saturday, June 3, Godwin set out by carriage with his young friend Basil Montagu, the illegitimate son of the Earl of Sandwich, to visit the Wedgwood family at Etruria. Evidently

Mary sent him off charged to report regularly and *entertainingly* about his progress; for on Monday, the 5th, he wrote:

I write at this moment from Hampton Lucy, in sight of the house and park of Sir Thomas Lucy, the great benefactor of mankind, who prosecuted William Shakespeare for deer stealing, & obliged him to take refuge in the metropolis. Montagu has just had a vomit, to carry off a certain quantity of punch, with the drinking of which he concluded the Sunday evening.

Is that the right style for a letter?

But presently he abandoned his chatter to discuss more personal and more important matters. "And now, my dear love," he asked,

what do you think of me? Do not you find solitude infinitely superior to the company of a husband? Will you give me leave to return to you again, when I have finished my pilgrimage, & discharged the penance of absence? Take care of yourself, my love, & take care of William. Do not you be drowned, whatever I am. I remember at every moment all the accidents to which your condition subjects you, & wish I knew of some sympathy that could inform me from moment to moment, how you do, & how you feel.

Tell Fanny something about me. Ask her where she thinks I am. Say I am a great way off, & going further & further, but that I shall turn round & come back again some day. . . . Montagu said this morning about eight o'clock upon the road, Just now little Fanny is going to plungity plunge. Was he right?

Godwin had indeed found the right style for a letter. Life with Mary was going far to make a real human being of him.

Back in London Mary was delighted with the letter, and she replied with equal warmth on the following day. She told him that she was touched by his writing so promptly, and she commended him on his epistolary style. "I find," she remarked,

you can write the kind of letter a friend ought to write, and give an account of your movements. I hailed the sunshine, and moon-light, and travelled with you, scenting the fragrant gale. Enable me still to be your company, and I will allow you to peep over my shoulder, and see me under the shade of my green blind, thinking of you, and all I am to hear and feel when you return. You may read my heart—if you will.

And in reporting on the state of her health she revealed once again how much his affection meant to her:

I was not quite well the day after you left me; but it is past, and I am well and tranquil, excepting the disturbance produced by Master William's joy, who took it into his head to frisk a little at being informed of your remembrance. I begin to love this little creature, and to anticipate his birth as a fresh twist to a knot, which I do not wish to untie. Men are spoilt by frankness, I believe, yet I must tell you that I love you better than I supposed I did, when I promised to love you forever—and I will add what will gratify your benevolence, if not your heart, that on the whole I may be termed happy. You are a tender, affectionate creature; and I feel it thrilling through my frame giving and promising pleasure.

Her concluding paragraph was even more revealing:

I am not fatigued with solitude—yet I have not relished my solitary dinner. A husband is a convenient part of the furniture of a house, unless he be a clumsy fixture. I wish you, from my soul, to be rivetted in my heart; but I do not desire to have you always at my elbow—though at this moment I should not care if you were.

And she signed herself, appropriately, as "Yours truly and tenderly."

Godwin was touched by Mary's frank disclosure of her affection. When he replied on June 10, he was reading the letter over for the fourth time. And he began:

You cannot imagine how happy your letter made me. No creature expresses, because no creature feels, the tender affections, so perfectly as you do; & after all one's philosophy, it must be confessed that the knowledge, that there is some one that takes an interest in our happiness, something like that which each man feels in his own, is extremely gratifying.

It was an extraordinary admission, and for the moment Godwin seems to have relaxed completely from his old staidness. Then suddenly he sends a message to Fanny:

Give Fanny the kiss I sent her, & tell her, as I desired you, that I am in the land of mugs. You wish, it may be, that my message had been better adapted to her capacity; but I think it better as it is; I hope you do not disdain the task of being its commentator.

No baby talk for Godwin, regardless of his wife's directions! And presently he had lost all his ease and tenderness, and had assumed again the role of the philosopher:

One of the pleasures I promised myself in my excursion, was to increase my value in your estimation, & I am not disappointed. What we possess without intermission, we inevitably hold light; it is a refinement in voluptuousness, to submit to voluntary privations. Separation is the image of death, but it is Death stripped of all that is most tremendous, & his dart purged of its deadly venom. I always thought St. Paul's rule, that we should die daily, an exquisite Epicurean maxim. The practice of it would give to life a double relish.

On the same day Mary was writing to Godwin: "Pray tell me the precise time—I mean when it is fixed—I do believe I shall be glad to see you!—of your return, and I will keep a good look out." And in her conclusion she begged him to take good care of himself, adding: "Now I have ventured on you, I should not like to lose you." Unfortunately, however, her letter was slow in arriving, and on Monday the 12th Godwin sent her a chilling reprimand for her apparent failure to write to him. "You have encouraged me to believe," he began austerely,

that some pleasure results to you, merely from thus obtaining the power of accompanying my motions, and that what would be uninteresting to another may, by this circumstance, be rendered agreeable to you. I am the less capable of altering my method, if it ought to be altered, as you have not dealt fairly by me this post.

His annoyance, cool as it seemed, was of course prompted by love and anxiety; and presently he told her so:

What am I to think? How many possible accidents will the anxiety of affection present to one's thoughts? Not serious ones, I hope; in that case, I trust I should have heard. But head-aches; but sickness of the heart, a general loathing of life & of me. Do not give place to this worst of diseases! The least I can think is, that you recollect me with less tenderness & impatience than I reflect on you. There is a general sadness in the sky: the clouds are shutting round me, & seem depressed with moisture: every thing tunes the soul to melancholy. Guess what my feelings are, when the most soothing & consolatory thought that occurs, is a temporary remission & oblivion in your affections!

Just as he finished writing the words, a letter from Mary arrived; and he closed cheerfully, telling her that he expected to be back in London on the following Friday or Saturday.

But on Thursday he and Montagu were still traveling in leisurely style through Warwickshire. They had stopped at Derby to pay their respects to Erasmus Darwin the poet and at Tamworth to visit Robert Bage, the manufacturer turned novelist. Perhaps, Godwin remarked, they would not reach home until Sunday. On Sunday evening he wrote again; they had traveled only to Cambridge, and their arrival was postponed another day.

But when Monday came, they failed to appear. Mary waited and waited. Her patience was strained to the breaking point. Finally it snapped. Just before midnight she scribbled off her angry thoughts as they occurred to her:

One of the pleasures you tell me, that you promised yourself from your journey was the effect your absence might produce on me. Certainly at first my affection was increased; or rather was more alive. But now it is just the contrary. Your latter letters might have been addressed to any body —and will serve to remind you where you have been, though they resemble nothing less than mementos of affection.

I wrote to you to Dr. Parr's; you take no notice of my letter. Previous to your departure, I requested you not to torment me by leaving the day of your return undecided. But whatever tenderness you took away with you seems to have evaporated in the journey, and new objects—and the homage of vulgar minds, restored you to your icy Philosophy.

. . . I am at a loss to guess how you could have been from Saturday to Sunday night travelling from C[ovcntr]y to C[ambrid]ge. In short—your being so late to night, and the chance of your not coming, shows so little consideration, that unless you suppose me a stick or a stone, you must have forgot to think—as well as to feel, since you have been on the wing. I am afraid to add what I feel. Good-night.

Then, having vented her wrath, she doubtless marched off to bed. Godwin could shift for himself.

But the storm soon blew over. When Mary next wrote to her husband five days later, on June 25, she had almost returned to "true *wifish* submission." He had apparently objected to her calling on his friend Holcroft, and she replied that he was "right in the principle; but a little wrong in the present application." She proceeded to defend herself and to assure him that she did not intend to "obtrude on" his social life. For apparently Godwin objected to her going to Holcroft's, not because he disapproved of his wife's calling on another man, but because he felt that Holcroft's house was his own preserve. They had agreed to avoid each other in public, and she had failed to adhere to the letter of the agreement.

But they did not avoid each other's company at home. On July 3 Mary wrote:

I have a design upon you this evening to keep you quite to myself (I hope nobody will call!) and make you read the play.

I was thinking of a favourite song of my poor friend, Fanny's—"In a vacant rainy day you shall be wholly mine"—&c.

There must have many such evenings during July and August, the last two months of Mary's pregnancy. She had discovered that "a husband is a convenient part of the furniture of a house," and Godwin had discovered that "after all one's philosophy, it must be confessed that the knowledge, that there is some one that takes an interest in our happiness . . . is extremely gratifying." And despite Mary's occasional "sickness of the heart" and Godwin's lapses into "icy Philosophy," they were being drawn ever closer together. Both awaited eagerly the birth of "little William," who, with such illustrious parents and in such a stimulating household, could not fail to be a prodigy.

Yet there was one serious interruption to their happiness, caused by a woman named Miss Pinkerton, who had developed a romantic attachment for Godwin and was making a nuisance of herself. Did Mary recall now how she had plagued the Fuselis only five years before? If so, she took an entirely different attitude toward the problem, now that her own "property" was threatened. Godwin was her husband, and she had no notion of sharing him— much less losing him. And when he tried to make light of the whole affair, she wrote to him:

I think you *wrong*—yes; with the most decided conviction I dare to say it, having still in my mind the *unswervable* principles of justice and humanity. You judge not in your own case as in that of another. You give a softer name to folly and immorality when it flatters—yes, I must say it— your vanity, than to mistaken passion when it was extended to another. You termed Miss Hays' conduct insanity when only her own happiness was involved—I cannot forget the strength of your expressions—and you treat with a mildness calculated to foster it, a romantic selfishness, and pamper conceit, which will even lead the object to—I was going to say misery—but I believe her incapable of feeling it. Her want of sensibility with respect to her family first disgusted me. Then to obtrude herself on me, to see affection, and instead of feeling sympathy, to endeavour to under-mine it, certainly resembles the conduct of the fictitious being, to whose dignity she aspires. Yet you, at the very moment, commenced a corres-pondence with her whom you had previously almost neglected. You brought me a letter without a conclusion—and you changed countenance at the reply. My old wounds bleed afresh. What did not blind confidence, and unsuspecting truth, lead me to—my very soul trembles. Sooner than endure the hundredth part of what I have suffered, I could wish my poor Fanny and self asleep at the bottom of the sea.

One word more—I never blamed the woman for whom I was abandoned. I offered to see her, nay, even to live with her, and I should have tried to improve her. But even she was deceived with respect to my character, and had her scruples when she heard the truth. But enough of the effusions of a sick heart. I only intended to write a line or two.

Mary was terrified at the prospect of another disappointment in love; but Godwin soon set her mind at rest. Although the affair seems to have remained unresolved for a month,[60] their letters in the meantime were usually friendly—so much so, indeed, that they even addressed each other as "papa" and "mama." But on August 9 Mary wrote a note to Miss Pinkerton and sent it to Godwin for his approval. "I do not now feel the least resentment," she assured him, "and I merely write, because I expect to see her to day or to morrow, and truth demands that I should not seem ignorant of the steps she takes to extort visits from you." "If you have the slightest wish to prevent my writing at all," she added, "—say so—I shall think you actuated by humanity, though I may not coincide in opinion, with respect to the measures you take to effect your purpose." Evidently Godwin approved the note, and it had its desired effect; for presently Miss Pinkerton wrote back: "At length I am sensible of the impropriety of my conduct. Tears and communication afford me relief." And there the matter closed—with Mary victorious.

Meanwhile she was not idle. She had three projects in hand: the novel *The Wrongs of Woman,* which she was constantly recasting and rewriting; a manual entitled "Letters on the Management of Infants"; and a new series of books for children. All were destined to be left incomplete and to be published in fragmentary form scarcely six months later in Godwin's edition of Mary's *Posthumous Works.*

It would be unfair to judge Mary's powers in the last months of her life by her work in *The Wrongs of Woman; or, Maria.* Though she had intended the book as her masterpiece and had "recommenced and revised the manuscript several times" (doubt-less at Godwin's urging), she was dissatisfied even with Part I, which she had managed to work into a semblance of its final form. In his Preface to the novel Godwin quotes from a letter which she wrote to a friend whom she had asked for criticism: "I am perfectly aware that some of the incidents ought to be transposed, and heightened by more harmonious shading; and I wished in some degree to avail myself of criticism, before I began to adjust my events into a story the outline of which I had sketched in my mind."[61] Yet all its faults do not stem from its lack of finish. The most casual reader can see that *The Wrongs of Woman* would never have been a great novel. Mary was more interested in ideas than in personalities; she wanted to create not a convincing pic-ture of life but a bold criticism of life, and the thesis of her novel was far more important to her than the novel itself.

As a result Mary's picture of life is painfully distorted. When the story opens, her heroine, Maria Venables, is confined to an insane asylum by her brutal husband, who seeks to claim for him-self the fortune which she has inherited from an uncle. At the asylum she meets Henry Darnford, who also has been confined by relatives eager to seize his inheritance. And when Maria is told that her only child, a daughter, has died—presumably because her father has neglected her—she turns to Darnford for consolation, and presently falls in love with him. In order to inform him about her past history, she confides to him the autobiography intended for her daughter—written to tell the girl about her mother's mis-fortunes and to warn her against the wrongs which all women are likely to suffer. The rest of Part I is taken up with Maria's long account of her early life and her unhappy marriage. And while the reader reads it over (supposedly with Darnford), he gradually loses touch with the love of Maria and her new friend, on which the plot of the novel hinges.

From the fragments of Parts II and III it is apparent that Darnford eventually became Maria's lover, that they escaped from the asylum and lived together, and that Venables impoverished them by suing for adultery and seduction (offering Maria an opportunity to inveigh against the "partial laws" which can chain a woman to a man whom she has learned to loathe). The sketches for the final chapters of the book suggest that Darnford soon became so concerned with attempts to recoup his fortune that he neglected Maria. Then, apparently, was to follow a grand climax when she, having become pregnant, attempted suicide by taking laudanum—only to be prevented by her faithful attendant Jemima, who arrived in the nick of time, leading with her Maria's daughter, who proves not to have died of neglect after all. Then of course Maria, like her creator before her, determines to live on for her child's sake.

The plot is, in substance, arresting; and, if properly developed, it might have been hair-raising. The episodes, certainly, have often a melodramatic intensity which would have won admiration in Mary's time, if not in ours. But at best the novel would have been theatrical rather than dramatic; the characters are unconvincing, and the whole picture of life is shallow and two-dimensional. Even Maria's autobiography, written in the first person, fails to convince the reader; for Mary uses it not to reveal her heroine's inner thoughts but to set down her own reflections on life. And those reflections are usually concerned with the now rather threadbare subject: the slavery of her sex.

Most of the faults of the novel, indeed, arise from Mary's preoccupation with her thesis. It dominates the book and determines almost every incident. The wrongs of woman confront the reader at each turn of the plot—not only the wrongs which Maria suffers from Venables and Darnford, but the wrongs which any woman may suffer from the tyranny of man. To drive home her point, Mary stuffs the novel with irrelevant incidents. Every woman who appears is sooner or later provoked to tell how she has suffered at the hands of men; and the central plot is often left unheeded while the reader is regaled with a story utterly irrelevant except as it illustrates the thesis of the book. Naturally no novel could succeed against such odds.

In the Preface Godwin maintained that the novel in its fragmentary state would have value in revealing the operations of a creative mind. Apparently it was somewhat admired in its own time. Though never reissued in England after its first appearance in the *Posthumous Works,* it was translated into French by B. Ducos in 1798 and published separately (as *Maria; or, the Wrongs of Woman*) in Philadelphia in 1799. But to a modern reader the incoherence of the fragments, the lack of continuity in the narrative, and (above all) the relentless emphasis on the thesis render the book scarcely readable. Its only interest lies in the occasional passages of Maria's autobiography which throw light on Mary's own early life. One wonders, incidentally, how much of her subsequent history would have been worked into the story if she had lived to finish it. Darnford clearly suggests Imlay; and Mary may have been planning to use incidents from her affair with him, perhaps even to quote from the letters which she had written to him and which he had returned.

But though Mary's novel was almost certainly doomed to failure, the "Fragment of Letters on the Management of Infants" might well, if completed, have proved to be a signal contribution to contemporary understanding of the problems of child care. Mary had already shown, in her writings and her occasional comments on rearing Fanny, that she disagreed with eighteenth century practices.[62] In the "Letters" she would have had an opportunity to assemble and publish her thoughts on the subject. And since her work was to have been revised by the surgeon Anthony Carlisle, it might have been accepted as authoritative and have had appreciable influence. Unfortunately, however, Mary finished only the table of contents and a fragment of her introductory letter. The table of contents indicates that she would have begun with the mother's pregnancy and discussed the care and training of the child through its second year at least. The introductory letter, written informally as if to a friend who had asked for advice, says that the best method of rearing children is that based on simplicity. Mary adds that, since one-third of all children born die in infancy, something must be wrong with the usual methods, and that she hopes to improve conditions among the middle class, confident that the lower class will follow their example. And that is all. How much Mary might have anticipated modern theories of child care can never be known.

Of the series of books for children (intended specifically for Fanny, now three years old) only the "Lessons" appear in *Posthumous Works*.[63] There are fourteen in all, obviously planned to teach a child how to read. The first two contain only lists of common words, but in the third the child is given a simple story expressed in sentences of two, three, or four monosyllables. Gradually, in the succeeding lessons, the sentences become more difficult, and the story is continued, always with the recurring moral (an old favorite of Mary's) that children must obey their parents until experience matures their judgment and enables them to act wisely for themselves. Compared with the *Original Stories,* written only nine years earlier, the "Lessons" offer one more bit of evidence of Mary's growth in wisdom. They are pathetic, too, for the story which runs through them concerns the Godwin family as Mary imagines their life will be after the new baby is born. Fanny, in the story, is four years old; her little brother William is a baby on his mother's knee; "Papa plays a pretty tune on the fiddle," and all is serene. Nothing is said of the miseries of the past, and Fanny is led to believe that her present "papa" has always been with them. On the outside of the manuscript of the "Lessons" Godwin found, in Mary's hand, the note: "The first book of a series which I intended to have written for my unfortunate girl"; and he concluded that the note must have been written "in a period of desperation, in the month of October, 1795."[64] That may well be. Perhaps Mary had written the first two lessons much earlier than those describing life in the Polygon. Or perhaps she scrawled the words shortly after her second baby was born, when she had abandoned hope of recovering.

Though the "Lessons" described life in the Godwin household as Mary expected it to be a year later, it doubtless reflects the contentment and happiness which the family enjoyed during the last weeks before her confinement. She had no fear of the ordeal ahead. Fanny's birth had not proved difficult for her, and she was confident that "William" would cause her no trouble. She assured Godwin that he could expect her downstairs for dinner the day after his son was born, and she expressed only scorn for ladies who indulged themselves in a month's confinement. She had engaged a Mrs. Blenkinsop, matron and midwife at the Westminster Lying-in Hospital, to attend her—partially, no doubt, as Godwin remarked in the *Memoirs,* because she was "influenced by ideas of decorum,"[65] but doubtless also because she wished to display her confidence in her own sex. She had called on Mrs. Blenkinsop several times during her pregnancy, and had also, it would seem, been examined by Dr. George Fordyce and Anthony Carlisle. But she was convinced that the responsibility in childbirth lay with the mother rather than with her attendants, and she was prepared to fulfill her duties with dispatch.

On Wednesday, August 30, at five o'clock in the morning, her labor pains began. To Godwin, who went as usual to his rooms in the Evesham Buildings, she wrote soon after breakfast:

I have no doubt of seeing the animal to-day; but must wait for Mrs. Blenkinsop to guess at the hour. I have sent for her. Pray send me the newspaper. I wish I had a novel, or some book of sheer amusement, to excite curiosity, and while away the time. Have you anything of the kind?

At about nine o'clock Mrs. Blenkinsop arrived and examined her. Mary was distressed that the pains were coming on so slowly, and she refused to go upstairs to her room, hoping perhaps that she could hasten her labor by remaining active. To Godwin she reported:

Mrs. Blenkinsop tells me that Every thing is in a fair way, and that there is no fear of the event being put off till another day. Still, *at present,* she thinks I shall not immediately be freed from my load. I am very well. Call me before dinner time, unless you receive another message from me.

And she kept herself busy and cheerful throughout the morning by writing notes to friends.

At two o'clock in the afternoon she retired at last to her room, and at three she wrote to Godwin: "Mrs. Blenkinsop tells me that I am in the most natural state, and can promise me a safe delivery —but that I must have a little patience." Godwin dined that day with Mr. and Mrs. Reveley, but he was back at the Polygon during the evening and was waiting in his parlor (Mary refused to allow him to witness the birth), when the baby was born at 11:20 P.M. It turned out to be a girl rather than the boy whom the parents had so confidently expected. But whatever disappointment Godwin may have felt on that score was soon forgotten when Mrs. Blenkinsop told him, shortly after two o'clock on Thursday morning, that Mary had not yet discharged the placenta. Godwin rushed immediately from the house and brought back Dr. Poignand, physician and man-midwife at the Westminster Hospital, who went to work immediately to remove the placenta. Presently he reported that, though it had broken in the process, he had managed to remove all the pieces.—But he was mistaken.

Meanwhile Mary had been in agony. She had lost a great deal of blood and had fainted again and again. Not until eight o'clock on Thursday morning did she find relief from her suffering. And she later told Godwin that she had never known such acute pain. Compared with it, she said, any pain which she had known in the past was nothing. She told him, too, that she never would have lived through the night had she not been determined not to leave him. From one who had so often courted death, this was a real tribute.

When Dr. Poignand stopped at the house later Thursday morning, Godwin told him that Mary wished to call in her old friend Fordyce for consultation. Poignand discouraged the idea, claiming that Dr. Fordyce could be of little help, the more so because he had never specialized in obstetrics. But Godwin sent for him none the less. He called at three in the afternoon and, after an examination, pronounced Mary out of danger. Consequently Godwin, who had remained in his wife's bedchamber practically all day Thursday, felt sufficiently encouraged to spend most of the following day away from home on business. When he returned, he found her doing well. The crisis seemed to have passed.

On Saturday Mary seemed weaker, but she showed no alarming symptoms. Godwin could rest content that she was receiving the best of care. Besides her usual servant Mary, she had Eliza Fenwick as nurse, and Drs. Poignand and Fordyce were visiting her every day. Anthony Carlisle, too, had stopped in voluntarily to offer his services, and thereafter he called regularly. Thus, though Mary seemed somewhat worse on Saturday evening, Godwin did not hesitate to spend Sunday on a round of calls with Basil Montagu. He was soon to repent of his long absence.

When he reached home at dinnertime, he found Mary much weaker. She had been worried at his being away so long, and had suffered a "shivering fit."[66] Godwin's sister Hannah and a friend, who had been invited to dinner, were asked not to come; and Mary requested that the meal be served in the ground-floor parlor rather than in the regular dining room directly beneath her chamber. That evening she suffered more chills; "Every muscle of the body trembled, the teeth chattered, and the bed shook under her."[67] It was the turning point. Mary later told Godwin that she had frequently felt herself on the very verge of death. And from that time forth she rallied only to relapse again.

By this time Mary was under the care of Dr. Fordyce. Dr. Poignand had resigned the case, offended because Godwin had seen fit to consult another physician. On Monday Fordyce ordered that the baby be taken off the breast. Puppies were brought in to draw off the mother's milk, and for all her weakness Mary was able to joke about the procedure. Godwin hovered about, eager to be of some help, hopeful of keeping up her spirits. And when he "intreated her to recover," she replied with "smiles and kind speeches."[68]

On Tuesday Fordyce called in Dr. Clarke, a surgeon with offices on New Burlington Street, thinking that an operation might save Mary's life. Probably he hoped that they might extract the fragment of the placenta which was slowly poisoning her system. But Clarke evidently saw that she was too weak to undergo an operation, for nothing was done. And her suffering dragged on.

The next day Fordyce ordered that she be given wine "rather freely" to dull her senses and relieve her pain. Godwin obediently plied her with it from four in the afternoon until seven in the evening, himself suffering all the while. He was tormented with the thought that he was trifling with all that he most loved. And when a servant carelessly remarked that in her estimation Mary was sinking "as fast as possible," he was almost beside himself with anxiety and grief. Doubtless urged by a compulsion to do something for her, he sent that evening for Carlisle, who came at once from a dinner party several miles away and remained at the house almost constantly while Mary lived. Then Godwin decided that she should have another nurse; and when she suggested writing to Mrs. Cotton, in Berkshire, he put her off, convinced that he would be unable to reach her until too late for her to be of any use. Instead he called in Mary Hays. He himself scarcely left his wife's room. Basil Montagu, James Marshal, George Dyson, and Eliza Fenwick's husband (supposedly the original of the improvident Ralph Bigod in Lamb's "Two Races of Men") were at his disposal day and night to perform the necessary errands. Yet despite the houseful of people eager to serve Mary, despite the faithful attendance of Carlisle and Drs. Fordyce and Clarke, Godwin dared not hope for her recovery.

Thursday, Friday, and Saturday seemed interminable. On Thursday morning Carlisle thought she seemed better, but Godwin determined not to be beguiled by false hopes; and that evening, when she seemed again on the verge of dying, he had, as he perversely phrased it, "reason to rejoice in the firmness of my gloomy thoughts."[69] By Friday Mary herself seemed to be resigned to death. But this time she did not luxuriate in the histrionics which she had so often exercised when convinced that she had not long to live. Now that she had found happiness in life, death no longer appeared as a welcome release. When her husband asked her some questions about raising the children, ineptly explaining that he must oversee their training until she recovered, she said only, "I know what you are thinking of."[70] And to Godwin's satisfaction she uttered "not one word of a religious cast."[71] Thomas Cooper of Manchester later reported that she showed "a distressing reluctance to quit the world."[72] But Godwin's painstaking account of her last days stresses always her gentleness and her patience. She was, he claims, affectionate and eager to lighten her attendants' labor. When they asked her to rest, she obediently closed her eyes and tried to breathe steadily as though asleep. And when her servant urged her to do something for which she lacked the needed strength, she said only, "Pray, pray, do not let her reason with me."[73]

The slow weakening process never faltered. Mary had scarcely a moment's respite from pain. Once when Godwin gave her a drug to relieve her suffering, she is supposed to have murmured, "Oh Godwin, I am in heaven"—and he to have answered, lapsing into his old character: "You mean, my dear, that your physical sensations are somewhat easier."[74] But if he so lapsed now and then, he was, most of the time, as tender and devoted a husband as any woman could ask. Mary knew it, and she rejoiced in her good fortune, however belated. And shortly before 7:40 on the morning of Sunday, September 10, when her heart at last ceased its struggle against pain and weakness, she whispered: "He is the kindest, best man in the world."[75]

At first Godwin could find no way to express what he felt. He had slept little in the past week. He had been called up at six o'clock on this last morning, and since then he had stood at her bedside watching her painful efforts to live. Now she was dead. Now he had lost what so recently he had gained. How could he hope to express what he felt? When he sat down to enter the event in the diary which he kept so methodically, he wrote only "20 minutes before 8" and a long series of dashes.[76]

Then came the lonely days of waiting for the funeral. Godwin kept to himself. Fanny and the baby had been sent to Mrs. Reveley's house. Marshal and Basil Montagu attended to all necessary details, and Godwin tried to fill the long hours by writing notes to inform his friends of Mary's death. To Holcroft he wrote:

> My wife is now dead. She died this morning at eight o'clock. She grew worse before your letter arrived. Nobody has a greater call to reproach himself, except for want of kindness and attention in which I hope I have not been very deficient, than I have. But reproach would answer no good purpose, and I will not harbour it.
>
> I firmly believe that there does not exist her equal in the world. I know from experience we were formed to make each other happy. I have not the least expectation that I can now ever know happiness again.[77]

Three days later he was carrying on a fruitless argument with a friend named Tuthil, who had declined to attend the funeral on the ground that it would be immoral for an unbeliever like himself to be present at a religious ceremony.[78] By September 14, when he replied to a letter of condolence from Mary's friend Mrs. Cotton, he had, he said, "half destroyed" himself with writing, and had found that "it does me more mischief than anything else."[79] Yet on the 15th he was still writing. Mary's funeral, which began at ten o'clock in the morning, was in progress; and still he wrote. He was too much prostrated to attend the service, and he sat alone in Marshal's lodgings, writing now to Anthony Carlisle to thank him for all his kindnesses during Mary's illness. "My mind is extremely sunk and languid," he told Carlisle.

> But I husband my thoughts, and shall do very well. I have been but once since you saw me, in a train of thought that gave me alarm. One of my wife's books now lies near me, but I avoid opening it. I took up a book on the education of children, but that impressed me too forcibly with my forlorn and disabled state with respect to the two poor animals left under my protection, and I threw it aside.

Then he proceeded to pay tribute to Carlisle's "clear and capacious" understanding, his "goodness of heart," and his "sweetness of manners." And he concluded almost plaintively: "If you have any . . . consolation in store for me, be at the pains to bestow it. But, above all, be severely sincere. I ought to be acquainted with my own defects, and to trace their nature in the effects they produce."[80] It is probably a unique document.

Mary was buried in St. Pancras Churchyard. It was less than six months since she and Godwin had stolen away to the old church to be married. On the headstone which he and some of her friends erected over her grave in the following year Godwin placed the simple inscription:

> Mary Wollstonecraft Godwin,
> Author of
> A Vindication
> Of the Rights of Woman:
> Born 27 April, 1759:
> Died 10 September, 1797.

Wisely he made no attempt to enumerate her virtues; they were familiar enough to the many who had enjoyed her friendship. As for her faults, he had practically forgotten them. If others recalled them, they were silent—for the present, at least. Imlay, whom her faults had betrayed for the cad that he was, had vanished from the scene. And Fuseli, who had been alternately amused and annoyed by her faults, wrote only: "Poor Mary!"[81] Yet Mary would probably have spurned his pity. She who had so often pitied herself and sought pity from others—she who had despaired of happiness and longed for death—had died a happy woman. Fuseli could hardly have imagined what only she and Godwin knew: that she had lived through years of frustration only to find the fulfillment of her nature in the last few months of her life.

CHAPTER X
Epilogue

Something resides in this heart that is not perishable.
—Letters Written ... in Sweden.

WHEN Mary's death was announced in the press, her faults were again almost completely overlooked. The anonymous obituary in the *Monthly Magazine* for September, 1797, was probably the most profuse in its praise of her: the author lauded her talents fulsomely and lamented her martyrdom. Then in the following month, the magazine contained a letter from Mary Hays informing readers that she had written the obituary and wished to be known as its author. Even the *Gentleman's Magazine,* which had ignored Mary's existence since the appearance of her *Rights of Men,* hailed her now as "a woman of uncommon talents and considerable knowledge." Apparently the editors felt that they could afford to be tolerant, now that Mary would no longer threaten the institutions they revered; and though they still bemoaned her political opinions and her morality, they generously admitted:

Her manners were gentle, easy, and elegant; her conversation intelligent and amusing, without the least trace of literary pride or the apparent consciousness of powers above the level of her sex; and, for soundness of understanding, and sensibility of heart, she was, perhaps, never equaled. Her practical skill in education was even superior to her speculations on that subject; nor is it possible to express the misfortune sustained, in that respect, by her children.[1]

Godwin must have been touched by such tributes, but they could not console him for his loss. In fact, if he read the obituary in the *Gentleman's Magazine,* he was only reminded of the baffling problem which confronted him: how was he to bring up the two children whom Mary had left behind? In the midst of his aching grief he must find a solution. Where could he find a woman of Mary's capacity to direct the care of his house and children? He could not imagine finding such another, much less one who would be willing to devote her powers to directing his household. The two little girls had been returned from Mrs. Reveley's house now. Fanny had been brought back on the day after her mother's funeral, and the baby—named, of course, Mary Wollstonecraft Godwin—had been returned on the day after that. Mrs. Fenwick had agreed to stay on at the house for a few days to take charge, but the arrangement was of course only tentative.

Probably Godwin believed that the new baby would demand especially careful training. If she were to inherit her parents' genius, she would certainly be a prodigy—such as only her dead mother could rear properly. She was a healthy child from the outset—"the finest baby I ever saw," Mrs. Fenwick reported to Everina Wollstonecraft[2]—but her father must have been more interested in her mind than in her body. And he probably read attentively the analysis of her character made by William Nicholson, who called at Godwin's house the day after the baby was brought home. "The outline of the head viewed from above, its profile, the outline of the forehead . . . are such as I have invariably and exclusively seen in subjects who possessed considerable memory and intelligence," Nicholson reported. "The base of the forehead, the eyes and eyebrows, are familiar to me in subjects of quick sensibility, irritable, scarcely irascible, and surely not given to rage. That part of the outline of the forehead, which is very distinct in patient investigators, is less so in her. I think her powers, of themselves, would lead to speedy combination, rather than continued research."[3] Godwin might well have reflected that here was indeed another Mary Wollstonecraft Godwin.

Eventually the supervision of the house and children was entrusted to a Miss Louisa Jones, one of his sister Hannah's friends. He himself vacated his office in Evesham Buildings and moved his study to Mary's former chamber, so that he would be able to keep in touch with affairs at home. Then he set himself to the task of rising above his sorrow. As a philosopher he disapproved of excessive mourning: twenty years later, when little Clara Everina Shelley died, he wrote to his daughter:

I sincerely sympathize with you in the affliction which forms the subject of your letter, and which I may consider as the first severe trial of your constancy and the firmness of your temper that has occurred to you in the course of your life. You should, however, recollect that it is only persons of a very ordinary sort, and of a very pusillanimous disposition, that sink long under a calamity of this nature. I assure you such a recollection will be of great use to you. We seldom indulge long in depression and mourning, except when we think secretly that there is something very refined in it, and that it does us honour.[4]

Accordingly, he now encouraged friends to call on him and welcomed their invitations to dinner. He made a point of spending his evenings away from home, and when he was not invited out, he often went to the theater rather than sit by himself at the Polygon. Yet he found that he could not easily force his griefs or his worries from his mind. And when he wrote to Mary's friend Mrs. Cotton on October 24, he was still overwhelmed:

I am still here, in the same situation in which you saw me, surrounded by the children, and all the well-known objects, which, though they all talk to me of melancholy, are still dear to me. I love to cherish melancholy. I love to tread the edge of intellectual danger, and just to keep within the line which every moral and intellectual consideration forbids me to overstep, and in this indulgence and this vigilance I place my present luxury.

The poor children! I am myself totally unfitted to educate them. The scepticism which perhaps sometimes leads me right in matters of speculation, is torment to me when I would attempt to direct the infant mind. I am the most unfit person for this office; she was the best qualified in the world. What a change. The loss of the children is less remediless than mine. You can understand the difference.[5]

He tried to proceed with the literary work which he had in hand, but he found that his thoughts constantly recurred to Mary. He tried to read, but he found that he could enjoy nothing but her books—which only fed his grief. From them he turned to the letters and unpublished papers which she had left behind her. And the result was that he reached a salutary decision: he would edit Mary's unpublished writings and would record her life while its details were still fresh in his memory. This would be his memorial for her; he would preserve for posterity all that could be preserved of the woman whom he had loved.

The *Posthumous Works of the Author of "A Vindication of the Rights of Woman,"* in four volumes, and the *Memoirs of the Author of "A Vindication of the Rights of Woman,"* in one, were published by Joseph Johnson early in 1798. The first contained the fragments of the three works which Mary had been writing during the last year of her life: the novel *The Wrongs of Woman,* the "Letters on the Management of Infants," and the "Lessons." Along with them Godwin published the essay "On Poetry and Our Relish for the Beauties of Nature" (already published in the *Monthly Magazine* for April, 1797), the "Letter on the Present Character of the French Nation" (written in Paris in 1793), and the unfinished "Cave of Fancy" (begun in 1787). To these papers obviously intended for publication he added Mary's letters to Imlay and to Joseph Johnson and a collection of what he called "Hints Chiefly Designed to Have Been Incorporated in the Second Part of the *Vindication of the Rights of Woman.*" Actually the "Hints" seem like a collection of maxims on various subjects which Mary had written over a long period. Only the first nine concern the position of women; the remaining twenty-three treat of matters related to education, religion, poetry, taste, and imagination. And though Mary, in one of the earlier "Hints," warns against the dangers of a romantic imagination, she later asserts boldly her confidence in the imagination. For example:

24: When the Arabs had no trace of literature or science, they composed beautiful verses on the subjects of love and war. The flights of the imagination, and the laboured deductions of reason, appear almost incompatible.

28: Mr. Kant has observed, that the understanding is sublime, the imagination beautiful—yet it is evident, that poets, and men who undoubtedly possess the liveliest imagination, are most touched by the sublime, while men who have cold, enquiring minds, have not this exquisite feeling in any great degree, and indeed seem to lose it as they cultivate their reason.

31: It is the individual manner of seeing and feeling, pourtrayed by a strong imagination in bold images that have struck the senses, which creates all the charms of poetry. A great reader is always quoting the descriptions of another's emotions: a strong imagination delights to paint its own. A writer of genius makes us feel; an inferior author reason.

These, together with Mary's reference to "rude Gothic grandeur" and her dissatisfaction with the lack of stimulus given the imagination by "Grecian buildings," sound like the product of what might be termed Mary's "Pre-Romantic period." And they show once again that she had discovered her natural sympathy with the new tendency in contemporary thought.

The sixteen "Letters to Mr. Johnson" published in the *Posthumous Works* have only autobiographical interest, but the "Letters [to Imlay]," seventy-seven in all, in Volumes III and IV, have been much admired for their literary merits. Godwin claimed that they "may possibly be found to contain the finest examples of the language of sentiment and passion ever presented to the world,"[6] and later writers have often echoed his praise. Surely few collections of letters have revealed so clearly the anguish of a mind at once frantic and articulate, and few have given more intimate glimpses of the pangs of disprized love. Yet their morbid sentimentality soon cloys, and their endless reiteration soon tires. The tenderness and delicacy of the early letters gives way to self-consciousness; as Mary grew unsure of Imlay's love, she became increasingly critical of him and insisted on detailing her own merits to prove that she deserved his respect and affection. She tried to make herself more "interesting"; and to do so, she dramatized herself and cultivated false rhetorical effects as she had done in her earlier letters to her sisters and George Blood. Certainly most of Mary's letters have more interest to a psychologist than to a literary critic, and they must have antagonized many a reader who has admired Mary's achievements or been moved by her personal history. Such a reader can see Mary at her best in the notes which she scribbled off to Godwin during the last year of her life. In Godwin she had found a man who valued her; with him she could be herself. She no longer cultivated "the language of sentiment and passion"; she eschewed overstatement for overtones; she abandoned her role of sufferer to chat or laugh or scold or whisper, much as she must have done in life. Unfortunately Godwin was unwilling to share these letters with others—or he may have regarded them as mere letters, and nothing more. At all events he left them unpublished and gave the world, instead, the letters to Imlay, which he considered to be *Literature*.

In the *Memoirs* Godwin remarked that it would be "an idle piece of delicacy to attempt to suppress a name, which is known to every one whom the reputation of Mary has reached,"[7] and accordingly he related her affair with Imlay in as much detail as he could furnish. In a sense it was a violation of trust, since Mary had promised Imlay that she would never attempt to throw the odium of the affair on him. But Godwin, understandably enough, wished to vindicate his wife. He felt no obligation to Imlay; perhaps he believed that such perfidy should be revealed. If so, he succeeded; Imlay was completely unmasked. And he was perhaps thoroughly embarrassed, for he seems to have disappeared from public notice. Nothing further is known of him except that he is probably the Gilbert Imlay who was buried in St. Brelade's Churchyard, on the island of Jersey, in 1828.[8] Perhaps he fled to Jersey to escape the infamy which the *Memoirs* brought to him.

Godwin wisely avoided apologizing for Mary in his biography of her. Instead, he presented as honest an account of her life as he could construct from his own knowledge, from her writings, and from information provided by friends like Hugh Skeys and Joseph Johnson. Mary's sisters, who might have aided him most, unfortunately disapproved of him and refused to help him in any way. But so far as he could make it, the *Memoirs* was accurate and complete. He made no attempt to gloze over the details of Mary's life which might scandalize conventional readers; he told all: her love affairs with Imlay and himself, her attempts at suicide, and her frailties of temper. The narrative was brightened, however, by his recognition of her powers, so different from his own, and by his devoted affection for her. Even his description of her final illness, which he told in all its agonizing detail, was ennobled by his recollection of his own suffering and despair, always set down with due restraint. The book was, as the American Henry Tuckerman later wrote, an "unaffected, manly, and truthful narrative"[9]—the tenderest and most humane piece of writing ever to come from Godwin's pen. It shows clearly that he was, as Coleridge claimed, "in heart and manner . . . all the better for having been the husband of Mary Wollstonecraft."[10] Thanks to his wife's conscious efforts, his literary style had been considerably enlivened; and thanks to his experience of love and sorrow, he had learned a new respect for human emotions. In fact, as his biographer F. K. Brown points out, Godwin virtually renounced, in the *Memoirs,* two of the cardinal tenets of *Political Justice*: the doctrine that "general benevolence" should replace personal affection, and the doctrine that reason alone can guide a man to right conduct.[11] And he showed more marked changes in the novel *St. Leon,* published in 1799. Nowhere, however, is his debt to Mary more specifically stated than in the pathetic last paragraphs of the first edition of the *Memoirs*:

The loss of the world in this admirable woman, I leave other men to collect; my own I well know, nor can it be improper to describe it. I do not here allude to the personal pleasures I enjoyed in her conversation: these increased every day, in proportion as we knew each other better, and as our mutual confidence increased. They can be measured only by the treasures of her mind, and the virtues of her heart. But this is a subject for meditation, not for words. What I purposed alluding to, was the improvement that I have for ever lost.

We had cultivated our powers (if I may venture to use this sort of language) in different directions; I chiefly an attempt at logical and metaphysical distinction, she a taste for the picturesque. One of the leading passions of my mind has been an anxious desire not to be deceived. This has led me to view the topics of my reflection on all sides; and to examine and re-examine without end, the questions that interest me.

But it was not merely (to judge at least from all the reports of my memory in this respect) the difference of propensities, that made the difference in our intellectual habits. I have been stimulated, as long as I can remember, by an ambition for intellectual distinction; but, as long as I can remember, I have been discouraged, when I have endeavoured to cast the sum of my intellectual value, by finding that I did not possess, in the degree of some other men, an intuitive perception of intellectual beauty. I have perhaps a strong and lively sense of the pleasures of the imagination; but I have seldom been right in assigning to them their proportionate value, but by dint of persevering examination, and the change and correction of my first opinions.

What I wanted in this respect, Mary possessed in a degree superior to any other person I ever knew. The strength of her mind lay in intuition.

She was often right, by this means only, in matters of mere speculation. Her religion, her philosophy, (in both of which the errors were comparatively few, and the strain dignified and generous) were, as I have already said, the pure result of feeling and taste. She adopted one opinion, and rejected another, spontaneously, by a sort of tact, and the force of a cultivated imagination; and yet, though perhaps, in the strict sense of the term, she reasoned little, it is surprising what a degree of soundness is to be found in her determinations. But, if this quality was of use to her in topics that seem the proper province of reasoning, it was much more so in matters directly appealing to the intellectual taste. In a robust and unwavering judgment of this sort, there is a kind of witchcraft; when it decides justly, it produces a responsive vibration in every ingenuous mind. In this sense, my oscillation and scepticism were fixed by her boldness. When a true opinion emanated in this way from another mind, the conviction produced in my own assumed a similar character, instantaneous and firm. This species of intellect probably differs from the other, chiefly in the relation of earlier and later. What the one perceives instantaneously (circumstances having produced in it, either a premature attention to objects of this sort, or a greater boldness of decision) the other receives only by degrees. What it wants, seems to be nothing more than a minute attention to first impressions, and a just appreciation of them; habits that are never so effectually generated, as by the daily recurrence of a striking example.

This light was lent to me for a very short period, and is now extinguished for ever![12]

Though the *Posthumous Works* was never reprinted in its entirety, the *Memoirs* went into a second (and somewhat revised) edition within a few months, and, as *Memoirs of Mary Wollstonecraft Godwin,* appeared in two American editions published at Philadelphia in 1799 and 1804. Meanwhile it had been translated into German by Christian Gotthilf Salzmann in 1799 and into French by "le Citoyen D*****n" in 1802.[13] But though the book found a reasonably wide audience, it and the *Posthumous Works* were received by critics with almost universal disfavor. To be sure, the *Analytical* loyally defended Mary's unconventional behavior and theories; but in doing so—and in expressing regret that Godwin had failed to *explain* the reasons for her principles—the reviewer attempted the very kind of apology which Godwin had disdained to write. Of other magazines, the *Monthly Mirror* was most favorable: its critic found the *Memoirs* tiresome because of its detail and *The Wrongs of Woman* too incomplete to be properly judged, but praised Mary herself and her letters to Imlay extravagantly.[14] Generally speaking, however, reviewers were scandalized to learn the details of Mary's private life; and even those who could excuse her unorthodox behavior agreed in damning Godwin's candor in revealing it.[15] Dr. Robert Bisset's *Historical Magazine* went so far as to pronounce the *Memoirs* the "most hurtful" book of the year 1798.[16] And even the best-disposed of reviewers would probably have approved the biographer William Roscoe's lines:

> Hard was thy fate in all the scenes of life,
> As daughter, sister, mother, friend, and wife;
> But harder still thy fate in death we own,
> Thus mourn'd by Godwin with a heart of stone.[17]

The claim was, of course, grossly unfair: Godwin's heart had never been tenderer than when he wrote the *Memoirs*. Yet he could scarcely have done Mary's reputation more harm if he had deliberately set out to vilify her.

In short order she became a symbol of the hated Jacobinism. The scurrilous organs of the Tory press turned on her with a vengeance and defiled her memory with grim glee. Somehow the young men of the famous *Anti-Jacobin*—including George Canning and John Hookham Frere, who had been students at Eton when Mary visited there in 1786—never attacked her. Though their magazine appeared weekly from November 20, 1797, to July 9, 1798, and though they occasionally attacked Godwin and Helen Maria Williams, they ignored the *Memoirs* and never once mentioned Mary. But the monthly *Anti-Jacobin Review and Magazine,* which succeeded the *Anti-Jacobin,* assailed her in its very first issue. The editors began by a scathing review of *The Wrongs of Woman,* concluding:

But as there have been writers, who have in theory promulgated opinions subversive of morality, yet in their conduct have not been immoral, Godwin has laboured to inform the world, that the theory of Mrs. Wollstonecroft was reduced to practice; that she lived and acted, as she wrote and taught.[18]

Then followed a slashing critique of the *Memoirs,* consisting of a summary of Mary's life with bitter comments on her every action. The reviewer found fault not only with her love affairs and her attempts at suicide; he even charged her with disrespect for her parents, with neglecting her pupils at Newington Green when she left them to nurse Fanny Blood at Lisbon, and with planning to emigrate to America so as to escape her creditors. And what he dared not state, he implied. For example: "The biographer does not mention many of her amours."[19] He found some consolation, however, in the thought that Mary's example might serve as a woeful warning to others. "Intended by [Godwin] for a beacon," he observed, "it serves for a buoy; if it does not shew what it is wise to pursue, it manifests what it is wise to avoid."[20] And in conclusion he attacked the *Analytical* for its favorable reviews of the *Memoirs* and *Posthumous Works* and promised to combat religiously all such evidences of Jacobinism wherever he found them. The *coup de grâce* came in the Index to the magazine, where under the heading "Prostitution" the editors inserted the direction: "See Mary Wollstonecraft."

Nor was this the only scathing review of the books which Godwin had prepared to honor the memory of his wife. The criticism of the *Memoirs* in the *European Magazine* was almost as severe. Its reviewer branded Mary as a "philosophical wanton," attributed her conduct to her neglect of religion, and prophesied that the book would be read "with disgust by every female who has any pretensions to delicacy; with detestation by every one attached to the interests of religion and morality; and with indignation by any one who might feel any regard for the unhappy woman, whose frailties should have been buried in oblivion."[21] He too found a moral lesson in the account of Mary's life; it illustrated effectively the dangers of defying the laws of society. To enforce his point he mentioned a scandal which had recently befallen the family of Mary's former employer, Lord Kingsborough. The scandal vaguely referred to was that of Mary Elizabeth King, one of the girls in Mary's charge during her year in Ireland. The trouble began when Henry Fitzgerald, the natural son of Lady Kingsborough's brother, fell in love with his young cousin.

Though married, he induced her to elope with him early in 1797; but they were discovered, and the girl was taken to Ireland. In October of the same year, however, Fitzgerald set out for Mitchelstown, determined to reclaim his beloved. But he was discovered at a hotel in nearby Kilworth by Lord Kingsborough and his son Robert; and after a brief encounter Kingsborough shot Fitzgerald. Because the old Earl of Kingston died presently and Lord Kingsborough succeeded him, he was tried by his peers in the High Court of Parliament and judged not guilty.[22] And there the story ended—for all but Mary Wollstonecraft. The *European Magazine* implied that the guilt was really hers, that she had perverted the mind of Mary Elizabeth King back in 1787. It seems incredible that any such hypothesis could be taken seriously; yet it evidently was. At least the *British Critic* revived the story a few months later and again charged Mary with responsibility for the tragedy.[23]

The attacks on Mary were by no means limited to reviews of the *Memoirs* and *Posthumous Works*. She never was caricatured in the cartoons of Gillray, who liked to sketch Godwin with the head of a jackass, but she was badly used in several satirical novels and poems of the period. In George Walker's novel *The Vagabond* (1799), a fairly good-natured attack on the "new philosophy," the hero finds no difficulty in winning the favors of a married woman named Mary who derives her theories of morality from *The Rights of Woman* and the *Memoirs* (to which the author refers in his footnotes). And when "A Democratic Review" remonstrated with him for his brutal treatment of Mary, he retorted in a note to later editions: "If repeating verbatim her own sentiments be brutality, then am I guilty. But if they mean that such sentiments brutalize a woman, I cannot help that."[24] In a similarly restrained vein was an article in the *Lady's Monthly Museum* for December, 1799, allegedly written by the mother of four daughters, all of whom had been debased by reading *The Rights of Woman*. The approach here hardly deserves to be called "satirical," since the article was apparently written in all seriousness and probably accepted in good faith by the readers of the *Museum*.

Often, however, Mary's critics were downright abusive. Consider, for example, a passage from Richard Polwhele's poem "The Unsex'd Females" (1798), in which she is presented as the leader of a band of shameless vixens intent upon emancipation:

> See Wollstonecraft, whom no decorum checks,
> Arise, the intrepid champion of her sex;
> O'er humbled man assert the sovereign claim,
> And slight the timid blush of virgin fame.
>   "Go, go (she cries) ye tribes of melting maids,
> Go, screen your softness in sequester'd shades;
> With plaintive whispers woo the unconscious grove,
> And feebly perish, as despis'd ye love.
> What tho' the fine Romances of Rousseau
> Bid the frame flutter, and the bosom glow;
> Tho' the rapt Bard, your empire fond to own,
> Fall prostrate and adore your living throne,
> The living throne his hand presum'd to rear,
> Its seat a simper, and its base a tear;
> Soon shall the sex disdain the illusive sway,
> And wield the sceptre in yon blaze of day; . . .
> Surpass their rivals in the powers of mind
> And vindicate *the Rights of womankind*."[25]

Then once again Mary's love affairs and her attempts at suicide are rehearsed; and Polwhele charges her with immodesty (because she has professed an interest in botany) and indecency (because she has urged women to take part in athletics).

Presently T. J. Mathias, author of *The Pursuits of Literature,* published another poem, *The Shade of Alexander Pope on the Banks of the Thames* (1799), which also attacked the radical writers of the period, driving its points home with frequent footnotes often so extensive as to leave room for only a line or two of verse on a page. Although Mathias had attacked Godwin in *The Pursuits of Literature,* he had said nothing about Mary. But latterly he had seen the *Memoirs* and the *Posthumous Works,* and like others he chose to regard them as manuals of vice. They should, he observed in one of his footnotes, be earnestly recommended to every father and mother, to every guardian and every mistress of a boarding school throughout the kingdoms of Great Britain, as "A convenient Manual of speculative debauchery, with the most select arguments for reducing it into practice;" for the amusement, initiation and instruction of young ladies from sixteen to twenty-five years of age, who wish to figure in life, and afterwards in Doctors Commons and the King's Bench; or ultimately in the notorious receptacles of *patrician* prostitution.[26]

And in the poem itself he wrote:

> Mark now, where bold, with fronts metallick shine
> *William* and *Mary* on one common coin:
> Full freedom to the genial bed restore,
> And prove whate'er Vanini prov'd before.
> Fierce passion's slave, she veer'd with every gust,
> Love, Rights, and Wrongs, Philosophy, and Lust:
> But some more wise in metaphysick air,
> Weigh the man's wits against the Lady's hair.[27]

Such abuse, in abominable taste when applied to a person able to defend himself, is unforgivable when written of a dead woman and her grieving husband. But considerations of taste played no part in determining what was to be said of the abhorred Jacobins. Ultra-Tories felt that no abuse was too coarse, no damnation too searing for them. One and all, the English Jacobins were considered agents of Robespierre or Bonaparte or whatever hated Frenchmen, dead or alive, one chanced to think of first. They had no right to claim common courtesy, and they were seldom accorded it. And Mary, whose morals were by ordinary standards deplorable, was a convenient whipping boy. Unscrupulous Tory writers raged at her, ignoring her political principles or deliberately confusing them with her moral theories. In 1800-1801 there were three novels—Dr. Robert Bisset's *Douglas; or, The Highlanders,* Charles Lucas's *Infernal Quixote,* and Sally Wood's *Dorval; or, The Speculator*—which presented the melancholy sight of a young woman corrupted by reading *The Rights of Woman.* And two other writers, Mrs. Jane West and the American Samuel Lorenzo Knapp, attacked Mary directly in *Letters to a Young Man* and *Letters of Shahcoolen.* But the low point in abuse of Godwin and his wife was reached by the *Anti-Jacobin Review,* which in the

Appendix to its ninth volume (1801) published a poem in Spenserian stanzas entitled "The Vision of Liberty" and containing these lines:

> Then saw I mounted on a braying ass,
> William and Mary, sooth, a couple jolly;
> Who married, note ye how it came to pass,
> Although each held that marriage was but folly?—
> And she of curses would discharge a volley
> If the ass stumbled, leaping pales or ditches:
> Her husband, sans-culottes, was melancholy,
> For Mary verily would wear the breeches—
> God help poor silly men from such usurping b - - - - - s.
>
> Whilom this dame the Rights of Women writ,
> That is the title to her book she places,
> Exhorting bashful womankind to quit
> All foolish modesty, and coy grimaces;
> And name their backsides as it were their faces;
> Such license loose-tongued liberty adores,
> Which adds to female speech exceeding graces;
> Lucky the maid that on her volume pores,
> A scripture, archly fram'd, for propagating w - - - - s.
>
> William hath penn'd a waggon-load of stuff,
> And Mary's life at last he needs must write,
> Thinking her whoredoms were not known enough,
> Till fairly printed off in black and white.—
> With wondrous glee and pride, this simple wight
> Her brothel feats of wantonness sets down,
> Being her spouse, he tells, with huge delight,
> How oft she cuckolded the silly clown,
> And lent, O lovely piece! herself to half the town.[28]

The result was that few right-thinking people dared to say a word in defense of Mary. Even Mary Hays's admiration flagged noticeably.[29] Her biographical sketch of Mary, in *Annual Necrology, 1797-8* (published in 1800) was markedly more restrained and apologetic than the obituary which she had so proudly contributed to the *Monthly Magazine* just after Mary's death. Three years later, when Miss Hays issued her five-volume *Female Biography,* Mary was omitted altogether, although Catherine Macaulay, Mme. Roland, and Mary Astell were all treated fully.

All this time, while the critics raged, Godwin had been living on at the Polygon working regularly in his study, where Opie's painting of Mary now hung, and going out frequently to visit friends or attend the theater. After he had finished work on the *Memoirs* and the *Posthumous Works,* he had written the novel *St. Leon,* the heroine of which is commonly accepted as an idealized reflection of Mary. In the Preface to the novel Godwin admitted that he had modified his opinions since the publication of *Political Justice.* "I apprehend domestic and private affections inseparable from the nature of man, and from what may be styled the culture of the heart," he wrote, "and am fully persuaded that they are not incompatible with a profound and active sense of justice in the mind of him that cherishes them."[30] And the whole book is, in a sense, a tribute to the "domestic affections"—a far cry from *Caleb Williams,* where the only character truly in love was the silly Emily Melville. "Man was not born to live alone," Godwin makes his hero observe; and in his description of the joys of love, his praise of the character of the heroine, Marguerite, and his account of St. Leon's grief at her death, the reader feels that the author is drawing on his own recent experiences. Certainly Godwin himself could have said with St. Leon: "This was the woman destined to crown my happiness, and consummate my misery. If I had never known her, I should never have tasted true pleasure. . . ."[31]

But however touching Godwin's change of heart may be, it was accompanied by a gradual weakening of his powers. Slowly he was slipping into the dismal anticlimax which clouded the last thirty years of his life. Though he was a better man for having been Mary's husband, he was a worse philosopher: she had shaken his faith in his very rational system of philosophy, had undermined his confidence in pure individualism. Henceforth he was often to retract, rarely to reconstruct. Though he pretended always to have utter faith in himself, he must have been conscious of his waning powers. He must have been pained, too, by the heartless attacks which his foes were launching against him and the woman whom he had loved. It is easy to deride Godwin's ignominious downfall, but on second thought anyone with a grain of human sympathy will feel more pity than amusement at his fate.

He was seldom free from domestic worries. As he had admitted himself, he was ill suited to the task of rearing the two little girls, much as he loved them. Miss Jones managed the household for a while, but eventually she resigned the job, perhaps because she had despaired of becoming the second Mrs. Godwin.[32] And from that time forward, the household was generally disorganized. There was a nurse to care for the children and a maid to keep house; and several of Godwin's lady admirers—Mrs. Reveley, Miss Jones, his sister Hannah, and others—took turns in supervising. It was a poor environment for the little girls, and it was made worse by Godwin's insistence that the house be quiet while he was working in his study. Mary Wollstonecraft would have deplored such a restriction. Coleridge remarked to Southey in December, 1799, that "the cadaverous silence of Godwin's children is to me quite catacombish, and, thinking of Mary Wollstonecraft, I was oppressed by it the day Davy and I dined there."[33]

Godwin himself knew what was lacking in his household. In *St. Leon* he had discussed at some length how his hero should go about choosing a "protector" for his daughters after their mother's death. And only six or seven months after Mary's death he himself made his first efforts to find a new wife. Though his action seems hasty, it by no means proves that he was unfaithful to Mary's memory. Not only did he need a woman to mother the children, but he also needed a companion to cheer him. His opinion of marriage had changed considerably; his brief taste of married life had taught him that "the knowledge, that there is some one that takes an interest in our happiness . . . is extremely gratifying." He had in fact become thoroughly enamored of wedded bliss, and his desire to marry so soon after Mary's death should doubtless be interpreted as a genuine tribute to her—the kind of tribute that only William Godwin would expect the world to understand.

Naturally he hoped to find a woman of talents commensurate with Mary's. He showed no interest in Louisa Jones, despite her apparent willingness to be wooed. But when he went down to Bath for a vacation in March, 1798, and met Harriet Lee, the novelist who with her sister Sophia was best known for their joint work in *Canterbury Tales,* he was immediately interested. Soon after he returned home, he wrote to her:

There are so few persons in the world that have excited that degree of interest in my mind which you have excited, that I am loth to have the catalogue of such persons diminished, and that distance should place a barrier between them and me, scarcely less complete than that of death. Indulge me with the knowledge that I have some place in your recollection. Suffer me to suppose, in any future production that you may give to the world, that while you are writing it, you will sometimes remember me in the number of your intended readers.[34]

Then he went on to suggest that she stay at his house under Miss Jones's chaperonage, next time she came up to London. But he received no answer to his invitation. By June 2 he had learned that Miss Lee had been to London and returned home without even notifying him that she was in town. So he wrote once more. This time he made five drafts of the letter (four of which he carefully filed away) before he found the proper words to express his feelings. Then:

I have been extremely mortified at receiving no answer from you, to the letter I wrote soon after my late excursion to Bath. I am not sure indeed whether, in perfect strictness I was entitled to an answer. But silence is so ambiguous a thing, and admits of so many interpretations, that with the admiration I had conceived for you, I could not sit down tranquilly under its discipline. It might mean simply that I had not been long enough your knight, to entitle me to such a distinction. But it might mean disapprobation, displeasure, or offence, when my heart prompted me to demand cordiality and friendship.[35]

And he asked her if he might call on her during the following week, when he was to be in Bristol for a few days. Miss Lee replied formally, consenting to see him.—But meanwhile she had studied his letter carefully and recorded this estimate of Godwin's character:

The tone of this letter appears to me to betray vanity disappointed by the scantiness of the homage it has received, rather than mortified by any apprehension of discouragement. If any offence was given by the former letter this is calculated to renew and increase it; for it is equally presuming without being more explicit, except in two sentences, so alien to the temper, or distant from the express reach of the rest, that they should be made under all circumstances to leave the letter. An alternative proposed by the second clause presents itself to me thus: this journey to Bristol has no reference to me; as far as that is concerned he visits me simply as an acquaintance; but his title to be received as such has been lost by his forwardness to employ the privileges, and claim the rights of a more endeared relation. The purpose of his journey is addresst to me, and it may be dictated either by humility or assurance. I doubt that the former interpretation would be given to a letter in which the same air and accent reign as in this.[36]

Godwin called when he reached Bath, and enjoyed what he called in his diary a "conference" with Miss Lee. She was admittedly interested in his suit, but she feared what her sister Sophia would think of the match, was worried about what "the world" would say, and wondered what would be the result of the union of a devout woman like herself and a skeptic like Godwin. And though he wrote at length to answer her objections and to dilate on the joys of married life, she finally persuaded him that he was wasting his time.[37]

For a while, then, Godwin marked time. But when Mrs. Reveley's husband died suddenly in July, 1799, he sprang to attention. He had long admired Maria Reveley, and she had shown more than a mere friendly interest in him. "When all obstacles interposed between us," he wrote to her presently, "when I had a wife, when you had a husband, you said you loved me, for years loved me!"[38] But under the shock of her husband's sudden death she retired to an attic room for a week, and she remained distressed for some time afterward. Godwin, however, failed to respect her mourning; and less than a month after Reveley's death he proposed that they marry. The lady was scandalized and sent back word that she considered the proposal untimely. Then Godwin, scandalized in turn at her conventionality, replied:

How my whole soul disdains and tramples upon these cowardly ceremonies! Is woman always to be a slave? Is she so wretched an animal that every breath can destroy her, and every temptation, or more properly every possibility of an offence, is to be supposed to subdue her?

This ceremony is to be observed *for some time*. What miserable, heartless words! What is *some time?* this phrase, upon which all feeling, all hope of anything reasonable is left to writhe, and to guess, as it can, when its sufferings shall have an end. You know in what light such ceremonies have been viewed by all the liberal and wise, both of my sex and yours.[39]

Yet Mrs. Reveley remained unmoved, and in his next letter Godwin was protesting at her cruelty:

You have it in your power to give me new life, a new interest in existence, to raise me from the grave in which my heart lies buried. You are invited to form the sole happiness of one of the most known men of the age, of one whose principles, whose temper, whose thoughts, you have been long acquainted with, and will, I believe, confess their universal constancy. This connection, I should think, would restore you to self-respect, would give security to your future peace, and insure for you no mean degree of respectability. What you propose to choose in opposition to this I hardly know how to describe to you. You have said you cannot live without a passion; yet you prefer a mere abstraction, the unknown ticket you may draw in the lottery of men, to the attachment of a man of some virtues, a man whom you once, whom you long believed you loved.[40]

But Mrs. Reveley refused to see her suitor, and presently she sent him word by Mrs. Fenwick that she felt herself unworthy of a man of such profound understanding.[41] Then again Godwin argued, but in vain. And when they finally met again in December, she was with Mr. Gisborne, whom she later married.

So once again Godwin was obliged to mark time until 1801, when Mrs. Mary Jane Clairmont moved into the house next to his in the Polygon. This time it was apparently the lady who made the first advances; at least she is reputed to have greeted him, the first time she saw him, with the cry: "Is it possible that I behold the immortal Godwin?"[42] She was doubtless influenced in his favor not only by her respect for his reputation but also by the need for finding a means of support for herself and her two young children. In any case Godwin, having at last found a willing subject, fell to courting with zest. Charles Lamb reported that he had grown "quite juvenile." "He bows when he is spoke to," Lamb wrote to John Rickman on September 16, "and smiles without occasion, and wriggles as fantastically as Malvolio, and has more affectation than a canary bird pluming his feathers when he thinks somebody looks at him. He lays down his spectacles as if in scorn, and takes 'em up again from necessity, and winks that she mayn't see he gets sleepy about eleven o'Clock. You never saw such a philosophic coxcomb, nor any one play the Romeo so unnaturally."[43] Two months later, on December 21, 1801, they were married; and the two Clairmont children, Charles and Clara Mary Jane (who preferred to be called Claire) moved with their mother to Godwin's house.

The new Mrs. Godwin was no Mary Wollstonecraft. Few women have gone down in history with so many unfavorable comments from famous friends. Occasionally strangers spoke well of her, but her most intimate acquaintances had scarcely a good word to say for her. Lamb called her a "damn'd disagreeable woman" and was wont to refer to her as "the Liar" or "the Bitch." Mrs. Fenwick said that she was "of all human beings . . . the object of my sincerest detestation." John Philpot Curran described her as "a pustule of vanity." And Shelley, his first wife Harriet, Crabb Robinson, Thomas Jefferson Hogg, and Coleridge all spoke in her disfavor. Even her two children by Clairmont seem to have cared little for her; and of her two stepchildren, Mary "detested" her, and even mild little Fanny confessed that she and Mrs. Godwin were "not great friends."[44]

Yet many of those who damned her admitted that she made Godwin a good wife. She supplied to their household the common sense which he lacked, she managed the publishing business which they inaugurated in 1805, and she supported her husband through the bitter years of his anticlimax. Meanwhile she held the strangely assorted family together—and that was an achievement in itself. She had in her charge the daughter of Imlay and Mary Wollstonecraft, the daughter of Godwin and Mary, a son and daughter by her previous marriage, and soon another son, William, by her second marriage. Hers was not an enviable lot! Yet she persevered, and despite occasional quarrels[45] she and Godwin managed to live a reasonably happy life together.

Godwin must, more than once, have made the inevitable comparison between his first wife and his second, but he was enough of a philosopher (or a realist) to know that he must make the best of his bargain. It was a relief for him to entrust the care of the children to her. He probably knew that she made a poor step-mother, and he admitted that the little girls were not being reared according to their mother's theories.[46] But as time went on, his financial difficulties absorbed more and more of his attention, and his family received ever less. And as his behavior became more reprehensible, he developed a perverse longing for respectability which seems to have made him conceal Mary's history from his two daughters. It may be, of course, that Mrs. Godwin discouraged talk about her husband's first wife—but it is more than likely that she disapproved of Mary's conduct before marriage, and that God-win himself eventually decided that his first wife was a poor model for growing girls to contemplate. At all events Fanny and Mary seem to have known very little about their mother before they met Shelley.

Godwin's apparent willingness not to talk about his dead wife was one more evidence of his anticlimax. The great individualist had lost his faith; the fearless radical had grown timid. He was writing second-rate children's books and third-rate tragedies and novels; his philosophical essays were little but retractions of what he had formerly written. Young men still honored him for what he once had been. Shelley was soon pouring hundreds of pounds into his pockets out of respect for the mind that had formulated the theories of *Political Justice*. But everyone knew that Godwin had long since fallen from his high place; he was, as Crabb Robinson said, "the worn-out philosopher who survived his philosophy."[47] Though he had once "blazed as the sun in the firmament of reputation," said Hazlitt, he had now "sunk below the horizon."[48] And if he was pathetic as a philosopher, he was almost contemptible as a man. He no doubt persuaded himself that money was so base that it mattered not how he came by it. Yet his reckless expenditures, his devious shifts to acquire money, his feeble excuses, and his ingratitude to his creditors are inexcusable. Certainly he as much as his wife helped to render the atmosphere at the Polygon—and later at the house on Skinner Street, to which they moved in 1807—strained and uncongenial. Was it Wollstonecraft nerves, Clairmont irritability, or Godwin improvidence that blighted the lives of Fanny and Mary? That is a moot question.

By the time the Godwin family had settled in the Skinner Street house Mary Wollstonecraft's name had been almost forgotten by the reading public. To be sure, in 1803 a hardy admirer had published anonymously *A Defence of the Character and Conduct of the late Mary Wollstonecraft Godwin, Founded on Principles of Nature and Reason, as Applied to the Peculiar Circumstances of Her Case; in a Series of Letters to a Lady*. But the book had proved to be more apology than defense. The author had argued that "extraordinary Geniuses are not to be estimated by common rules" and maintained that, though Mary had erred in judgment, her intentions were pure and her principles grounded in reason. Without trying to condone her errors and with patent disapproval of Godwin's frankness in the *Memoirs,* he tried to judge Mary impartially and to recognize her merits. But the reviewers were scarcely grateful for his pains. The *Monthly Review* announced that since its editors were too old-fashioned to believe in a separate morality for geniuses, they would not examine the merits of the book.[49] The *British Critic* asked why anyone should want to revive the story of Mary Wollstonecraft now that she had been forgotten.[50] And the *Anti-Jacobin Review* remarked:

The writings of that noted person are already fast descending to the gulph of oblivion which so soon absorbs the efforts of ingenuity to outrage common sense; but as many of our readers may have forgotten the details either of her writings or history, to recall them to our memories we rummaged a closet into which we throw literary lumber, and found her *Rights of Woman* in company with Tom Paine's politics and theology; Thelwall's eloquence; the dramatic poetry of Holcroft; and Godwin's philosophy.[51]

But instead of examining the principles of *The Rights of Woman,* the reviewer rehearsed Mary's history once again in an attempt to prove that her conduct was by no means based on nature and reason—that, in fact, she was no better than a prostitute.

His was the last word to be said about Mary for some time. Like Mary Hays's *Female Biography,* Matilda Betham's *Dictionary of Celebrated Women* (1804) contained no mention of her. And by the time Chalmers's "revised and enlarged" edition of the *General Biographical Dictionary* appeared in 1812-17, she was apparently no longer regarded as a dangerous influence.[52] She had been dead for nearly two decades by that time, and none of her controversial works had been republished since before 1800. The editor was, therefore, able to achieve a kind of philosophical detachment and to pronounce what he doubtless considered the decision of posterity on Mary Wollstonecraft Godwin. In this generous frame of mind he expressed admiration for her talents but lamented her ungovernable passions and her rapid shifts from Fuseli to Imlay to Godwin. And he declared that, for all her powers, she was "a voluptuary and a sensualist."

In the meantime Mary's two daughters—"les Goddesses," Godwin called them—were growing to young womanhood. In 1812 Fanny was eighteen and Mary was fifteen, and they were allowed to meet some of the distinguished visitors who came to call on their father. They had their duties and their pleasures, both of which were quite different from the sort that prevailed in most London households. Part of their duty was to read and criticize the juvenile books submitted for publication by the family press. And one of their pleasures recalls Godwin's own childhood, when he delivered sermons from his highchair. On February 15, 1812, Aaron Burr recorded in his journal a visit at the Godwins' to hear little William, then nine years old, deliver his weekly lecture.

Having heard how Coleridge and others lectured, he would also lecture; and one of his sisters (Mary, I think) writes a lecture, which he reads from a little pulpit which they have erected for him. He went through it with great gravity and decorum. The subject was "The influence of governments on the character of a people." After the lecture we had tea, and the girls danced and sang an hour, and at nine [I] came home.[53]

In October of the same year another ardent young disciple, Percy Bysshe Shelley, came to call with his wife, having learned only shortly before that the author of *Political Justice* was not, as he had supposed, dead. The young poet seems hardly to have noticed Mary, but he was much interested in Fanny. And his wife reported to her friend Catherine Nugent that they had seen the daughter of "that dear Mary Wolstoncroft," whom Percy so much admired. "She is . . . very plain, but very sensible," she wrote. "The beauty of her mind fully overbalances the plainness of her countenance."[54] Fanny was shy, too, and sensitive: her stepsister, Claire Clairmont, remarked when she read Henry Mackenzie's *Man of Feeling* that the hero would have made a good husband for Fanny.[55] She was doubtless the most tractable of the five children in the Godwin household, and Godwin seems to have loved her for it; certainly he seems never to have grumbled at the expense of caring for her.[56] Unfortunately, along with Fanny's gentleness and sensitivity, went a decidedly melancholy nature. It had been her misfortune to inherit her mother's temperament rather than her beauty. And, like her mother, she began worrying early in life. "Now do not be melancholy," Claire wrote to her in 1815; "for heaven's sake be cheerful; so young in life and so melancholy!"[57] But Fanny could not easily alter her nature, however much she might wish to; and in 1816 she wrote to her half sister Mary: "I cannot help envying your calm contented disposition, and the calm philosophical habits of life which pursue you, or rather which you pursue, everywhere."[58]

Fate had been kinder to Mary. She was slight, like her mother, with piercing gray eyes and waving hair "of a sunny and burnished brightness,"[59] but she had been blessed with a cheerier disposition. She was sensitive, though, and imaginative; and already she had the itch to write. "As a child I scribbled," she wrote later, in the Preface to *Frankenstein;* "and my favourite pastime, during the hours given me for recreation, was to 'write stories.' Still I had a dearer pleasure than this, which was the formation of castles in the air." Yet she and Fanny probably knew very little about their mother, and they seem never to have seen their aunts Everina and Eliza. Godwin had met them at Hugh Skeys's house in Dublin in 1800 and had brought back presents from them to the girls,[60] but the ladies themselves probably did not see their nieces until nearly twenty years after Mary Wollstonecraft's death.

Although Mary and Shelley must have met when he first visited her father in 1812, they did not fall in love until June, 1814, when she was not quite seventeen. Shelley declared his love while the two were visiting Mary's mother's grave in St. Pancras Churchyard, and there they met often and read together (of all books!) her father's essay "On Sepulchres." From the beginning, as Harriet Shelley averred,[61] Shelley was attracted to the girl by her name—Mary Wollstonecraft Godwin—which he had long revered. When in 1817 he honored her in the Dedication to *The Revolt of Islam,* he wrote:

> They say that thou wert lovely from thy birth,
> Of glorious parents, thou aspiring Child.
> I wonder not—for One then left this earth
> Whose life was like a setting planet mild,
> Which clothed thee in the radiance undefiled
> Of its departing glory; still her fame
> Shines on thee, through the tempests dark and wild
> Which shake these latter days; and thou canst claim
> The shelter, from thy Sire, of an immortal name.

He may also have told her more about her mother's history when he tried to persuade her to disregard convention and elope with him.

Before long she consented, and early on the morning of July 28, 1814, they stole away with Claire Clairmont and crossed the Channel to Calais. There they were overtaken by Mrs. Godwin, who tried in vain to dissuade the girls from their adventure. Then began the strange tramp through France and Switzerland, with Shelley writing back to his wife to urge her to join them. Then the return to England, the moving from place to place, hounded by debts and infamy. Mary was reading her mother's books, doubtless encouraged to do so by Shelley; in them she could find the story of another noble spirit whom the world had failed to understand.

Meanwhile Fanny, who had been visiting in Wales when the

elopement took place, was back in Skinner Street—and discon-
solate. Mary and Claire had managed to escape from their depressing environment, but she had still to endure it. She may have
heard only recently that Godwin was not her real father, and
been distressed to think how long she had been a burden to him.
In 1816, when she was twenty-two years old, she was temporarily
cheered by talks with George Blood, her mother's old friend, and
Robert Dale Owen, a later admirer of Mary Wollstonecraft.[62]
Both men spoke in high praise of the mother whom she could not
recall, and Blood told her anecdotes about Mary as a young woman. He seems to have had hopes of inducing Eliza and Everina
Wollstonecraft to take Fanny to live with them in Dublin and to
teach in their school. On July 29, 1816, she wrote to Mary that their
aunt Everina was to be in London during the following week,
"when my future fate will be decided." But she added in a tone
strongly reminiscent of her mother's old complaints: "I am not
well; my mind always keeps my body in a fever; but never mind
me."[63]

Everina doubtless decided that Fanny was too much of a risk;
she had not only her mother's scandal to live down, but her sister's and Claire's as well. She would never do as a teacher in a
school for young ladies.—So Fanny grew more morose. She could
see no possible escape from her hapless existence. Perhaps, as some
have claimed, she too loved Shelley, and was crushed by his preferring her half sister. But she had sorrows enough, without that
additional one, to overwhelm a much hardier spirit. She felt alone
and unwanted, as her mother had often felt; and to her, as to her
mother, suicide seemed the obvious escape. Early in October, 1816,
she left home, apparently to visit her aunts in Dublin. Presently
she wrote from Bristol to both Godwin and the Shelleys: "I depart
immediately to the spot from which I hope never to remove."[64]
And though Godwin and Shelley set out separately to prevent her,
they were stopped by an item in a Bristol paper announcing the
suicide of an unknown young woman who had taken laudanum

on the night of October 9 at the Mackworth Arms Inn in Swansea. She had left a note:

I have long determined that the best thing I could do was to put an end to the existence of a being whose birth was unfortunate, and whose life has only been a series of pain to those persons who have hurt their health in endeavouring to promote her welfare. Perhaps to hear of my death will give you pain, but you will soon have the blessing of forgetting that such a creature ever existed as . . . .[65]

The name seemed to have been torn away and burnt, but the newspaper account reported that her stockings were marked with a "G." and her stays with the letters "M. W." There could be no doubt that it was Fanny. Yet Godwin, eager to avoid further scandal in the family, returned home without claiming her body. He told her friends that she had died suddenly of a pulmonary ailment while visiting her aunts. And her only epitaph was Shelley's lines:

> Her voice did quiver as we parted;
> Yet knew I not that heart was broken
> From which it came, and I departed
> Heeding not the words then spoken.
> Misery—O Misery,
> This world is all too wide for thee!

A month later Harriet Shelley threw herself into the Serpentine. On December 29, soon after her body had been recovered, Shelley and Mary were married. Then Godwin, whose degradation was now complete, took heart. He who had been rigidly honest in his dealings with his first wife and in his biography of her, had since become utterly dishonest. Witness his lies to conceal Fanny's suicide. Witness his refusal to see Shelley after the elopement, but his willingness to accept his money—provided it did not come to him in a signed check. Godwin rejoiced now at his daughter's success and, in a letter to his brother, bragged that she had married a baronet's son.[66] The old spirit had indeed "sunk below the horizon." Even Mary Shelley, shocked at her father's willingness to deal with Shelley only through an attorney, could comment only *"Oh philosophy!"*[67]

Mary's troubles did not end when she added "Shelley" to her

distinguished name. Debts still hounded her and her new husband; she was constantly confused by the conflict between his notions of morality and the rest of the world's. Children were born but to die. Was it a punishment for her sins? Shelley proved to be less and less a comfort to her; he found new "soul's sisters"— Claire, Emilia Viviani, Jane Williams—wherever they went. Was it because she failed to give him the happiness he sought? He shunned company when she craved it—he wore a jacket when others did not—he was growing ever more unconventional. Or was the real trouble that, like her father, she was herself becoming more conventional, more concerned about the approval of the world? "Farewell!" Godwin had written to her in 1818. "Be useful, be respectable, be happy!"[68] And she must have been painfully aware that she was nothing of the kind.

In 1822 came the horrible blow: Shelley's drowning. Perhaps their relations were strained at the time. If so, she must conceal that fact from the world. She had been the "chosen mate of a celestial spirit"; now she would "justify his ways."[69] Then followed the dreary years of widowhood, with Mary Shelley striving always to clear her husband's name of infamy. As if to prove her affection for him, she mourned elaborately: her journals echoed the rhetorical extravagance which had characterized her mother's letters years before. She became more and more enamored of sorrow— until people forgot how lighthearted a girl she had been. Even in 1819, after the death of her son William, Leigh Hunt had written to her: "I need not say how it grieves me to see you so dispirited. Not that I wonder at it under such sufferings; but I know, at least I have often suspected, that you have a tendency, partly constitutional perhaps, and partly owing to the turn of your philosophy, to look over-intensely at the dark side of human things."[70] Now that tendency grew more marked. In 1827 her father complacently told her: "Would to God you were my daughter in all but my poverty! But I am afraid you are a Wollstonecraft."[71]

A Wollstonecraft? Perhaps. But not a Mary Wollstonecraft. To be sure, the daughter had developed her mother's melancholy nature, but she lacked her mother's fearless honesty. Surprisingly enough, the one member of the family who seemed most like Mary Wollstonecraft was Claire Clairmont. Fanny resembled her mother only in her melancholy disposition; Mary, in her appearance and later in her melancholy. Yet it was small wonder that Mary Wollstonecraft's two daughters seemed anticlimactic. As Claire said, "In our family, if you cannot write an epic poem or a novel that by its originality knocks all other novels on the head, you are a despicable creature, not worth acknowledging."[72] But though Fanny spared herself from living out her anticlimax, Mary, like her father, lived on—withdrawing more and more from the spirit of her mother. She could never forget that her son was an English gentleman, that he would some day be a baronet. She wrote furiously to gain the money to insure him a conventional education, and she prayed God that he might be made to think like other people. And as her legacy to him, she did her utmost to make herself, his father, and her parents seem like the kind of forebears who would not disgrace a gentleman of his position. Only when he had at last inherited his title and his fortune, when she had chosen for him a wife who showed proper reverence for his family, did she relax and achieve a sort of contentment. And long after she had died, Lady Shelley, her son's wife, proudly wore an amethyst ring said to have been Mary Wollstonecraft's,[73] and kept in the manor house at Boscombe, in a recess in her boudoir known as "The Sanctum," bracelets made from Mary Wollstonecraft's hair.[74] Nearby, in the churchyard of St. Peter's, in Bournemouth, lay the bodies of Mary and Godwin, having been removed there from the old graveyard at St. Pancras in 1851, when the railroad was put through.[75] Certainly Mary would have been ironically amused could she have known of these posthumous honors. In her own time she had had little to do with titled folk except when she served as governess in Lord Kingsborough's family.

She would have been touched, though, at her daughter's unflagging devotion to her memory. When in 1823 Mrs. Kenney (former wife of Thomas Holcroft) told her that she had "grown very like" her mother, she wrote to Leigh Hunt: "This is the most flattering thing any one c[oul]d say to me."[76] Godwin's reverence, too, would certainly have moved Mary—his faithfulness in keeping her portrait ever near him, and his request in his will that he be buried "as near as may be" to her.[77] And though she might have grieved for the loss of his principles, she would have been able to forgive him much when she saw that he ever retained some of the gentle affectionateness which she had taught him. His kindness to the members of his own family—especially to poor Fanny —and his eagerness to help the young people who sought him out would, in Mary's eyes, have compensated for many of his failings.

As time went on, her memory was rescued from the mire into which it had fallen. To be sure, a Dr. William Gibbons, a Hicksite Quaker, singled her out as a melancholy example of the "new philosophy" in his *Exposition of Modern Skepticism* (1829), and he gave the world again an account of her love affairs and her attempts at suicide, urging parents to make her a horrible example to their children. Yet slowly opinions of Mary's character showed growing tolerance. Mrs. Anne Elwood's biographical sketch of her in *Memoirs of the Literary Ladies of England* (1842) was almost wholeheartedly sympathetic. Mrs. Elwood was cautious of direct praise, and she could not wholly ignore the bad example which Mary had set. "If error even in a Mary Wollstonecroft could not be overlooked," she asked in the last sentence of her essay, "what woman can hope to offend with impunity against the laws of society?"[78] Yet she gave Mary the most favorable notice accorded her since the appearance of the *Defence* in 1803. Thirty-four more years were to elapse, however, before any thorough reinterpretation of Mary's life and work was attempted. Then, in 1876, Charles Kegan Paul, who had access to the Shelley family papers, printed in his biography of Godwin several of Mary's early letters to her sisters and George Blood in an attempt to prove that she was a truly devout woman. He dismissed the affair with Fuseli as groundless, maintained that Mary had failed to marry Imlay because marriage was impossible for an English citizen in Paris in 1793, and similarly glozed over or apologized for all the "irregularities" of Mary's history which might offend Victorian readers. Unfortunately his evasions and apologies were repeated in most of the dozen or more popular biographies of Mary published during the next half century. Thus at long last Mary was vindicated—almost canonized. But the saintly lady who emerged in the process was hardly recognizable.[79] And Mary would scarcely have thanked her worshippers for their efforts to explain away her unconventionality. Shortly before she died she wrote in a letter to a friend:

> Those who are bold enough to advance before the age they live in, and to throw off, by the force of their own minds, the prejudices which the maturing reason of the world will in time disavow, must learn to brave censure. We ought not to be too anxious respecting the opinion of others.— I am not fond of vindications.—Those who know me will suppose that I acted from principle.—Nay, as we in general give others credit for worth, in proportion as we possess it—I am easy with regard to the opinions of the *best* part of mankind.—I *rest* on my own.[80]

The vindication of Mary's character came too late, however, to permit her ideas to have any profound influence on the course of the feminist movement of the nineteenth century. During the early years of the movement *The Rights of Woman* seems to have been little read; for although there were four editions of the book between 1833 and 1856, there were none thereafter until 1890. Of the women who led the fight for emancipation few seem to have been aware of her. And of those who mentioned her in their writings, some were distinctly hostile. Harriet Martineau dryly declared that "the Wollstonecraft order . . . do infinite mischief; and, for my part, I do not wish to have any thing to do with them"; and she added that she did not regard Mary as "a safe example, nor as a successful champion of Woman and her Rights."[81] Emma Willard also disapproved of Mary, claiming that by her conduct she had hindered the advancement of the feminist cause.[82] Margaret Fuller considered her a melancholy example—"a woman whose existence better proved the need of some new interpretation of Woman's Rights, than anything she wrote."[83] Others revered Mary's memory but apparently hesitated to express their reverence publicly. When Frances Wright Darusmont wrote to Mary Shelley in 1827 to enlist her interest in the utopian colony at Nashoba, she remarked that she was prompted by her respect for Godwin and Mary Wollstonecraft.[84] Elizabeth Cady Stanton read *The Rights of Woman* with enthusiasm in 1840, although it was, as she said, "tabooed by orthodox teachers." And when she met Lucretia Mott in London a few months later, the two women eagerly discussed "Mary Wollstonecraft, her social theories, and her demands of equality for women."[85] Later, in September, 1855, Mrs. Mott wrote in a letter to a friend: "I have long wished and believed that the time would come, when Mary Wollstonecraft and Frances Wright, and Robert Owen, would have justice done them, and the denunciations of bigoted sectarianism fall into merited contempt."[86]

Public recognition of Mary's share in the feminist movement was, however, delayed until after the publication of Kegan Paul's biography of Godwin in 1876. Elizabeth Robins Pennell's *Life of Mary Wollstonecraft,* published in 1884, was the first full-length biography of Mary and the first attempt to estimate her contribution to feminism; and it doubtless led to the re-issue of *The Rights of Woman* in England by Mrs. Henry Fawcett in 1890 and in America by Mrs. Pennell herself in 1892. Meanwhile, in 1889, the massive three-volume *History of Woman Suffrage,* by Elizabeth Cady Stanton, Susan B. Anthony, and Matilda Joslyn Gage, had appeared. And although Mary's contribution to the feminist cause was dismissed in a few lines of the opening chapter of the book, her name stood first in the list of dedicatees.

With or without Mary's aid, the good work had gone forward. One by one women had realized what she had maintained long before: that they were being denied their natural rights to freedom and happiness. Their strongest support came from John Stuart Mill's *Subjection of Women,* published in 1869. Yet the slow reform was due not to any one book or any one leader but to the general revolution in philosophy, politics, and social structure throughout Western Europe and the United States. Hundreds of plucky women contributed to the movement: some sought the franchise, others demanded to be admitted to colleges and medical schools, still others sought to retain control of their own property after marriage, to retain custody of their children when separated from their husbands, or to help determine the educational policies of their communities. After Mill's book had appeared, however, women's rights were defined and their goals clarified. Thereafter the course of reform scarcely swerved. Yet Mary Wollstonecraft had no part in determining Mill's theories. He never mentioned her; indeed he regarded his wife as the first feminist. But though Mary had little traceable influence on the course of female emancipation, no one can estimate how much her theories and example may have inspired workers in the cause. She was a pioneer in the movement if not actually a leader; and *The Rights of Woman,* which has gained the immortality of an Everyman edition, must be regarded as an original, if not an influential, book.

It is, however, Mary's personality that has kept her memory alive. Surely dozens of readers have thrilled to her history or been fired by her example for every one who has read his way through *The Rights of Woman.* There was indeed, as she said, something residing in her heart that was not perishable; and it was her heart, more than her mind, that made her a great woman. True, she had many faults: she was impulsive, hypercritical, and egotistical. Yet as Godwin said, her errors "were connected and interwoven with the qualities most characteristic of her genius":[87] her impulses were generous, her critical mind enabled her to penetrate to the root of an evil, and her egotism strengthened her to fight for what she believed to be right. Even when she was most exasperating, Mary was never mean—and she was never dull. She was alert and vibrant, always interested in new ideas; and if she had lived a few years longer, she might well have helped to rally the new forces of Romanticism. She was, above all, a woman of great personal charm, once she had rid herself of the brashness displayed in the years of her first successes. And her charm was not the placid charm which rises from beauty and graciousness alone; it was the positive, energetic charm of a courageous woman eager to serve humanity.

Notes

Chapter I

1. Except when otherwise specified, all biographical information in this chapter is derived from the letters of Mary Wollstonecraft now in the possession of Lord Abinger, and from the first two chapters of William Godwin's *Memoirs of the Author of "A Vindication of the Rights of Woman,"* which was published in London in two editions in 1798 and re-issued as *Memoirs of Mary Wollstonecraft Godwin* in two American editions published at Philadelphia in 1799 and 1804. Throughout my book I have cited the modern edition of the *Memoirs* edited by W. Clark Durant and published in 1927 by Constable and Company, Limited, of London, and Greenberg of New York. This edition is the most easily available and the most helpful to the scholar, because it lists the variants between the first and second English editions and also contains an extensive Supplement of miscellaneous information about Mary Wollstonecraft.

Only two of Mary Wollstonecraft's letters written during the first twenty-one years of her life survive in the collection of Lord Abinger. Except for occasional hints from later letters, Godwin's *Memoirs* is the only source of information about her early life. At my request Mrs. Margery Beckingham of London investigated the records of the various parishes in which the Wollstonecraft family lived, but was able to find no new information about births, marriages, or deaths in the family. Apparently there is no way of checking Godwin's accuracy in the *Memoirs*. Yet the book can probably be accepted as reliable; for although he met Mary only after she reached maturity, he forehandedly asked her about her earlier life and even jotted down notes on the information which she furnished him. He also questioned other friends who had known her before he met her. However, Mary's two sisters, who might have been most helpful, refused to aid him; they were probably scandalized at Mary's belated marriage, and they naturally disapproved of Godwin's desire to inform the world about her unconventional life.

2. Godwin spells the name *Dixon* in the *Memoirs;* but it is spelled *Dickson* in the letters of Mary and her sisters. Everina Wollstonecraft revealed a scrap of information about her mother's family in a letter of November 1, 1835 [?] to her niece Elizabeth W. Berry of Crows Nest, Sydney, N.S.W.: "Your Grandmother was an Irishwoman and some of her Nephews you must have seen at your father's house. One, George Dickson, was an officer in the army—Edward Sterling Dickson was a Navy Officer—He was a Midshipman with the Duke of Clarence, and became an Admiral, when the Duke became a King. . . ." The rest of the letter is missing. The surviving fragment is preserved in the Mitchell Library of Sydney and is reprinted here by permission of the Trustees of the Library.

3. Mary never knew whether she was born in London or in the Epping Forest. Her birth is not recorded in the register of Christchurch, Spitalfields.

4. See the Chronological Table prefacing Durant's edition of Godwin's *Memoirs,* p. xiv. Durant states that James Wollstonecraft was "bapt. February 23" at the Parish Church of St. Margaret's, Barking. The records of this church were not available when Mrs. Beckingham sought to consult them for me.

5. *Memoirs,* p. 14.

6. Mary Wollstonecraft, *Letters to Imlay,* No. XV. These letters are available in three editions: they first appeared in Volumes III and IV of the *Posthumous Works of the Author of "A Vindication of the Rights of Woman"* edited by Godwin in 1798, and they have been published in later editions by C. Kegan Paul (London, 1879) and Roger Ingpen (London, 1908). For ease of reference I shall refer to these letters by number, since all three editions agree in the order in which the letters are printed, but vary in pagination.

7. In referring to her failure to get a hoped-for position at Lorient, in France, Eliza Wollstonecraft Bishop wrote to her sister Everina on January 30, 1793: "Did I not tell you? that the L'Orient Castle would soon moulder away or fall like our Geneva Fabrics —Mother's Cottage in the New-World, or the still more stately Edifice, that Jammey once crossed the Pacific ocean to Erect for his *helpless* sisters!!"

8. *Mary, a Fiction,* London, 1788, pp. 16-17. I have occasionally made use of this novel and the later *Wrongs of Woman; or, Maria* (first published in fragmentary form

in the first two volumes of Mary's *Posthumous Works* in 1798) to supplement the limited information available about Mary's early life. Since both are obviously only partly autobiographical, they cannot be accepted as reliable accounts of the events of her life; yet they sometimes suggest reactions which a biographer cannot ignore.

9. *Mary*, pp. 12-13.

10. The same, p. 30.

11. The letters were published as a supplement to *English Exercises*, a textbook published at York in 1801 by Miss Massey under the pseudonym "Jane Gardiner." Mrs. Anne Elwood was perhaps referring to these letters when she quoted a "well-known living writer" as saying: "I have seen a series of letters written by her when very young, and living at Beverley, which evinced neither knowledge nor precocious talent, and think she did not attain the great faculty she afterwards evinced, until she was nearly thirty" (*Memoirs of the Literary Ladies of England*, London, 1843, II, 153). A copy of *English Exercises* was extant in 1870, but it has since been lost (see *Notes and Queries*, Ser. IV, vi, 341-42, and Vol. 146:102), and no other copy has been located. Durant reported in the Supplement to his edition of the *Memoirs* that he had "vainly searched, both here and in England, for a copy of the book," and I have done the same with as little success.

12. Supplement to *Memoirs*, p. 150.

13. This is the only letter to Miss Arden surviving among Lord Abinger's manuscripts. I have been unable to locate the "considerable number of Mary Wollstonecraft's letters written before she went to Lisbon . . . [and] addressed to a Miss Arden," of which Edward Dowden had transcripts in 1900. (See his letters of May 27, 1900, and October 13, 1905, reprinted in *Letters about Shelley*, ed. R. S. Garnett, London, Toronto, and New York, 1917, pp. 215 and 258.) Neither the letters themselves nor the transcripts seem to have survived.

14. *Thoughts on the Education of Daughters: with Reflections on Female Conduct, in the more Important Duties of Life*, London, 1787, pp. 69-70.

15. *Mary*, pp. 15-16.

16. Mary put the same words into the mouth of the dying mother of the heroine of *The Wrongs of Woman; or, Maria*. (See *Posthumous Works*, I, 174.)

17. See Eliza W. Bishop's letter of January 30, 1793, quoted above, note 7.

18. *Letters to Imlay*, No. XXXII.

Chapter II

1. Except when otherwise specified, all biographical information in this chapter is derived from the letters of Mary Wollstonecraft and Fanny Blood now in the possession of Lord Abinger, or from Godwin's *Memoirs* (ed. Durant), pp. 23-39. Some of the letters quoted have already been printed in C. Kegan Paul's *William Godwin, His Friends and Contemporaries* (London, 1876), I, 166-85, but I have followed always my own transcripts, since Paul's are often inaccurate. Concerning his errors in dating several of these letters, see Durant's Supplement to *Memoirs*, p. 161.

2. *Mary*, p. 35.

3. This information is given, without mention of its source, in Paul's *William Godwin*, I, 165.

4. P. W. Clayden, *The Early Life of Samuel Rogers*, Boston, 1888, p. 1.

5. Information about Price is derived from Roland Thomas's *Richard Price* (Oxford and London, 1924) and from Clayden's *Early Life of Samuel Rogers*.

6. This may well have been the house which Mary rented for her school.

7. Information about Thomas Rogers and his family is derived from Clayden's *Early Life of Samuel Rogers* and Samuel Sharpe's *Some Particulars of the Life of Samuel Rogers* (London, 1859).

8. Clayden, p. 7.

9. Thomas, p. 49.

10. Clayden, p. 9.

11. *Memoirs*, p. 28.

12. See Mary's reviews of Abbé de Lille's *The Garden* (*Analytical Review*, VIII [1790], 174-78) and of Arthur Murphy's *Essay on the Life of Samuel Johnson* and the

anonymous *Character of Dr. Johnson* (*Analytical Review*, XIII [1792], 268-73).

13. See Miss Elizabeth Nitchie's article "An Early Suitor of Mary Wollstonecraft" (*PMLA*, LVIII [1943], 163-69). Miss Nitchie points out that Mary's affair with Water-house might have begun in Bath in 1778-80 or 1787 at Newington Green. Mary's letters suggest that it almost certainly ended (and probably began) during her stay at the Green. (See my discussion, pp. 41-43.)

14. After Mary's death the ring was given to her daughter Mary. (See Mrs. Julian Marshall's *Life and Letters of Mary Wollstonecraft Shelley* [London, 1889], II, 52.)

15. *Letters Written during a Short Residence in Sweden, Norway, and Denmark,* 1st American ed., Wilmington, Delaware, 1796, pp. 62-63.

16. *Memoirs,* p. 36.

17. *Mary,* pp. 80-81.

18. *A Vindication of the Rights of Woman,* London, 1792, pp. 316 and 278 n.

19. *Thoughts on the Education of Daughters,* pp. 24-25.

20. The same, pp. 99-100.

21. P. 84

22. P. 91.

23. P. 89.

24. P. 79.

25. Pp. 82-83.

26. Pp. 77-78.

27. Pp. 74-75.

28. P. 74.

29. P. 84.

30. P. 111.

31. P. 52.

32. P. iv.

33. The two letters containing the information and quotations given in this para-graph and the next are both dated July 6. Since one of the two was obviously written several days before the other, I have treated them separately without assigning a date to either.

34. *Thoughts on the Education of Daughters,* p. 72.

Chapter III

1. Except when otherwise specified, all biographical information in this chapter is derived from the letters of Mary Wollstonecraft now in the possession of Lord Abinger, or from Godwin's *Memoirs* (ed. Durant), pp. 39-44. Some of the letters quoted have already been printed in Kegan Paul's *William Godwin, His Friends and Contem-poraries,* I, 185-90, but I have followed my own transcripts, since Paul's are often in-accurate. Concerning his errors in dating several of these letters, see Durant's Supplement to *Memoirs,* p. 161.

2. Arthur Young, *Autobiography,* ed. M. Betham-Edwards, London, 1898, p. 79.

3. Young attributed his discharge from his position with the Kingsborough family to the friction between the couple. First, he claimed, Lady Kingsborough was persuaded by a Mrs. Thornhill (who wanted Young's job for her husband) that Lord Kingsborough was in love with Miss Crosby, the children's governess at the time. Then after Miss Crosby had been discharged, Mrs. Thornhill allegedly persuaded Lady Kingsborough that Young was aiding Miss Crosby to win His Lordship's affection—and at the same time persuaded Lord Kingsborough that Young was in love with Her Ladyship. (See *Autobiography,* p. 79.) Gordon Goodwin, in his *DNB* article on Lord Kingsborough, states that the couple lived apart for several years before His Lordship died in 1799.

4. *Memoirs,* p. 40.

5. Arthur Young, *A Tour through the Kingdom of Ireland,* London, 1780, II, 57.

6. Mary's letters of this period contain frequent references to the lawsuit without making clear exactly why she was suing Roebuck. In one of her letters from Newington Green she says that she hopes not to leave the Green until the settlement of the "suit about the children's money." In the *Memoirs* Godwin says at one point that "the de-rangement of her father's affairs daily became more and more glaring; and a small

independent provision made for herself and her sisters, appears to have been sacrificed in the wreck" (p. 25); and later: "She was engaged in a contest with a near relation, whom she regarded as unprincipled, respecting the wreck of her father's fortune" (p. 72). Perhaps Mary's father paid out his daughters' funds to settle his own debts, and Mary sued to regain the money on the ground that it was not truly her father's. Yet her remarks on the subject in her letters never suggest that either Everina or Eliza was to receive any part of the proceeds of the suit.

7. *Letters Written . . . in Sweden, etc.*, p. 21.

8. Letters to Johnson, No. I (*Posthumous Works*, IV, 61-62).

9. *Mary*, pp. 60-61.

10. The same, p. 108.

11. P. 185.

12. P. 19.

13. Sig. A-lv-A-2.

14. Pp. 145-46.

15. Pp. 6-7.

16. Pp. 62-63.

17. Pp. 148-49.

18. Sig. A-2-A-2v.

19. See *A Vindication of the Rights of Woman*, pp. 383-84 and 399-400. Note also that the mother of the heroine in *Mary* fondles her dogs and neglects her children.

20. Letters to Johnson, No. IV (*Posthumous Works*, IV, 69).

21. Godwin met Lady Mountcashell (as Margaret King became after her marriage) during his trip to Dublin in 1800. He gave a striking description of her in a letter to James Marshal, reprinted in Paul's *William Godwin*, I, 369-70. In later years she was separated from her husband and lived in Italy with George William Tighe; and under her pseudonym "Mrs. Mason" she was an intimate friend of the Shelleys after they went to live at Pisa in 1820.

22. Letters to Johnson, No. II (*Posthumous Works*, IV, 63-65).

23. Letters to Johnson, No. III (*Posthumous Works*, IV, 66).

24. *Posthumous Works*, IV, 99.

25. The same, pp. 117-18.

Chapter IV

1. *Mary*, pp. 131-32.

2. Leslie Stephen, *History of English Thought in the Eighteenth Century*, London, 1876, I, 380.

3. Except when otherwise specified, all biographical information in this chapter is derived from the letters of Mary Wollstonecraft now in the possession of Lord Abinger, or from Godwin's *Memoirs* (ed. Durant), pp. 44-49. Some of the letters quoted have already been printed in Kegan Paul's *William Godwin, His Friends and Contemporaries*, I, 191-93, but I have followed my own transcripts, since Paul's are often inaccurate.

4. Here and elsewhere information about the publication of Mary's later books is, when no other evidence is offered, derived from the semi-annual "Catalogue of Books Published" in the *Analytical Review*.

5. *Original Stories*, ed. E. V. Lucas, London, 1906, p. 4.

6. The same, p. 3.

7. P. 13.

8. P. 25.

9. P. 5.

10. Pp. 86-87.

11. Pp. xvii-xviii.

12. Letters to Johnson, No. IV (*Posthumous Works*, IV, 67-68).

13. Editions were published in London in 1807, 1820, and 1835, and in Dublin in 1803. The latest edition, that of Mr. E. V. Lucas, proves nothing about the popularity of the book, since it was published only as a literary curiosity.

14. *Original Stories*, ed. Lucas, p. 71.

15. See *Letters Written . . . in Sweden, etc.*, p. 203.

16. *Original Stories*, ed. Lucas, p. 50.

17. Thomas Wright, *Life of William Blake*, Olney, Bucks., 1929, I, 20.

18. The same, p. 21.

19. See Grace A. Ellis, *A Memoir of Mrs. Anna Laetitia Barbauld*, Boston, 1874, I, 114.

20. Information derived from Joseph Johnson's manuscript note on the life of Mary Wollstonecraft, now, in the possession of Lord Abinger. A greatly altered version of the note appears in Paul's *William Godwin*, I, 193-94.

21. See Letters to Johnson, No. VIII and XV (*Posthumous Works*, IV, 75 and 91).

22. Godwin does not list Geddes as one of Mary's friends; yet she could hardly have failed to know him, since he was a member of Johnson's inner circle of friends. As for Fuseli, Mary may not have met him until later. John Knowles, Fuseli's biographer and literary executor, claims that they met in 1790.

23. Leigh Hunt, *Lord Byron and Some of His Contemporaries*, London, 1828, II, 34.

24. See *Gentleman's Magazine*, LXXII (1802), 588-90.

25. See John Mason Good, *Memoirs of the Life and Writings of the Reverend Alexander Geddes, LL.D.*, London, 1803, pp. 300-01 and *passim*.

26. See *Original Stories*, ed. Lucas, p. 27, and *Analytical Review*, II (1788), 223.

27. Letters to Johnson, No. IX (*Posthumous Works*, IV, 77).

28. Letters to Johnson, No. XIV (*Posthumous Works*, IV, 89-90).

29. The same, p. 89.

30. Letters to Johnson, No. IX (*Posthumous Works*, IV, 76-78).

31. For a discussion of the nature and extent of Mary's work for the *Analytical*, see my article "Mary Wollstonecraft, *Analytical Reviewer*," PMLA, LXII (1947), 1000-09. Here and elsewhere, in my discussion of Mary's contributions, I assume that she wrote all the articles signed M, W, or T. My reasons for attributing these reviews to her are set forth in my PMLA article.

32. See Mary's reviews of Charlotte Smith's *Ethelinde* (December, 1789) and Mrs. Bennet's *Agnes de Courcy* (January, 1790).

33. See Letters to Johnson, No. XIV (*Posthumous Works*, IV, 89).

34. See Letters to Johnson, No. IX (*Posthumous Works*, IV, 73-74).

35. Jacques Necker, *Of the Importance of Religious Opinions*, tr. Mary Wollstonecraft, London, 1788, pp. 75-76.

36. In later years Mary lost her respect for Necker and his book. In her *Historical and Moral View of the Origin and Progress of the French Revolution*, Volume I (London, 1794) she wrote: "Not content with the fame he acquired by writing on a subject, which his turn of mind and profession enabled him to comprehend, he wished to attain a higher degree of celebrity, by forming into a large book various metaphysical shreds of arguments, which he had collected from the conversation of men, fond of ingenious subtilties; and the style, excepting some declamatory passages, was as inflated and confused as the thoughts were far fetched and unconnected" (pp. 61-62).

37. *Analytical Review*, III (1789), 47-48.

38. The Stockdale translation was made from a French translation of the original German. Since Mary seems to have studied German only shortly before she translated *Elements of Morality* in 1790-1791, she too may have been working from the French.

39. My information about the title and contents of the book is derived from a review of it in the *Analytical Review* for June, 1789. In transcribing Joseph Johnson's manuscript note on Mary's life Kegan Paul incorrectly listed this book as "French Reader," and his error has been often repeated.

40. *Memoirs*, pp. 50-51.

41. The book was issued anonymously by Johnson in 1790.

42. The *Analytical Review* for December, 1789, and April, 1790, contained a two-part review of Holcroft's translation with selections from it presented alongside specimens of a translation "of our own" to illustrate Holcroft's inaccuracies. Though the review (signed "Y. Y.") is probably not Mary's work, the specimens may well have been taken from her uncompleted translation.

43. See the reviews of *Letters to a Young Lady* in the January issue and *Rudiments of Taste* in the April issue.

44. See John Knowles, *The Life and Writings of Henry Fuseli*, London, 1831, I, 164.

45. Letters to Johnson, No. X (*Posthumous Works,* IV, 79).

46. See Letters to Johnson, No. IV (*Posthumous Works,* IV, 68).

Chapter V

1. Except when otherwise specified, all biographical information in this chapter is derived from the letters of Mary Wollstonecraft and Eliza Wollstonecraft Bishop now in the possession of Lord Abinger, or from Godwin's *Memoirs* (ed. Durant), pp. 52-53 and 62-63. Three of Eliza Bishop's letters have been reprinted in Kegan Paul's *William Godwin, His Friends and Contemporaries,* I, 196-99, but I have followed my own transcripts, since Paul's are often inaccurate.

2. Richard Price, *A Discourse on the Love of Our Country,* 2nd ed., Dublin, 1790, pp. 54-55.

3. Price was referring to the storming of the Bastille, not, as Burke supposed, to the attack on the Queen's apartments at Versailles on October 6, 1789.

4. *A Vindication of the Rights of Men, in a Letter to the Right Honourable Edmund Burke,* London, 1790, p. iv.

5. The same, pp. 25-26.

6. P. 7.

7. See *Memoirs,* pp. 51-52.

8. *A Vindication of the Rights of Men,* pp. 19-20.

9. The same, pp. 144-45.

10. P. 94.

11. The Whitehall *Evening Post* announced the second edition of Mary's *Rights of Men* on December 14, 1790.

12. For the reviews cited, see *Analytical Review,* VIII (1790), 416-19; *Monthly Review,* New Series, IV (1791), 95-97; *Critical Review,* LXX (1790), 694-96; and *Gentleman's Magazine,* LXI (1791), 151-54.

13. Salzmann returned the compliment by translating Mary's *Rights of Woman* into German in 1793; and after her death he translated Godwin's *Memoirs.*

14. See the dates affixed to the plates in the first edition.

15. See Mary's review of *Problems Exemplified and Illustrated by Pictures from Real Life* in the *Analytical Review* for September, 1790.

16. Compare C. G. Salzmann, *Moralisches Elementarbuch* (Leipzig, 1785-87), I, 22, 32-33, and 246, and *Elements of Morality* (Philadelphia, 1796), I, 58 and 71, II, 68-69.

17. Compare Salzmann, I, 137, and Mary's translation, I, 185-86.

18. Compare Salzmann, I, 401, and Mary's translation, II, 248.

19. Compare Salzmann, I, 14, and Mary's translation, I, 50.

20. Compare Salzmann, I, 261, and Mary's translation, II, 86.

21. The Philadelphia edition contained a letter from four faculty members of the University of Pennsylvania assuring the publishers that they "will run no risk" in reprinting *Elements of Morality.* Durant, in his Supplement to Godwin's *Memoirs* (p. 201), suggests that the letter may have been inserted to counteract the effect of the "Introductory Address to Parents," in which parents were urged to "speak to children of the organs of generation as freely as we speak of the other parts of the body."

22. *Analytical Review,* III (1789), 459.

23. See Mark Schorer, *William Blake: The Politics of Vision,* New York, 1946, pp. 216-20 and *passim.* I am not convinced, as most biographers of Blake seem to be, that the poem "Mary," which Blake probably wrote in 1803, was inspired by his recollections of Mary Wollstonecraft. Nor can I find any reason to credit the legend that Blake wished to introduce Mary into his household as the nucleus of "a community of wives." I suspect that the legend is a garbled version of Mary's disastrous experience with Blake's friend and fellow-artist Fuseli.

24. Thomas Wright, *Life of William Blake,* I, 21.

25. *Memoirs,* pp. 63-64.

26. Godwin says that the girl was "about seven years of age" (*Memoirs,* p. 49); but Mrs. Mark Leavenworth, a Connecticut Yankee who knew Mary in London in 1791-92, described the child as "an orphan Girl, which the dying mother of the Child an East Indian gave her to bring up . . . aet. 11." At least so she is quoted in *The Literary Diary of Ezra Stiles, D.D., LL.D.* (ed F. B. Dexter, New York, 1901), III, 502.

27. See *Letters to Imlay* (ed. C. Kegan Paul, London, 1879), pp. xxi-xxiii, and compare *The Love-Letters of Mary Hays (1779-1780)* (ed. A. F. Wedd, London, 1925), pp. 224-25.

28. *Analytical Review*, XI (1791), 528.

29. The same, IX (1791), 182-83.

30. The letter was reprinted in the *New York Magazine*, II (1791), 713-14.

Chapter VI

1. The *Vindication of the Rights of Woman* was published early in 1792, or possibly at the end of 1791, and Mary was evidently working on it in November (as she implies on p. 281 of the first edition). Yet on page 236 she wrote: "When I first thought of writing these strictures I anticipated Mrs. Macaulay's approbation . . .; but soon heard with the sickly qualm of disappointed hope; and the still seriousness of regret—that she was no more!" Since Mrs. Macaulay died on June 22, 1791, Mary must have been planning her book for some months before she actually began writing it.

2. See especially Mary's attack on Burke's *Philosophical Enquiry into the Origin of Our Ideas of the Sublime and Beautiful* in *A Vindication of the Rights of Men*, pp. 105-08.

3. See Ephesians 5: 22-24 and I Timothy 2: 11-14.

4. James Boswell, *The Life of Samuel Johnson*, ed. G. Birkbeck Hill, Oxford and New York, 1887, V, 226 n.

5. Mary R. Beard, *Woman as Force in History*, New York, 1946, p. 95.

6. The same, p. 100.

7. *Henry Esmond*, Bk. I, Ch. XII.

8. *The Letters of Philip Dormer Stanhope, the Earl of Chesterfield, with the Characters*, ed. John Bradshaw, London, 1892, I, 141-42.

9. *Life of Johnson*, ed. Hill, III, 286-87.

10. Quoted in Durant's Supplement to *Memoirs*, p. 216.

11. Lady Mary Wortley Montagu, *Letters, 1709-1762*, Everyman's Library, London and New York, pp. 414 and 454.

12. James Fordyce, *Sermons for Young Women*, 11th ed., London, 1792, I, 185.

13. The same, II, 163.

14. I, 272.

15. Edmund Gosse, *Gray*, English Men of Letters Series, London, 1918, p. 9.

16. See also the *Tatler*, No. 61, 141, and 248, and the *Spectator*, No. 53 and 66.

17. See Swift's "Letter to a Very Young Lady on Her Marriage," his fragmentary essay "Of the Education of Ladies," and Addison's *Spectator*, No. 10. Note also that in Bk I, Ch. 6, and Bk IV, Ch. 8, of *Gulliver's Travels* Swift implies that he approves of the same education for both sexes.

18. An expanded translation of the introduction to this essay was published as "An Occasional Letter on the Female Sex" in the *Pennsylvania Magazine* in 1775 and has often been attributed to Tom Paine. Concerning the real authorship of the piece see Frank Smith, "The Authorship of 'An Occasional Letter on the Female Sex,' " *American Literature*, II (1930-31), 277-80.

19. After Mary's death her friend Mary Hays wrote: "It is but justice to add, that the principles of [*The Rights of Woman*] are to be found in Catherine Macauley's [*sic*] Treatise on Education" (*Annual Necrology, 1797-8*, London, 1800, p. 422). Miss Hays's claim was repeated in George G. Cunningham's *Lives of Eminent and Illustrious Englishmen* (Glasgow, 1835-37, VI, 248), but since then it seems never to have been noticed.

20. *A Vindication of the Rights of Woman*, London, 1792, p. viii.

21. The same, p. 25.

22. Quoted in *The Rights of Woman*, p. 175.

23. Quoted in the same, p. 190.

24. *The Rights of Woman*, p. 39.

25. The same, p. 87.

26. P. 196.

27. P. 223.

28. P. 54.

29. P. 236 n.

30. P. 106.
31. P. 291.
32. P. 335.
33. Mary announced in the Advertisement to her *Rights of Woman* that she was preparing a second volume of her work, but Godwin states that he found among her papers after her death nothing that could be certainly identified as a continuation of the book.
34. *The Rights of Woman*, p. 409.
35. The same, p. 22.
36. P. 236.
37. P. 133.
38. Quoted in Supplement to *Memoirs*, pp. 218-19.
39. For the reviews mentioned in this paragraph see *Analytical Review*, XII (1792), 241-49, and XIII (1792), 481-89; *General Magazine*, VI (1792), 187-91; *Literary Magazine*, I (1792), 133-39; *New York Magazine*, IV (1793), 77-81; and *Monthly Review*, New Series, VIII (1793), 198-209.
40. Quoted in Supplement to *Memoirs*, p. 217.
41. Matthew L. Davis, *Memoirs of Aaron Burr*, New York, 1836, I, 363.
42. *Letters of Anna Seward*, Edinburgh and London, 1811, III, 117.
43. See Supplement to *Memoirs*, p. 216.
44. Hannah Cowley, *A Day in Turkey*, Dublin, 1792, Sig. A-2.
45. See *The Letters of Horace Walpole*, ed. Mrs. Paget Toynbee, Oxford, 1905, XV, 131-32, 337-38.
46. *A Sketch of the Rights of Boys and Girls*, London, 1792, p. 18.
47. The same, p. 63.
48. *A Vindication of the Rights of Brutes*, London, 1792, p. 15.
49. The same, p. 103.
50. *Selections from the Letters of Robert Southey*, ed. J. W. Warter, London, 1856, I, 180.
51. Judith Sargeant Murray, *The Gleaner, a Miscellaneous Production*, Boston, 1798, III, 188.
52. Fordyce's book, first published in 1765, appeared in a fourteenth edition in 1814; Gregory's, first published in 1774, "attained the popularity of a chap-book," according to the *Cambridge Bibliography of English Literature*. There seems to be no record of its editions, but the last was apparently published in 1877.
53. I cannot give an exhaustive list of Mary's literary allusions because she often refers only to "a grave philosophical reasoner" or "an eminent orator" as the author of a quotation which she uses.
54. *The Rights of Woman*, p. 424.
55. See Preface to *Memoirs*, pp. xxxvii-xli.
56. *Memoirs*, p. 27.
57. *The Rights of Woman*, p. 236.
58. The same, p. 112.
59. P. 246.
60. P. 142.
61. P. 37.
62. P. 114.

Chapter VII

1. Except when otherwise specified, all biographical information in this chapter is derived from the letters of Mary Wollstonecraft and Eliza Wollstonecraft Bishop, or from Godwin's *Memoirs* (ed. Durant), pp. 57-78. Quotations from Mary's letters to Imlay (No. I-XXII) are copied from Kegan Paul's reprint of them, published at London in 1879; quotations from Mary's letters to her sisters or from Mrs. Bishop's letters to her sister Everina Wollstonecraft are copied from the originals now in the possession of Lord Abinger. Kegan Paul has reprinted a few of these letters in *William Godwin, His Friends and Contemporaries*, I, 205-20; but I have preferred to follow my own transcripts because his are often inaccurate.

2. See John Knowles, *The Life and Writings of Henry Fuseli,* I, 164-65. This anecdote has often been repeated to illustrate how frugally Mary lived in her first house on George Street. But as Durant has pointed out in his Supplement to *Memoirs* (p. 215), Talleyrand visited England from January to March, 1792, after Mary had moved to Store Street.

3. See *A Vindication of the Rights of Woman,* pp. 150-52.

4. Charles's report was relayed by Eliza Bishop to their sister Everina in a letter dated July 3, 1792.

5. *Annual Necrology, 1797-8,* p. 460.

6. Copied from a manuscript letter in the possession of Miss Anne F. Wedd of London.

7. Copied from a manuscript letter in my possession, thanks to the generous gift of Miss Wedd, who printed it in her edition of *The Love-Letters of Mary Hays,* p. 224.

8. Though Kegan Paul (*William Godwin,* I, 207-08) and Elizabeth Robins Pennell (*Life of Mary Wollstonecraft,* Boston, 1884, 180-85) deny that Mary was ever infatuated with Fuseli, there is every reason to believe that John Knowles's account of the affair, in his *Life and Writings of Henry Fuseli,* is substantially correct. The letters which Knowles quotes sound like Mary's work, and no one has presented a shred of proof that they are not authentic. In fact Godwin is said to have asked Knowles to mention Mary "very slightly . . . or not at all" in his biography of Fuseli (see Paul, *William Godwin,* II, 297), and Mary's grandson, Sir Percy Florence Shelley, who bought from Knowles the letters allegedly written by Mary to Fuseli, emphatically refused to allow Mrs. Pennell to examine them. (See Durant, Supplement to *Memoirs,* pp. 186-87.) The truth is undoubtedly that the Shelley family was eager to conceal the scandal and that Kegan Paul co-operated with them in trying to cover all traces of it. In copying the manuscript note about Mary's life written by Joseph Johnson, Paul omitted two important passages without indicating his omission. After describing her stay in the house at George Street and her frequent visits to his house, Johnson wrote: "F. was frequently with us." And after telling of her move to Store Street, he added: "Here her exertions seem to have been palsied, you know the cause." Certainly the omission of these two sentences suggests that Paul was trying to conceal facts which he knew to be true. (For his version of Johnson's note, see *William Godwin,* I, 193-94.)

Undoubtedly Mary's letters to Fuseli were destroyed soon after Sir Percy Shelley bought them from Knowles. The only trace of them among the papers now in Lord Abinger's possession is a note from Knowles to Sir Percy, dated February 1, 1886, saying that he encloses "a pencilled note which you ought I think to possess" (evidently one which he failed to turn over to Sir Percy when the letters were sold) and "a short note from Lord Jeffries to Fuseli which you may like to have." The note from Jeffries, dated September 10, 1797, reads: "One who loved you, & whom I respected, is no more. Mrs. Godwin died this morning." But the "pencilled note" is missing. Probably it too was disposed of.

9. *The Rights of Woman,* p. 160.

10. *Thoughts on the Education of Daughters,* p. 88.

11. All quotations from Mary's letters to Fuseli are copied from the transcripts given by Knowles in his *Life and Writings of Henry Fuseli,* I, 163-70.

12. See Barlow's letter to his wife dated June 6, 1792, and preserved in the Harvard College Library.

13. See discussion above, page 50 and note, and compare Mary's reviews of Johnson's *Sermon . . . for the Funeral of his Wife* (*Analytical Review,* I [1788], 467-68) and his *Sermons on Different Subjects* (*Analytical Review,* V [1789], 64-67).

14. *The Rights of Woman,* p. 224.

15. See *Annual Necrology, 1797-8,* p. 424.

16. Letters to Johnson, No. XVI (*Posthumous Works,* IV, 93-94).

17. *Posthumous Works,* IV, 43-45.

18. The same, p. 50.

19. Pp. 48-49.

20. See Supplement to *Memoirs,* pp. 248-52.

21. George Imlay [*sic*], *A Topographical Description of the Western Territory of North America,* 2nd ed., London, 1793, pp. 172-73.

22. All biographical information about Imlay is derived from two sources: Ralph L. Rusk's "The Adventures of Gilbert Imlay," *Indiana University Studies*, No. 57, Bloomington, 1923, and the Introduction to *Four New Letters of Mary Wollstonecraft and Helen M. Williams,* ed. B. P. Kurtz and Carrie C. Autrey, Berkeley, Calif., 1937.

23. *Topographical Description,* pp. 54-55.

24. Gilbert Imlay, *The Emigrants,* London, 1793, III, 3.

25. The same, II, 41.

26. The copy of the first edition of Godwin's *Memoirs* now in the Cornell University Library contains this manuscript note on the final page of the book: "Mr. Imlay was tall & rather awkward in his walk—very cheerful & highspirited—he wrote a novel which he attempted to publish." The title-page of the book bears the name "John Powle," who may have been the original owner of the book.

27. Roger Ingpen, in the Preface to his edition of Mary's *Letters to Imlay* (p. xv), claims that Helen Maria Williams had been Imlay's mistress. Mary seems to have known of at least one of her lover's previous affairs, for she referred in her letters to the "cunning woman" whom he was used to, and to the sacrifices which he had made for "a woman you did not respect." (See Letters to Imlay, No. XXII and XXXVII.)

28. *Analytical Review,* XII (1792), 505.

29. Kegan Paul (*Letters to Imlay,* pp. xxxviii-xxxix) and Mrs. Pennell (*Life of Mary Wollstonecraft,* pp. 199-201) claim that the registration was the only kind of marriage possible for Mary because she would have been liable to arrest if she had applied for a marriage certificate and declared her nationality. Godwin, in his *Memoirs* (pp. 70-71), maintains that Mary objected to marriage because she did not wish to involve Imlay in "family embarrassments to which she conceived herself exposed." But Mary's own statement, in the letter to Ruth Barlow quoted in the following paragraph in the text, proves that she needed no pretext for her failure to marry Imlay, that in fact she rejoiced in her freedom from marriage bonds.

30. *Four New Letters,* p. 41.

31. *Memoirs,* p. 75.

32. See Supplement to *Memoirs,* pp. 243-44.

33. See Amelia Alderson's letter to Mrs. John Taylor quoted in Cecilia Lucy Brightwell's *Memorials of the Life of Amelia Opie* (Norwich and London, 1854), p. 49. Miss Alderson says that Imlay announced the news to Mary. If so, his departure for Havre must have taken place later than mid-August, the time set by Paul (*Letters to Imlay,* p. 47). Paul dates only one letter of this period earlier than November. That one, tentatively dated September, mentions "this comfortless weather."

34. See Letters to Imlay, No. XI and XIV.

35. Virginia Woolf, "Four Figures—III: Mary Wollstonecraft," *The Second Common Reader,* New York, 1932, p. 173.

36. Paul (*Letters to Imlay,* p. xli) says that Mary went to Havre late in 1793; Godwin (*Memoirs,* p. 77) dates her removal January, 1794. Mr. Kurtz and Miss Autrey have proved from the letters that Godwin's dating is correct and that the dates of Letters XI-XVIII in Paul's edition of *Letters to Imlay* are incorrect. (See *Four New Letters,* pp. 52-56.)

37. *Four New Letters,* p. 39.

38. The same, p. 41.

39. P. 43.

40. Supplement to *Memoirs,* pp. 262-63.

41. In the Advertisement to the book Mary says that she has already written "a considerable part" of "two or three more volumes." Godwin reports, however, that he found no trace of the manuscript among her papers after she died. (See *Memoirs,* p. 69 n.)

42. *An Historical and Moral View of the Origin and Progress of the French Revolution,* London, 1796, pp. v-vi.

43. The same, pp. 512-13.

44. P. 335.

45. Pp. vii-viii.

46. P. 512.

47. P. 135.

48. P. 33.

49. P. 325.

50. P. 161.

51. Mary actually quoted most from *Etats Généraux; ou, Récit de ce qui s'est passée aux Etats Généraux, depuis le 5 mai 1789 au 1er septembre,* later published as the first three volumes of the *Journal des Débats et des Décrets.*

52. Adams's comments are recorded in the *Bulletin of the Boston Public Library,* IV, v, 4-13, and in an article by Elizabeth Luther Cary in *The Lamp,* XXVI (1903), 35-40.

53. The reviews referred to in this paragraph are as follows: *Analytical Review,* XX (1794), 337-47; XXI (1795), 8-17; *Monthly Review,* New Series, XVI (1795), 393-402; *Critical Review,* New Arrangement, XVI (1796), 390-96; and *British Critic,* VI (1795), 29-36.

Chapter VIII

1. Except when otherwise specified, all biographical information in this chapter is derived from Godwin's *Memoirs* (ed. Durant), pp. 79-96; from Mary's account of her Scandinavian trip in *Letters Written during a Short Residence in Sweden, Norway, and Denmark;* from the letters of Mary and her sister Eliza Bishop now in the possession of Lord Abinger; and from Mary's letters to Imlay, No. XXIII-LXXV. Quotations from Mary's letters to her sisters or from Mrs. Bishop's letters to her sister Everina Wollstonecraft are copied from the originals; quotations from Mary's letters to Imlay are copied from Kegan Paul's reprint of them, published at London in 1879. Since Godwin failed unaccountably to include any letter No. LXXII when he published the letters in *Posthumous Works,* his numbering of the letters which follow (No. LXXIII-LXXV) differs from that of Paul.

2. Quoted in translation in Supplement to *Memoirs,* p. 247. Immediately after the passage quoted in the text, Madame Schweitzer added: "I must confess that this erotic absorption made such a disagreeable impression on me, that all my pleasure vanished." It would be idle, however, to conclude from this isolated instance, that Mary was an inveterate flirt. No other acquaintance accuses her of coquetry.

3. Quoted in Supplement to *Memoirs,* p. 253.

4. Copied from the original letter now in the possession of Lord Abinger.

5. *Posthumous Works,* III, 91 n.

6. The name of Imlay's insistent partner, like all proper names, is left blank in the letters as Godwin published them. It may have been Joel Barlow. If so, Mary may have fallen out with him and his wife because of Imlay's gradual estrangement. Her last surviving letter to Ruth Barlow seems to have been written in the fall or winter of 1794. (See Supplement to *Memoirs,* p. 265.) Yet Barlow seems to have thought kindly of Mary as late as July, 1796. (See *Four New Letters of Mary Wollstonecraft and Helen M. Williams,* ed. Kurtz and Autrey, p. 25.)

7. Mary quotes this passage in her Letter to Imlay, No. LXXVI, saying that it was written "before I returned to England." G. R. Stirling Taylor, in *Mary Wollstonecraft: A Study in Economics and Romance* (London, 1911) assumes that it was written just before Mary's return from her Scandinavian tour in 1795. But her letters of that period show that she returned to England without any urging from Imlay, that in fact she was not even sure that he would consent to see her. (See Letters to Imlay, No. LXVII and LXVIII.)

8. See the two affectionate letters which Mary wrote to Archibald Hamilton Rowan (reprinted in Supplement to *Memoirs,* pp. 292-94). Evidently Mary had stopped temporarily at the house which she had occupied during her residence at Havre. She seems to have arranged for Rowan to occupy it while waiting for passage to America and to have offered it to a family named Russell until she succeeded in renting it. Evidently Mary was concealing from her friends the strained state of her relations with Imlay, for she wrote to Rowan: "In spite of my impatience to meet a friend who deserves all my tenderness, I have still a corner in my heart where I will allow you a place, *if you have no objection."*

9. Mary held no grudge against Eliza; and when presently she left for Sweden, she charged Imlay to send what money he could to her two sisters and her father (perhaps as payment for her discharging his affairs in the Scandinavian countries). She later

reprimanded him for his failure to fulfill his promise. (See Letters to Imlay, No. LXXV.) Probably Mary and Eliza never met or corresponded again. After Mary's death Godwin seems not to have notified Eliza directly; but in the letter which Eliza Fenwick wrote, at his request, to Everina, there is a postscript: "Mr. Godwin requests you will make Mrs. Bishop acquainted with the particulars of this afflicting event. He tells me that Mrs. Godwin entertained a sincere and earnest affection for Mrs. Bishop" (Paul, *William Godwin*, I, 283).

10. The document, now in the possession of Lord Abinger, is reprinted in Paul's *William Godwin*, I, 227-28.

11. Kegan Paul, in his edition of the Letters to Imlay, dates Mary's first letter from Hull May 27, her second May 28, and her third June 12. But Godwin (*Memoirs*, p. 82) claims that she was in the house provided by Imlay until June 6. Undoubtedly Godwin is right; it is unlikely that Mary would have written on two successive days and then waited two weeks before writing again. Moreover, in Letter No. XLIV Mary mentions receiving "yours of the 9th" and in a postscript adds, "Your second letter reached me about an hour ago." This suggests that Imlay's first letter after Mary's departure was written on the 9th—and he would hardly have dared to wait two weeks before writing! Incidentally, if the dates of Mary's first two letters from Hull are changed, her delay there is reduced from twenty-five days to eleven.

12. *Letters Written during a Short Residence in Sweden, Norway, and Denmark*, 1st American edition, Wilmington, Delaware, 1796, p. 111.

13. The same, p. 119.

14. P. 133.

15. P. 197.

16. P. 209.

17. See the passage from Joseph Farington's Diary quoted in Supplement to *Memoirs*, p. 298. Farington (or Farringdon), a member of the Royal Academy, lived at 35 Charlotte Street, Rathbone Place, a few houses from the lodgings which Mary occupied before her departure on her Scandinavian trip.

18. Imlay's words are quoted in Mary's Letters to Imlay, No. LXX.

19. John Knowles, *Life and Writings of Henry Fuseli*, I, 169.

20. Godwin (*Memoirs*, p. 96) wrote of this play: "It was offered to both the winter-managers, and remained among her papers at the period of her decease; but it appeared to me to be in so crude and imperfect a state, that I judged it most respectful to her memory to commit it to the flames."

21. Godwin (*Memoirs*, p. 96) claims that the volume was published at the end of 1795, but the title-page of the first edition gives the date of publication as 1796, and the *Analytical Review* lists it among books published during the first six months of 1796.

22. Kegan Paul, in his edition of *Letters to Imlay* (p. 142) claims that the *Letters Written . . . in Sweden, etc.* "formed a part" of her regular correspondence with Imlay during her journey. It is highly improbable, however, that Mary would have put Imlay to the expense of postage for the twenty-five bulky letters which make up her volume. The *Letters* seems, rather, to have been a journal kept throughout her journey and intended first for Imlay's eyes. She addresses him from time to time as "my friend" and makes many references (especially to her unhappiness and to his preoccupation with business) which only he could fully understand.

How much she revised the journal before publishing it is impossible to determine: the only clear instance of revision is her remark, after describing a lonely landscape in Sweden: "for it was summer, you remember" (p. 45). There is also one probable bit of interpolation from her letters to Imlay: the passage beginning "How am I altered by disappointment!" (p. 144), which appears almost word for word (and much more appropriately) in Letters to Imlay, No. L. (Note too that the quotation from *King Lear* in the footnote to p. 144 of the *Letters Written . . . in Sweden, etc.* appears also in Letters to Imlay, No. XLIX.) Mary intimates in the Advertisement to her book that she rejected the idea of careful revision because she "perceived that I could not give a just description of what I saw, but by relating the effect different objects had produced on my mind and feelings, whilst the impression was still fresh." And her vagueness about her traveling companions confirms the impression that she had done little revising: at first she seems to be traveling alone; then, on p. 7, she speaks of Marguerite without introducing her to the reader, and on p. 12 she refers for the first time to "my babe" without any explanation.

23. *Analytical Review,* V (1789), 41. Compare VII (1790), 375.
24. *Letters Written . . . in Sweden, etc.,* p. 204.
25. The same, p. 37.
26. P. 31.
27. P. 99.
28. P. 140.
29. P. 20.
30. P. 111.
31. P. 37.
32. Pp. 54-55.
33. P. 62.
34. See p. 200.
35. Quoted in Supplement to *Memoirs,* pp. 306-07.
36. For the reviews and reprinted excerpts cited see *Monthly Magazine,* I (1796), 279-81; *Analytical Review,* XXIII (1796), 229-38; *Critical Review,* New Arrangement, XVI (1796), 209-12; *New Annual Register for 1796,* pp. 248-49; *Monthly Review,* New Series, XX (1796), 251-57; *British Critic,* VII (1796), 602-10; *Universal Magazine,* XCVIII (1796), 108-13; *Scots Magazine,* LVIII (1796), 627-28; and *New York Magazine,* VIII (1797), 23-25.
37. This edition may, as Durant suggests (Supplement to *Memoirs,* p. 302 n.), have been reprinted from the copy of the book which Mary sent to Archibald Hamilton Rowan while he was living at Wilmington.
38. *Memoirs,* p. 84.

Chapter IX

1. Except when otherwise specified, all biographical information in this chapter is derived from the letters of Mary Wollstonecraft and William Godwin now in the possession of Lord Abinger, or from Godwin's *Memoirs* (ed. Durant) pp. 95-123. Some of the letters quoted have already been printed in Kegan Paul's *William Godwin, His Friends and Contemporaries,* I, 241-69, 272-73; but I have followed my own transcripts, since Paul's are often inaccurate.
2. Quoted in Supplement to *Memoirs,* pp. 300-01.
3. See *The Love Letters of Mary Hays,* ed. A. F. Wedd, pp. 1-7.
4. *Letters to Imlay,* ed. Kegan Paul, p. li.
5. *Memoirs,* p. 103.
6. *An Enquiry concerning Political Justice,* London, 1793, II, 850.
7. Paul, *William Godwin,* I, 30-31.
8. The same, p. 32.
9. Cecilia L. Brightwell, *Memorials of the Life of Amelia Opie,* pp. 59-60.
10. *Memoirs,* pp. 97-98.
11. Letters to Imlay, LXVI (erroneously numbered LXVII in *Posthumous Works*). Kegan Paul, in his edition of the Letters to Imlay, dates this letter "December, 1796." But Godwin, in his *Memoirs* (p. 91) claims that Mary's last letter of appeal to Imlay was written after his return from Paris—that is, in February or March, 1797.
12. Letters to Imlay, No. LXVII (LXVIII in *Posthumous Works*).
13. *Love Letters of Mary Hays,* ed. Wedd, p. 10.
14. The apology was added in the second edition of the *Memoirs.* See Durant ed., p. 98.
15. See Paul, *William Godwin,* I, 154.
16. *Memoirs,* p. 99.
17. *Memorials of the Life of Amelia Opie,* p. 62.
18. See Letters to Johnson, No. XI-XIII (*Posthumous Works,* IV, 81-88). Mrs. Pennell, in her *Life of Mary Wollstonecraft* (pp. 109-13), assumes that these letters were written soon after Mary first settled in London. But the phraseology of the letters—her references to her "unprotected situation," her "almost broken heart," and her "disinterestedness" —suggests that the letters were written when Mary was recovering from the blow she suffered when she learned at last that she could never regain Imlay's love.

19. *Memoirs,* p. 98.

20. F. K. Brown, *William Godwin,* London and Toronto, 1926, p. 116. This letter seems to be the only extant letter from Mary to Godwin not now in the possession of Lord Abinger. Unfortunately the late Professor Brown, who did not have access to the Abinger Manuscripts, did not record where he found it.

21. See F. K. Brown, *William Godwin,* p. 118.

22. See *The Rights of Woman,* p. 160.

23. *Memoirs,* p. 99.

24. The same, p. 100.

25. P. 100.

26. See Supplement to *Memoirs,* p. 312.

27. Copied from the original letter now in the possession of Lord Abinger.

28. Edward Dowden, *The French Revolution and English Literature,* New York, 1897, pp. 86-87.

29. Mary's first contribution to the *Analytical* after her return from Scandinavia was a review of Mrs. Inchbald's *Nature and Art* in the issue of May, 1796. The June and July issues of the magazine contained no articles signed "M." (the only one of her three regular signatures which she used after her return), but in August she reviewed Fanny Burney's *Camilla;* in September, a volume of letters from France; and in October, four novels and a book of instructions for parents. None of these articles throw light on Mary's thinking at this time. She seems now to have regarded reviewing as mere hack work and not as an outlet for her real talents.

30. See her requests that Mary Hays review *The Gossip's Story* (*Love Letters of Mary Hays,* ed. Wedd, p. 240) and that Godwin review *Vaurien* (Paul, *William Godwin,* I, 244).

31. *Love Letters of Mary Hays,* ed. Wedd, p. 240.

32. This letter and the others by Amelia Alderson referred to in this paragraph are now in the possession of Lord Abinger.

33. Supplement to *Memoirs,* p. 302.

34. *Memoirs,* p. 101.

35. *Posthumous Works,* IV, 161-62.

36. The same, p. 168.

37. P. 171.

38. Pp. 174-75.

39. *Complete Works of William Hazlitt,* ed. Howe, XVII, 111-12.

40. F. K. Brown, *William Godwin,* pp. 117-18. No one else seems to have remarked on the paralysis of Mary's eyelid, unless Godwin was referring to it when he mentioned "the malicious leer of your eye" in his letter from Norwich quoted on pp. 340-41.

41. Brown, *William Godwin,* p. 118.

42. *Memoirs,* p. 103.

43. *Memorials of the Life of Amelia Opie,* pp. 61-62.

44. *Letters to Imlay,* ed. Paul, p. lv.

45. Paul, *William Godwin,* I, 235.

46. The same, p. 240.

47. Pp. 237-38.

48. P. 240.

49. For Mrs. Inchbald's later correspondence with Godwin, see Paul, *William Godwin,* I, 276-79, 350; II, 77, 142; and James Boaden, *Memoirs of Mrs. Inchbald* (London, 1833), II, 29-30, 82-83.

50. Knowles, *Life and Writings of Henry Fuseli,* I, 170.

51. Quoted in Supplement to *Memoirs,* p. 315.

52. Quoted in the same, pp. 313-14.

53. *Memorials of the Life of Amelia Opie,* p. 63.

54. The same, p. 61.

55. Quoted in Supplement to *Memoirs,* pp. 313-14.

56. Except for a review of the novel *Edward* in the January issue, Mary had made no contribution to the *Analytical* since the previous October. The May reviews, none of which deserves special comment, were her last contributions to the magazine.

57. Paul, *William Godwin,* I, 361.

58. See Knowles, *Life and Writings of Henry Fuseli,* I, 170, and 365.

59. See *The Correspondence of Robert Southey with Caroline Bowles,* ed. Edward Dowden, Dublin and London, 1881, p. 63.

60. Miss Pinkerton's note of apology (now in Lord Abinger's possession) is dated July 9, but Godwin (who added dates to most of Mary's letters to him after her death) assigns the later notes on the subject to the month of August. Though he may have erred, he was usually very conscientious in such matters—and he had his carefully kept journal to remind him of the events which took place on a given day. It is not improbable, of course, that Miss Pinkerton, in her distraught state of mind, misdated her note.

61. *Posthumous Works,* I, Sig. b2-b2v.

62. Mary's system of rearing Fanny had apparently attracted some attention. In a letter dated August 28, 1796 (now in the possession of Lord Abinger), Amelia Alderson wrote: "A very amiable clever friend of mine who is on the point of bringing forth a first child on the delightful banks of Ul[l]swater, is desirous of knowing *in detail,* your means of inuring Fanny to a thin dress in this cold climate. I have sent her all the information on the subject which I am in possession of, with my testimony as eye witness to the success of your plan, as exhibited in the strong, well-formed limbs, & florid complexion of your child—but I wish to receive from *you,* the particulars she requests. Will you favour me with them?"

63. These lessons were reprinted in a separate volume entitled *Lessons for Children* published by Joseph Johnson in 1798.

64. *Posthumous Works,* II, 175.

65. *Memoirs,* p. 112.

66. Mrs. Pennell reprints, in her *Life of Mary Wollstonecraft* (pp. 353-54), a note by Henry Reveley concerning a quarrel between a man and his wife which supposedly took place on the day before Mary's death and which brought on her final relapse. But as Mrs. Pennell herself points out, the story is unlikely. The quarrel might, however, have taken place, as Edward Dowden suggested (*Letters about Shelley,* ed. R. S. Garnett, pp. 93-94), on Sunday, when Godwin was away from home, and have occasioned the relapse which Mary suffered then. Or it might have taken place on the Friday before her confinement when, as Godwin states in the *Memoirs* (p. 112), Mary was "somewhat indisposed . . . , the consequence, I believe, of a sudden alarm."

67. *Memoirs,* p. 116.

68. The same, p. 118.

69. P. 120.

70. P. 122.

71. P. 121.

72. See *The Diary of William Dunlap,* Collections of the New York Historical Society, New York, 1930, I, 212.

73. *Memoirs,* p. 122.

74. *Letters to Imlay,* ed. Paul, pp. lix-lx.

75. See the letter of Eliza Fenwick to Everina Wollstonecraft printed in Paul's *William Godwin,* I, 282-83.

76. See Paul, *William Godwin,* I, 275.

77. The same, pp. 275-76.

78. See the same, pp. 283-84.

79. P. 280.

80. Pp. 285-86.

81. Knowles, *Life and Writings of Henry Fuseli,* I, 170.

Chapter X

1. *Gentleman's Magazine,* LXVII (1797), 894.

2. See Paul, *William Godwin, His Friends and Contemporaries,* I, 283.

3. The same, pp. 289-90.

4. Edward Dowden, *The Life of Percy Bysshe Shelley,* London, 1886, II, 232.

5. Paul, *William Godwin,* I, 281.

6. *Posthumous Works,* III, Sig. 5.

7. *Memoirs*, p. 68.

8. Richard Garnett, author of the article on Imlay in the *Dictionary of National Biography*, published the inscription on the tombstone and the record in the parish register in the *Athenaeum*, No. 3955 (August 15, 1903), pp. 219-20.

9. Henry T. Tuckerman, *Characteristics of Literature, Second Series*, Philadelphia, 1851, p. 274.

10. *Letters of Samuel Taylor Coleridge*, ed. E. H. Coleridge, Boston and New York, 1895, I, 316.

11. See F. K. Brown, *William Godwin*, p. 133.

12 *Memoirs*, pp. 123-26. In the parallel passage in the second edition of the *Memoirs* Godwin attributed the differences between Mary and himself partly to the basic differences between the sexes.

13. Note also the German translation by Therese Schlesinger-Eckstein published in 1912, Durant's edition published in London and New York in 1927, and the re-issue of Durant's edition with a preface by John Middleton Murry published in New York in 1930.

14. Mary's relations with the *Monthly Mirror* were curious. Back in 1796, when the magazine was brand new, the editors had asked Joseph Johnson for biographical information about her and had been curtly refused. "The highest compliment you could do Mrs. Wollstonecraft," he had said, "would be that of *saying nothing about her*." But the editors of the *Mirror* were not to be put off so easily; and they published an engraving supposedly made from a portrait of Mary (see discussion in Supplement to *Memoirs*, pp. 327-32), described Johnson's "insolence" in detail, promised a biography of Mary in the near future, and lauded her as the champion of her sex. The promised biography did not appear until after Godwin's *Memoirs* had been published. Then the editors presented a summary account of Mary's life, derived from the *Memoirs*, and praised Mary lavishly. Yet shortly afterwards, when Johnson published her *Lessons for Children*, the *Mirror* reviewed the book with praise for Mary's mental powers and her teaching ability, but added that cautious teachers would beware of the ideas of one so fond of innovation and so opposed to all institutions.

15. See *British Critic*, XII (1798), 228-35; *Gentleman's Magazine*, LXVIII (1798), 186-87; *Monthly Review*, New Series, XXVII (1798), 321-27; *Critical Review*, New Arrangement, XXII (1798), 414-19; *Monthly Magazine*, V (1798), 493-94; *New Annual Register for the Year 1798*, p. 271; and *Monthly Magazine and American Review*, I (1799), 330-35.

16. *Historical Magazine*, I (1799), 34.

17. The lines as given were written from memory on a blank leaf of a copy of the *Memoirs* by Dr. William Shepherd and recorded in *Notes and Queries*, III, viii, 66.

18. *Anti-Jacobin Review and Magazine*, I (1798), 93.

19. The same, p. 97.

20. P. 94.

21. *European Magazine*, XXXIII (1798), 251.

22. The story is told in James R. O'Flanagan's *The Munster Circuit* (London, 1880), pp. 140-48. The sequel to the story is rather amusing: Mary Elizabeth King took refuge at the home of a Welsh clergyman, where she lived under an assumed name. One day she told him her life history, fully expecting him to order her to leave his house. But he allowed her to remain, and not long afterwards they were married.

23. See *British Critic*, XII (1798), 230.

24. George Walker, *The Vagabond*, 1st American, from 4th English, ed., Boston, 1800, p. 116 n.

25. Richard Polwhele, *The Unsex'd Females*, London, 1798, pp. 13-15.

26. T. J. Mathias, *The Shade of Alexander Pope on the Banks of the Thames*, London, 1799, pp. 47-48.

27. The same, pp. 44-50.

28. *Anti-Jacobin Review and Magazine*, IX (1801), 518.

29. Apparently the only other contemporary women to offer a word of defense of Mary after her death were Anna Seward and the youthful Eliza Southgate, and both of them did so only very cautiously in personal letters. See *Letters of Anna Seward*, V, 73-74, and Eliza Southgate Bowne, *A Girl's Life Eighty Years Ago*, ed. Clarence Cook, N.Y., 1888, pp. 61-62.

30. William Godwin, *St. Leon,* London, 1816, I, ix-x.

31. The same, pp. 89-90.

32. See Paul, *William Godwin,* II, 57.

33. *Letters of Samuel Taylor Coleridge,* ed. E. H. Coleridge, I, 321.

34. Paul, *William Godwin,* I, 299.

35. The same, p. 300.

36. P. 301.

37. Godwin's later letters to Miss Lee are printed in Paul, I, 302-10.

38. The same, p. 335.

39. Pp. 333-34.

40. P. 335.

41. See Godwin's reply, printed in Paul, I, 336-38.

42. The same, II, 58.

43. *Letters of Charles and Mary Lamb,* ed. E. V. Lucas, New Haven, 1935, I, 273-74.

44. The opinions of Mrs. Godwin quoted in this paragraph can be found in *Letters of Charles and Mary Lamb,* ed. Lucas, I, 275, 304, 317; II, 112; Edith J. Morley, ed., *Henry Crabb Robinson on Books and Their Writers* (London, 1938), I, 14, 235, 441; *Letters of Percy Bysshe Shelley,* ed. Roger Ingpen (London, 1909), I, 407 n., 435 n.; II, 536; *Letters of Samuel Taylor Coleridge,* ed. E. H. Coleridge, II, 466; *Letters of Edward John Trelawny,* ed. H. Buxton Forman (Oxford, 1910), p. 200; and Mrs. Julian Marshall's *Life and Letters of Mary W. Shelley,* I, 165, 188.

45. See Paul, *William Godwin,* II, 98-99 and 187-88.

46. See the same, p. 213.

47. Edith J. Morley, ed., *Henry Crabb Robinson on Books and Their Writers,* I, 426.

48. *Complete Works of William Hazlitt,* ed. P. P. Howe, XI, 16.

49. See *Monthly Review,* New Series, XLV (1804), 447-48.

50. See *British Critic,* XXI (1803), 690-91.

51. *Anti-Jacobin Review and Magazine,* XV (1803), 183.

52. There was, however, one isolated (and irate) poetic outburst against Mary in Thomas G. Fessenden's *Ladies Monitor,* Bellows Falls, Vermont, 1818, pp. 58-60.

53. *The Private Journal of Aaron Burr, during His Residence of Four Years in Europe, with Selections from His Correspondence,* ed. M. L. Davis, New York, 1838, II, 307.

54. *Letters of Percy Bysshe Shelley,* ed. Ingpen, I, 363.

55. See R. Glynn Grylls, *Claire Clairmont,* London, 1939, p. 47.

56. Kegan Paul (*William Godwin,* I, 229) claims that Imlay never paid either principal or interest of the bond which he settled on Fanny.

57. Edward Dowden, *Life of Shelley,* I, 521.

58. The same, II, 52.

59. See the descriptions of Mary by Thomas Jefferson Hogg and Edward Trelawny in *The Life of Percy Bysshe Shelley,* ed. Humbert Wolfe (London, Toronto, and New York, 1933), II, 148 and 173, and that by Claire Clairmont in R. Glynn Grylls's *Claire Clairmont,* p. 254.

60. See Paul, *William Godwin,* I, 373. Godwin wrote from Dublin to his friend Marshal, who was staying with the children: "I love Aunt Bishop as much as I hate (you must not read that word) Aunt Everina." Probably the feeling was mutual. Everina may have suspected his relationship with Mary when she visited her sister in London in February and March, 1797. Shortly afterward, when Godwin visited the Wedgwood family while Everina was acting as their governess, she received him coolly. (See Paul, *William Godwin,* I, 254 and 258.) And many years later, in a letter dated September 30, 1835 [?], she told her niece Elizabeth W. Berry, of Crows Nest, Sydney, N.S.W.: "[Your aunt's] genius . . . indeed *was great* though some of her essential *sentiments* changed sorrowfully during her Residence in Paris—and her subsequent union with Godwin was woeful and most afflictive to her many, many Friends." (The letter is preserved in the Mitchell Library of Sydney and reprinted here by permission of the Trustees of the Library.)

61. See Newman Ivey White, *Shelley,* New York, 1940, I, 348-49.

62. See Dowden, *Life of Shelley,* II, 23-24 and 40.

63. The same, pp. 41-42.

64. Mrs. Marshall, *Life and Letters of Mary W. Shelley,* I, 167-68.

65. Paul, *William Godwin*, I, 242.

66. See the same, p. 246.

67. *Mary Shelley's Journal*, ed. Frederick L. Jones, Norman, Okla., 1947, p. 21.

68. Lady Shelley, *Shelley Memorials*, London, 1859, p. 102.

69. Quoted in the preface to T. J. Hogg's biography of Shelley. See *The Life of Percy Bysshe Shelley*, ed. Humbert Wolfe, I, 5.

70. Mrs. Marshall, *Life and Letters of Mary W. Shelley*, I, 250.

71. Paul, *William Godwin*, II, 299.

72. Mrs. Marshall, *Life and Letters of Mary W. Shelley*, II, 248.

73. See R. Glynn Grylls, *Mary Shelley*, London, New York, and Toronto, 1938, p. 261. Actually the ring was probably the "pritty mourning ring with an emethist and 2 sparks" sent by Godwin's mother to the younger Mary after her mother's death. (See Paul, *William Godwin*, I, 326.)

74. See Grylls, *Mary Shelley*, p. 253.

75. The monument still stands in the public park which has replaced the old graveyard.

76. *Letters of Mary W. Shelley*, ed. F. L. Jones, Norman, Okla., 1944, I, 258.

77. Roger Ingpen, *Shelley in England*, Boston and New York, 1917, p. 612.

78. Mrs. [Anne] Elwood, *Memoirs of the Literary Ladies of England*, London, 1843, II, 152.

79. Mary's reputation has only recently been subjected to a sharp attack in Ferdinand Lundberg and Marynia F. Farnham's *Modern Woman: The Lost Sex* (New York and London, 1947). The authors have psychoanalyzed her across the gap of a century and a half and have concluded that her life and work were actuated by "penis-envy." But no one familiar with Mary's history is likely to take their diagnosis seriously. In the first place they seem to have carried their researches into Mary's life no further than *This Shining Woman*, the fictionalized biography by "George R. Preedy" (Gabrielle M. Long), and their lurid summary of her career contains at least a dozen factual errors and several very questionable bits of interpretation. In the second place, their diagnosis seems to be based wholly on a fragment of a sentence from *The Rights of Woman* which they have wrenched from its context, ignoring the limiting statements which Mary subjoined. And finally, they maintain that in asking for equality of the sexes, she and later feminists were actually insisting that men and women are identical. And they proceed to catalogue the male and female sexual organs in order to prove that the sexes are not identical!

80. *Annual Necrology, 1797-8*, p. 455.

81. Harriet Martineau, *Autobiography*, ed. M. W. Chapman, Boston, 1877, I, 303.

82. See Alma Lutz, *Emma Willard, Daughter of Democracy*, Boston and New York, 1929, pp. 31-32.

83. Margaret Fuller Ossoli, *Woman in the Nineteenth Century*, Boston, 1855, pp. 75 and 77.

84. See Mrs. Marshall, *Life and Letters of Mary W. Shelley*, II, 168-81.

85. *James and Lucretia Mott: Life and Letters*, ed. A. D. Hallowell, Boston and New York, 1884, p. 187.

86. The same, p. 357.

87. *Memoirs*, p. 97.

Index